FRANCE SINCE THE REVOLUTION

FRANCE

SINCE

THE REVOLUTION

Donald J. Harvey

THE FREE PRESS, *New York*

COLLIER-MACMILLAN LIMITED, *London*

First Printing

To my daughter Nanette

whose patience and understanding far exceed

her eleven years

ACKNOWLEDGMENTS

Freud's description of creative works as sublimated or neurotic manifestations could make an author most uneasy or irrelevant in explaining the original impulses leading to the writing of his book. In deference to Freud, without necessarily agreeing with his views, I shall avoid burdening the reader with the dark forces of my happy childhood and adolescence that might have been the basis for the following book. I shall acknowledge my debts in all sincerity and in a traditional manner.

To Professor Herbert H. Rowen of Rutgers, I express my gratitude for setting down the initial guidelines and for offering rigorous and illuminating counsel in the early stages of the task. To Professor Eugen Weber of the University of California at Los Angeles, I extend my thanks for his constructive criticism, encouragement, and inspiring scholarly example. The faults and weaknesses of my book stem from my failure to follow my friends' good counsel and fine example.

To my wife, Jacqueline, who can brush more truth and wisdom and harmony and perception on canvas than I could ever portray on a printed page, I shall acknowledge my debts personally. Let it be known publicly, however, how eternally grateful I am for her constant and intelligent aid and for the fact that, through the protracted program of planned authorship, she survived.

Donald J. Harvey

CONTENTS

ACKNOWLEDGMENTS   vii

1. on purposes, hypotheses, and approaches   *1*
2. the background and nature of the French
   Revolution (1789–1814)   4
   the old regime   *4*
   from frustrated reform to successful revolt   *13*
   ten years of revolutionary ferment (1789–1799)   *32*
   the Napoleonic synthesis (1799–1814)   *56*
3. the quest for a permanent regime (1814–1870)   65
   the Bourbon Restoration and its repudiation (1814–1830)   68
   the Bourgeois Monarchy and its overthrow (1830–1848)   77
   the life and death of the Second Republic (1848–1852)   *91*
   the Second Empire and its collapse (1852–1870)   *98*
4. the strange birth and vigor of the Third
   Republic (1870–1914)   *112*
   the politics of making and maintaining the republic   *113*
   economic changes and their consequences   *144*
   France in the imperial race   *155*
   France and the world powers   *160*
5. the trials and tribulations of the Third
   Republic (1914–1939)   *174*
   the great illusion (1914–1918)   *174*
   the 1920s' quest for security at home and abroad   *201*
   domestic strife and appeasement without peace: the 1930s   *228*

6. **the regeneration of a nation: France since 1939** *256*

phony war, military defeat, and political collapse (1939–1940) 257

occupation, Vichy, Free France, Resistance, Liberation
(1940–1944) 266

the founding and foundering of the Fourth Republic
(1944–1958) 284

the origins and operations of the Fifth Republic (1958–   ) 320

RECOMMENDED READINGS *343*

INDEX *351*

1.

ON PURPOSES, HYPOTHESES, AND
APPROACHES

FIVE republics, two empires, and several constitutional monarchies ago, the French launched a revolution to reform the long-established Bourbon regime. Accompanying the search for appropriate political forms since 1789, the French enjoyed or deplored an historical experience variously marked by economic stagnation and progress, social immobility and realignment, colonial expansion and contraction, foreign glory and defeat, and cultural contributions of generally high quality. This book is ambitiously designed to narrate and interpret these half-dozen facets of French historical experience since 1789.

Without wishing to substitute new myths for old, I shall approach these half-dozen facets or problems in a relativistic way. The very nature of each historical problem faced by the French was modified by the presence of the other problems of the day. The burning, agonizing issue of one particular moment did not have the same intensity at some other moment. Since the very character of a problem is transformed by its interrelationships with other issues, the problems were consciously or unconsciously arranged on a scale of priorities that varied in successive moments of modern French history. The Frenchman, persuaded of the virtues of republicanism in time of international calm and domestic tranquility, easily voted monarchist in the 1871 moment of foreign peril and social stress. The pacifist of July, 1914, embraced militarism in

August, 1914, when he thought *la patrie* was in danger or when he hoped to gain a social transformation through war's turmoil.

A relativist approach to modern French history demands special caution in assigning any one single cause to the unfolding events in France since the Revolution. Marxist socioeconomic factors undoubtedly determined many French institutions and ideas at certain moments during the past two hundred years. But, at other moments, concepts, ideas, standards, and principles appeared more significant as the causes shaping events. To materialism and idealism must be added the sometimes exaggerated presence of a special national French psychology that gives a peculiar stamp to the French historical experience. At still other moments, clashing socioeconomic interests, rival ideologies, and national psychology were patently disregarded by the political leaders of France, who seemed to make the state a private club with political life a game in which every member (but not the ordinary citizen, of course) received his turn at bat or, at least, a cozy seat in the publicly supported dugout.

Like any sound hypothesis of historical analysis, the principle of relativism makes one wary of accepting the customary labeling of Frenchmen as right, center, or left. If "the right" designates traditionalist, conservative, reactionary, militarist, clerical, property-conscious citizens and "the left" designates innovating, revolutionary, radical, pacifist, secular, socialist Frenchmen, then French history will remain thoroughly baffling. For French history has been replete not with the phenomenon of complete rigidity in the membership or values of the so-called right or left, but with the equally common changing, switching, reversing tendencies of Frenchmen grouped in these categories. The right of 1788, composed of the land- and office-holding aristocracy, manifested many of the attributes usually ascribed to the left. The aristocrats of the right, not the bourgeois, peasant, or proletarian of a presumable left, were the innovating, reforming, radical elements who opened the gates to revolution in 1789. Within a year, of course, the agitating, power-seeking right, aghast at the spreading revolution in which other interests of theirs were jeopardized, reassumed their conservatism and closed ranks with the monarchy they had so frontally attacked. So, too, during the 1930s, the French right dropped its thumping militarist, anti-German stance of the previous decades to espouse the appeasement of Nazi Germany lest war bring further social ferment and loss of property rights in a socialist Bolshevik France. Relativism thus applies to the treatment of right and left groupings in France; the composition and policy of each faction depended on the circumstances, problems, or issues foremost at a particular moment.

Since these and other hypotheses and approaches have validity only with reference to the reality of French historical experience, this book will present numerous details of the interacting problems and issues involved. Selected for emphasis will be the search for a stable political structure; the economic and social adjustment to industrialization; the formulation and implementation of a foreign and military policy appropriate to the varied interests of France in a dynamically changing world; the quest for empire and the debate over colonial policy; and finally, the role, status, and contributions of the intellectuals.

2.

THE BACKGROUND AND NATURE
OF THE FRENCH REVOLUTION

The old regime

MODERN French history begins with the old regime and its revolutionary overthrow at the end of the eighteenth century. Old-regime institutions, habits, customs, and practices were abandoned or modified at a varying pace after 1789. What to preserve and what to discard was decided sometimes by conscious calculation and sometimes by an uncharted complex of needs, pressures, or neglect at particular moments.

What was the exact nature of the old regime that had such deep roots in centuries of monarchical experience, collapsed so suddenly in 1789, persisted in certain respects long after its demise, and attracted supporters for its revival throughout the nineteenth and early twentieth centuries? A complex society, the old regime theoretically was based on the premise of divine right. God had endowed the monarch with an omnipotence that no subject could challenge without defying God and King. No delegation of power could be considered permanent or could diminish the divinely derived royal prerogative. Louis XIV, XV, and XVI possessed complete sovereignty – legislative, executive, judicial, administrative, military. The Estates-General – the traditional French parliament representing the three estates of clergy, nobility, and commons – had not met since 1614. Laws were thus but the decrees of the King, drawn up by himself or advisors chosen by and responsible to him

4

alone. The *parlements,* quasi-judicial, quasi-administrative organs
in Paris and the provincial towns, did possess a recognized function
of registering royal decrees before they could be considered valid
and enforceable. Yet, the *parlements'* check on the royal will could
be overcome by the mere presence of the King and his personal
command to register the decree. The monarch stood, too, at the
apex of the social pyramid and even directed closely the activities
and appointments of the Church, often to the derogation of papal
authority. In theory, therefore, the monarch was absolute, sharing
his power with no one.

But practice did not conform with the theory of centralized
absolutism, and this became increasingly apparent during the eighteenth century. Feudal manorial law and ecclesiastical canon law
coexisted with royal law. Justice was dispensed not only by the
King's officials, but also by the feudal lords and the clergy. Services
and taxes were due not only to the crown, but also to the lord and
the Church. A strong, dedicated, interested, or ruthless ruler might
have been able to exercise the powers that theoretically rested in
his hands, but neither Louis xv nor Louis xvi possessed the necessary
qualifications. As a result of their weakness, the multiple functions
of state were fulfilled by the ambitious nobility and clergy. This
so-called "refeudalization" of the old regime manifested itself in
the dominance of the aristocracy at Versailles, in the courts, and in
the provincial offices. Formerly recruited from the bourgeoisie in
the days of Louis xiv, the persons in the King's councils, the intendants of the provinces, the members of the *parlements,* the ranking officers of the armed services, and the higher clergy were noble
in title by the 1780s – whether of old feudal blood (the nobility of
the sword) or of the purchased variety (the nobility of the robe).

The fact of plural benefits inherent in membership in the nobility or clergy lends even greater significance to the nature of the
social structure of the old regime. It is accurate but deceptive to
describe eighteenth-century society as divided into three estates or
classes. The frictions within a particular estate often were more
pointed than the conflicts between estates. The identity and har-

mony of interests across estate lines, too, were sometimes closer than those existing within a chosen estate. A description of each estate should make these truths self-evident. The approximately one hundred thousand clergymen in the First Estate included the entire hierarchy of the Roman Catholic Church in France – from the cardinals, archbishops, and bishops down to the parish priests and other churchmen in the secular clergy; to these must be added the heads and members of the regular monastic orders. Dedicated as it might have been to a common creed, pledged to service and obedience to the Church organization, the clergy was nevertheless torn by differences in social background and disputes about the nature of its function and contact with laymen.

By the eve of the Revolution, the leadership of the Church was entirely in the hands of sons of noble families. Not a single bishop in all France came from the Third Estate. Worthy and spiritual though many a bishop or abbot may have been, his outlook and attributes were derived from the landed aristocracy. To the sacerdotal, educational, and philanthropic functions of the upper clergy was added the management of the immense properties of the Church – estimated at 10 percent of the land in France. Even where a bishop was not the lord of a village and thus faced with the same concerns as his aristocratic brothers and cousins with secular lands, he was responsible for the efficient operation of the Church lands in his custody.

Unlike the upper echelons of the Church hierarchy, the parish priests and the great majority in the monastic orders were commoners, rural or urban. But their sympathy or, at least, familiarity with the needs and interests of the peasant or townsman stemmed from more than their class origin. Through his performance of the sacraments and his duties as teacher, tithe collector, dispenser of poor relief, and keeper of the records of births, marriages, and deaths in the parish, the priest had more than passing contact with his wards. Many a priest or monk could be seen tilling the soil, harvesting the crops, pressing the grapes, or generally working alongside the peasants, farm hands, and serfs, thus more completely sharing their experiences. For the material well-being of his parishioners, especially in seasons of bad harvests, the priest might not be in full agreement with his superiors on questions of the amount due the diocese or the amount to be re-allocated to his parish. The difficulties and hardships of urban and rural parishioners were usually more directly obvious to the priest than to the more distant bishop.

If the First Estate exhibited less social cohesion than its spiritual unity might imply, the Second Estate, the nobility, displayed similarly divisive elements. Rated socially at the top of the Second Estate was the traditional nobility of the sword, the nobility of blood. Barring the indiscretion of an ancestral duchess, eighteenth-century dukes could proudly trace their lineage back to the Middle Ages. The social distinction of noble blood was not necessarily accompanied by extensive wealth or sizeable incomes, however. Although many of the nobility of the sword possessed substantial lands that yielded handsome revenues, others were obliged to marry below themselves socially to keep up financially. Less enterprising or more disdainful noblemen chose to maintain the purity of their blood line even if it meant a shabby existence. Titles and scanty associated privileges were all that distinguished these impoverished noblemen from neighboring peasant proprietors.

Increasingly intermingled by marriage and time with the nobility of the sword was the newer nobility of the robe. During the seventeenth and eighteenth centuries, wealthy bourgeois or royal favorites purchased or were rewarded by patents of nobility. This type of title was frequently connected with holding office in the leading administrative and judicial courts, such as a *parlement,* or in some other form of public service. Despised by the lesser nobility of the sword, the new nobles insinuated themselves into the moderately good graces of the upper nobility – often thanks to their supply of daughters with beautiful dowries.

Amounting to 96 percent of the nation, the Third Estate was the the most heterogeneous of the three estates. Fixed descriptive social categories for these twenty-three million commoners, who ranged from the richest of Parisian bankers to the poorest of Breton peasants, can be highly misleading. To designate the bourgeoisie, for example, as an exclusively urban class is to ignore the members who inhabited the rural villages or had wide and practical interests in agriculture. To lump under a single subheading the whole of the peasantry as a socially differentiated class totally unfamiliar with bourgeois capitalistic methods or values is also to distort the social realities of the old regime.

Most prominent in the Third Estate were those bourgeois whose wealth and ambition might even have led them to abandon their fellow commoners and buy their way into the nobility. Content or not with their social status, the top level of the Third Estate included the heads of financial houses and insurance firms that were to be found in Paris, inland trading centers, and port towns. On a par with these prosperous financiers were the merchants who directed the large-scale movement of raw materials, farm produce, or finished goods for the domestic, colonial, or foreign market. Still too early for the widespread industrialism of the following centuries, there were nevertheless already some few "captains of industry" in eighteenth-century France who were involved in mass production in shipbuilding, metallurgy, and certain textiles. It was not uncommon for the financier to be the merchant who was simultaneously the industrial capitalist. These merchants and financiers were perched on the highest rungs of the ladder of the Third Estate.

The problem of evaluating the tangible and intangible rewards of the professional sector of the bourgeoisie creates anew the difficulty of assigning categories and hierarchies within the Third Estate. The incomes of many lawyers, doctors, journalists, civil servants, intellectuals, or artists may have equalled that of a merchant or fallen below that of a thriving bootmaker. Yet, the status and intangible gratifications – was it social or psychological or did the lines blur? – are as hard to determine as those of a bankrupt aristocrat who protected his children from marriage with social-climbing, nonaristocratic suitors.

On lower rungs stood the more typically French bourgeois: the artisan, craftsman, shopkeeper, and tradesman. Again, there often existed an overlap of function. The artisan might practice his skill on the very premises where he or his watchful wife retailed the product. A more successful member of this group might employ skilled workmen to meet an expanded demand or might hire shop helpers to allow his wife the leisure to bloom in a more luxurious middle-class fashion.

Forming the urban proletariat of the Third Estate were the journeymen and apprentices who might have aspired and even secured promotion to a superior rank in the crafts. Such would be an unlikely fate for skilled workmen in the few factories, ship-yards, or mines that anticipated the larger establishments of the nineteenth and twentieth centuries. In this very small class of pro-letariat, there were also unskilled workmen, shop helpers, and domestics, who would swell the number of the unemployed by joining unemployables and beggars in times of economic dis-tress.

The agricultural counterpart of this last-named group would include five million rural proletarians. Serfs (who were far less numerous than in other contemporary continental European soci-eties), migratory or seasonably employed farm hands, landless tenants, and sharecroppers all worked the lands of peasant, bour-geois, noble, or clerical owners and comprised a sizeable portion of the Third Estate as one moved back up the ladder of the society in the countryside. Although outright ownership was complicated by manorial land-tenure arrangements affording many privileges to the local nobility, approximately 30 to 40 percent of the land was in the hands of the fifteen to twenty million socially superior peas-ants. The quantity and quality of the peasant holdings, however, varied widely. A flourishing farmer of Normandy was a peasant, but he lived like a prince compared to his equal in neighboring Brittany. Many peasants with small holdings were obliged to hire themselves out as wage earners in order to survive. On the other hand, others had such extensive property that they were compelled to hire hands, rent part of their land, or arrange for tenants or sharecroppers. Possessors of almost as much of the land as the peasants, many bourgeois were deeply and directly involved in agriculture, whether as resident or as absentee landlords.

Extremely heavy royal, ecclesiastical, and manorial demands fell on the persons and incomes of both the landed and landless rural Frenchmen. As the nobility and clergy, from a desire to ape the bourgeoisie or for other reasons, proceeded to increase their cash returns by more modern methods of farming or by reviving long-forgotten medieval rights over the provincial populace, the lot of the agricultural Third Estate became more and more desperate.

Shared membership in the Third Estate, or even in the First or Second, obviously did not guarantee shared interests. The wide range of differences within the Third Estate engendered serious clashes, actually and potentially. Even in the upper reaches of the bourgeoisie, there would be disharmony between a wealthy manufacturer and a shipping magnate; the manufacturer would press for tariff protection against cheaper English-made goods, whereas the shipping magnate urged abandonment of all restrictions on commerce in order to fill his bottoms regardless of the origin. For the bourgeois with extensive interests in both enterprises, schizophrenia might result from the attempt to satisfy his dual concerns. At the other end of the scale, prolonged periods of unemployment could easily sharpen the latent or overt resentment of the urban or rural proletariat against its own estate's property-owning employers.

The multiple conflicts within specific estates and classes and the frequent accord across estate or class lines should not obscure the fact that membership in the First or Second Estate did carry privileges that went far beyond mere status value. An aristocrat or clergyman possessed certain positive rights, probable advantages, and definite relief from various burdens. No nobleman or cleric could be mustered into the army, obliged to render personal services, or pay certain taxes. Among the probable advantages accruing to the first two estates was the likelihood of appointment to high public office in the civil, military, or ecclesiastical institutions of the old regime. The Third Estate was generally excluded from these positions of power. On the local political scene, too, the provincial Estates and *parlements* were the instruments of noblemen and clergymen. Ecclesiastical courts existed to mete out justice to those churchmen who might still demand and secure "benefit of clergy." The economic advantage of belonging to the First or Second Estate involved exemption from such taxes as the *taille* and entitled one to tax those in the Third Estate (by tithe, tolls, dues, or other means). Although many well-to-do or well-connected bourgeois obtained similar exemptions from the *taille,* seignorial financial demands on the populace became ever more strictly enforced during the latter part of the eighteenth century. Through these and other economic and political privileges, the two highest orders imposed on France a localism particularly abhorrent to the market-conscious bourgeoisie and a burden especially heavy on the lower levels of the Third Estate.

Despite social frictions and anachronistic customs, the economic growth of eighteenth-century France was striking. Scientific methods of cultivation and stock-raising had improved the quality and quantity of agricultural production – the most significant sector of the contemporary economy. New markets and expanding old ones had stimulated a vigorous foreign, colonial, and domestic trade. In most instances, the volume and value of this trade quintupled over the sixty-year period from the 1730s through the 1780s. Production of finished goods mounted to supply the enlarged markets, even though the outlets remained chiefly local. Investment opportunities proliferated, often mixing indistinguishably with speculation on the Paris and provincial exchanges.

Benefits from this burgeoning economy were, however, very unevenly distributed among and within the three estates. Most bourgeois could note with cheer that the prices of goods and commodities in the 1780s had risen 65 percent over their 1730 level. The aristocracy, clergy, and land-owning (not land-renting) bourgeoisie had even more cause for joy: rents had risen 98 percent. The tolls and tithes obviously yielded greater returns in addition to the rents on land leased out by the nobles and clergy to bourgeois and peasant entrepreneurs. Most harassed were the agricultural and urban wage earners who could have noted statistically that the eighteenth-century price inflation far outstripped their mere 22 percent increase in wages.

If the economic growth was striking, it was also cyclical. The last third of the period revealed serious decline and numerous weak spots. The decade preceding the Revolution witnessed a decline in productivity, a slackening of commercial activity, and a rapid rise in unemployment. Especially serious was the 1788 crop failure, which capped the already depressed decade. Deprived of agricultural surpluses for possible cash sale, peasant and bourgeois farm owners were less able to purchase the goods of townsmen. Poor harvests also reduced the employment opportunities of field and vineyard workers, whose misery was multiplied. The commercial and industrial middle classes found vanishing markets for the goods they produced, processed, or handled. Cutbacks in production led to a reduction of bourgeois profits and jobs for their workers. Scarcity of basic foodstuffs led to a sharp increase in prices at the very moment when unemployment deprived the proletariat of money to buy bread.

Although the general image of economic well-being was a true one for the old regime, grave, inherent inequities were exaggerated by the agricultural disasters of 1788 and the commercial and industrial depression.

Vitality rather than liberty and hostility to rather than support of the old regime marked the expression of the eighteenth-century French philosophes, essayists, playwrights, and other literary figures. Their vision of the good — and perhaps even perfect — society ill matched the one that they inhabited and criticized. Paradoxically, despite the frequent fate of exile or expurgation of their works, these authors seemed surprisingly free to bemoan the censorship practiced by the crown and the clergy. Many enlightened noblemen joined with even greater numbers of bourgeois publicists to recommend sweeping political, social, and economic reform of the old regime. Condorcet, Turgot, Voltaire, and a host of others openly or under the thinnest camouflage recommended fundamental changes in the existing system. Even from creative works not primarily designed to be didactic or socially conscious, there also poured forth bitter comments on the injustice and inequality inherent in the privileged order of the day. Beaumarchais might have been principally concerned with internal dramatic and comic tensions in his *Marriage of Figaro,* but many theater goers went home as impressed by the valet's Gallic jibes at the easily outsmarted and ridiculed aristocrats. Yet, this corrosive content did not prevent the play from being released by the censor and performed in 1784 over the six-year opposition of Louis XVI.

By the end of the eighteenth century, there existed a body of literature that could not help but sharpen the awareness of literate Frenchmen — noble and bourgeois — to the flaws of the old regime and, in addition, concrete proposals for its modification. The range was wide — from the penetrating but often timid analysis by Montesquieu of the forms and essence of government to the denunciatory, inflammatory, anticlerical tracts of Voltaire and the more revolutionary social and political diatribes of Jean-Jacques Rousseau.

The informed sectors of the French population approached the 1780s with a keen realization that the old regime in practice fell far short of the espoused ideal of the eighteenth-century philosophe. These and less informed Frenchmen might have longer and passively suffered injustice and grievances if the deepening fiscal crisis and accentuated economic distress had not combined to give the old regime the appearance of inefficiency, inadequacy, or insanity. In these circumstances, the Revolution took place.

From frustrated reform to successful revolt

TO INTERPRET the coming of the French Revolution and the collapse of the old regime in 1789, a wide range of more or less respectable causal choices is available. Surveying the old regime from the end of Louis XIV's reign in 1715 to the fateful 1789 of the rule of Louis XVI, observers of some or no particular profession have claimed to find the origins of the Revolution in material conditions and situations. For such determinists, the conscious or unconscious quest of classes, groups, institutions, or individuals for radical revision of the political, social and economic order inevitably led to revolution. On the other hand, analysts of an idealist bent explain the coming of the French Revolution by citing the influence of the stirring and subversive ideas of enlightened philosophers and their adherents. To throw off the yoke of tyranny, the people rose and sought to create a society in the image of enlightened concepts and principles. Possibly the volume of ink poured out discussing these two broadly opposed causal positions has equalled the amount of blood spilled bringing about the actual Revolution in 1789.

In the materialist school, there are many teachers. According to the Marxists and near-Marxists, the Revolution inexorably took place as the result of long-developing changes in the mode of production and distribution. The application of capitalist methods to commerce, finance, manufacturing of the eighteenth-century variety, and even agriculture had produced a middle class of greater size and self-awareness than had existed in old feudal France. Thwarted by the rules, regulations, and customs that were relics of an archaic local, manorial, aristocratic, ecclesiastical order, the new bourgeoisie sought by revolution to capture the state and to transform the society into vehicles suitable to its new prosperous world of pre-industrial capitalism. Excluded from posts of political or administrative significance, deprived of privileges and rights that the "decadent" nobility and clergy monopolized, exhilarated by several generations of financial success, the bourgeoisie revolted to protect and advance its propertied interests.

Joined to this disgruntled class was the mass of the exploited – the journeymen, apprentices, peasants, agricultural laborers, and serfs. Medievally appropriate guild restrictions had become insurmountable barriers to the promotion of the interests of those who could not even move to the status of a frustrated eighteenth-century master craftsman or artisan. Among the agriculturally exploited classes, the technically free peasant, becoming infected often by capitalistic methods and motives, wriggled uncomfortably in the knots of feudal obligations tied by noblemen and clergymen. With renewed influence at Versailles and in the local areas, the privileged orders were enabled to perpetuate old claims and revive lapsed ones on the landed freemen of the Third Estate. And the unfree, landless proletariat of rural France was harassed to the point of revolutionary desperation by the socioeconomic dichotomies of the old regime. By these standards, how could the nearly twenty-three million members of the Third Estate – from the wealthiest financier to the most impoverished farmhand – long resist engaging in revolutionary activity against the half-million uncompromising, privileged Frenchmen who directed the ruling institutions of state, Church, and army and who attempted to impose their class-derived standards and ways of behavior on the multitude?

Socioeconomic factors were recognized by other materialist interpreters of the French Revolution, but the political and social "scientists" have preferred to shift the weight of causation to the inadequacy, ineffectiveness, or insanity of the old regime's governmental or social apparatus. Rather than focus on socioeconomic drives, these commentators point to the inability of the local and central governmental officials to resolve the problems facing the body politic or to maintain authority over the citizens – privileged or unprivileged. In this sense, the old regime was doomed to fall and be replaced by a more efficient, more appropriate form of government. It was time for a change.

Diametrically opposed to these and other materialist interpreters are the idealists, who are convinced that the French Revolution in particular was fomented by the concepts, principles, and formulas of eighteenth-century philosophes. The political, social, and economic revisions sought by Frenchmen in 1789 were conceived in the minds of intellectuals and artists like Voltaire, Monte-

squieu, Rousseau, and even Beaumarchais. Without the stimuli of
the pithy, vitriolic remarks of Voltaire, the incisive, analytic comments of Montesquieu, the fulminations of Rousseau, and the popular antiprivilege stage remarks of Beaumarchais' *Figaro,* the
citizens of the most materially blessed nation of Europe would
never have budged from what might have been an existentially
absurd personal state of being but, in comparison with that of
other Europeans, was an elevated way of living. Stimulated and
instructed by the ideas contained in the essays, plays, and other
intellectual or artistic works of the eighteenth century, the French
could no longer live within the confines of the old regime. Its
pattern was demonstrably out of focus with the vision of the supposedly perfect society proposed and sketched out by the critics of
pre-1789 France.

The materialist and idealist theories suggested above as well as
those of tangential, derivative, or peripheral schools must all stand
the test of verification by the actual events of the last years of the
old regime. It is from these events that one must ascertain the
Frenchmen's adherence to or abandonment of enlightened ideals,
the fixity or flexibility of class interests, and the strength or weakness of political coalitions.

The storming of the Bastille, the popular uprisings in provincial towns, and peasant rioting in rural France have long entranced
gatherers of facts and tellers of tales. These acts of violence of July,
1789, however, were preceded by equally revolutionary if less violent developments. The issues and problems that produced the
drama of July 14, 1789, were different from those of the preceding year. So, necessarily, were the attitudes and alignments of individuals, classes, and estates as they faced the issues and problems
of the late 1780s.

Cause or catalyst, the crisis over the government's finances precipitated the collapse of the old regime. By 1788, expenditures far
exceeded revenues, with an anticipated deficit of 20 percent. The
debt incurred by the government of Louis XVI was swollen by
grants to the American revolutionaries, by lavish court life, and by

the ordinary expenses of military and civil administration. The servicing of the debt – the mere payment of interest on what had been borrowed – accounted for more than half of the expected revenues for 1789. Radical measures seemed essential to avoid bankruptcy and to balance the budget. Successive ministers had attempted reform of the fiscal system since 1776; they succeeded only in resorting to further borrowing.

The alternatives for resolving the fiscal crisis were vividly clear and demonstrably unfeasible. Reduction of expenditures was one possibility; repudiation of the debt, another; increase of revenues, a third. Pruning costs at Versailles would not substantially solve the problem and would only antagonize the aristocrats who fed so well at the public (or royal) trough. Besides, the vacillating King could be easily induced to reject such proposals. Neither the Queen nor her courtly entourage would lightly submit to such austerity. For all these reasons and for fear of jeopardizing the security of France, economies in the military establishment were deemed inappropriate.

The second road to fiscal safety was to repudiate or refund the outstanding debt. By this means, a tremendous saving could be made. Support for this policy could easily have been secured from the old aristocracy, which held few state bonds. The danger lay in the hostility of the new noblemen, who were influential in the *parlements,* and the bourgeois, whose favor for future borrowing had always to be considered. Furthermore, in the depression-ridden moment of 1788, the French business community was in no financial condition to afford additional loss of capital or income. Already kindled by eighteenth-century ideas and sentiments, they might be too enflamed by losses to their wallets.

The inability to decree and pursue either of these courses of action or the third – increasing state revenues – led to a paralysis of reform, thereby compounding the evil by further borrowing. How, indeed, could state revenues have been increased? Almost all the members of the Third Estate were in economic distress. To increase taxes on the near-bankrupt bourgeois, the wageless working-man, the crop-deprived peasant, or the hard-hit agricultural worker would have produced little revenue and much resistance. Dire need and reason pointed the finger at the privileged classes as a relatively untapped and fruitful source of revenue. Reformer after reformer during the 1780s had attempted to revise the tax system in France. Regional and even intra-estate differences were important, but the greatest degree of tax inequality lay in the exemption of the first two estates. The clergy and the nobility were natural targets for the King and his finance ministers. The promised yield was, in their cases, well worth strenuous effort.

With the fiscal crisis as the issue of the moment during the late 1780s, the King and his ministers moved to formulate and register the appropriate decrees. The privileged class, however, manifested their objections in many ways. They watered down the reforms when they were discussed in the consultative assemblies convoked by the King in 1787. Sufficiently represented by their estate-mates in the Paris and provincial *parlements,* the old and new aristocracy frustrated the royal program by refusing to register the sections of the decrees that would submit the first two estates to equality of taxation. Influential at Versailles, the nobility also acted to undermine the King's confidence in his own reforming intentions. In the provinces, the King's agents, the intendants, were either too weak, too badly supported, or too assimilated locally to be effective against the will of the aristocrats. And what was the royal army but an instrument officered by the very noblemen who protested the potential loss of privilege?

Desperate for money, the King responded with extreme measures. He deprived the *parlement* of much of its jurisdiction and power. A new Plenary Court was entrusted with the duty of registering royal decrees. Other extensions of royal power followed. Exile, arrest, or suspension was the fate of leading court officials who had spearheaded the aristocrats' protests.

What had been a fiscal problem was now widening into one of structural reform and royal disregard for the rights of all Frenchmen. On an individual and institutional basis, the privileged classes took political advantage from the broadening of the crisis. The aristocracy astutely rallied popular support in the common cause against the alleged despotism of the monarch. From the professional sector of the bourgeoisie to the hired rural help, the Third Estate joined the agitation against the arbitrary actions of Louis XVI. Speaking for "the people" in the summer of 1788, the aristocrats forced the King to schedule a meeting of the Estates-General for May, 1789. A revolution against the old regime had truly taken place; not since 1614 had this representative body been convened. The radical, tradition-breaking, agitating left of the moment appeared indubitably to be composed of noblemen and clergy.

A battle had been won, but the war was not over. The King had acknowledged the need to consult the representatives of the nation in order to secure the necessary taxes. The nation was united but only superficially and temporarily. Stemming from the vast differences in background, attitudes, and interests of the first two estates' membership, contradictions appeared in their recommendations. More significantly, the Third Estate began to ponder the implications of the aristocrats' victory over the King.

In September, 1788, the *parlement* of Paris threatened to rob the Third Estate of the spoils of the common struggle against the King. The pronouncement raised a storm of indignation from the Third Estate. The Estates-General, declared the *parlement,* should be constituted as it had been in 1614. For its particular purposes, the aristocracy interpreted this ruling to mean voting by order, voting by estate. Thereby, the closely associated clergy and nobility would easily be able to overrule the Third Estate, dominate the Estates-General and thus rule the kingdom. The elation of the aristocracy was matched by the despair of the Third Estate. What had been achieved but an exchange of masters? Instead of decree by the King, legislation by clergymen and nobility would regulate the lives and property of all Frenchmen. Despite the altruistic declamations of many noblemen and churchmen on relinquishing tax privileges, others of the First and Second Estate hedged, hemmed, and hawed. With political power vested in an Estates-General dominated by these estates, the resolution of the fiscal crisis or any subsequent problem might not suit the Third Estate.

From September, 1788, until May, 1789, the persisting and deepening fiscal crisis was overshadowed by the Third Estate's attempts to acquire more substantial political weight in the coming meeting of the Estates-General. A technically insignificant but potentially crucial gain was made in December, when the government allowed for a doubling of the representation of the Third Estate. Approximately three hundred deputies of the First Estate, and three hundred of the Second could anticipate the presence of six hundred of the Third Estate. The gain was of no importance, however, as long as voting would be by separate estates and not by head in joint meeting. Even if the Third Estate had quintupled the number of its representatives, it could still be outvoted two to one under a rule of voting by order. Of course, if the Third Estate ever succeeded in obtaining the vote by head, the December decision of "doubling" would shift the political dominance in the Estates-General from the First and Second to the Third Estate. This was especially foreseeable since enough enlightened noblemen and clergy would be likely to side with the commoners. For the moment, nevertheless, the indecisive King would issue or cause to be issued no precise ruling on voting procedure.

Before the real victory of voting by head could be achieved, elections had to be held and programs drawn up. On both counts, the aristocracy fared badly in the elections of the First Estate. Parish priests, whose social origins inclined them to sympathy with the commoners, won many seats desired by the nobility-affiliated upper clergy. In the Second Estate, by sheer numbers and influence in the local areas, the provincial noblemen were the winners over the enlightened court nobility. More pregnant for the future were the results in the Third Estate. The professional and the wealthy elements of the bourgeoisie captured control of the entire estate. Thanks to their literacy, talent, status, and influence — to say nothing of the complicated and indirect electoral system — the numerically inferior middle class would represent the rural and urban masses of Frenchmen.

Election of deputies was not the sole political activity in France in the early months of 1789. Each estate was occupied also with framing *cahiers*, lists of grievances and recommended reforms from the varied regions and classes. Although there were many differences in intent and content, the *cahiers* did reflect basic points of agreement. All estates recorded their affection and loyalty to the monarch as the head of the French state, respect for the rights of property holders, and devotion to the Church as a nationally binding institution. That these statements were not mere lip service may be judged in part from the critical suggestions contained in the *cahiers*. That the King should exercise exclusive right to impose taxes was universally rejected. That he should tamper with the related rights of property was also considered inappropriate. In another area, too, the King had demonstrably aroused unanimous protest. He had infringed arbitrarily on many individual and civil rights (arrest, judgment, imprisonment) to the dissatisfaction of enlightened and unenlightened Frenchmen. The proposed limitations on the power of the King were not intended, however, to deprive him of the people's professed love or his many important governmental functions.

The impression of national unity fades on closer reading and analysis of the *cahiers*. Only the First Estate frequently inserted a desire for continued censorship. The Second joined the First in reiterating a hard position on retaining "traditional dues," a term differently understood and often opposed in the grievance lists of the Third Estate. Many a *cahier* of the Third Estate provocatively asserted the demand for voting by head in the forthcoming Estates-General, implying the commoners' quest for political power.

The measured tones of the *cahiers* were less indicative of the split between the estates than were the strident notes of the rash of pamphlets that appeared in late 1788 and early 1789. The famous *What Is the Third Estate?* by the Abbé Sieyès dispelled any fanciful idea that the aristocratically inspired Revolution was complete in the eyes of their erstwhile partners. To Sieyès and to increasing numbers of Frenchmen, the Third Estate was the nation. The minimum demand was to secure "an influence at least equal to that of the privileged classes. . . ." More extravagantly, the Abbé threatened that the Third Estate "will form a National Assembly. . . ."

With battle lines being drawn between the aristocracy and the bourgeoisie and with the King still uncommitted on voting procedures, the deputies began to gather at Versailles in the spring of 1789. No concrete program was forthcoming from Louis XVI's address to the inaugural session of the Estates-General on May 5. From the speeches delivered by his officials (Keeper of the Seals Barentin and Finance Minister Necker), no real reform agenda could be discerned. What was crystal clear on that and subsequent days was that the King sided with the privileged classes in their hope of retaining the custom of meeting separately and voting by estate, not by head. Some few firebrands in the Third Estate wished an immediate showdown on this issue. The moderates and conservatives prevailed, preferring delaying tactics and negotiations with the upper two estates.

One full month of pursuing this latter policy strengthened the position of the Third Estate. Greater unity was achieved among its disparate elements. Sizeable numbers of the clergy and a small fraction of the nobility expressed sympathy for the cause of the commoners, thus weakening the front of the first two estates. On June 17, the Third Estate voted to arrogate to itself the title and several functions of a "National Assembly." More than 80 percent of the deputies were willing to take the plunge. Only a parliamentary maneuver prevented the First Estate from joining the Third two days later, when a majority of the clergy voted favorably on such a motion.

Threatened with an isolated minority status, the nobility and upper clergy hastened to seek the good favor of the King. The revolutionaries of 1788 who had sought to wrest power from the King now had to enlist his services and acclaim his authority in order to maintain minimal political weight, to say nothing of seignorial financial privileges.

Before the King and his council could or would express themselves, the Third Estate made an even more dramatic gesture than that of June 17. Barred from its regular meeting place on June 20 — not by what was assumed to be the repressive intent of King or council, but by workmen performing routine repair work on the hall — the Third Estate thronged angrily into a nearby indoor tennis court. The famous oath taken there reaffirmed the June 17 intention to act as a National Assembly. As a threat and challenge to the King and the hostile aristocrats, it was further resolved that,

. . . all members of this Assembly shall at once take a solemn oath never to separate but to meet in any place that circumstances may require, until the constitution of the kingdom shall be laid and established on secure foundations; and that after the swearing of the oath each and every member shall confirm this indefeasible resolution by signing with his own hand.[1]

All but three deputies did so sign; one refused and two abstained. The Third Estate was firm, the Third Estate was nearly unanimous, but the Third Estate was not yet officially recognized as a National Assembly. Within two days, the majority of the clergy and a faction of the nobility joined in the sessions of the self-styled National Assembly.

The King at last declared the court's opinion at the royal session of June 23. Concession was piled on concession. To the Estates-General he promised the right to control the budget; to legislate on basic administrative changes; to establish freedom for the individual, the press, and internal trade; and to abolish the many personal services due the King (such as the *corvée* — obligatory work on the roads). For these matters, as well as for those of general interest, the Estates-General would be permitted to meet jointly and vote by head. The King appeared willing to accept the

[1] Quoted in Georges Lefebvre, *The Coming of the French Revolution*, trans. R. R. Palmer (Princeton, N.J.: Princeton University Press, 1947), p. 85.

role of a limited monarch. The Estates-General would be a major political force in the formation of French institutions and practices.

Certain reservations made these possibilities less attractive to the Third Estate. The King was not willing to yield to the Estates-General the right to vote by head on "the ancient and constitutional rights of the three orders, the form and constitution of future Estates-General, feudal and manorial property, and honorific privileges and useful rights of the first two orders." [2] Religion and Church organization would come under the jurisdiction of the Estates-General only with the prior agreement of the clergy. Even equality of taxation would require the separate and voluntary action of the privileged orders. The end of the King's speech spelled also the end of the commoners' hopes. He ordered the estates to separate and to deliberate separately about the royal conception of the new France.

The temper of the delegates of the Third Estate was not suited to such hedged offers. The sugar coating of influence in some important affairs of state was too thin to make palatable the pill of the privileged orders' continued political and social supremacy. The nobility and churchmen would still be the arbiters of change on such crucial items as tax exemption, constitution-making, and feudal privilege. What if the aristocracy and clergy objected to suggested reforms in these fields? It was likely. Would the King apply pressure to force the first two estates to yield? It was not likely. Even the moderate, conservative members of the Third Estate seemed to realize how bitter the medicine would be if they followed the King's prescription.

Unwilling to sacrifice the opportunity of gaining leverage on all major decisions, unwilling to remain in an acknowledged status of social inferiority, unwilling to trust either the King's unwavering support of reform or the aristocracy's altruism, the Third Estate held firm for a recognition of a National Assembly dominated by the bourgeoisie and empowered with rights to frame a constitution

[2] Quoted in Lefebvre, p. 86.

and to share in governing France. Physical force alone could budge them from their principles, interests, and seats. Guards were dispatched to the hall for this very purpose.

At this crucial moment, the personality of a man determined the shape of history. Whether from weakness or miscalculation or kindness or indifference or all combined, the King refrained from having his adamant subjects chased and shot. Not only did he ignore the blandishments and insistence of the court, but he even ordered the nobility and clergy to join the Third Estate on June 27 to constitute themselves as a single, "National Constituent Assembly." By firmness, unity, and some manifestations of popular support, the bourgeoisie had effected a bloodless revolution.

To translate this tactical and strategic success into tangible, operative laws of the land required the good will and cooperation of the embittered aristocracy in the Assembly and of the hapless monarch in Versailles. The bourgeois members, along with most of the clergy and some of the nobility, wished to proceed slowly and carefully toward a reasonable, moderate, constitutional future. Evidence mounted that the King was according more than a casual audience to those aristocrats and churchmen who considered the defeat of June 27 as a strictly temporary setback. In early July, troop movements from the provincial and frontier areas of France alarmed the Assembly at Versailles and the Paris populace. Secret meetings at court increased the suspicions and fears of the deputies that their victory would be shortlived. Seeming confirmation of these suspicions came on July 11 when one of the darlings of the bourgeoisie, Necker, was dismissed in a reshuffling of the King's ministry.

A long-enduring coalition crystallized in July of 1789. Aristocrats and upper clergy attached themselves to the King for their own and the royal cause. Abandoning their revolutionary stance of 1788, the privileged classes and their royal ally represented a formidable power bloc. Administrative, judicial, military, and ecclesiastical control was technically in their hands. The traditional subservience of the people to the sword, the cross, and the scepter might also be expected to buttress their authority. Against this array of strength, what counted the legal ability, oratorical skill, and business acumen of the middle-class majority in the threatened National Assembly? Additional forces were deemed essential to sustain the Third Estate's parliamentary success. By design and spontaneity, they materialized to save the National Assembly and to furnish the future with a symbol by which the Revolution could be easily identified. Parisian mobs provided the muscle and the Bastille, the symbol. Historians should neither disregard nor over-rate those legends by which later actions are motivated, programs formulated and promoted, hopes inspired, and stones and streets transformed into near-religious relics.

If the nervous middle-class deputies of the menaced National Assembly had impelling reasons to enlist the aid of the mob, the lower classes of Paris had equally strong but different ones for engaging in revolutionary action. Artisans and shopkeepers were as disturbed as their journeymen, apprentices, and hired help by the depression that had reduced their ability to sell their wares. Food shortages and the high cost of grain and bread were even more disconcerting to the increasing numbers of unemployed in the capital. The July 12 news of Necker's dismissal intensified popular discontent. Did the government intend to refuse measures that might alleviate the misery of the people? The efforts of royal troops to halt protesting paraders and to disperse noisy gatherings were met with indignation. In a growing number of instances, factions of the French Guards, recruited often from the very classes whose misery had led them to violence, intervened against the King's troops and mingled sympathetically with the mob. Burning and pillaging many public buildings, the crowds momentarily forced the withdrawal of the military and the police. Barricades were hastily erected.

Without arms, the populace might have found it difficult to thwart a concentrated, surprise attack. The search for grain and food supplies became a search for weapons and ammunition. The need for defense against royal cavalry units sparked a quest for all possible means to frustrate the rumored large-scale punitive action planned by King and court. Gun shops were raided. Ammunition was collected. Royal depots of arms and ammunition were tempting targets. Bastions from which royal forces could issue were viewed with suspicion. The Bastille conveniently fell into both categories. To disarm the Bastille of its menacing cannon and to expropriate its supplies would reduce the retaliatory opportunities of the King and ensure the safety of the Parisians. Seizure of the Bastille was further justified by the popular but erroneous conviction that the fortress was a Devil's Island for victims of despotism.

With the limited purposes of dismantling its offensive armaments and distributing its store of weapons, the mobs marched to and milled about the gates of the Bastille. Misunderstanding rather than plot better explains the bloody storming, seizing, and burning of the fortress. The tensions of the crowd outside could not await the conclusion of the polite and prolonged negotiations of its spokesmen within the walls. The garrison was too apathetic and inadequate to do more than provoke an easily provoked mob. The governor, the Marquis de Launay, was a microcosmic Louis XVI who could never choose the correct moment to be either repressive or permissive. Stirred by the street-corner speeches of bourgeois, impelled by their own "class interests" (of which they were undoubtedly less conscious than they were of their immediate hunger and joblessness), swept up in the excitement of the moment, the Parisian crowds demonstrated their capacity for ferocity. "The people" had asserted themselves, flouted the authority of the King, and rendered unlikely his disbanding the National Assembly.

In the provincial towns and in rural France, similar outbursts preceded or followed the July 14 fall of the Bastille. Royal officials in administrative and judicial posts were rudely displaced by ambitious bourgeois. Their success was attributable to their own efforts and to the same type of popular uprising that had won the day in Paris. Peasants conducted their own countryside vendetta against the privileged classes and the crown. Châteaux were burned, noblemen harassed, royal agents attacked. The July, 1789, outburst was motivated partly by the desire to destroy the feudal charters on which aristocrats based their traditional and persisting seignorial demands. Crop failures and rural unemployment during 1788–1789 made the impositions of lord and King even more hateful. Fear was a factor, too. The peasants were convinced, by their own intuition and by swiftly spreading rumors, that the nobility was leagued with the King. Troops and bands of beggars, vagrants, and brigands were all reportedly being grouped to restore the order of yesteryear, shattered by the Third Estate's ascendancy in the National Assembly. In fact if not in law, the peasants had liberated themselves from feudalism and many aspects of royal authority.

Reports of the widespread disorder during the "Great Fear" filtered into Versailles. The bourgeois in the National Assembly were grateful for the buttressing of their position vis-à-vis the King and court. The majority of the delegates were nevertheless fearful of sliding into an anarchy that might threaten their emerging economic and social pre-eminence. To recognize the peasants' gains without encouraging further attacks on property, several deputies planned to introduce appropriate bills at the meeting of August 4, 1789. In an unanticipated orgy of decree-making, the emotion-swept National Assembly concluded its session the following morning. Liberal noblemen and parish priests joined the representatives of the middle class to proclaim the end of the feudal system. Voted out of existence, without compensation to the possessors, were such traditional rights and privileges of the clergy and nobility as the tithe, tax exemption, manorial justice, public office-holding, hunting and fishing, labor services, and holding serfs. Money payments were to compensate the privileged classes for the loss of the manorial dues, which included charges for use of the lord's mill, wine-press, and so forth. Municipalities, provinces, and many corporate institutions suffered the revocation of their charters and special rights and monopolies. Private property as such remained undisturbed by the flood of decrees that issued from the National Assembly on August 4 and 5 and on the following, less frenzied days.

The next step in the Revolution was the framing of a Declaration that would serve many purposes. Not only would it provide an apologia for the sometimes violent events that had already transpired, but also it would be a legal and philosophical charter for the constitutional reforms that were necessarily forthcoming. The preamble to the August 26 *Declaration of the Rights of Man and Citizen* recognized that man possessed certain "natural, inalienable and sacred rights. . . ." These rights were defined in the second of the seventeen clauses as "liberty, property, security and resistance from oppression." More specifically, all Frenchmen were guaranteed equal treatment before the law; freedom of speech, press, and religious opinion; and inviolability of property. Limitation of these and other liberties was legitimate only by due process of law and in such cases where one man's exercise of his liberty jeopardized his neighbor or the public order. Since sovereignty now inhered in the nation, the law was the expression of the people or their representatives. Separation of powers was proclaimed as essential as the guarantee of rights. By the formulation of the Declaration of Rights, the National Assembly sanctioned and consolidated in law the gains achieved by revolutionary action. In law as well as in fact, the old regime was shorn of its authoritarian, inegalitarian characteristics.

The King remained, however, and there was no mystery about his hostility to the Declaration of Rights and the August 4–5 decrees. But there was conjecture about whether he would accept and sign them or oppose them openly by refusing his signature or adherence. The rift between Louis xvi and the Assembly was widened during the negotiations about the veto powers that would be allowed the King. Political tensions mounted during the month of September. The monarch refused to take action on the Assembly's decrees. He insisted on an absolute veto and called the Flanders Regiment to Versailles. A pre-Bastille day atmosphere prevailed.

Noble and clerical opponents of the revolutionary changes linked their cause ever more firmly with the King's. Even some wealthy bourgeois deputies rallied to the King or, at least, appeared lukewarm toward the Assembly's effort to infringe further on royal authority. For these delegates, the Revolution had been won. There was nothing to gain and much to lose by further violence. Other deputies felt differently and coordinated plans with sympathetic Parisian politicians, journalists, and agitators to force the King's hand. For this purpose, the recently formed National Guard seemed an unreliable or inadequate weapon. Its commander, Lafayette, was by no means inclined to bloody engagement with royal forces. The volunteer members of the Guard were mostly well-to-do citizens, those who could afford the obligation to purchase their own uniforms. As in July, the Parisian masses would be needed.

The crowd was willing. Similar political fears, identical economic factors, and the same play of mob psychology that had brought about the fall of the Bastille accounted for the October Days. Better organization and more careful direction by bourgeois groups and clubs were the distinguishing mark of the October 5 march to Versailles. A rowdy, howling mob of women hurled rocks and oaths along the route from Paris to the palace. Bread, bread, and more bread seemed to be their objective. Oral guarantees by the King that grain supplies would be immediately made available in Paris did not appease the demonstrators. Neither did royal adherence to the Declaration of Rights and the August decrees. The mob would be calmed only by having the King and his family move to Paris. Under the watchful eye of "the people," the King would perforce be amenable to the general will. He would be less able to use his remaining instruments of power against constitutional and legislative reforms. He would be removed from the anti- or counterrevolutionary influence of many aristocrats and clergymen. A jubiliant crowd accompanied him (and wagonloads of grain) on the unsought trip from Versailles, and the King was installed in the Tuileries on the night of October 6. The National Assembly soon followed, thus making the entire government highly sensitive to the opinions and passions of the Parisian populace. The mob was king.

Revolution on a national scale had occurred. In urban and rural France, the old regime was dead — or, at least, mortally wounded. The label of exclusive responsibility can not be pinned on any single individual, group, or class. Each class played an active or passive role in the rapidly unfolding events of 1788–1789. Initially, the aristocrats had appeared to be the revolutionary party, dealing a blow to the old regime by forcing the King to call an Estates-General. Successively, middle-class elements emerged as the radical left, forcing the nobles to the center and right as the original revolutionaries felt compelled to support the regime they had so vehemently criticized months earlier. The popular uprisings of July and October, sometimes directed and organized by the bourgeoisie, sometimes erupting spontaneously, introduced the peasants and lower classes as activists. In the face of the potentially dangerous masses, previously leftist bourgeois shifted to a center or right position, abandoning their former collaborators in the Third Estate. Thus, to hold any particular class responsible for the Revolution or to categorize it as being right, center, or left, one must be precise as to the moment — day, month, and year.

Even at those precise moments when a single class or individual might be adjudged the protagonist of a key event, multiple forces were operative. To view the origins of the Revolution solely in socioeconomic terms of class conflict is to possess good but not perfect vision. An undeniable clash of interest in organizing economic life existed between the privileged classes and the Third Estate in the old regime and certainly played a role in bringing on the Revolution. Nevertheless, a common political front was managed in the summer of 1788 when peasants apparently overlooked the aggravations and burdens of seignorial demands. The bourgeois, too, seemed to ignore those feudal remnants of tolls, taxes, and tithes that restricted their economic advancement or reduced their profits. Again in July, 1789, aristocrats, bourgeois, and peasants were unable to appreciate the essence or implications of property-holding. Instead, the "capitalist" middle class and the land-owning peasantry incited the propertyless masses. With a fine disregard for the canons of Karl Marx, the French petty bourgeois and the proletarian of shop and farm eagerly joined their bourgeois and peasant exploiters. A significant historical event was apparently being determined by forces or factors other than a conscious struggle for class interests. If socioeconomic determinists insist on the event having transpired by unconscious manifestation of a basic conflict, perhaps Freud or Jung would be a more helpful guide than Marx.

1789–1799

Ten years of revolutionary ferment

SEVERAL fundamental problems commanded the attention of the French nation during the decade bracketed by the fall of the Bastille on July 14, 1789, and the Bonapartist coup of 18–19 Brumaire (November 9–10, 1799). Ten years of experimentation did not resolve the French political problem. (But, with the exception of a few years, have the nearly two hundred years since 1789 been more fruitful?) To decree a shift of sovereignty from the monarch to the entire French nation was simple. To devise effective and acceptable institutions to govern the country was not so simple. How was the general will of the people to be made manifest? What was to be the form of the government? Regardless of form, who would wield the decisive powers of state when and if they were separated in accordance with the avowed intention of the Declaration of Rights? How equal were all citizens to be in respect to voting and office-holding? What would be the arrangements for local government and for the administration of the realm? Where was the line to be drawn between the jurisdiction of the state and that of "nonpolitical" social, economic, religious, and cultural institutions?

While seeking answers to these and other aspects of the political question, the French nation simultaneously sought the right prescription for its fiscal health. The financial ills of the state may have been inherited from the old regime, but they were intensified by the commotion of the early revolutionary years and aggravated by the drain of the war effort of the 1790s. Suggestions for a cure were numerous. Some were economically sound but politically un-

feasible; others were practical politically but financially unrewarding; still others were acceptable only because of the urgency of
military defense.

The measures adopted in 1789 and 1790 to resolve the fiscal
problem opened the door to deep-seated and long-enduring controversy over religious life. At stake was the institutional and even
the spiritual position of the Roman Catholic Church in France.
The status and role of the Church, its relationship to the state, and
its doctrine became issues about which Frenchmen argued and
fought.

The problem of war was also significant in itself and served to
precipitate action or discussion in other fields. Reorganization of
the military forces, their training, leadership, and employment required careful consideration. The needs of the army in defensive
or offensive operations were obviously matters of political and
economic concern. Furthermore, Frenchmen of the decade were
compelled to determine a policy for the conquest, annexation, or
occupation of non-French lands and peoples.

Although these and other problems may be abstracted for
separate analysis, they were inextricably interrelated in the actual
experience of the French. The problem of political reorganization
was complicated by the economic and social ramifications of possible solutions. Religious reform was inextricably involved in the
effort to resolve the fiscal crisis. The origins, nature, and effects of
the foreign wars were closely linked to all the other problems of
the decade.

Each problem evoked a wide range of suggestions for a "proper"
solution. Many factors determined the Frenchman's stand as a
radical, moderate, or conservative – if indeed he had any stand at
all. Political, social, or economic interests of a personal or class
nature might have influenced him. Ideology might have lured him
into the left, center, or right. However, numerous Frenchmen who
stood on the left on one particular issue were staunchly on the right
when another problem came to the fore.

For purposes of description and analysis, the revolutionary

decade of 1789–1799 may be divided into three periods: 1789–
1792, 1792–1795, 1795–1799. The logic as well as the artificiality
of this separation should become evident as the discussion of the
events unfolds. During the first period, 1789–1792, the political
responsibility of the National Assembly was twofold. On the one
hand, the deputies were engaged in drafting a constitution that
would carry out the instructions in the *cahiers,* conform with the
principles of the Declaration of Rights, and anticipate the long-
range needs of the French nation. Simultaneously, the constitution
makers shouldered the task of making and implementing the day-
to-day decisions necessary in running a government.

The deputies produced the Constitution of 1791 to define the
structure and function of the component parts of the new French
government. Tradition was maintained in the figure of the King.
Revolutionary change was clearly indicated in the limitations on
his absolute authority as well as in the establishment of institutions
that subverted the old regime. Although sovereignty was inherent
in the nation and vested in its representatives, the powers of government were dispersed, if not entirely separated. The King had the
right to conduct diplomatic relations even if the final decisions
belonged to the representative body. Over the armed forces, too,
the King maintained nominal leadership and an appointive prerogative subject to parliamentary approval. The King was circum-
scribed also in the choice and control of his ministers and advisors,
or "cabinet." He could nominate his favorites, but their installation
was valid only with the Assembly's approval. Each royal decree
required the countersignature of one of the ministers, who were, in
turn, fair game for interpellation by the Assembly. Over certain
acts of Parliament, the King possessed a substantial veto. For the
duration of two sessions of the chambers, the monarch could suspend the enactment of nonconstitutional, nonfinancial measures.

The Constitution of 1791 granted predominant weight to the
representative, elective, unicameral Parliament. Despite the stated
powers of the King, the Assembly had the final say on the appointment of diplomatic and military chiefs, ratification of treaties,

decisions on war and peace, and expenditures for the military establishment. The Parliament alone had the right to decide on constitutional and fiscal matters, the King's veto being inapplicable. The King had no formal check on the rights, privileges, and tenure of Parliament and its members. Parliament was "permanent, inviolable, and indissoluble" once elected by the citizens. According to the Constitution, however, citizens were divided into two categories: active and passive. The rights inscribed in the Declaration of Rights were guaranteed to all citizens, but political privileges such as voting and office-holding were accorded only to active citizens. Property-holding or tax-paying was the criterion for an "active" rating. Electoral procedures of an indirect, two-step nature were adopted along with special qualifications for the eligibility of candidacy for deputies and electors. By these definitions and devices, the number of active, voting citizens was reduced to little over 4,000,000. In the step before the choice of deputies, there were merely 50,000 electors.

Through principled conviction, Machiavellian astuteness, or fear of creating too many enemies on the left or right, the middle-class constitution makers did not project their unquestionable political primacy into the judicial area. Passive citizens were rewarded by a court system that carried out the expression of equality found in the Declaration of Rights. Whatever the defects of a judiciary elected on the same "undemocratic" basis as the Parliament, the courts of law were not headed by venal or appointed officials. Independent of both Assembly and King, the judicial branch was to be guided by rules and procedures of egalitarian and humanitarian character. No longer enmeshed in the plural jurisdictional toils of King, intendant, clergymen, and lord, and no longer subject to fees for hearing and judging his case, the most passive citizen found his humble social status no bar to an elevated consideration of his crimes or torts.

Administratively, too, the reformers moved in the direction of simplification and uniformity. Replacing the old regime's nobility and clergy who shared or disputed administration with the royally appointed intendants, local officials were now elected. The thirty-odd provinces were henceforth divided into eighty-three departments that were subdivided into districts, cantons, and communes. Although centralized direction replaced elective practice by 1792, the administrative units have remained until today.

Economic and social reforms were substantial, too, during the period 1789–1792. Mercantilist controls on commerce, industry, and agriculture were relaxed or abolished, helping to free the individual and to make a national unit of economic life. Although protective tariffs against foreign goods were retained, the grain trade within France was freed, and internal customs and toll barriers were eliminated. The termination of monopolies and exclusive economic privileges theoretically permitted every Frenchman to enter the profession, career, or trade of his choice. In this respect, the final suspension of the guilds, voted in the Le Chapelier Law of June, 1791, was also intended to be a boon. This same law, subsequently re-enforced by other decrees, foreshadowed the highly individualist tendencies of nineteenth-century economic liberalism. Unions were outlawed, as were collective efforts by workingmen to bargain, petition, demonstrate, or strike. Even the possibility of charitable and educational functions by workingmen's associations was denied.

Fiscal reforms proceeded apace. Inequality of taxation was ended. Indirect taxes, such as the detested salt tax, were abolished. In their place were legislated direct taxes, payable by all Frenchmen, on land, industry, and commercial enterprises. Drastic revision of the tax system brought practice into line with revolutionary theory but did not bring much-needed revenues into the treasury. In fact, the many reforms tended to compound the curse that had helped bring on the Revolution. Frenchmen were apparently reassured in their resistance to tax-paying by the slogans and principles of their deputies. The flight of capital from France made even more febrile the government's financial condition.

Inadequate tax yields and the inviolability of private property led the Assembly to seek relief by seizing and selling the property of the greatest single corporate body in France – the Church. This action must not be construed as an antireligious or even anticlerical attack. The Church was not destroyed nor was theology affected. What was needed in 1789–1790 was money. The sale of Church land would fill this need. Meanwhile, negotiable notes called *assignats* were issued with the lands as collateral. The *assignats* were soon after declared to be legal tender. The criticism frequently leveled against this operation could be justified only later in the decade. On purely economic grounds, in 1790 the operation was sound. Only when the printing presses outstripped the possible receipts from the sale of the lands was a dangerous situation created. Only, too, when the state moved into the reorganization of Church administration and even into religious beliefs and practices was there serious division of opinion in France.

If the fiscal problem necessitated the confiscation of Church property, the despoiling of the Church dictated a reformation of the state's religious policy. The disappearance of the Church's capital and revenue prevented it from being able to function independently. Unless it were to withdraw from all but perfunctory ceremonial performances, the state would be obliged to become increasingly involved in religious affairs. Since the deputies of 1789 were not the anticlerical, antireligious fire eaters of later French generations, the Assembly moved to buttress the Church's position. When the Assembly seized the Church's property, the state assumed the responsibility of paying salaries to the clergy and supporting the Church's activities in worship, charity, and education. Pensions were provided for members of the regular clergy whose monasteries were disbanded. The unaffected teaching and charitable orders received state aid.

The Civil Constitution of the Clergy, framed finally on July 12, 1790, and accepted ten days later by the King, was essentially a measure designed to reorganize the secular clergy. Paralleling the new administrative arrangement of France, the ecclesiastical body was divided into eighty-three dioceses, coinciding with the departments. The Pope was stripped of administrative authority but remained unchallenged as spiritual head. The bishops and subordinate parish priests, however, were to be elected by the citizens instead of being appointed by their hierarchical superiors. The French nation now selected its own religious officials; the French state paid their salaries.

As public servants, the clergy was asked on November 27, 1790, to take an oath of allegiance to the new Constitution, of which the Civil Constitution of the Clergy was an integral part. Thereby, the deputies hoped to translate the basic legislation into administrative practice, to force the hesitant Pope to pronounce himself on the revolutionary changes, and to replace resistant churchmen with more sympathetic elected bishops and priests.

To the dismay of the deputies, their legislation on the Church provoked a more violent response than that elicited by any of their other reforms. Divisions and dissatisfaction were created or manifested that boded ill for a lasting revolutionary settlement beyond the religious one. Whatever the relationships among the issues, the French reaction to the treatment of the Church serves as an excellent point of departure for an examination of responses to all the major reforms of the 1789–1792 period.

Calm had attended the Assembly's initial reforms of the Church pertaining to the abolition of the tithe, the annates, the monastic orders, and the confiscation of Church property. The Civil Constitution of the Clergy was drafted in an atmosphere of friendly deliberation. The King accepted these changes without overt hostility. The Pope, accustomed although opposed to the radical measures to which the eighteenth century had subjected him, seemed not to be an insurmountable obstacle in the negotiations that were being conducted between him and the revolutionary government. The majority of the French clergy seemed to anticipate without undue alarm important revision of the Gallican Church. Nevertheless, when the oath of allegiance was demanded in 1790, the upper clergy was nearly unanimous in rejecting adherence. Only seven bishops in all France subscribed. Even among the lower clergy, generally more attuned to the Revolution than their superiors, half of the parish priests refused to swear fidelity to the Constitution. Partly to frustrate any ecclesiastical reform and partly to escape implicit state domination, more than half the clergy became nonjuring or refractory; fewer than half were juring or constitutional. So substantial were the numbers of recalcitrant clergy that the bewildered Assembly was unable to replace them with elected officials without entirely disrupting the sacramental system for the laity.

Frenchmen of many classes rallied in support of the refractory churchmen. The devout King became irreconcilably opposed to the bourgeois reformers, especially when the Pope, on March 11, and April 13, 1791, officially pronounced himself against the principles of the Revolution and the Civil Constitution of the Clergy. Aristocrats, associated with the clergy by blood, ideas, or both, hastened to the side of nonjuring churchmen. Ties of tradition, belief, or temperament bound large sections of the peasantry to the parish priest who chose to refuse the oath. Regional rather than class differences, however, were far more significant in locating the Church's allies against the state. Much of the west (Brittany and the Vendée), north, and east (Alsace) of France was particularly staunch. Elsewhere, the reformation of the clergy proceeded smoothly according to the Assembly's plans.

There began to appear in revolutionary France a right-wing clerical faction (composed of King, aristocrats, peasants, and bourgeois) that united against the moderate reform of the Assembly. From the increasingly heated debate on church–state relations, there also emerged a left wing that objected to the deputies' efforts as being too moderate, too tepid. In the Parliament and in Jacobin Clubs, members of the professional bourgeoisie professed ideological attachment to a more anticlerical position than most deputies would allow as tenable or feasible. For these children of Voltaire, the Church ought not to be handled with kid gloves but rather with the mailed fist in order that Frenchmen, like it or not, be liberated from the shackles of unreason to soar to a secular heaven of harmony. The stage was being set for the great debate on church and state that would perplex the French nation for more than a century.

The sale and distribution of Church lands complicated the Frenchmen's position on the religious issue. Although half the clergy resisted the oath of allegiance and the subjection to state control, far fewer agreed with their colleagues that the tithe be restored or that the confiscated property be returned. Many peasants and bourgeois had displayed rightist tendencies by siding with the nonjuring priests. These same laymen, however, were adamantly leftist and anticlerical whenever any suggestion arose that they should disgorge the parcels of Church land they had acquired or were in the process of acquiring.

On legislation other than religious of 1789–1792, Frenchmen had equally good grounds to take sides. Considering the material and ideological background of the literate bourgeois architects of the French world, it should not be surprising to find a polarized reaction to the political reforms of the period. The King had never fully accepted or adapted himself to the concept or practice of submission to or cooperation with the representative body of his nation. His good intentions were highly conditioned and sometimes negated by his own preconceptions of royal rule and his sometimes correlated, sometimes discordant attachment to the hunt, his wife, and his hobbies. As a man so variously pulled and tied, Louis XVI was an important force in the crystallizing right of 1789–1792. By incapacity or inability to act the executive role as the disembodied figurehead or the cooperative participant in the constitutional monarchy of his day, Louis became an antirevolutionary rightist. Members of the aristocracy, whose displacement from posts of central and local authority was not requited by the satisfaction of an impulsive or cerebral liberalism, had their special reasons for enlisting in the right-wing opposition to the political France structured by the bourgeois deputies of the Assembly.

Frustrated in political aspirations rather than stripped of former power were the left-wing opponents of the Constitution of 1791. Denial of suffrage would probably not have bothered the inarticulate, "passive" citizen if certain universally minded bourgeois had not projected their democratic and disruptive vision. Extension of suffrage was a less radical portion of this vision than the mounting republicanism of left-wing circles. The ill-concealed repugnance of the King to the Constitution frightened Jacobin Frenchmen. An uncooperative King could and did obstruct the smooth, efficient operation of parliamentary government. Conviction was growing among radicals that the monarchy would have to be replaced by a republic in order to consolidate the revolutionary gains. Many a bourgeois who associated himself with the left on this issue, however, would shy away from the left's anticlerical, antireligious stand.

Discontent over the economic and social program of the bourgeois Assembly could also have contributed to the formation of a French right and left. Loss of privilege placed the aristocracy at the helm of the right. The bourgeois center's reforms evoked a leftist response from other bourgeois, who were principally concerned for ideological reasons. The interests of the masses were poorly served by the economic and social individualism so dear the middle-class victors of 1789. The mass of the aggrieved — propertyless Frenchmen who were to be found in the lesser bourgeoisie and in the rural and urban working class — was not at first organized or fully conscious of its predicament. It could often be attracted by the leadership of the right or the left. Many workers were activated by the nobility's or clergy's call to return to the traditional order, and many were stirred by the promises and measures of radical bourgeois leaders, such as Maximilian Robespierre. The latter course seemed more appealing, since the left offered advantages not forthcoming from the right. The right was still too tainted with the possession of old-regime privilege to have more than local success between 1789 and 1792.

Political, religious, economic, and social issues of material or ideological origins were dividing the French nation into diverse, shifting groups by 1792. The domestic situation, combined with the foreign one, helped precipitate two interconnected events of extraordinary importance: the outbreak of war and the end of the monarchy. In turn, these two developments intensified the rifts within the nation.

The multiple reforms of the Revolution did not seem to pose a threat to the security of other European states in 1789. In fact, the last days of the old regime and the first ones of the Revolution had witnessed a withdrawal of France from its traditionally ascendant position on the continent. An empty treasury, an indecisive King, and preoccupation with internal activities had militated against a forceful foreign policy. The Belgian uprisings against Austrian rule in 1788–1790 passed without vigorous response in France. The relatively bloodless arrival of reform in Europe's most powerful state seemed to presage an era of cooperation and peace with Austria, Prussia, and Russia, whose monarchs were paying at least lip service to enlightened principles.

Suspicions of doubt crept into this illusionary Eden when the Alsatian nobility and the European rulers realized the implications of the Revolution's abolition of feudal and manorial rights and privileges. By the ambiguous but valid Peace of Westphalia of 1648, Alsace had been ceded to France on condition that the French guarantee the rights, privileges, and immunities of the resident nobility. Presumably, these aristocrats, retained legal connections with agencies of the Holy Roman Empire. The spontaneous decrees and the more calculated Declaration of Rights of August, 1789, could be technically considered as unilateral abrogations of international obligations. European apprehensions were enhanced by the revolutionary treatment of Avignon. Long a papal possession that included Frenchmen in an area surrounded by still more French nationals, Avignon was finally annexed by the National Assembly. The objections of the head of the Church had no weight against the French deputies' respect for the wishes of the local populace.

The decision of April 20, 1792, of the Legislative Assembly was an example of contradictory, opposite elements arriving at a single, harmonious conclusion: war. That it would be a long war was inconceivable to all the promoters. That its effects would reach Washington, Moscow, and unborn distant capitals was ill anticipated.

That it would lead to untold unity and unbelievable dispute within the French nation in the 1790s, 1890s, and perhaps 1990s was not even dimly foreseen.

Less from temperamental bellicosity than from political ambition, Louis XVI provoked war. He initiated and maintained communications with heads of European states and with French émigrés in order to reverse the revolutionary tide at home. The correspondence with these foreign and expatriate enemies was strangely received. Hapsburg Austria's Holy Roman Emperor Leopold was militarily cool to his little sister Antoinette's recurrent appeals for aid. Big brother-in-law was not too receptive either to those right-wing noblemen who had fled France to use their Rhineland havens as sanctuaries or launching bases for a recapture of their homeland. The Emperor and the other monarchs were nevertheless under internal pressure to take some kind of positive action against revolutionary France.

The sword of war had two edges. If it was the desired instrument of the King and nobility to return to the old regime, it was also the weapon sought by the bourgeois majority to oblige the King to play a more cooperative role as constitutional monarch or to pierce through to a republican France. Convinced by 1792 that the monarchical experiment was a political failure and a menace to the gains of the Revolution, the Girondin faction in the Assembly believed that a foreign war would demonstrate to the nation these deputies' sound but undocumented, intuitive impression that the King was a traitor. The vote for a declaration of war encountered little opposition. One objector was a bright young man named Robespierre who embraced a doctrinaire pacifism at that juncture. The conduct of a foreign war was now added to the many issues over which the French divided, grouped, or debated during the second period of the Revolution, 1792–1795.

The 1792–1795 period was infinitely more radical than the earlier or following eras. The republican form of government was introduced, centralization of administration was resumed, political rivalries were sharpened, and the Reign of Terror took place. Economic and social measures more familiar to the twentieth century than to the eighteenth were decreed. Social customs and religious habits underwent striking change. War complicated the problems and heightened the excitement of those years. Organization of a nation in arms seemed mandatory. Nationalism became a force as potent as the revolutionary liberal program in its impact on France, the rest of Europe, and the world. In all these changes, a note of pragmatic immediacy can be detected, but there also inhered a mystique of an ideological, almost theological, missionary quality.

The all-pervading but not always determining factor of war hastened the end of the monarchy — and the monarch. The Girondins had guessed right, although sometimes for the wrong reasons. Military operations proceeded abominably from the very beginning. Two months after the April, 1792, declaration of war, Prussia joined Austria and subjected French armies to several reverses. With victorious allied troops massed at the frontiers, the invasion of France was heralded by a provocative manifesto signed by the coalition's leader, the Duke of Brunswick. Over his signature was an émigré-inspired pronouncement to the people of Paris that the city and its inhabitants would be subject to the most dire punishment if any harm came to the King or his family while the foreign troops marched to reestablish his authority. The populace was inflamed to fury by this statement, instead of being reduced to submissiveness. The radical section heads captured the municipal government of Paris. The illegal Commune took extraordinary steps to avert local catastrophe and a return to the old regime. The insurrectionists stormed the royal residence in the Tuileries on August 10 leaving a scene of carnage and pillage. The King saved his life but not his throne by seeking temporary asylum with the Assembly. The Assembly, however, was helpless against the well-organized and powerful Parisian municipal government, the Commune, some of whose chieftains were made temporary executives of the French state. In the absence of the right and center deputies, the Assembly voted overwhelmingly to arrest the King, nullify the Constitution of 1791, and order universal male suffrage.

Before the newly elected Convention could meet on September 22, 1792, to begin its work, further violence racked the capital. To the great numbers of criminals and nonjuring priests in the Paris prisons were added, after August 10, innumerable aristocrats who were suspected of close connections with the defunct royal cause. Incarcerated, too, were noblemen presumed treasonable because of their attachment to relatives fortunate enough to be émigrés. With the rumored and often real progress of Prussian troops across the French frontiers and towards Paris, the citizenry experienced a "Fear" similar to that of 1789. Inflamed by the passions and success of August 10 and alarmed over the possibility of a city-wide jailbreak of aristocrats and clergy who might constitute a fifth column for the advancing regular columns of repression, the revolutionary leaders of the Commune contained themselves no longer. The "September massacres" occurred. Better directed than on previous great days, groups of Parisians gathered at the crowded prisons to release thousands of inmates for summary trial, conviction, and death. Little regard was held for enlightened principles or practices. The higher principles of republicanism and national security seemed to excuse low practices, but, then, the higher principles of the nobility and the clergy threatened to be implemented by methods as low.

The traumatic events attending the birth of the First French Republic were a prelude to a hectic lifetime. From 1792 to 1795, politics followed a frenzied pattern. A bitter struggle took place between the bourgeois factions — the Girondins and the Montagnards. The Girondins had constituted the left in 1791–1792 by their opposition to the royalists, aristocrats, and clergy. With the overthrow of the monarchy and the imprisonment or elimination of dissident noblemen and churchmen, the Girondins wished to conserve the new representative, bourgeois republic they had succeeded in establishing. Supported by the provincial and Parisian well-to-do middle classes, the Girondins were loath to introduce legislation that would regulate or control economic life. War was an inadmissible excuse to engage in dangerous economic and social experimentation. The Montagnards, on the other hand, had political and ideological motives to abandon the position their bourgeois background should have instilled in them. The Montagnards had ridden into power by expressing the wishes and organizing the strength of the popular elements – petty bourgeoisie and working class. To disregard the interests of their constituents and backers would be to jeopardize their place and importance in the Convention. No mere power-conscious Machiavellians, the Montagnards possessed traits of secular saints and missionaries and seemed illuminated by the vision of a democratic society they wished to install in France.

The upshot of the six-month duel between the Girondins and the Montagnards was the proscription of the former and the subjection of the Convention to the latter by April, 1793. Although nominally the Convention remained the representative governing body for the sovereign French nation, committee rule became the norm from 1793 to 1794. The Committee of Public Safety and the Committee of General Security were selected from the membership of the Convention and derived their executive powers from that body to which they were theoretically responsible. The Convention functioned as a report-receiving, petition-hearing, rubber-stamp body for the public and for the ruling cliques of the Mountain.

During the ascendancy of the Committees, political decisions were carried out locally by appointive agents of two sorts. Gone or superceded were the elective local officials who typified the 1789 attempt to create a federal, decentralized France. Instead, the Convention reassumed the direction of Louis XIV and foreshadowed Napoleonic and modern France's drive toward a well-knit, centralized, unitary state. Imperfect instruments though they were, the special agents on particular missions and the permanent resident agents were charged by the National Convention's Committee of Public Safety to transmit the spirit and letter of Parisian directives into every corner of France. The local Jacobin Clubs, purged like the Convention of effective Girondin or moderate elements, served as recruiting offices and watch dogs to keep a chaste local administration.

In the capital, the Committees were burdened by crushing decisions of state, tortured by wrenching crises of conscience, and rent
by personal rivalries. A collective-rule spirit, not a Stalinist one,
pervaded governmental operations in 1793 and early 1794. Differences of opinion among the "Commissars" were checked by the
sense of a common domestic and foreign mission. Trouble arose
from the attempt to keep tight controls over dissenting factions
whose vested interests might interfere with the war effort or the
democratic program. Dantonists and Robespierrists were like angels
dancing on the head of a pin. The distance between the two was far
less than that between them and their audience. Robespierre was
able to outmaneuver and remove Danton by the spring of 1794. The
victor, however, enjoyed only a few months of power. A prolonged
tenure for Robespierre was rendered impossible by opposition from
many sources – the clerical, aristocratic right in the Vendée, the
bourgeois right under the ex-Girondin deputies in the south and
west, the proletarian left headed by newly arisen egalitarian figures,
and the overwhelming unorganized mass of people revolted by the
excesses of the Terror.

With the fall and guillotining of Robespierre in the summer of
1794, political authority reverted to the Convention, but internal
quiet did not return immediately to France. During the Thermidorean Reaction of 1794–1795, it was the turn of the right and
center to display its immoderation. On the road back to parliamentary government, with personnel and policies reminiscent of
1789–1792, the Terrorist purgers were now purged and deprived
of their positions, their lands, and often their lives. Many clerical
and lay émigrés returned from abroad or rose to the surface from
underground haunts. By 1795, the Convention was politically dominated by a center inclined to the right rather than by a center held
under the spell of the left.

The politics of 1792–1795 had not been a game played in a
vacuum. The participants had been deeply involved in the scramble
for the seats of power at the expense of equally ambitious contenders. Personal or factional appetites were conditioned and whetted

by a compelling interest in resolving the economic, social, and military problems of the period. More nebulous and perhaps even more determining were the ideological premises and goals of these seekers of power, these reformers of society, these strategists of war. A failure to recognize the multiple drives of these men or the plural pressures of the era can result only in a sterile academic exercise, to say nothing of an imperfect perception of human (in this case, French) experience.

The economic and social legislation – or decrees – of 1792–1795 provides one of many foils to demonstrate this hypothesis. Edict piled upon edict in the design to transform or regulate the economy. Decree followed decree in the desire to reform society. Prices and wages were fixed, goods were requisitioned or rationed, property was confiscated, human resources were mobilized, calendars were changed, old holidays gave way to new. There existed no blueprint for constructing a collectivist or socialist society. Many measures were dictated by an ideological stance, but not to be overlooked were war needs and the political necessity of currying favor with the popular elements in Paris whose support was essential to perpetuating the Committees' rule.

The September 29, 1793, Law of the Maximum decreed, among other things, a nationwide ceiling on basic commodities and wages. A maximum on grain had already been fixed earlier in the year. Before using our twentieth-century sophistication and selective memories, let us look at the circumstances under which this step was taken. Rising prices and lagging wages made it increasingly difficult for artisans, journeymen, apprentices, and the rural and urban worker to buy bread and other staples. Shortages in certain areas created opportunities for profiteering by peasant producers and middlemen. The pressure on the government to remedy the situation was doubled by the need to make extensive but inexpensive purchases for the armed forces. A sense of social justice, too, contributed to the enactment of the Law of the Maximum. For, on August 23, 1793, the modern nation in arms was born. According to that day's decree:

1. From this moment until that in which the enemy shall have been driven from the soil of the Republic, all Frenchmen are in permanent requisition for the service of the armies.

The young men shall go to battle; the married men shall forge arms and transport provisions; the women shall make tents and clothing and shall serve in the hospitals; the children shall turn old linen into lint; the aged shall betake themselves to the public places in order to arouse the courage of the warriors and preach the hatred of kings and the unity of the Republic.

* * *

5. The Committee of Public Safety is charged to take all the necessary measures to set up without delay an extraordinary manufacture of arms of every sort which corresponds with the ardor and energy of the French people. It is, accordingly, authorized to form all the establishments, factories, workshops, and mills which shall be deemed necessary for the carrying on of these works, as well as to put in requisition, within the entire extent of the Republic, the artists and workingmen who can contribute to their success. . . .

* * *

7. Nobody can get himself replaced in the service for which he shall have been requisitioned. The public functionaries shall remain at their posts.[3]

The ensuing organization of the nation for war impelled the government to suspend the operation of the natural law of supply and demand as a means of setting prices and wages. The mass of citizens engaged in the common effort would be otherwise unable to secure essential goods available only to the well-to-do. The Law of the Maximum thus demonstrated more an attempt to maintain popular support for a political faction and to institute wartime rationing than to chart the future for a socially egalitarian society.

The decrees of Ventôse, Year II (March, 1794), provide a better

[3] F. M. Anderson, *The Constitutions and Other Select Documents Illustrative of the History of France, 1789–1907*, 2nd ed. (Minneapolis, Minn., 1908), pp. 184–85. Quoted in Thomas C. Mendenhall, Basil D. Henning, and Archibald S. Foord, *The Quest for a Principle of Authority in Europe, 1715–Present* (New York: Holt, Rinehart & Winston, 1948), p. 76.

but still inaccurate example of pure socioeconomic determinism. Robespierre and his colleague, Saint-Just, inspired this move to distribute property among the poor. Without introducing the vote-getting or morale-boosting considerations of this "socialist" meas-ure, it was not inherently too great a departure from the stand of the day. According to the decrees, "the property of patriots" was sacred. Only the land of three hundred thousand suspects — emi-grated or resident enemies of the nation — would be affected. Trials before special tribunals would take place. If found wanting in their loyalty to the Republic on the home or war front, they would suffer the loss of their holdings. The title of these properties would revert not to the state, not to collective groups, but to selected poor indi-vidual Frenchmen. The new holders would be endowed with the same sacrosanct right of private property enjoyed by all loyal citi-zens, rich or poor. Patriotism, not property, was the test.

Hitherto unstressed in this account has been the contribution of the French Revolution to modern nationalism and the role of na-tionalism in the Revolution. In 1789, there was proclaimed an era of equal rights for all Frenchmen — indeed, for all men. Within the realm, hereditary and social privilege was abolished. The kingdom contained citizens, not subjects, whose personalities and properties might vary but whose equal civil and legal status was not to be dis-turbed by birth, wealth, or creed. Bound to the King and his dynasty as a symbol of their Frenchness until 1789, the people were urged to transfer their loyalty to the more impersonal concept of a French nation and, in 1792, a French Republic. Such identification was complete in many but not all Frenchmen.

An important factor in the events of 1789–1792, nationalism became even more prominent in 1792–1795 and succeeding eras. Once it superseded mere attachment to a fatherly absolute monarch, nationalism invaded all fields. The many reforms of 1789–1792 were rooted in a mixed political, social, and economic soil. Nation-alism was also an element. It was to achieve a more perfect national unity, too, that the administrative reorganization was effected and that the religious changes were instituted. On all levels, nationalism was a more consciously present consideration in 1792–1795. Perhaps the vacuum left by the guillotined symbol of Frenchness was so extensive that a host of substitutes had to be invented to fill the space. How compelling seemed the search for an enlightened unity in society to match the popularized versions of the unity in nature and science. The Law of the Maximum and the Decrees of Ventôse manifested a desire for national unity as much as for political power, economic programming, or wartime success. All citizens were to be provided with basic necessities; all citizens were to be furnished the outward signs of grace and national togetherness. In the place of local, separate practices and customs, the Convention authorized the establishment of national ones. Although other causes existed, the force of nationalism helped usher in new forms of dating the year, dressing the person, and edifying the soul. Once introduced, the new fashions (clothing, anthem, flag, art, education, holidays) tended to offer common experiences to the whole nation.

Modern nationalism and the French revolutionary wars kept close company, each stimulating the other. The very nature of the war effort was a goad to nationalism. Total mobilization of manpower and other resources obliged Frenchmen to engage in activities beyond the manor, parish, or province. Victory or defeat at the front excited the citizens of every region. Once aroused, nationalism combined with liberalism to reshape the ways of war. Between 1792 and 1795, there appeared portents of what total war might be. Only six months after the outbreak of war, the new Republic cloaked it in the mantle of an ideological crusade. In the November 19, 1792, Declaration for Assistance and Fraternity to Foreign Peoples, the Convention offered "fraternity and assistance to all peoples who shall wish to recover their liberty, and charges the executive power to give to the generals the necessary order to furnish assistance to these peoples. . . ." [4] One month later, the French government defined its position more precisely in its December 15 Decree for

---

[4] See Leo Gershoy, "Readings" in *The Era of the French Revolution, 1789–1799* ("Anvil Series"; Princeton, N.J.: D. Van Nostrand Company, Inc., 1957), p. 152.

Proclaiming the Liberty and Sovereignty of all Peoples. The Convention,

> faithful to the principles of the sovereignty of the people, which do not permit it to recognize any of the institutions which bring an attack upon it, and wishing to settle the rules to be followed by the generals of the armies of the Republic in the countries where they shall carry its arms,[5]

decreed a long list of eleven instructions. The first and the last are worth citing:

> 1. In the countries which are or shall be occupied by the armies of the Republic, the generals shall proclaim immediately, in the name of the French nation, the sovereignty of the people, the suppression of all the established authorities and of the existing imposts and taxes, the abolition of the tithe, of feudalism, of seignorial rights, both feudal and *sensuel*, fixed or precarious, of *banalités*, of real and personal servitude, of the privileges of hunting and fishing, of *corvées*, of the nobility, and generally of all privileges.

*   *   *

> 11. The French nation declares that it will treat as enemies the people who, refusing liberty and equality, or renouncing them, may wish to preserve, recall, or treat with the prince and the privileged castes; it promises and engages not to subscribe to any treaty, and not to lay down its arms until after the establishment of the sovereignty and independence of the people whose territory the troops of the Republic have entered upon and who shall have adopted the principles of equality, and established a free popular government.[6]

On February 13, 1793, Lazare Carnot, the member of the Committee who worked so hard as "Organizer of Victory," gave a speech that revealed French intentions more nakedly. According to Carnot, "nations are . . . in the political order what individuals are in the social order: like the latter they have their respective rights; these rights are independence, security abroad, unity at home, national honor. . . ." If a people were deprived of these "primary interests"

---

[5] *Ibid.*

[6] Anderson, pp. 130–32; quoted in Mendenhall *et al.*, pp. 82–83.

by force, that people had the right to regain them by the same
method when possible. Unless certain conditions were met, Carnot
stated that "no annexation, increase, diminution, or change of any
territory whatsoever can take place in the extent of the Republic. . . ." The conditions included the consultation with the local
residents and the need to consider the interests and security of the
state. In a magnificent gesture, Carnot admitted that "the right of
each nation is to live isolated if it pleases, or to unite with others
if they wish it, for the common interest. We French recognize as
sovereigns only the people themselves; our system is not domination,
but fraternity. . . ." More menacing was his claim that "the old
and natural frontiers of France are the Rhine, the Alps, and the
Pyrenees; the parts which have been taken from it have been taken
by usurpation. . . ." [7] It was the self-proclaimed right of the French
to seize these unjustly lost lands.

The war begun in April, 1792, for national and revolutionary
survival had already acquired a missionary aspect of spreading nationalism and liberalism beyond the French frontiers of 1789. A
door was being cautiously opened, too, for territorial acquisitions
more typical of the remaining years of the 1790s and the Napoleonic
era than of 1792–1795.

The third and last period of the revolutionary decade (1795–
1799) followed the transitional Thermidorean Reaction. Liquidation of Committee rule and its associated radical decrees and spirit
proceeded apace with the establishment of so-called moderate institutional forms and balanced approaches. Authority slipped into
new hands under the Directory, but the new leaders nevertheless
had to face old problems similar to those faced by their differently
oriented predecessors.

Constitutionally, the regime of 1795–1799 would be considered
conservative if not reactionary by certain latter-day standards. Property limitations on suffrage and office-holding, ascription of substantial powers to a more exclusive upper house of a bicameral
parliament, responsibility of ministers to the executive body of five

[7] Mendenhall *et al.,* p. 83.

Directors rather than to the more representative lower house, as well as other innumerable restrictions based on age, property-holding, marital status – these and other hedging qualifications might mark the period as one of denial of liberal or democratic aspirations. Yet, contemporary and subsequent generations of Europeans – and especially those since the war of 1914 – have only a dubious right of judgment.

In the context of what had already happened and what was to happen in modern French (and European) history, the Directory manifested a tight-rope-walking agility rarely found in previous or following governments. Perhaps the early years of the Third and the later years of the Fourth Republics demonstrated comparable talent. The great feat of the Directory was to survive the onslaughts from the left and from the right while at the same time dealing with difficult domestic and foreign problems. Resentful of the entrenchment of the bourgeoisie in the seats of power, the right marshalled its strength and used it openly in the Vendée and other provincial regions, furtively and obstructively in the capital. Royalist followers of the Comte de Provence (Louis XVIII) engaged in similar attacks on the bourgeois Republic. The Parisian proletariat found a true class leader in Babeuf, whose organization was nevertheless destroyed after an ill-supported uprising in 1796. With the left deprived of effective leadership and the right held in check, the Directory passed legislation and molded institutions designed to undercut the extremists and to build a moderate republican France.

Strenuous efforts – some daring, some pedestrian – were made during 1795–1799 to resolve the persistent fiscal problem and to stimulate the economy. The public debt was refunded, the budget was pruned, the monetary and tax system was overhauled, and regulation and requisition were astutely tempered by supports and aid to French business enterprise. Improvement in the government's financial condition was noted by 1799, stemming partly from these reforms but more from the loot and tribute exacted from conquered territories.

If waging war was a factor in achieving a certain fiscal stability, the political survival of the Directory was increasingly dependent on reliance on (or succumbing to) the military authorities. Civil–military relations until 1795 had been dominated by the Parliament or its Committees. The Convention was supported by the Parisian populace. So armed, the Convention or the Committees could defy regional and class opposition and yet survive. The Directory represented the more delicate example of self-preservation of a regime by playing polar groups against each other to enlist the grateful acquiescence of a center desirous of public tranquility. But the maneuvers and tricks of the Directory were too modern to be appreciated by the well-armed and disloyal opposition. To support the decisions to invalidate elections, to disqualify subversive parliamentarians, to maintain the experiment in cautious, bourgeois government, the Directory turned to the army over which it presumed it had control. Time and time again, coup after coup, the new-wave officers had demonstrated a self-effacing loyalty to the Republic. When the Directory summoned aid in 1797 from General Napoleon Bonaparte, who had helped consolidate the regime by his well-known "whiff of grapeshot" of 1795, had he not sent a worthwhile subordinate? The dispatched general had threatened and subdued those disparate elements who desired a restoration of kings or committees, of royalism or radical republicanism.

In the field of foreign affairs, two trends were discernible. On the one hand, policy was undergoing a significant change; on the other hand, the military chiefs were making their presence more perceptible. With regard to the modification of policy, the missionary zeal so exuberantly expressed in the propaganda decrees of 1792 and 1793 was being transmuted by 1795–1799 into a more traditional expansionism. Annexation within the "natural frontiers" had already been initiated by the National Convention. Avignon, then Belgium, the Rhineland, Savoy, and Nice had thus been considered fair game for integration within the French state before 1795. When the Republic advanced beyond the natural frontiers, it had used the gains as diplomatic pawns in forcing concessions on members of the hostile coalitions. Under the Directory, however, the balance of European power was further shattered by the establishment of nominally independent but actually subservient republics in Holland, Switzerland, and Italy. Exploitation rather than liberation more and more marked the treatment of the absorbed peoples in the enlarged French Republic and vassal states.

In the formulation of these shifting policies, the generals played an ever larger role. After 1795, the military tail began to wag the political, diplomatic dog. Previously, peace treaties, like that of Basel in 1795, were made possible by the prowess of the generals but were negotiated and concluded by the civil authorities. A new pattern was set in 1797. The objectives and extent of the Italian campaign were determined more by the field commanders than by the lay strategists in Paris. The provisions of the Treaty of Campo Formio (October, 1789) were as much dictated to the Republic's Directory as to the Austrian enemy. It was the loyal republican Napoleon Bonaparte who confronted his home government with the fait accompli of a preliminary treaty he had designed without consulting his civilian superiors. Although chiefly interested in the more limited ambition of rounding out the natural frontiers, the Directory nevertheless yielded to the blandishments of Bonaparte and the temptation of extending French influence beyond those frontiers into the Italian Peninsula.

1799–1814

The Napoleonic synthesis

THE KIND but bumbling Louis XVI, the equally well-intentioned but often unsubstantial Lafayette, the shrewd but overly intriguing Mirabeau, the host of dedicated but sometimes fanatic figures of the Terror, the almost purposely anonymous Directors – all had many commendable private and public virtues, but none had sufficient stature to command the French nation during its revolutionary decade. Robespierre alone could be considered to be a forceful personality with broad vision and capacity for sustained leadership.

Time was somehow out of joint for these mediocrities, or the men
were out of joint with their time. In 1799, however, the moment
seemed appropriate, although not inevitably propitious for a man
who possessed the qualities and yearning for strong leadership.
Napoleon Bonaparte, like Barkus, was willing to lead, whether the
nation was willing or not to be led.

Political power has often been won by means of the ballot, the
bullet, or the boudoir. Napoleon Bonaparte's journey was no exception. He was already a military hero of battles against domestic
and foreign enemies of the Republic; no harm had been done to his
image by his boudoir exploits and marriage with Josephine Beauharnais, the ex-mistress of Director Barras; the ballots would
await the introduction of plebiscites to confirm the popularity of
the coup of 1799 and Napoleon's subsequent transformations of
governmental forms.

Napoleon came to power by a coup d'état – that of 18 and 19
Brumaire, Year VII (November 9 and 10, 1799). Dissension and
fears within the Directory accounted for this plot to revise the
format of the Republic. Not Napoleon but the ever lingering Abbé
Sieyès and the ever present upper bourgeois elements in the legislative body despaired of stability. Their recent experience seemed to
have taught the plotters that General Bonaparte was a pliable,
devoted servant of the Republic. Had they overlooked or de-empha-
sized his offhand manner of dictating the Peace of Campo Formio?
Presumably, his presence as a republican partner in the assassination of the Directory would help make the coup a safe and popular
one. Miscalculations by intriguing politicians and interested factions have produced twentieth-century heads of state of worse
repute than Napoleon.

Campaign promises have a dismal record of fulfillment; programs proposed by perpetrators of coups d'état have often suffered
the same fate. The avowals contained in the proclamation issued
the morrow of the November 9–10, 1799, coup by the consuls of
the Republic were exceptions to the rule. The new leaders swore to
bring domestic and foreign peace to France by suppressing the civil

disturbances in the Vendée and in Brittany, concluding an honorable peace with the foreign enemies, framing a constitution, codifying the laws, and stabilizing finances. By 1804, every one of the pledges had been fulfilled. To these accomplishments were added a sweeping reorganization of the educational system and a long-lasting settlement of the religious question.

To suppress the organized rebellion in the west of France, Napoleon concocted a successful blend of cajolery and coercion. Relaxation of many of the strictures against resident and émigré noblemen and clerics preceded the offer of a general amnesty to the rebels. Enough dissidents heeded these siren calls to enable Napoleon's army to capture, kill, or scatter the remaining hard core of anti-republican elements within a few months. Individual and group protests continued to stem from the western regions, but Napoleon definitely ended the mass threat to the nation's unity and strength.

A more fragile peace, little more than a truce, was secured with the external enemies, Austria and England. Through smashing military victories and astute diplomacy, Napoleon was able to impose the Peace of Lunéville on the Austrians in 1801 and the Peace of Amiens on the British in 1802. These treaties confirmed and extended the gains made by the French in 1797 at Campo Formio. French designs on Holland, Switzerland, the Rhineland, and the Italies were overtly approved by the Austrians and tacitly approved by the British. The latter even restored to the previous sovereigns all their recently gained colonies except Ceylon and Trinidad. Napoleon had ended hostilities with substantial gains for the French and the vassal states.

At home, meanwhile, a new constitution had been expeditiously framed, and, by January, 1800, the legislature was holding regular sessions. Napoleon possessed extensive but not absolute power. Sharing executive duties with two others, Napoleon nevertheless was designated as First Consul. The right to initiate legislation was assigned to the consuls, not to the bicameral Parliament. No law was effective, however, without the approval of both houses. The Directory's practice of ministerial responsibility to the executive and not to the representative body was continued. The effectiveness of universal male suffrage was nullified by the highly complicated and indirect system of selecting legislators. The appointment of local officials, called "prefects," strengthened the hand of the First Consul and capped the centralizing tendencies of the late 1790s, to the lasting frustration of the federal aspirations of the early years of the Revolution.

An enduring contribution by Napoleon was the codification of law. In 1804, there was promulgated the Civil Code, followed during the Empire by the Code of Civil Procedure (1806), the Commercial Code (1807), and the Code of Criminal Procedure and the Penal Law (1810). Ten years of revolutionary activity had prepared the way for these reforms, but it was essentially the keen interest and personal direction of Napoleon that saw the work done. In many respects, the Codes reflected a consolidation of revolutionary gains. The individual retained his recently won equality before the law, his liberty to choose his own profession, and his freedom of conscience. For better or for worse, the secular state asserted its supremacy. Many of the more radical social innovations of the revolutionary decade were discarded. The worker, for example, was placed at a definite disadvantage by the Codes and enforcing laws. Despite some very real benefits for the individual, the Codes represented also a resurgence of strong authority — the man over the woman, the father over the family, the state over the individual. This, as well as other contemporary reforms, apparently suited the interests and wishes of the majority of Frenchmen of that day and future ones.

Equally palatable to many Frenchmen was Napoleon's stabilization of the government's finances. By centralizing tax assessment, levying, and collecting as well as centralizing note issuance, government financing, and credit in the private Bank of France, Napoleon helped produce a more orderly fiscal situation. As under the Directory, however, the amount exacted from the peoples in annexed or satellite lands, unknown to us, was a crucial item in the budget. It must be remembered, too, that the French armies spared the treasury heavy expenditures by their well-developed technique of living off the land in many theaters of operations.

Military events helped make possible still another, and unpromised, accomplishment by Napoleon — the Concordat of 1802. French domination of the Italian Peninsula and the absence of any counterbalancing power put the Pope's temporal holdings and even his spiritual leadership at the mercy of Napoleon. Powerless to resist the will of the First Consul, the Pope could engage only in dilatory tactics in the negotiations Napoleon initiated in 1800. For his part, the French leader desired a settlement of the thorny religious issue in order to extend his authority at home and to reduce potential opposition to his regime. Domestic tranquility was in danger and foreign ambitions might be thwarted as long as the anticlerical and, at times, anti-Christian policies of the Revolution were in effect. Disaffected, refractory clergymen could always rally substantial support for hostility towards the government. Insecurity marked the mood of peasants and bourgeois whose acquisition of Church lands had not yet received an official blessing from the Pontiff. On the other hand, a storm of protest might arise if the First Consul repu-' diated religious freedom in coming to an accommodation with the Church.

The Concordat of 1802 was a compromise that definitely favored the long-standing Gallican traditions in France but did not sacrifice the interests of the Pope or the clergy. The Pope was guaranteed his temporal possessions in Italy and his authority to install (although not to nominate) French bishops, who, in turn, were restored the power of appointment of the lower clergy. The Pope conceded the loss of the tithe and the Church lands in return for which the French state would pay the salaries of French churchmen. Catholicism was recognized not as the sole established Church, but rather as the religion of the consuls and the great majority of Frenchmen. The government reserved the right to impose police regulation on worship for the purpose of maintaining public order. This ambiguous clause enabled Napoleon to append severe limitations on the Concordat in the form of certain "Organic Articles." Thereby the Consulate and successive regimes were authorized to censor papal bulls, edit the Catechism, deny admittance to papal legates, and regulate the number of seminaries. The Church was now officially reconciled to the Republic, the divisions within the Church were healed, the ownership of expropriated lands was indisputably in lay hands, and the French state possessed important and recognized controls over Church organization and practices.

That the Concordat was not a prelude to perpetual bliss in church–state relations was symbolized by the nature of the coronation ceremonies for the French Emperor. On December 2, 1804, the Pope was present at Notre Dame Cathedral ostensibly to crown Napoleon and thus sanction the elevated status of Bonaparte. At the crucial moment, Napoleon seized the crown from the Pope, crowned himself, and then proceeded to crown Josephine as Empress. Such unorthodox behavior was nothing compared to his subsequent treatment of Church officials, papal prerogatives, and even his own divorce proceedings. In the style of Henry VIII, Napoleon importuned one of his archbishops to allow a divorce in order to permit another marriage – that with Marie-Louise of Austria. Napoleon went on to earn himself excommunication; the Pope, "imprisonment" and loss of temporal holdings. The Pope's surprising firmness toward the Emperor and the Emperor's hostile actions against the Pontiff nevertheless did not lead to an abrogation of the Concordat, which remained in effect for a century.

Although still devoting considerable energy to domestic affairs, Napoleon became increasingly involved in foreign ventures. Military operations and diplomatic offensives were dovetailed with economic warfare to extend French hegemony over Europe. Farther and farther beyond the Rhine, the Pyrenees, and the Alps, Napoleon sent French armies, administrators, and family to conquer, reform, or rule. As a tool of military strategy and as a method of securing revenue, the Continental System was devised. Nearly all Europe, including Russia, was embraced in this effort to counter the British blockade, to cut off British markets and sources of supplies, and to stimulate French and continental economic enterprise. Resistance to French domination from the threatened dynasties and the exploited nations of Europe finally was decisive in defeating Napoleon on the field of battle and toppling him from his exalted position in France. Napoleon was overthrown as head of state in 1814 by foreign, not domestic, enemies.

At home, Napoleon had somehow managed to surpass the endurance record of his revolutionary predecessors. First among the three Consuls in 1799, Consul for life in 1802, Emperor in 1804, Napoleon steadily improved his political position and, at each stage, secured the outward endorsement of the entire nation. The official count in the election results – or plebiscites – favoring his inauguration as First Consul was 3,011,007 to 1,562; as Consul for life, 3,568,885 to 8,374; as Emperor, 3,572,329 to 2,579. Twentieth-century observers have become understandably but sometimes unduly jaded by their own experiences with such so-called irrefutable proofs of "the people's will." The modern state's persuasive and coercive instruments are too well known to accept uncritically such landslide victories. Nevertheless, awareness of attendant electoral trickery, bribery, and brute force should not blind the sophisticated to the very, very real and broad appeal of the plebiscite seekers.

Napoleon's success in securing and maintaining stability for his regime was certainly due in part to his invention or exercise of ultramodern totalitarian techniques: reliance on a loyal army to crush domestic as well as foreign opponents, use of police spies to root out disaffected groups, control of propaganda tools to mold public opinion, and introduction of methods to ensure favorable electoral results. National pride in French victories was a binding element, too. But Napoleon's success may be attributed just as much to the sweeping reforms that satisfied the great majority of Frenchmen and isolated the rightist and leftist opposition.

On the right, the royal family and its immediate adherents continued to inveigh against the illegitimacy of Napoleon's rule. Too many Frenchmen were secured in their material and metaphysical interests, however, to furnish followers for these or other fringe malcontents. The French peasantry was now completely assured of title to newly acquired Church lands, not only by unilateral revolutionary confiscation but by signed and sealed agreement with the papal owner. Religious or associated frictions could hardly be made issues if the Holy Father, the Gallican churchmen, and the state were in accord. Clergymen were being directed by their Roman superior to abide by the commands of their government. Clerical reconciliation was accompanied by a substantial reconciliation of the nobility, further disconcerting the leadership of the right. Restoration of a court hierarchy implied a formality gratifying to the aristocracy. Equally pleasing were the appointments, promotions, pensions, and other material benefits.

Wooing real and potential enemies on the right did not lead Napoleon into becoming the seducer seduced. He did not become so enthralled by the charm of the aristocracy as to fall under its spell. He kept the doors of social advancement wide open to nonaristocratic Frenchmen of talent. Educated, wealthy, and ambitious members of the bourgeoisie were enabled to satisfy their social yearnings alongside the aristocracy through placement in civil and military posts and installation in the Legion of Honor.

Napoleon provided more than social inducement to keep the bourgeoisie from heading a rightist or leftist opposition. Ousted from the role of policy maker, the bourgeoisie nevertheless continued to dominate the administration of France. The financial, religious, legal, educational, and other reforms contained the letter and spirit of much the middle class had sought by radical or reactionary activity during the revolutionary decade. Subsidies, bounties, tariffs, and other aids were offered the business community. Governmental help was one factor that purportedly contributed to the prosperity of the age. With Napoleon as head of state, the bourgeoisie felt that it inhabited a stable political order in which its social status and economic well-being were guaranteed. As a social class, the workingmen had the least reason to support Napoleon. But, deprived of leaders and organization by the repressive action of the Directory and the unrelaxed vigilance of Napoleon, the proletariat found it impossible to manifest its hostility. The general prosperity of the period, too, undercut much of the basis for urban discontent.

Napoleon's genius was to synthesize, often with creative insight and execution, certain tendencies of the old regime, much of the program of the eighteenth-century enlightened philosophes, and some of the fundamental reforms of the revolutionary decade. Napoleon's welding together of diverse elements favored *égalité* and *fraternité* at the expense of *liberté*. Authority and centralization were more typical than representative rule and individuual freedom. If the Napoleonic legend contains the partial fulfillment of revolutionary ideals, it also includes the practice of dictatorship. Excesses of repression evoked criticism from many contemporary intellectuals of the upper and middle classes. But where could they enlist support to unseat Napoleon when the bulk of the aristocracy, clergy, peasantry, bourgeoisie, and proletariat had been mollified by substantial gains or kept down by effective agencies?

The evil genius of this dynamic, brilliant, and often enlightened despot was the egoist drive that blinded him to the consequences of his military and foreign policy. The same fate thus overtook Napoleon's rule as that that was to abbreviate the duration of Hitler's Thousand Year Reich. After 1814, with the brief exception of his One Hundred Days' return in 1815, Napoleon Bonaparte would contemplate rather than direct the French and European scene. On St. Helena, he still worked to glorify his name. He created a myth about his place in history by weaving the threads of truth, half-truth, and untruth into a mantle that subsequent great men have tried to wear with less success.

3.

THE QUEST FOR A PERMANENT REGIME

IN THE SUCCESSION of governments established in France between 1814 and 1870, the French roughly repeated the pattern of 1789 to 1814. During the French revolutionary and Napoleonic eras, the old regime was displaced by a constitutional but still Bourbon monarchy; that, in turn, was supplanted by a Republic that was saved by Napoleon Bonaparte only to be converted by him into an Empire. During the two generations after 1814, a Bourbon Restoration was supplanted by another constitutional but Orleanist monarchy in 1830; and it, in turn, was also transmuted into a Second Republic in 1848 and transformed by its "savior," Louis Napoleon, into a Second Empire by 1852. The Empire, in turn, was repudiated in 1870 after its ruler lost a battle at Sedan. That the Empire was not succeeded again by a Bourbon Restoration was as much the fault of monarchists as the doing of republicans (see Chapter 4). No one form of government seemed to win the permanent loyalty of the majority of Frenchmen, nor even a cohesive minority able to retain the instruments of power.

The litter of regimes and constitutions that cluttered early and mid-nineteenth-century French history was the by-product of many forces. Exclusively political considerations figured largely. The vast majority of Frenchmen might have justifiably resented the constitutions and institutions of Bourbon and Orleanist monarchs because of the restriction of the suffrage and office-holding to an infinitesimal few. More corrosive of the monarchical form, however, was the alienation of a substantial portion of its original supporters. Factions within the ruling classes helped wreck their own system of government by their special pleading. The monarchs killed monarchy, too, by ignoring or refusing to abide by the axiom that even despotic governments can survive against a disruptive faction and a hostile mass if they command the police and military establishments. Unfortunately for the persistence of the monarchical form, the political enemies of the Kings neutralized or actually commanded the army and the National Guard. The disaffected elements of the ruling classes had these agencies of force at their disposal and added the barricades and parades of the mob, easily rallied for reasons of its own discontent. Replacing a regime, however, proved more arduous than displacing it. The anatomy of revolution reveals how simply a united revolutionary front can disintegrate in the attempt to create a government satisfactory to its disparate elements. Nothing fails like success.

The inability to achieve political stability during 1814–1870 can be traced to other than political sources. There is much truth in the allegation that French political troubles stemmed from the confluence of political, religious, and economic revolutions. Unlike the British and the Americans, the French had not arrived at a consensus on a form of government or a church–state accommodation before being engulfed by the Industrial Revolution. In the absence of fundamental accord on the appropriate form of government, disputes over other issues endangered not only the ministry of the moment, but also the entire regime. His Majesty's Opposition was not necessarily a loyal opposition, but one that preferred a republic to a monarchy, an Orleanist to a Legitimist Bourbon King, or a Bonapartist Empire to anything else. Squabbles over economic and social questions as well as foreign-policy, religious, and ideological matters thus became disproportionately significant. And the personalities and characters of the dramatis personae can not be denied their weight in the frustrating search.

When economic questions were raised, the agreement of even the upper classes on the ideal political form evaporated. The dispute over title to confiscated Church and émigré property, for example, set the clergy and aristocracy against the enriched bour-

geoisie during the Bourbon Restoration after 1814. The final resolution of the problem – a 1,000,000,000 franc indemnification
– did little to keep the middle-class and well-to-do peasant tax-
payers firm in their loyalty to legitimate monarchy. Later, too, the
bourgeoisie, enamored of the order and protection proferred by the
Second Empire, felt nevertheless aggrieved by Napoleon III's free-
trade policy as well as his paternalistic encouragement of labor
organization. Conversely, the political ambitions of property-conscious bourgeois often seduced them into unnatural alliances with
the propertyless proletariat against regimes backed by other propertied classes.

Instability of regime during the 1814–1870 era also stemmed
from basic disagreement on the question of church–state relations.
By giving too few or too many favors to the Church, the Kings and
the Emperor of the French aroused protests from clerics and anti-
clerics. The clericalism in aristocratic and upper-bourgeois circles
was decried by anticlerical sectors of the bourgeoisie. Louis Philippe's frequently laic posture was severely criticized by many royalists who despised the monarch on other grounds. Napoleon III's
encouragement of parochial education struck horror in the hearts
of the middle-class advocates of secular public schooling. Satisfied
clerics, in turn, were aghast at the Emperor's diplomatic and military aid to Italian unification, which jeopardized the Pontiff's hold
over the Papal States.

Even on the more purely secular level, the conduct of foreign
affairs produced serious divisions in the successive regimes seeking
permanence in France from 1814 to 1870. Bourbon intervention in
the Spanish Revolution of the 1820s may have been a strategic and
tactical success, but many French liberals among the groups otherwise supporting the regime had no stomach for using French troops
to destroy the moderate constitution beyond the Pyrenees. The rise
and spread of the Napoleonic legend in the 1830s and 1840s
created, with its nationalist overtones, dissatisfaction with the
Orleanist King's uninspiring, yielding foreign policy. Napoleon
III's uneven efforts to pursue the international aspects of the legend

he was supposed to inherit and represent resulted in no greater unity. The Mexican fiasco was a feeble forerunner of the disaster that awaited the Emperor in his fumbling German policy. As much the prisoner as the formulator of an ultimately rigid stand against the Prussians, Napoleon III brought about the collapse of his own regime by his engagement in the Franco-Prussian War. But, failure to have gone to war equally might have imperiled his chances of continuity in face of the nationalism engulfing so many classes of French society.

The interplay of personality is often discounted in historical analysis as the theoretically impersonal forces of liberalism, socialism, and nationalism are paraded as the disruptive factors in the French quest for permanent political forms. The enigmatic and often contradictory nature of Napoleon III cannot be ignored, however. And, perhaps, the worsening illness that gnawed at him helped eat away, too, the firmness on which the Empire might otherwise remain founded. Less discomfited and distracted by his pain, Napoleon III might have directed more and drifted less in the fatal German question. The overthrow of the Bourbon Restoration might have been avoided, too, by a monarch less dogmatic than Charles X. Perhaps intelligence, tact, and moderation were elements of greater significance than generally recognized in helping his older brother, Louis XVIII, to perform a feat unmatched by any other ruler of France from 1789 to 1870: dying a natural death in office. From the ensuing and admittedly selected narrative of French history from 1814 to 1870, the reader himself may judge the relative weight of the numerous factors producing instability in France.

1814–1830

The Bourbon Restoration and its repudiation

UNDER the auspices of the victorious Allies but careful not to appear their lackey, Louis XVIII received a warm weclome from his

war-weary subjects when he returned from exile in England to assume the throne in the spring of 1814. From the graciousness of his
majestic heart and the calculation of his pragmatic mind, he
immediately granted a constitution to his people. Had his older
brother, Louis XVI, as graciously offered as much to the rebellious
noblemen and the power-seeking bourgeois in 1788, France might
have been spared the events of 1789. The Bourbon Restoration did
not entail a complete return to the wicked and chaotic ways of the
old regime, as so many detractors among liberal nineteenth-century
historians claimed. Neither was it the recapturing of the idyllic but
never existent harmony and solidarity imagined by the revisionists
or apologists of the Restoration and old regime.

The *Charte* (or Constitution) of 1814 provided for a bicameral
Parliament whose upper house consisted of nominees of the King.
The lower house was elected by a sharply limited number of citizens. So high was the property qualification for voting that fewer
than one hundred thousand Frenchmen enjoyed the privilege and
only a tenth of these could be deputies in the Chamber. The two
bodies were empowered to vote on tax and other legislation, but
technically cabinet ministers were responsible to the King. In addition to delineating the representative institutions, the Constitution
contained guarantees of most civil rights and religious freedom,
although no formal Declaration of Rights or Bill of Rights was
promulgated. Also confirmed were the rights of private property,
specifically including the titles to lands acquired by the confiscation
of émigré and ecclesiastical holdings during the preceding decades.
Administratively, Louis retained the system of the French revolutionary and Napoleonic districts and appointed officialdom. In
practice, he also retained in their posts the same prefects, mayors,
and other personnel of the replaced regime. To placate a still larger
sector of the populace, the King offered to assume the public debt
and to honor the pensions, obligations, and titles of the Empire.
Most articles of the Civil Code, too, were carried forth as long as
they did not overtly conflict with the new Constitution. The public
clamor for peace and the King's generous or astute proclama-

tion augured well for the general acceptance of the restored Bourbon monarchy.

From 1814 until his death in 1824, Louis XVIII trimmed and tacked adroitly to ride out the rising storm of opposition. The Bourbon Monarchy capsized in 1830 when Charles X directed it on a collision course. Several events and developments made Louis XVIII's reign difficult and Charles's impossible. Trouble derived chiefly from the One Hundred Days' return of Napoleon and the ensuing White Terror, the factionalism in Parliament, the assassination of the Duc de Berri, the indemnification laws, the intensified clericalism, and finally, the foolish political measures of Charles X.

Louis XVIII was installed for less than a year when Napoleon returned from Elba for the renowned One Hundred Days. Apathy counted as much as outright hostility toward the monarch in enabling Napoleon to march back to power and his last battle. Many elements in the army and civil service had, it is true, been disaffected by Louis XVIII's policies of retrenchment and favoritism to the émigrés. Consequently, many officers and enlisted men rallied to the Emperor and most of the prefects and minor officials remained at their local posts. The great mass of the French, however, did not feel stirred either to hail Bonaparte enthusiastically or to resist him. The second and final abdication of Napoleon followed swiftly on his defeat at Waterloo. At this "second Restoration" of Louis XVIII, heavier recriminations were enacted against Frenchmen than had been the case in 1814. As punishment for the renewal of hostilities, the Allies pushed back the French frontier to its 1789 rather than its 1792 line. The Saarland and other ultimately valuable properties were lost. An indemnity of 700,000,000 francs was also imposed, along with military occupation of parts of France. The lenient peace treaty that France had negotiated in 1814 was thus made more punitive. On the domestic level, the One Hundred Days provoked a White Terror. The long pent-up fury of the émigré aristocrats and clergy, contained in 1814, vented itself on the officials and private citizens who allegedly aided Napoleon's return. Thanks to the efforts of Louis XVIII, who tempered the violence, and to the connivance of many of his ministers, who helped potential victims elude "justice," the number of deaths was kept to the hundreds.

The King's more general policy of moderation was hampered not only by the pressures of the émigrés during the White Terror, but also by their election victory in 1815. Despite the careful planting of electors and official candidates of moderate ilk, the enfranchised few voted in an Ultra-Royalist majority to the Chamber of Deputies. Dubbed the *Chambre Introuvable,* this émigré-dominated body faulted the King on his inadequate purge of Bonapartist and liberal officials, his deafness to demands for indemnification of property losses during the Revolution, and his failure to award the Church a more favored position in state and educational affairs. In many respects, the Ultra-Royalists were seeking not a return to the *ancien régime,* but a resumption of the aristocratic revolt of 1788 for more political authority on the local and national level. Leadership for the cause was provided by the Comte d'Artois, younger brother and heir of the childless Louis.

With no desire to turn France over to an aristocratic-clerical rule and thus offend both the majority of the population and the onlooking Allies, Louis xviii resisted the Ultras from 1816 to 1820. He dissolved the Chamber and, in 1816, secured a more congenial Parliament; he replaced ministers in the face of Ultra objections; and he remained unmoved by outcries for further purges or indemnification. In this moderation, he was assisted by center groups and even the left-of-the-moment liberals. Readers of nineteenth-century European history will recall that the liberals of the age were scarcely democratic. Sensitive though they were to prescribed civil and religious liberties of all citizens, they were opposed to extending suffrage or office-holding to the masses. As long as freedom of speech, press, assembly, and religious observance was not jeopardized and as the propertied classes retained the franchise and access to public office, the Bourbon monarch could count on their support. The sound financial measures of Louis xviii also enhanced his status among the upper bourgeois parliamentarians, as did his strik-

ing success in raising monies to pay off the war indemnity to the
Allies and securing removal of the occupation forces by 1818.

The assassination of the Duc de Berri in 1820 gave the Ultra-
Royalists leverage against Louis. The young Duke, last-presumed
heir to the Comte d'Artois, had nevertheless foiled the assassins:
the Duchess was already pregnant. Seven months later, she produced the "miracle child," the Comte de Chambord, who very
nearly headed another Bourbon Restoration as Henry v during the
1870s. Embittered by the personal tragedy and the contemplation
of the extinction of the Bourbon line, the Ultras pressed their reactionary campaign more successfully after 1820. It was now the
turn of the center and the left to witness acts and policies inimical
to their interests. By 1830, the reactionary trend could be reversed
only by revolution.

Revision of the electoral laws in 1820 favored the rural landholding aristocrats and deprived many of the bourgeoisie of their
votes. Enabled thereby to recoup their 1816 loss of a majority in
the Chamber, the Ultras in 1821 obliged the King to replace the
moderate Duc de Richelieu with their choice, Joseph Villèle. Prime
Minister for five years, bridging the reigns of Louis XVIII and
Charles X, Villèle went too far in his conservatism for the center
and left and not far enough for the extreme right. Over the opposition of the liberal but otherwise royalist factions, he urged the King
to intervene in the Spanish civil war. Ferdinand VII had been forced
by mutinous troops and bourgeois dissidents to accept a moderate
constitution in 1820. The Concert of Europe, meeting at Troppau
and Laibach in 1820–1821, had formulated the Troppau Protocol
as a general statement against revolutionary changes in European
regimes. The French government had only halfway associated itself
with the Protocol's insistence on the right to intervene in the internal affairs of states where revolutionary changes had taken place.
Ferdinand's pleas for fraternal aid from his French Bourbon counterpart were underscored by Russian and Austrian preparations for
a Spanish crusade. Liberals at home and statesmen in Britain inveighed against armed intervention on behalf of the autocratic

Ferdinand. England and the United States had obvious reasons of trade, security, and ideology to prefer either a weak Spanish government or one sympathetic to the republican, nationalist aspirations of Latin America. In France, after careful consideration and planning, Villèle and Louis xviii chose intervention in Spain and ordered French troops to a brief and bloodless expedition that reasserted the Spanish King's divine and constitutionless rights. Many Frenchmen found it distasteful that France, the land of the Revolution, should act so contrary to the mild principle of constitutionalism. Worse sensations were to be experienced in France itself by the liberals.

Before his death in September, 1824, Louis xviii had assented to the drafting of legislation that would finally indemnify the émigrés for their revolutionary property losses. Under Charles x, the bill became law, arousing strenuous protest from the bourgeois holders of state bonds, on whom the burden of payments would fall. In deference to their objections, the total amount of 1,000,000,000 francs was scaled down to approximately 6–700,000,000 francs, and the method of financing was revised to spread the charges. Although the émigrés did not receive full compensation for their confiscated lands and although bourgeois wealth was not the sole source of payment, the liberal middle class viewed this operation of the Bourbons as undue favoritism.

On the church–state question, the Restoration trod on the sensitive toes of the liberals with increasing weight after 1820. To the clergymen and noblemen trooping back to France in 1814, the time seemed propitious for the Church to recoup its lost position in political, educational, social, and spiritual matters. Fulfillment of the vision appeared promised by the outlook of King and commoner. What institution would be more serviceable to the restored Bourbons and the returned aristocrats in rallying the populace? Even to the bourgeoisie, frightened by the excesses of the Revolution and Napoleon, what institution could better guarantee social stability? What institution more admirably fitted the Romantic emphasis on emotional, mystical, intuitive paths to truth? Rural France became again the domain of aristocrat and clergyman, joined frequently by family ties, economic interest, political outlook, and social attitudes. The heads of state, Charles x more than Louis xviii however, deferred to the bishops and Church orders in political favoritism, control over education, and social functions. Evidence of the revival of clerical influence mounted under Louis and multiplied under Charles. Secondary education became the province of the clergy; higher education fell to the direction of an outstanding ecclesiastic; lay teachers, lecturers, and professors were closely supervised where allowed to remain in the educational system right up to the Sorbonne.

The reunion of church and state so ornately manifested in the colorful coronation of Charles x in the Rheims cathedral in 1825, the re-intrusion of the Church in the administration of education so ruthlessly exploited by the dismissal of Guizot and others from university posts — these highlights of clericalism proved glaringly offensive to the bourgeoisie and liberal Frenchmen. Perfectly willing to re-embrace the Church as a spiritual guide and a guarantor of social peace, the liberals abhorred the privileges of the Church in politics and education. Charles x and his Ultra-Royalist, clerical clique were obliged to make concessions to liberal opinion. Temporarily, he abandoned the purge of lay teachers, the sufferance of unauthorized Church orders, and the censorship of liberal journals. The climate of opinion, too, was changing during the late 1820s. Adherents of Romanticism — that nearly indefinable cultural phenomenon that seemed to nourish such contradictory movements as liberalism and reaction, nationalism and international brotherhood — began to desert the clerical and Bourbon cause by 1830. Perhaps the spokesmen of Romanticism were essentially seeking a stable matrix within which diverse individual experiences would be possible. When the Church with the Bourbons acted to repress rather than release individual expression, to fix Frenchmen in a rigid or monolithic order, then did the Romantics transfer allegiance to a more constitutional monarchy and even to republicanism.

The Bourbon Restoration might have survived the slings of out-

raged liberals and moderates, however, but for Charles x's incredibly solid political stupidity and his blind adherence to divine-
right principle and practice. By-elections to the Chamber in 1827
had introduced a bloc of opposition deputies equal in number to
the government's supporters. Charles formed a new cabinet in 1829
headed by Jules de Polignac and composed of notorious Ultra-
Royalist, clerical partisans. Bitterness inside and outside Parliament became endemic in 1829 and 1830, as the general elections
approached. Charles refused to reconstitute the ministry, which he
claimed, with legalistic correctness but little acumen, to be responsible to himself alone. A personal royal appeal to the voters for support of the official candidates was accompanied by the usual
behind-the-scenes electoral pressures and juggling by the King – to
no avail. In June and July, 1830, the fewer than one hundred thousand enfranchised Frenchmen gave a two to one majority to center
and leftist opposition candidates. Both Parliament and the propertied public had repudiated the Polignac ministry. The moment
was perhaps more crucial than most historians admit, for had
Charles bowed to the victorious liberals and moderaters, the Bourbon Monarchy would have been transformed from a constitutional
to a parliamentary regime, with cabinets subject to parliamentary
rather than royal control. Except for an infinitesimally few deputies,
the parliamentary opposition had not yet placed the dynasty in
question.

Where conecessions might still have assured the perpetuation of
the Bourbon regime, Charles chose repressive, reactionary measures. Such was the import of the Four Ordinances published on
July 26, 1830. The newly elected, recalcitrant Chamber was dissolved; seventy-five thousand of the one hundred thousand qualified
lost the franchise; the press was subject to severe censorship; and
new elections were called. Many liberal and conservative bourgeois,
who had been merely critics of government policies since 1814, now
became enemies of the regime. If the King and the Ultras succeeded
in executing the Four Ordinances, the bourgeoisie would be assigned to political oblivion. Deprived of its right to choose repre-

sentatives for a Chamber that had but limited power, curtailed in its ability to express its opinions in the public press, the bourgeoisie raised the standard of revolt.

The former partners in the Bourbon Restoration moved immediately to enlist the support of classes and groups that had not enjoyed even the restricted suffrage of 1814–1830. The entry of the lesser bourgeoisie, professional groups, workers, and students – all with grievances of their own – radicalized the dispute with the King. Demands were heard not merely to force the King's withdrawal of the Ordinances, but to replace the Bourbon with an Orleanist or to establish a republic. At the barricades on July 28 and on the streets the following day, wealthy bourgeois Parisians joined artisans, workers, reconstituted units of the National Guard disbanded by Charles in 1827, and hordes of students. The physical power of the demonstrators was enhanced when several regiments of the army deserted the King. The troops remaining loyal were obliged to abandon the city after suffering several hundred casualties. Two thousand Parisians, too, died in the street fighting of July 29.

In revolt against autocracy but not for democracy, the bourgeois leaders strove to check possible radicalism or republicanism. Convinced that a constitutional monarchy would provide greater protection for their social and economic interests and greater opportunities for their political ascendancy than a republic, the wealthy insurrectionists sought a king. One was available, and to him they quickly offered the throne. The choice was the Duc d'Orléans, descendant of a brother of Louis xiv and therefore not in the "legitimate" line of succession like Charles x and his grandson, the miracle child of 1820. Unobtrusively residing in a Paris suburb, the Duc d'Orléans was approached also by Charles x, who wanted his cousin to act as regent until the ten-year-old heir could rule as Henry v. The bourgeois backers of the Orleanist, however, persuaded the Duke to head their side.

No more articulate or organized for their special interests than the English crowds that two years later pressured Parliament into passing the liberal but not democratic Reform Bill, Parisian mobs watched the Duke's procession through Paris on July 30 as he rode to the Hôtel de Ville. There, in a well-staged scene, the crowds dropped their apathy for enthusiasm when the popular Lafayette, chief of the reformed National Guard, embraced the King and assured his kingship. The reconvened Chamber of Deputies confirmed the symbolic accession on the following day; Charles abdicated on August 2; the Duke officially accepted the throne as Louis Philippe on August 9. The Bourbon Restoration was repudiated; an Orleanist, bourgeois, constitutional monarchy supplanted it.

1830–1848

The Bourgeois Monarchy and its overthrow

PROVIDED with a new King, the French were soon furnished with a new Constitution in 1830. It was inevitable that the new Constitution would limit the prerogatives of the King, reduce the powers of the aristocracy, and assail the position of the Church. It was inevitable, too, that the new Constitution would guarantee the civil and religious liberties of all Frenchmen and assure the political domination of the upper bourgeoisie over the lower middle class and workers. The Constitution was basically formulated, after all, by the last Chamber of Deputies elected under Charles x. Chosen on the basis of the Restoration's narrow suffrage and purged of those Ultra-Royalists who refused allegiance to Louis Philippe or who were harried out of its sessions, the rump Chamber of liberal bourgeois deputies framed a document in the image of their ideology and interests. The Ultras and Legitimists were discredited; the lower-class companions of the barricades were powerless without a leader, an organization, or a coherent program.

Unlike 1814, the Constitution of 1830 was not the presumed gift of a kind monarch, but a declared right of the French nation. The status and powers of the monarch were reduced from those enjoyed by his Bourbon predecessors. Louis Philippe would have to be satisfied to be the symbolic heir of the Revolution rather than of the Bourbons; he was designated King of the French instead of King of France, and he had to accept the tricolor instead of the white Bourbon flag emblazoned with the fleur-de-lis. More concretely, the Constitution deprived Louis Philippe of the power to set aside the laws and rule by decree or to enjoy exclusive rights of initiating legislation. Only by implication, however, were the ministers considered responsible to the Chamber rather than the King.

The Parliament emerged a more powerful but only slightly more representative body. Retaining the two-house form of the Restoration, the constitution makers allowed the lower house to share with the King in the initiation of legislation. Although the qualifications for office-holding and suffrage were lowered, they were still essentially based on taxation of land. Nearly two hundred fifty thousand Frenchmen gained the vote, more than double the number allowed by the Restoration, but this was only 3 percent of the number that universal male suffrage would have provided. The continued emphasis on landholding might seem surprising and contradictory to bourgeois interests. Although many members of the commercial, financial, and industrial bourgeoisie were admittedly excluded from political life, the upper bourgeois citizen in trade, banking, and manufacturing had long been aping his betters by acquiring country estates and was thereby entitled to vote and hold office. The Reform Bill of 1832 in England would not be much more radical in the extension of suffrage. Other circumstances related to the landed aristocracy would enhance the relative political power of the bourgeoisie.

By legislation forthcoming in 1831 and only foreshadowed in the Constitution of 1830, the upper house of Parliament was more radically transformed than the lower. No longer would the Peers, coequal in law-making powers with the Chamber, be a stronghold for the hereditary nobility. The King was given the right to nominate the members of the upper house, which he proceeded to pack with favorites recruited from leading bourgeois and non-Legitimist noble families.

Excluded from elected or appointed office in Parliament, the nobility soon found itself replaced by the Orleanist aristocracy or bourgeoisie in the army, Church, and civil service. By virtue of their extensive landholding, the great noble families might have continued to do election battle with their competitors and form a parliamentary opposition. They added to the isolation imposed on them in the political and administrative realm by their own self-chosen withdrawal. What has been termed an *émigration intérieure* took place after 1830, wherein they retired to their châteaux in the countryside or their townhouses in the Parisian Faubourg Saint-Germain. There, they awaited the turn of the tide. Forty years passed in this vigil until they re-emerged during the 1870s only to fumble their opportunity to restore a Legitimate regime.

As the base for more laicism than ever displayed under the Restoration, the Constitution of 1830 defined Catholicism no longer as the religion of the state but merely as the religion professed by the majority of Frenchmen. Reflective of another grievance against the Bourbons, censorship was abolished and freedom of the press guaranteed. In 1831, another part of the revolutionary settlement was formalized – the official re-organization of the National Guard with membership confined to taxpaying bourgeois citizens who elected their own officers. Even though the government contributed the money and administrators of the Guard, the middle class now possessed an excellent weapon with which to resist royal encroachments on its newly confirmed dominance. The National Guard could and would be used, too, against any threats from the lower classes.

Rather than by a strict chronicle, the highlights of the Bourgeois Monarchy may be more conveniently portrayed by examining the causes of its revolutionary overthrow in 1848. As in 1830, divided interests and counsel within the groups and classes in power opened the door to revolution. By 1848, Louis Philippe could count among his opposition many of the bourgeoisie who had originally supported him. Other forces had been at work, however, to give a more radical and bloody mark to the 1848 upheaval than had been noted in the three-day, textbook, near-Glorious Revolution of 1830. To the liberalism that had earlier been a factor was added a stronger ferment of nationalism and socialism. A far more serious depression than the mild recession of the late 1820s also volatilized the situation after 1846.

In the Parliaments elected on the narrow base described in the 1830 Constitution, deputies soon gravitated to one of two principal factions: the party of resistance or the party of movement. Substantial agreement existed between the two groups on anticlerical legislation and the pursuit of a laissez-faire policy, as well as its corollary, the suppression of proletarian disorder. But the party of resistance encountered heavy fire from the progessivists on its conduct of foreign affairs, its steady denial of political reform, and its provocative curbing of civil liberties.

Widening the rift between the two factions was the insistence by the party of resistance that the Revolution of 1830 had produced the ideal type of government for France. François Guizot, leader of the conservatives, opposed any reform of Parliament and any extension of suffrage. During the 1840s, as the King identified himself more and more closely with Guizot and the party of resistance, loyalty to the regime itself seemed associated with adherence to the governmental party. The party of movement, with Adolphe Thiers as one of its shining lights, was provided with ammunition in its battle for reform by the King's electoral chicanery and some glowing examples of corruption in high places. Official lists of candidates and governmental pressures in elections were old stories to the French readers of the public press. Outright bribery at the polls, tampering with the returns, and arbitrary redistricting (jerrymandering) seemed more extraordinary. Yet, these operations were becoming the common practice of the King and his ministers. By the mid-1830s, Louis Philippe had even more distorted the limited representative and independent nature of Parliament. He had suborned nearly half of the unsalaried deputies by appointing them to lucrative or influential posts in the cabinet, judiciary, diplomatic service, or general administration. Whether from the lack of moral fiber or the presence of greater temptations, corruption appeared more frequently during the reign of Louis Philippe than under the Restoration. The trial, conviction, and attempted suicide of a Minister of War in 1847 was but one example played up by orators and pamphleteers to show the shabby deals for contracts and favors linking public officials with private interests.

Frustrated in the parliamentary drive for electoral reform and disgusted by the revealed and suspected cases of corruption, the party of movement began to wage its campaign against the government by extraparliamentary means during the late 1840s. Banquets were arranged that turned into political rallies of bourgeois deputies and journalists. In speeches and toasts, the King and the party of resistance became targets of severe criticism and ridicule. Guizot's response in early 1848 — prohibition of the banquets — helped detach the party of movement from the monarchy and gave the opposition a highly popular appeal. Bourgeois deputies could pose as champions of liberty against a government and King who suppressed freedom of speech, press, and assembly.

The increasingly strident tones of nationalism as well as the louder voice of liberalism also served to create disharmony among the ruling classes of the July Monarchy and to excite the disenfranchised against the regime. Louis Philippe had at first in 1830 achieved much popularity at home by aiding the Belgians in their liberal and national revolt against their Dutch King. Through Anglo-French military and diplomatic intervention, the Belgians secured an independent status. Cooperation with England turned to rivalry on such other issues as the Near Eastern Question, wherein French interests in Egypt clashed with British. Louis Philippe catered poorly to French nationalist sensibilities when he inclined to a subservient position toward Great Britain rather than a dynamic confrontation. The King ousted Thiers from the premiership over this policy during the 1830s, and Thiers engaged thereafter in a running battle with Guizot on the alleged weakness of the

King in foreign affairs. On the continent, the French state could scarcely be close friends with the autocratic monarchies of Austria, Prussia, or Russia. But Louis Philippe refused to make them enemies, either; appeals from Polish rebels and Italian nationalists were turned down lest the Russian or Austrian rulers become hostile to France. By 1848, French prestige was at a low ebb.

That the Bourgeois Monarchy's yielding, cautious international stance was at variance with the French nationalist spirit of the 1830s and 1840s was attested to by the rise and spread of the Napoleonic legend. By tricks of selective memory, by dint of careful seeding by Napoleon in exile, by cultivation in the hands of Bonapartist followers, and by the words and deeds of the young nephew, Louis Napoleon, the Napoleonic legend flourished during the 1840s. Forgotten were the bloodshed, the turmoil, and the despotism of the Empire. Only the glory and grandeur of France and the consolidation of revolutionary gains were recalled. On St. Helena, Napoleon had whiled away his last years penning this favorably colored description of his intentions and achievements. The heroic exploits of a France dominating Europe stood in marked contrast to the timid gestures of King Louis Philippe, who ruled a state he guided in isolation. Although no one could claim that *la patrie* was in danger, no one could pretend either that the resources of the kingdom were used to display French greatness. Aging army officers and prefects of the Napoleonic era heard with nostalgia and gratification the bourgeois deputies' criticism of Louis Philippe's drab foreign policy. Frenchmen of all ages and occupations might have found a vague distraction from the ennui that the poet Lamartine described as prevailing under the Bourgeois Monarchy.

Nationalism and the Napoleonic legend as contributions to the overthrow of the July Monarchy must nevertheless not be exaggerated. These forces probably acted more as intangibles undermining affection for the regime than as precise and positive rallying points. The government weathered its few foreign-policy crises. The appearance of Louis Napoleon as head of liberal and nationalist uprisings or coups in France and elsewhere in Europe during the

1830s and 1840s seemed more farcical than serious. No large or cohesive organization was partisan to his comic-opera sallies into Boulogne or Strasbourg. Not until after the Revolution of 1848 did he become the chief beneficiary of the legend, and then political and social reasons undoubtedly outweighed the nationalist–military–foreign policy appeal.

Socialism, on the other hand, like liberalism, did represent a movement that, by 1848, was more than a state of mind. Leaders had arisen, groups formed, and followers abounded for opposing the Bourgeois Monarchy. The opportunities for expression and implementation of socialist ideas would have been negligible if the ruling propertied classes had been solidly united under Louis Philippe. When the doctors disagreed among themselves, however, the patient was doomed to more than liberal medicine in 1848. The party of movement's assault on the monarchy paved the way for bourgeois advocacy of political republicanism seconded by the masses for purposes of social and economic experimentation.

By 1848, several varieties of socialism had been propounded. Two different, but not always distinctly separate, sources for the many types were discernible: ideological–humanitarian impulses of a secular or religious origin and material conditions deriving from industrialism. To many advocates of socialist programs, the concepts of the French Revolution were interpreted as or transmuted into a liberty, equality, and fraternity of social and economic significance instead of connoting purely political, civil, and nationalist values. Often indifferent to the existing political institutions and even to the implications of the Industrial Revolution, socialists thus oriented preoccupied themselves with schemes of social reorganization of agricultural and artisanal France.

Charles Fourier, for example, had recommended, during the Napoleonic era and the Restoration, the establishment of self-contained communities of several hundred members each. In these phalanxes, the individual would apply his skill in farming or crafts to provide his own and his fellows' basic needs. Social rearrangements accompanied the reorganization of economic life in these relatively self-sufficient settlements. Traditional family patterns were replaced by polygamous relationships and by common care and raising of the offspring. The social attitudes of peasants and craftsmen and the minimal attention given the urban worker did as much as the hostility of the ruling classes to limit adherence to Fourier's and other "utopian" socialist proposals.

Less secular in origin and application and, perhaps more stimulated by the misery of the new proletariat, a type of Christian Socialism issued from a few Catholic clerics and laymen. Prominent among these was the Abbé Félicité de Lamennais. Principally concerned with the presumed loss of Church appeal because of its close affiliation with the Bourbon Restoration, this one-time royalist inveighed against the monarchy and proposed an extreme ultramontanism as well as separation of church and state. An enemy, too, to the bourgeois liberalism that gave scant comfort to the exploited masses, Lamennais preached a dynamic social mission for the Church. Principles of Christian brotherhood should guide the Church toward the goal of social justice for all men of all classes. The generous but ill-defined approach was obviously poorly received by those who might have made it a success. Lamennais' ultramontanism offended the Gallican clergy, who had no desire to yield further jurisdiction to the Pope. The Pope bristled at the implications of separating the Church from the state, and the bourgeoisie was by no means ready to make the necessary concessions to the workers. The workers themselves, as farm or factory hands, distrusted the Church, in which so small a fraction of clergymen shared Lamennais' social conscience.

From religious sources, too, but more directly oriented to the needs of the urban proletariat, was the contribution of another Catholic, the laymen Philippe Buchez. To him, hypocrisy or, at best, paternalism typified the Church's social policy. Instead, the Church should take the lead not merely in moral suasion from the pulpit, but also overt sponsorship and support of workingmen's associations that would own the means of production and distribution. Although failing to enlist much Church aid, he was able to organize a few such groups and even to become elected as President of the National Assembly during its brief existence in 1848.

Combining moral fervor with a keen realization of the ways of industrialism, Henri, the Comte de Saint-Simon was one of the most outstanding socialist thinkers before Karl Marx. Saint-Simon's last book, *Le Nouveau Christianisme* (1825), revealed basic spiritual values of Christianity rather than sectarian religious ones. Brotherly love as exemplified by Christ should replace Catholic and Protestant tolerance of cutthroat competition and wage-slave treatment of labor. No mere platitudinous moralist, Saint-Simon went on to advocate sweeping changes in economic and social organization, which he felt were more attuned to the technological progress of the age. Unlike many of the utopian socialists of pre-1848 Europe, he accorded a large role to the state. The state, however, should not be directed by the traditional monarchs, aristocrats, clergy, or even bourgeois lawyers and professionals. For politics, to Saint-Simon, was a sterile game in which rulers, noblemen, and deputies quarreled on peripheral questions of religion, suffrage, tariffs, and foreign affairs. Ignored or mishandled was the true concern of a nation: the proper organization of its economic activity. In Saint-Simon's judgment, man's attribute of reason and man's acquisition of an advanced technological apparatus made possible a hitherto unachievable prosperity for all. Only by a rational and planned system, however, could this be accomplished. Although private property would be respected, the state would be the instrument for regulating, coordinating, and often determining the appropriate production and distribution of goods. The state obviously would have to be in the hands of engineers, technical experts, and scientists, or, at least, the government would have to defer to them.

Scarcely shocking to the twentieth-century Frenchman familiar with Popular Front programs or Monnet Plans at home and New Deals or Five-Year Plans abroad, Saint-Simon's proposals elicited little favorable response from the dominant classes of Bourbon and Orleanist France. The landed aristocracy and the clergy would hardly yield their waning influence to technocrats any more than would the entrenched bourgeois deputies of the July Monarchy. Nor would the merchants, industrialists, and bankers of the 1830s and 1840s be likely to trust the control of their enterprises to a state that might act in contradiction to their individual, short-term interests.

Although not without moral indignation stemming from the observation of an imperfect implementation of revolutionary ideals or religious teachings in the socioeconomic practices of the day, Louis Blanc represented a socialist whose ideas most intimately reflected the petty bourgeois and proletarian plight in an industrializing society. According to Blanc, the ultimate goal was to transform the capitalist system into a collective economy in which each person would contribute according to his ability and receive according to his needs. To arrive at this end, the intervention of the state would be essential. The state, preferably as a republic in which the government was democratically installed through universal male suffrage, would establish social workshops in all sectors of the economy – especially in industry – that would be under the control of the workers. Private business would be slowly supplanted, replaced by public and collective enterprises. Approaching Marxism in certain goals if not in methods, Blanc's *Organisation du Travail* (1840) and subsequent pleading earned him the largest following of any socialist in France by 1848. There was no well-organized or effective party attached to his cause, however. Formation of the workshops would have to depend on sympathetic politicians, and the deputies of the Bourgeois Monarchy's Parliament obviously did not come under this heading. The events of 1848 revealed that deputies chosen by universal male suffrage needed to be bullied to maintain even blurred copies of Blanc's social workshops.

The emerging socialism, the intensified liberalism, perhaps even the revived nationalism – all constituting latent or manifest challenges to the Bourgeois Monarchy – derived not only from an elaboration of French revolutionary ideology or Christian principles, but also from the consequences of economic change. During the first half of the nineteenth century, the methods of production and distribution in agriculture, industry, and commerce underwent substantial modification. These economic changes in turn affected the social structure, bringing into existence or increasing the presence of new elements of the bourgeoisie and proletariat. These classes made ever more insistent demands for political recognition and consideration for their social and economic needs. The Bourgeois Monarchy was thus subjected to greater stress from within and graver threats from without. The slow and uneven nature of economic change in France, however, provided the opportunity for reactionary or conservative forces to contain radicalism or, at least, to limit its gains should a revolution occur.

In the manufacturing of textiles, in mining, metallurgy, and transportation, the most striking innovations took place; in agriculture, the least. As a result of wider use of steam power, production rates tripled or quintupled in cotton, coal, and iron under the July Monarchy. Although no match for contemporary British developments, French use of raw cotton mounted from 28,000,000 kilograms in 1831 to nearly 65,000,000 in 1846. Coal production rose from 1,500,000 tons in 1829 to 5,153,000 in 1847; iron, from 751,000 tons in 1833 to 1,658,000 in 1847. Altogether, the French used nine times as many steam engines in 1847 as in 1833, but the English had already in 1826 a sixfold greater horsepower capacity than the 1847 figure of the French. More elaborate furnaces had been introduced, too, in smelting processes, but almost 90 percent of French iron was still treated in small charcoal furnaces in 1848. Traditional methods persisted also in textiles other than cotton or silk and in the luxury trades that absorbed the major portion of French capital and labor assigned to manufacturing.

Improvements in transportation were widespread, but lagged far behind those in Great Britain, Belgium, and the German states. The much-vaunted road and canal network of France was extended to enable the transport of heavier industrial freight, but the British and Germans surpassed the French in rail construction. A mere 38 kilometers in 1831, the French railway system had 1,921 available in 1848 with an additional 4,000 under way. By then, however, Britain already possessed more than 6,000 kilometers of rail lines and Prussia 3,400. The July Monarchy had done much to stimulate railway development. By the Railway Law of 1842, the government assumed responsibility for providing the land and constructing the substructure of the roadbed, tunnels, and bridges; private companies were to lay the rails, manufacture rolling stock, and build the stations. Once in operation, the government allowed private enterprise to lease the government's property until such time as the state would buy back the private sector to form a national system.

Although agriculture underwent fewer changes than other sectors of the economy, there nevertheless were several instances of progress. In some regions, the diversification, introduction, or spread of new crops proceeded rapidly between 1815 and 1848. Potato production quintupled during this period, and, from 1829 to 1847, wheat production nearly doubled. Under the protection of high tariffs against cane sugar, the sugar-beet industry flourished, to the advantage of humans and livestock. Rotation of crops, use of fertilizer, improved methods of stock-breeding and stock-raising, and government-sponsored educational programs all helped raise the level of agriculture in some areas of France. Essentially, however, French agriculture remained fixed in its pre-1815 ways. The revolutionary land settlement and its confirmation under the Restoration had tended to fix the rural population and to discourage innovation. Although much land had been confiscated from the nobility and clergy, its distribution had not greatly affected the peasants. Some few increased or consolidated their holdings, but the bourgeoisie had purchased the bulk of the land and had it farmed or leased it in small parcels. The chief contribution of the Revolution had been to assure the peasant of his full title to the land and free him from seignorial dues. Instead of encouraging large-scale farming or a drift into the urban labor market, as had been the effect of the enclosure movement in England, the French Revolution made the peasant comfortable in his new status and old ways. By 1848, therefore, more than 75 percent of the population still inhabited rural areas, whereas England's population was almost equally divided between rural and urban areas.

The restricted nature and scope of the economic changes in France from 1815 to 1848 produced but mild modification of the social structure and provided but limited bases for liberal reform or socialist programs. The most rudimentary of child labor laws passed in 1841 was unenforced. Distress existed and disorders broke out under the Bourgeois Monarchy only to be put down easily by the government, the National Guard, and employers' actions. During the mid-1830s, Lyons was a center of disturbances; workers organized resistance to wage cuts, extended use of machinery, and deplorable conditions in the silk industry. Elsewhere, retention of anti-union legislation, government sympathy with capitalists' interests, and insufficient numbers militated against effective labor organization or successful strikes. *Compagnonnage,* a relic of artisan guild arrangements, mutual aid and fraternal societies, and political clubs and labor journals formed the principal vehicles for voicing labor's discontent. It was evident that artisan and proletarian pressures for suffrage or for socioeconomic reform were foredoomed to containment as long as the bourgeois and landholding classes remained harmoniously joined together and associated with the regime. Together, the King and the propertied classes possessed the instruments of political, administrative, economic, and military power essential to their dominance.

By 1848, much of this harmony had dissolved, less because of issues of socioeconomic policy than because of political differences. That many elements of the aristocracy, clergy, peasantry, and bourgeoisie had grounds for apathy or hostility toward the regime has already been indicated. Legitimism, clericalism, nationalism, Bonapartism, liberalism, and socialism had lured many Frenchmen away from the Orleanist monarchy. Without necessarily operating as the direct cause of a revolutionary movement against the King, a depression during 1846–1847 helped to discredit the regime further in the eyes of its adherents and to sharpen the tempers of its enemies.

During 1846–1847, disaster in agriculture induced or coincided with a sharp decline in commerce, slackening industrial production, and severe reverses in finance. Crop failures similar to those throughout Europe at the time not only imperiled the peasants' economic position, but also resulted in intensified distress among urban workers. Soaring prices for the scarcer food supply and spreading unemployment – as factories closed down and trade shrank – combined to create even greater discontent than usual in the cities of France. Bankruptcy and collapse of the stock market created a panic atmosphere among the bourgeois manufacturers, merchants, bankers, and investors. The monied classes hastened to liquidate their speculative portfolios of railway and industrial securities. Depositors withdrew savings from banks at a rapid rate, leaving the Bank of France, for example, with only 57,000,000 francs in January, 1847, where there had been more than 300,000,-000 francs in June, 1845.

Economic conditions, however, seemed to improve by the end of 1847 and cannot be said to have directly ignited the revolutionary fire of 1848. Nevertheless, they did serve to add fuel to the conflagration once it was started by the bourgeois reformers' provocative demands, the fusillade on the boulevards of Paris, and the ineptitude of the government.

The Revolution of 1848 began on February 22 when demonstrators massed for a protest march against the government, which had just banned a scheduled banquet of bourgeois liberals. Barricades were set up by workers and students and some rioting broke out. The National Guard was called up but quickly showed its alignment with bourgeois reform rather than with the Bourgeois Monarchy. Yielding to the pressure from the mob, the King on the following day dismissed the detested Guizot, replacing him with Molé. This gesture mollified some of the bourgeois protestors but few of the more radical demonstrators. The crowds continued to roam the boulevards. In the evening of that day, the 23rd, the situation deteriorated. A shot was fired either by a rioter or by one of the infantry or cavalry. Fright overcame the troops, and a volley from them killed a still-undetermined number of demonstrators. The shocked crowd gathered up the dead and hauled the bodies of the martyrs in a wagon through the streets of Paris with torches to light their way. Too late, the King appointed Thiers as minister on the 24th. The crowd had already seized the Hôtel de Ville, the King abdicated in the afternoon, and a Republic was proclaimed. Louis Philippe slipped quietly away to England after declaring his young grandson, the Comte de Paris, to be his successor. The chastened and intimidated Chamber of Deputies declined the Monarch's suggestion. Instead it chose several ministers who joined with delegates of the crowd at the Hôtel de Ville to form a provisional government for the Second French Republic.

1848–1852

The life and death of the Second Republic

ALTHOUGH their numbers were hardly proportional to their respective contributions in making the Revolution, bourgeois reformers and proletarian delegates dominated the eleven-man committee of the provisional government. To the panel that included conservative and moderate republicans like Lamartine, Crémieux, and Garnier-Pagès, chosen by the outgoing Chamber of Deputies, were added socialists or social republicans from the Hôtel de Ville: Blanc, Flocon, and Thomas. Seven members considered the Revolution terminated. They wished merely to consolidate the political gains by drafting a constitution that would guarantee civil rights, establish truly representative government, and offer universal male suffrage. The minority of three, and sometimes four when Lamartine was so moved, was more radical, aspiring to institute a socialist society or, at least, a sweeping program of social legislation. While the issue of the moment had been political, the bourgeoisie and the proletariat could constitute a cohesive left. As the order of the day turned to the social question, the unity evaporated, revealing the bourgeoisie's presence on the right.

The workers, swollen in number by two decades of mild industrialization and aggravated by the depression of 1846–1847, refused
to disband promptly as they had done in 1830. The bourgeois
majority on the ruling committee deemed it expedient to make
otherwise distasteful concessions. At the workers' insistence and
desirous of alleviating unemployment, the government proclaimed
"the right to work" and established National Workshops before
the end of February. Ostensibly but only superficially patterned
after the ideas of Louis Blanc's social workshops, the National
Workshops were in effect nothing more than stopgap relief projects.
The unemployed of Paris and increasing numbers of jobless Frenchmen attracted to the capital from the provinces were given a pittance
to plant trees, clear parks, repair fortifications, and engage in
sundry municipal tasks. Any activity that might vaguely compete
with private enterprise was studiously avoided. These halfway measures pleased no one. Socialists were disappointed in the perversion
of their schemes; artisans and craftsmen objected to the senseless
manual labor to which they were assigned; the bourgeoisie and
peasantry bemoaned the tax increases necessary to support the projects.

The political task of transforming the provisional government
into a permanent republican form was also rendered difficult by
socialist and radical pressure. Workers' demonstrations in March
forced the committee to postpone briefly the scheduled general elections. When they finally did take place at the end of April, the
results showed how little the Paris Revolution and the radical
demands had struck root in the country at large. Elected by universal male suffrage, the Assembly that would be responsible for
framing a constitution and forming a government was conservative
if not reactionary in its membership. Of the nearly 900 seats, only
100 were captured by the socialist or radical republican left. Moderate republicans, representing rural and urban propertied classes,
won more than 400 places. Approximately 400 deputies were
exponents of monarchism: 300 Orleanists and 100 Legitimists.

The fears of the working-class and socialist elements were soon realized. In May, a demonstration was bloodily suppressed after the crowd had initially invested the Chamber, which had refused to reiterate the right to work. A more shattering blow was in the offing a month later. The rural and bourgeois deputies began to disband the National Workshops. On June 22, the government decreed the following alternatives for the workers: enlistment in the army or return to the provinces where payments would still be available. In a frenzied, desperate response, the Parisian mobs raised the red flag on barricades and at street corners. Under command of the republican General Cavaignac, the army and National Guard detachments from the provinces smashed the uprising with a relentlessness and finality that ended any chance of proletarian insurrection for a generation. Death, exile, or imprisonment was the fate of probably ten thousand Frenchmen. The propertied classes had overwhelmed the unpropertied in the capital; rural France had prevailed over urban. The Republic might survive, but it would necessarily be subservient to landowners and businessmen. Democracy might retain a political guise but not a social or economic one.

With Cavaignac appointed to executive and military leadership and with the social republicans eliminated from the political scene, the moderate republicans and monarchists in the Constituent Assembly completed the Constitution of the Second Republic by the autumn of 1848. Order, stability, and possibly facilitation of a Bourbon or Orleanist restoration seemed to motivate the constitution makers. The short life of the Constitution and the bias of its framers, however, should not blind the observer to its essentially democratic features. Although it is true that the popularly elected President, as executive, was invested with important powers and had the ministers responsible to himself, he was curbed in many ways. He was not authorized to take personal command of the army, to run for re-election after his four-year term, to dissolve Parliament, to exercise an absolute veto over legislation, or to abrogate the Constitution. In this Constitution of checks and balances, the unicameral Parliament, elected by universal male suffrage every three years, was assigned exclusive right to make the laws and to decide between war and peace. To enhance their independence of the executive and to avoid the abuses of the Bourgeois Monarchy, deputies were to receive salaries and denied concurrent appointment to administrative jobs. That this Constitution, reminiscent of the American one and foreshadowing the Fifth Republic's, did not long survive was due as much to the undemocratic predilections of the deputies elected to the new Assembly as to the ambitions of the first President, Louis Napoleon.

Nephew to Napoleon I by virtue of his father Louis of Holland's being a brother to Napoleon and step-nephew because of his mother Hortense Beauharnais' being the daughter of Josephine, Louis Napoleon was both victim and perpetrator of the Napoleonic legend. Early in life, he had resolved to restore what he considered to be the essential features of his uncle's contribution. During the 1830s and 1840s, Louis wrote numerous pamphlets revealing both his adherence to the legend begun on St. Helena and the blueprint conceived by the nephew for subsequent political and social action. Discounting the bloody wars of conquest as a mere defensive reflex against reactionary coalitions, young Louis preferred to emphasize the liberal and nationalist aspects of his uncle's rule. Efficient government and capable administraiton along with popular sovereignty expressed through plebiscites rather than through parliamentary or other representative forms seemed to be the testament and the goal. Order and authority would secure private property, but a greater social consciousness on the part of Louis led him to a paternalistic concern for the economically underprivileged. His tract on the extinction of pauperism could have given heart to the workers without making the bourgeois tremble. No more than the privilege of birth would the privilege of wealth entail undue advantages in a state headed by a Bonaparte. Protected from anticlerical excesses but not favored with political and social ascendancy, the Church would also be secure in the society. United, orderly, prosperous, and godly at home, the French would earn glory in the international field. By example and by encouragement of liberal and

national movements rather than by aggressive and acquisitive wars,
French prestige would soar among the delivered nations of Europe.
Under the direction of a Bonaparte, France would ride the liberal,
national wave of the future.

In 1848, the magic of Louis Napoleon's name more than the
wide circulation or following of his formulated ideas accounted for
his election to the Presidency of the Second Republic. Sound political judgment and sheer good luck played a role, too. Louis Napoleon was careful not to offend the republican Assembly by his
threatening presence in the summer of 1848, even though he had
been somehow elected as deputy by write-in votes. Because he had
tactfully withdrawn to England, he was fortunately not associated
with either side in the insurrection and repression of the June Days.
By the fall of 1848, he could return to France and present his
person with clean hands and wide Bonapartist attraction. To the
peasants, gentry, bourgeois, and churchmen who wanted a government of authority, he was an ideal candidate. To the workers who
were paralyzed by fear of further repression and exploitation, he
offered relief and hope. Other candidates – General Cavaignac,
poet Lamartine, radical republican Ledru-Rollin – had proven
themselves too partisan in the events of February through June,
1848. Louis Napoleon reaped a fall harvest of nearly 5,500,000
votes; Cavaignac garnished only 1,500,000; Ledru-Rollin, 350,000;
Lamartine, a pitiful 17,000.

Whether Louis Napoleon's oath to uphold the Constitution was
hypocritical and ringed with reservations or whether he sincerely
made the pledge only later to plan the move from the presidential
Elysée to an imperial home in the Tuileries is a moot point. That
he proceeded astutely to ingratiate himself with sizeable numbers
of Frenchmen by his political activity, economic pronouncements,
foreign policy, and religious views is beyond doubt. As his legal
term of office was expiring, it became clear that a coup d'état
would be required to overcome the Assembly's reluctance to extend
his tenure constitutionally. By that time, however, his popularity
was sufficient to leave the deputies helpless.

Once installed as President, Louis Napoleon quickly built up
an organized popular following through a subsidized press, well-
arranged speaking tours and personal appearances throughout the
country, and newly formed clubs and leagues of army and civilian
partisans. With the Parliament elected finally in May, 1849, the
President showed himself to the experienced deputies as an adroit
politician and not the cipher he had been considered. The membership of the new legislature was heavily conservative, counting
among the 750-man body about 550 Orleanists, Legitimists, Bonapartists, and moderate republicans. The surprising presence of 180
radical but not socialist republicans was unable to disturb the
propertied majority or the ambitious President. Louis undercut
possible discontent in the Assembly by the judicious choice of
Orleanist ministers for his cabinet. He maintained, too, in the
administration the Orleanist prefects and mayors. Offense to the
Legitimists was limited by his encouragement of the institution
dear to them – the Church. Napoleon ranged himself with the
entire amorphous conservative majority of monarchists and republicans by censoring radical journals and repressing subversive organizations.

On the religious question, Napoleon cultivated much support
not only from the Legitimists, but also from the previously and
subsequently anticlerical bourgeoisie. The memory of the events of
1848, especially the June Days, was still vividly fresh in the middle-
class mind. The otherwise detested or suspected Church seemed for
the moment to be institutionally suited to prevent social upheaval.
When republican forms seemed endangered a generation later, not
by a monarchist-clerical right, the bourgeois would adopt a different
stance; but 1850 was not 1880. In 1850, Louis Napoleon could
win wide praise for aid to the Church through the Falloux Law.
By this law, authorized religious groups were permitted to establish
primary and secondary schools as well as institutions of higher
learning. The ascendancy of the University and the public schools
was further reduced by re-introducing clergymen into teaching and
administrative posts in imitation of the Restoration. The Church's

position abroad was buttressed, too, by Napoleon's somewhat reluctant but appreciated military intervention. French forces were dispatched to Rome in 1849 to destroy the Roman Republic and to reassert papal authority over the city and the Papal States.

To earn a reputation as champion of the forces of order and yet to emerge as hero to liberals and democrats might seem a difficult feat. The forces of order in the Assembly, however, not only made it simple for Louis Napoleon, but also enabled him to extend his Presidency in 1851 and to proclaim himself Emperor in 1852. Frightened lest the by-elections of April, 1850, be a forecast of radical republican success in the general elections forthcoming two years later, the Assembly took a dangerous step. It passed a law that denied the vote to approximately three million Frenchmen. Claiming to be the upholder of the Constitution and the rights of the deprived lower classes, Louis Napoleon set himself against the conservatives in the legislature. In anticipation of his own expiring term, the supporter of democratic suffrage proposed a constitutional amendment to permit his re-eligibility for the Presidency. A majority, but not the three-fourths necessary, agreed to the bill in July, 1851, leaving Napoleon the prospect of retirement or illegal seizure of power. He chose the latter.

The opposition was easily rendered powerless against the coup d'état neatly planned and executed on the night of December 1–2. In command of a loyal army and solidly supported by the civil service, Napoleon had already weaned to his side or neutralized a large number of the original monarchist, clerical, and bourgeois backers of the hostile deputies. The working class seemed unlikely to resist the Bonapartist coup on behalf of parliamentarians who had refused its social demands and deprived it of its vote. More protofascist than democratic in pattern, a proclamation officially announced to the public the dissolution of the Parliament, a resumption of universal male suffrage, and a plebiscitary call on the people to accept or reject the new regime and a constitution to be drafted by its leader.

By immediate and harsher repression than warranted by the

scattered resistance and by purges of greater thoroughness than dictated by the circumstances, the otherwise tender-hearted Louis Napoleon and his zealous lieutenants sought to assure the solidity of his regime. Through intimidation, apathy, or persuasion, nearly 7,500,000 Frenchmen favored the December, 1851, coup and new Constitution and only 600,000 dissented. One year later, even fewer votes were cast against the brief amendment that made the President-dictator an Emperor, Napoleon III.

1852–1870

The Second Empire and its collapse

THE CONSTITUTIONS offered in the plebiscites made a mockery of representative government although retaining many of its forms. Virtually all executive and legislative power was assigned to the President and then the Emperor. The cabinet was responsible to him alone. The Emperor had the right to appoint all members to the Senate, the upper house of the bicameral Parliament, which he scrupulously did by packing it with military and religious figures and other favorites. The principal function of the Senate was to reject laws it considered unconstitutional. The popularly elected lower house could discuss and accept or reject bills, but it could not introduce or amend any. By means of governmental pressure well-known in previous regimes, the Second Empire hoped to direct the voters' choice of legislators by advancing official candidates who held exclusive access to government agencies and funds and by jerrymandering the reduced number of electoral districts. The *Conseil d'Etat* was revived, its members appointed by the Emperor and given the power to draft laws once the bills introduced by the Emperor were passed by the Legislative Assembly. Amendment to the Constitution was possible only by suggestion of the Emperor and endorsement by a plebiscite.

During the remaining years of the 1850s, the political life of France was characterized by the authoritarian features sketched above. From 1860 to the eve of the Franco-Prussian War in 1870, however, noteworthy revision of the Constitution and a high degree of relaxation of other rules occurred. Apologists for Napoleon III have claimed that he had always harbored liberal political intentions and had merely awaited propitious circumstances to fulfill them. Adversaries have looked to the concessions as capitulations to hostile domestic forces that might otherwise attempt to topple his regime. The ambiguous and frequently contradictory nature of Louis Napoleon might lend support to both views simultaneously. Whatever the mixture of reasons for the liberalization during the second decade of the Second Empire, certain freedoms reappeared and a parliamentary system did emerge.

With minor exceptions, full amnesty was decreed in 1859 for all political prisoners and deportees. Restrictions on the press, which had been imposed in the aftermath of the Revolution of 1848, were substantially removed by the law of 1868. During the same year, trade unions were permitted to organize, extending the legalization of strikes and the right of temporary labor association authorized in 1864. By a series of decrees or laws during the years 1860, 1867, and 1870, the two houses of Parliament were the greatest beneficiaries of the Emperor's calculation, largesse, or weakness. By 1870, the Senate received coequal legislative powers with the lower house and the right of public rather than secret debate. The lower house was accorded the hitherto denied right to initiate bills, to scrutinize and vote the budget, and to choose its own officers.

Acceptance of this ill-disguised but slowly relenting dictatorship may be attributable in part to the institutional controls in the Emperor's hand and to his retention of the sole instruments of power. With the National Guard disbanded, the loyal army and the envigorated police could detect and meet almost any challenge put to its chief. Acceptance stemmed also from the prosperity not hitherto enjoyed in nineteenth-century France. Many bourgeois were hostile to Napoleon III for his free-trade policy and his Saint-Simonian approach to economic problems. Many workers, too, were

suspicious of the property-protecting regime that ruthlessly put
down strikes on the one hand and aided the cause of trade unionism on the other. Nevertheless, the urban classes were largely
mollified by the striking economic expansion and full employment
of which the Emperor was both beneficiary and architect.

Financial, railway, industrial, and commercial growth was
phenomenal during the Second Empire. Both by direct state expenditures and by the encouragement of semipublic and private banks,
Napoleon III extended the credit facilities of France enormously.
Founded or fostered during the Empire, such institutions as the
Crédit Mobilier, the *Crédit Foncier,* the *Crédit Lyonnais,* and the
Crédit Agricole helped channel the savings and investments of rural
and urban Frenchmen into railroad development, industrial establishments, foreign and domestic trade, and agricultural improvement.

Where France had but half the rail trackage of the German
states and less than a third of Britain's in 1848, the 1870 mileage
showed the gap narrowed. On the eve of the Franco-Prussian War,
the French rail system measured 17,500 kilometers as compared
with 19,580 in Germany and 24,500 in England. Over the same
time span, the domestic mining of coal doubled; consumption rose
threefold. The use of steam power in factories and mines increased
even more, and annual production in Le Creusot iron works alone
mounted from 18,000 tons in the poor year of 1847 to 133,000
tons twenty years later. Although cotton textiles failed to match the
gains of other industries, partly as a result of competition from
England, French silk, wool, and worsted goods greatly improved
their record. Trade in these and other French products soared to
new heights; imports quadrupled and exports tripled. In agriculture, the wine industry particularly benefited, especially aided by
Napoleon's 1860 free-trade agreement with the British, who purchased nearly four times as much wine in 1864 as in 1857.

In one of the most vast urban renewal projects of modern times,
Napoleon III revealed most clearly his Saint-Simonian tendencies
by enlisting specialists and technicians in the service of the state.

Despite the resistance of the bourgeoisie because of the high costs and unorthodox methods involved, Napoleon's plans for the renovation of the city of Paris were executed by the talented although sometimes officious Baron Haussmann. The business, scientific, and artistic communities combined their respective skills in the mixed public–private enterprise of large-scale construction. Demolition of congested neighborhoods was followed by the building of wide, tree-lined boulevards flanked by up-to-date private dwellings, office buildings, sidewalk cafés, department stores, and an opera house. Parks and elaborate sanitation facilities were installed. New bridges spanned the Seine. Uneasy though they were about the enormous costs and often deprived of cheap housing and narrow alleys easily barricaded, the bourgeois and workingmen of Paris nevertheless enjoyed the stimulated economic activity and the full artisanal and manual employment produced by these public works.

Napoleon III's astute political operations and his generally salutary socioeconomic policies might have maintained him as Emperor and guaranteed a Bonapartist succession for the heir born in 1856. Ineptitude or frightfully bad luck in the conduct of foreign affairs denied this future. Although ever conscious of his Bonapartist background and the urge for French prestige, he exhibited no overwhelming desire or intention to lead France and Europe into the mass wars for which his uncle had been notorious. The three major wars of the Second Empire were either "accidental" in origin, as was the case of the Crimean War in 1854; limited in scope, as was the Italian War in 1859 from which he quickly disengaged himself when escalation threatened; or imposed on the Emperor by external circumstances and jingoism at home, as was the Franco-Prussian War of 1870. That he blundered and stumbled into these wars was indisputable. That he planned and entered them with relish is untrue, except for the Italian War.

As President of the Second Republic, Louis Napoleon could not resist involvement in the "monkish quarrel" in the Holy Places. Without recalling the glorious participation of French crusaders, French interest in the Near East was no Bonapartist invention. As

protector of Christian privileges in the Holy Places within the Ottoman Empire, the French President and then Emperor exerted
pressure on the Sultan to ensure Roman Catholic rather than
Greek Orthodox jurisdiction. Devout Catholics in France as well
as nonpracticing patriots were gratified by Napoleon's success in
extracting from the Sultan a public pronouncement that Roman
Catholics would have special and superior rights in the Holy
Places.

The chapter might have been closed with this addition to French
prestige in 1853 but for the intervention of Russia in the affair.
The Russian Tsar undertook to champion the opposite religious
faction. By his sponsorship of the Orthodox clergy, he hoped to
make territorial, commercial, or military gains in the Balkans, Black
Sea, or Straits. From the sidelines, as a satisfied party, Napoleon
watched with growing uneasiness the deterioration of Russo-
Turkish relations and the increased diplomatic attention of Britain.
Probably with irregularly promised support from the British Ambassador, the Sultan rebuffed Russian threats and lures. In exas-
peration, the Tsar put pressure on the Sultan by invading the
Danubian Principalities of Wallachia and Moldavia. Desirous
neither of the Sultan's being obliged by the Russians to rescind the
pronouncement favoring Roman Catholics nor of England's being
the sole beneficiary of upholding the Ottoman Empire, Napoleon
III felt compelled to associate the French fleet with the British as a
counterchallenge to the Tsar. When the Russians refused to withdraw their forces from the Ottoman Empire's Principalities, a
Russo-Turkish war began. Some months later, in March, 1854, the
British and the French threw in their lot with the Sultan.

After months of desultory land and sea engagements and fruitless diplomatic efforts, Anglo-French armies invaded the Crimea in
September, 1854. The remainder of that year and almost all of the
next proved an agonizing nightmare for the troops battling for
possession of the peninsula. Neither the ministrations of Florence
Nightingale nor the poetry of Alfred, Lord Tennyson, could
glamorize this small-scale but intense war. By early 1856, allied

victories and the threat of Austrian intervention pressed the Russians to sue for peace.

From the Congress that met in Paris rather than Vienna in February and March, 1856, Napoleon III obtained more personal and national prestige than specific spoils. Primarily of interest to England, the Ottoman Empire, and Austria, provisions of the peace treaty set back Russia in the Balkans, the Straits, and the Black Sea. Amplification of maritime law was of secondary importance to the French. On one point, however, Napoleon contributed heavily; he fostered the initial measures that would lead eventually to the national unification and independence of a Rumanian state formed from the Principalities of Wallachia and Moldavia. Less concrete results rewarded Napoleon's sympathetic sponsorship of Sardinia for a hearing of Italian national ambitions.

More fruitful in yield yet more fraught with danger to France than the Crimean War was Napoleon III's war against Austria on behalf of Italian unification. It was also more attributable to his planning and execution. In describing Napoleon's role in 1859, too much attention has been accorded to his miscalculations and backsliding betrayal, too little to his motivating vision. He was convinced, personally and as heir to the Napoleonic legend, that liberalism and nationalism should and would be the pattern for the European state-system of generations to come. Under a Bonaparte, it was France's mission to encourage these movements where possible and to place French resources at the disposal of subject nationalities, who, in turn, would offer France unqualified gratitude and possibly tangible compensation. To stand aside while these movements reformed the map of Europe would result in isolation or enmity from the evolving nation–states. To allow Austria, in particular, to consolidate her hold over Italy would not only frustrate liberalism and nationalism, but also would enhance the power of Austria to deny potential French expansion in the German states that Austria headed.

Persuaded by ideological and material considerations, Napoleon III undertook to negotiate secretly with the Sardinian Kingdom's minister, Camillo Cavour. At Plombières in July, 1858, Napoleon revealed himself more cognizant of the dangers of French involvement than his critics care to admit. For to create a tightly united Italian Kingdom, under the House of Savoy or any other single dynasty, might ultimately threaten French security on the continent and in the Mediterranean. The papal temporal position, too, might be jeopardized, further to the disadvantage of Napoleon's domestic position. Napoleon took precautions against such contingencies by agreeing at Plombières to the formation of only a loose confederation of Italian states under the titular headship of the Pope. Sardinia, enlarged by a projected annexation of Lombardy and Venetia, would form the most powerful of the four states. A Central Kingdom of the Duchies of Parma, Modena, and Tuscany; the Papal States; and the Kingdom of the Two Sicilies would constitute the remaining parts. Thereby, Italian national aspirations would be satisfied and the potential threat to French or papal interests mitigated. In return for French military aid against the Austrian masters of Italy, Napoleon was promised the provinces of Nice and Savoy (subject to a plebiscite in each) and a dynastic marriage between Napoleon's cousin, Prince Jerome, and King Victor Emmanuel's daughter, Clotilde (subject to the young lady's assent). In a stipulation as much foreshadowing the methods of twentieth-century dictators as reminiscent of those of sixteenth-century Machiavelli, French armies would march only if Austria was made to appear the aggressor.

But for the persistence and cunning of Cavour and the incredibly stupid diplomacy of Austria, the Italian question might have become the subject of a general European Congress instead of a war. Among the great powers, England especially was pressing the alternative of deliberation upon Napoleon. Cavour managed to keep the Emperor to his commitment to the end, however, by a near-blackmail threat of publishing the correspondence between the two "conspirators." It was Austrian stupidity that saved the day for Cavour and paved the way for war. Justifiably provoked by Cavour's surreptitious encouragement of draft-dodging in her Italian provinces of Lombardy and Venetia and infuriated by Sardinian mobilization, Austria submitted an ultimatum to Sardinia. Neither Sardinia in 1859, Serbia in 1914, nor most sovereign states in any era would be likely to find such an ultimatum acceptable. Austria had probably intended it to be unacceptable; Cavour was delighted to declare it so. The giant Austrian Empire appeared the aggressor against the pygmy Sardinian kingdom. France, under the terms of the Pact of Plombières, joined Sardinia. The war was begun.

Within three months, French and Sardinian armies had beaten Austrian forces back into a limited but defensible set of fortresses in northern Italy. With several victories behind and success tantalizingly ahead, Napoleon III suddenly deserted the common cause and unilaterally negotiated an armistice with Emperor Franz Joseph at Villafranca in July. The Austrians were forced to cede Lombardy but not Venetia to Sardinia and to recognize the confederated Italy established on paper at Plombières. A nearly apoplectic Cavour was left with the alternative of incomplete victory or continuation of an impossible war alone against Austria. He resigned for a brief while when his monarch chose discretion.

Napoleon's betrayal may be less harshly judged if notice is given to the stunned Cavour's sly undermining of the pact to which he had assented. In international relations as in domestic affairs, alignments and coalitions are highly relative to the issues at stake at the moment. The action required to satisfy French (and Italian) interests of state in July, 1859, was different from that demanded in April, 1859, or July, 1858, when the Pact of Plombières was conceived. As Austrian forces withdrew from the client states in central Italy in the spring of 1859, nationalist societies showed themselves more than a match for the local authorities. In the absence of Austrian backing, the Dukes and their aristocratic-clerical retinues were easily ousted. Aided and abetted by Cavour, the new provisional governments and liberated peoples of the Duchies clamored for annexation to the Sardinian kingdom with obvious intentions of forming a highly centralized Italian state. What might be the fate of the Pope in his restive lands? French interests of state and Napoleon's domestic position seemed ill served by continuing the war. Equally impelling reasons for Napoleon's defection at Villafranca were found in the Prussian mobilization moves. That state, as well as several other members of the German Confederation over which Austria presided, had initially harbored unspoken pleasure at the prospect of Austrian involvement in the Italian War. An Austria preoccupied or slightly crippled might give wider latitude to an independent or even nationalist course in the Germanies. An Austria thoroughly defeated, however, would be no bulwark against French thrusts into the Rhineland.

From the venture in Italy, Napoleon salvaged much and lost much. Unquestionably, French prestige rose as a result of the defeats inflicted on Austrian armies. The promised dynastic marriage did take place. Nice and Savoy were eventually ceded to France. The Pope was protected in his temporal possession of the city of Rome and its environs, although not in the more extensive properties of the Papal States. On the other hand, Austria was obviously antagonized by the French contribution to her decline. The new Italian kingdom attributed to France its failure to acquire Venetia and its inability to use Rome as its capital. The British were suspicious of Bonapartist ambition. In the German states, however, there lurked the greatest menace to France as an outcome of the Italian War. German nationalists and Prussian expansionists began to presume from the Austrian defeat that the head of the Confederation was more vulnerable than her reputation, size, and resources might indicate.

Outside Europe, Napoleon III employed French military and administrative agencies to extend French influence. In Indochina, Syria, and Mexico, Catholic missionaries or clerical interests were protected with energy. Strategic and economic motives were evident, too, as Napoleon III absorbed Cochin-China, made Cambodia a protectorate, wrested concessions from China, and supported Ferdinand de Lesseps' construction of the Suez Canal. Although the Emperor relaxed the French grip on Algeria, he expanded French control over such West African territories as Senegal. Profiting from the United States' involvement in the Civil War, Napoleon began in 1861 to make real his dream of a canal through a Central America tied closer to France politically and culturally. A French-sponsored regime in Mexico under Maximilian of Austria received financial, diplomatic, and military aid until local opposition and the reunited United States called a halt to this undertaking.

If Napoleon III's Italian policy and overseas exploits had brought only mixed blessings to the Second Empire, his German policy was an undiluted disaster. French, British, and Russian inaction in the Danish War of 1864 had enabled Prussia and Austria to seize and share the provinces of Schleswig and Holstein. While Otto von Bismarck, Chancellor in Prussia, prepared diplomatically and militarily for a showdown fight with Austria for control in the German Confederation, Napoleon III busied himself with plans to extract the greatest possible benefits for France.

Since he was not adamantly opposed to a liberal and more national arrangement beyond the Rhine, he was sympathetic to Bismarck's overtures at their Biarritz meeting in 1865. Bismarck, in turn, seemed eager to comply with one of Napoleon's requests, namely that Italy should be made a partner to Prussia and should be awarded Venetia for her efforts. Napoleon might thereby regain his dubious reputation as a champion of Italian unification. The price of French neutrality in the event of an Austro-Prussian duel, however, involved compensation Bismarck would not specifically offer. To maintain the European balance of power and to enhance France's status — Bismarck's gains were anticipated to bring Prussia on a par with Austria — Napoleon sought Rhineland or Belgian territory and was shrewdly given the impression of assurance. This much-criticized and certainly ill-advised French offer of neutrality was based on opinions shared by most European statesmen and military experts. They all judged that Austrian strength was equal or possibly superior to Prussian. Consequently, a war between the two states would be a long, drawn-out affair. In the stalemate foreseen, Napoleon III hoped with little effort to become the arbiter of the struggle and to dictate a settlement of the German question highly advantageous to the French. With an army assiduously trained and equipped by Bismarck during the 1860s and by the effective use of its rail network, Prussia was able in seven weeks to overrun many of the north German states and to inflict a stunning defeat on Austria at Sadowa. By imposing his measured will on more impetuous colleagues, Bismarck ended the war promptly without subjecting Austria to a Carthaginian peace. Cession of Venetia to Italy and exclusion from German affairs were the extent of Austrian losses. No indemnity, no further territory was demanded of the grateful Austrians. France and the other European powers were presented with a fait accompli that left no room for diplomatic or military maneuver.

While Bismarck proceeded to annex many of the north German states, to associate with the remaining ones in a Prussian dominated North German Confederation, and to negotiate offensive–defensive alliances with the independent south German states, Napoleon pleaded for fulfillment of the implied promises of Biarritz. Bismarck refused outright to consider French acquisition of the left bank of the Rhine, but he did not reject offhand possible French gains in Luxembourg and Belgium. At the wily request of Bismarck, the French Ambassador Benedetti committed the cardinal sin of putting these French demands into writing. Four years later, the French would sorely regret the advantage Bismarck would take from this act.

Refused concrete compensation in 1866 and frustrated again in 1867 by Bismarck's role in blocking the purchase of Luxembourg from the proprietary King of Holland, the French used the Spanish Succession as a means of diplomatic retaliation against Prussia. In 1870, Prince Leopold of Hohenzollern-Sigmaringen declined and then, as a result of Bismarck's connivance, accepted the Spanish government's offer to fill the vacant throne. French expressions of alarm at encirclement by the distant dynastic connection between the King of Prussia and Prince Leopold were highly exaggerated. As a pretext to repair damaged French prestige and honor, however, the issue could serve admirably. By its strenuous protest to the Prussian head of the Hohenzollerns, the French government forced Leopold to withdraw his candidacy. Bismarck was deeply disappointed by his King's submission to the French.

The petulant and foolish French refused to let the matter drop. Napoleon's advisors instructed Ambassador Benedetti to press the Prussian King for a renunciation in perpetuity of any Hohenzollern candidacy to the Spanish throne. The vacationing King preferred the pleasures of the resort town of Bad Ems to the incessant importuning of the nagging Benedetti, and, in a casual telegram to his Chancellor in Berlin, said so. By careful editing and publication of the dispatch, Bismarck created the impression on both sides of the Rhine that respective French and German national sensibilities had been offended. The Parisian press and its readers, members of the French Parliament, administrators, and factions at court urged Napoleon to respond with vigor. With much reluctance, he declared war on July 19 and decreed the doom of the Second Empire.

Napoleon no more succeeded in war than he had in diplomacy. French military reforms were incomplete; French diplomatic isolation was total. Bismarck had kept Austria friendly to Prussia by lenient treatment in 1866; he had assured Russian neutrality by aid in suppressing Polish insurrections during the 1860s; he had detached England from any possible French alignment by publishing in London the 1866 document revealing French designs on Belgium. The south German states, in military alliance with Prussia, felt more threatened by French aggrandizement than by Prussian. Napoleon's defense of the Pope in Rome denied the Italian kingdom as an ally to the French.

Despite the isolation of France in 1870 and the recent victory of Prussia over Austria in 1866, most Frenchmen felt optimistic about their chances for military success. Even the majority of foreign observers rated the French military machine higher than the German. The French quickly realized their inferiority in numbers of effectives, in training and most equipment, and in strategic planning and execution, however. The relatively small professional French army availed itself less of reserve components than the Prussian. French artillery was speedy in delivering fire and in making tactical moves, but the Prussians had the advantage of heavier and massed weapons. More modern small arms and the French soldiers' personal courage were insufficient to offset the Prussian organization, matériel, and command. By late August, Marshal MacMahon had been defeated and driven back in Alsace, and Marshal Bazaine had been forced to take cover in the fortified region of Metz. On September 2, the French Emperor, at the head of the French armies near Sedan and accompanied by a surgeon in the event of a recurrence of his enervating bladder disturbance, witnessed the rout of his troops and surrendered himself and eighty thousand men to the enemy. It was a defeat from which the Second Empire would not recover.

On September 4, 1870, two Paris deputies led a mass of demonstrators to the Hôtel de Ville and proclaimed a Republic. Earlier that day, mobs had surged into the Palais Bourbon and forced the remaining legislators to decree a formal end to the Second Empire. The demise of the Empire and the birth of the Republic were induced by long-developing maladies made especially manifest by the Empire's involvement in the Franco-Prussian War.

To survive as a regime, the Second Empire required one or a combination of resources: an impelling leader, a dedicated body of politicians and administrators, a loyal military or police organization, a massive popular following. By September 4, 1870, the Empire could claim none of these. The ailing Emperor was in the hands of the enemy. Neither the Empress nor any other notable figure would or could step forward to establish a regency. Legislators and bureaucrats evinced no great interest in continuing their association or identification with the demonstrably inefficient Empire. Officers and men loyal to Napoleon III were either prisoners themselves or waging losing engagements far from the cities where political decisions were being made. The public was shocked by the military disaster. The Emperor had placed in jeopardy the security and integrity of France.

The Empire's direction — or mis-direction — of the Franco-

Prussian War was not the exclusive factor in bringing down that regime. The Empire had already alienated many of its supporters before 1870. Napoleon's successive concessions during the 1860s had not fully satisfied the liberal reformers but had whetted the appetite of radicals who yearned for a republic. The misadventure in Mexico had estranged many private citizens and public figures, and the legislated but unimplemented military reforms had confused the army by the summer of 1870. The war thus precipitated the death of the declining Second Empire and the birth of a republic.

To arrive as a regime, the Third Republic profited from the bankruptcy of the Empire and added to its chances the promise of positive action. What monarchists or remaining Bonapartists feared to do, republicans could do with impunity: invoke the historical memories of the Revolution's call to the nation to repel the invader. Provided with a stirring, dramatic leader like Léon Gambetta, backed by enthusiastic citizens, and initially successful in attracting officers and recruiting soldiers, the war-born Republic seemed sound.

4.

THE STRANGE BIRTH AND VIGOR OF THE THIRD REPUBLIC

FROM the 1870 proclamation of the new Republic to the 1914 declaration of war, the French were confronted by four kinds of problems: political, economic and social, imperial, and international. Political forms and practices required definition. Not until 1875 was the balcony-proclaimed Republic given organic structure. Not until 1879 did the republican-dominated Parliament secure ascendancy over the potentially monarchical executive. Not until the early 1900s, however, had the Republic overwhelmed the rival institutions in which antirepublican elements were entrenched — the Church, the army, and numerous monarchist organizations. As the threat from this so-called right diminished after 1900, the challenge to the republican establishment emerged from the left.

Simultaneous with the turbulent politics of founding and preserving the Third Republic were the mounting tensions of French economic and social life. The growth of existing industries and the appearance of new ones often had a disturbing effect on traditional craft manufacturing. Agricultural disasters or backwardness wrought havoc in the rural areas. The social structure and mores were strained by the swelling numbers of new bourgeois and proletarian Frenchmen whose demands, aspirations, and habits hardly fitted with those of the existing order.

Imperial and international problems were also pressing. The Parliament, the army, and the Church were but a few of the institutions involved in determining the nature and degree of the French commitment to colonial acquisition and management. Statesmen and citizens had also to reflect on the new status of a France defeated in 1871. Responsible officials had to formulate and implement a foreign policy that would satisfy French interests of state in continental Europe and overseas.

Although each of the cited problems might arbitrarily be defined and treated separately, each had an important bearing on all the others. Domestic politics and foreign policy, for example, were often closely linked. To strengthen the French position against Germany, an anticlerical republic rather than a Church-affiliated monarchy might be more likely to associate with the new Italian kingdom that had rendered the Pope a "Prisoner of the Vatican." Yet, as in previous and subsequent periods, Frenchmen who were violently at odds over one particular problem readily joined together when a different issue arose. The political antipathy of monarchists to republicans did not prevent their political affinity against socialist challenges to private property or military preparedness.

The politics of making and maintaining the Republic

A GOVERNMENT of National Defense was formed in September, 1870, by private agreement among the Parisian Republic makers rather than by consultation with the French people for whom the Republic had just been proclaimed. War's dislocation and Bismarck's refusal to suspend hostilities precluded any chance of holding elections for the formation of a popularly designated government.

The assignment of the Presidency to General Louis Jules Trochu, the Military Governor of Paris, gave the impression of solidity and order to many timorous Parisian and provincial bourgeois as well as to the distant but influential rural notables. The cautious, conservative Ernest Picard's inclusion in the government helped fortify this impression. As Minister of Interior, Léon Gambetta could and did function overtly to organize the nation for defense and covertly to place republican officials in important local posts. The moderate republican Jules Favre assumed the Vice-Presidency and crucial Ministry of Foreign Affairs. In deference to the Parisian crowds that had been so instrumental in the transformation of September 4, editor Henri Rochefort found his way into the government. Adolphe Thiers was one important figure whose skepticism kept him from seeking or accepting a ministry. His political and patriotic sense however, induced him to serve France as ambassador-at-large.

With some few exceptions, Frenchmen participated in or rallied to the Government of National Defense in September, 1870, more for the defense of France than for the sake of any particular form of government. The strongest political passion was undoubtedly disillusionment with the Empire rather than a desire of a republic or monarchy. Even such a rabid republican as Gambetta devoted more attention to the conduct of the war than to the search for constitutions. Even strong partisans of monarchy were willing to enlist in the armies being recruited by the Paris-proclaimed Republic. Skeptics, cynics, and opportunists existed on both sides of the political fence, but then this is an account of French history.

To redress the unfavorable military situation after Sedan, the Government of National Defense had some significant resources at its disposition. Since some of these forces were not readily available to Napoleon III, there was room to believe that the new government might succeed against the Prussians where the Empire had failed. Marshal Achille Bazaine still had a sizeable undefeated army when Napoleon III surrendered. Other Imperial regulars still in the field could be re-enforced by a revitalized National Guard and a nation-wide call to arms. With Charles de Freycinet as his deputy, Gambetta directed much of the military organization and planning. Heavy reliance was placed on the besieged army under Bazaine at Metz to tie up German forces that might otherwise break through the defenses of besieged Paris or disrupt the training of recruits for the Army of the Loire. If Bazaine kept the Germans distracted in the east, Gambetta assumed that the Germans around Paris could be scattered by a coordinated attack by the French armies from without and the Parisian garrison from within.

With headquarters in Tours after his spectacular October 9 balloon escape from Paris, Gambetta moved strenuously to pursue these military goals. He roved France and supervised the recruiting, training, and equipping of the Army of the Loire. Within Paris, scattered contingents of regulars and a reconstituted National Guard manned the city's defenses and worked with the populace in preparing barricades against the Prussian besiegers. The National Guard admitted working-class as well as traditional middle-class elements. Such an innovation as payment to members of the Guard was due not only to the need for manpower, but also to the hope of resolving the explosive social problem of unemployment in the surrounded capital.

Until the end of October and even through early November, Gambetta's approach seemed feasible. However, Bazaine's surrender at Metz on October 28, whether by malicious treason or unfortunate necessity, seriously lessened French chances of success. Relieved from Metz, German armies reached the Paris region before the Army of the Loire could exploit its astonishing November 9 victory near Orléans. Thereafter, inadequate matériel, manpower, and command led the French to defeat after defeat. Sorties by the Paris garrison were repulsed, and conditions in the capital deteriorated at an alarming rate.

As French military fortunes declined, French political difficulties rose. The Government of National Defense, already physically separated by residence in three places (Paris, Tours, and Bordeaux), became increasingly divided over the choice between continuing the war or seeking peace. The ultra-republican Gambetta represented the faction urging war to the bitter end. Some conservative members, including Foreign Minister Favre, were more inclined to come to terms with the Germans. An official like Thiers, who had not even in September been an avid supporter of a war policy, found more sympathy for his peace stand by January, 1871. The

French public, too, and particularly the provincials, became more and more apathetic in seconding Gambetta and more and more emphatic in opposing the struggle. Dying for a lost cause held no appeal for the French peasant. To rural notables and even to some September republicans, examples of political radicalism and social strife seemed to be appalling forerunners of revolutionary upheaval. Would not the entire social fabric of France be in shreds if the war were continued? Unable to impose his war policy on the government or on the majority of the French people any longer, Gambetta bitterly bowed to the armistice accepted by the Paris delegation of the Government of National Defense on January 26, 1871. After resigning from the government, he prepared to campaign for the general elections that he had failed to delay.

On February 8, 1871, the French voted overwhelmingly for peace. To express this intention, they were compelled to cast their ballots for monarchist or conservative republican candidates rather than for ultra-republicans who persisted in their advocacy of war. Nevertheless, as Denis W. Brogan observes:

> The general confusion combined with the "scrutin de liste" to produce very odd electoral combinations. Thus the Bouches du Rhône, home of extremes, chose Radicals like Pelletan and Gambetta, the most famous of its native sons, Thiers, the Papal Zouave and hereditary Royalist hero, General de Charette, the moderate Republican, Grévy, and that ghost of 1848, Ledru-Rollin! [1]

Whatever the intentions of the voters, monarchists outnumbered republicans by more than two to one in the new National Assembly. In that body of more than 600 members, more than 400 were monarchists and approximately 80 were conservatives with no staunch commitment either to monarchy or republic. Moderate republicans numbered 100, and the Gambetta-variety republicans counted a mere 40. A splinter of 20 Bonapartists was also seated. Thiers was

---

[1] Denis W. Brogan, *France under the Republic, 1870–1939* (New York: Harper & Row, 1940), p. 78.

immediately selected as "the Chief Executive Power of the French Republic," and was able to conclude an informal Pact of Bordeaux whereby the major factions agreed to delay any action on the formation of permanent forms for the government.

With a clear mandate to secure peace, the National Assembly made peace. It voted on March 1 to accept the preliminary terms drawn up in Versailles. Final confirmation took place on May 10 with the signing of the Treaty of Frankfurt. By its provisions, the Germans procured all of Alsace and part of Lorraine, an indemnity of 5,000,000,000 francs ($1,000,000,000), the right to occupation of certain areas, and permission for a triumphal march through Paris in lieu of title to the fortress city of Belfort.

Having disposed of its obligation to the majority of Frenchmen by terminating the war, the new Provisional Government faced the hostile minority that had opposed peace-making. Resentment was especially marked in Paris and other large cities such as Lyons and Marseilles. Had the rural provincials so heavily represented in the Assembly made a wholehearted effort to relieve the besieged capital during the war? Had Thiers any right to allow the Prussians to march in arrogant procession through the city, which had not been conquered but had surrendered or had possibly been betrayed?

War or peace was not the only issue giving rise to dissatisfaction among elements in Paris. What was the significance of the Provisional Government's move from its initial seat in Bordeaux to Versailles instead of Paris? Was this a downgrading of the capital city of Republics and a foreshadowing of a royal restoration by the rural aristocracy and clergy? The government offended economic as well as military and political sensibilities. By declaring an end to the wartime moratorium on payments of rents, bills, and debts and by refusing further pay to the National Guard, the National Assembly showed obvious disregard for the interests of lower bourgeois and proletarian Parisians. In these incendiary circumstances, the government attempted to remove cannon from the Montmartre and other artillery parks on March 17–18. Disgruntled on so many grounds, the Parisians were provoked into open insurrection and inaugurated the Commune. Karl Marx's claim notwithstanding, the Paris Commune had obviously not been the product of class struggle alone, although economic and social factors were present in the amalgam of causes.

The leadership and the program of the Commune were no more Marxist than its origins. Once the Provisional Government lost control of Paris, authority fell to the Central Committee of the National Guard and to the Municipal Council (the Commune) elected on March 26. The leaders of both these bodies were predominantly lower middle class — artisans, shopkeepers, and professionals — and only one adhered to Marxian socialism. The remainder were radical in the Jacobin or Proudhonian sense. Insofar as there existed any well-defined program, the Commune proposed a federal rather than centralized Republic and a vociferous anticlericalism. The rights of private property remained inviolable.

Thiers, and a most obliging National Assembly, worked relentlessly against the insurrectionist Commune. He could easily count on the monarchist majority and also found support from the moderate republican minority, for despite the rivalry of the parliamentary opposites on the question of regime, moderate republicans like the four Juleses — Favre, Ferry, Grévy, and Simon — had no taste for the radical republicanism of the Commune. Even ultra-republicans like Georges Clemenceau, Louis Blanc, Victor Hugo, and Léon Gambetta became unwitting allies of the monarchists by refusing unanimous adherence to their fellow republicans of the Commune.

Two months of siege and assault operations by the regular troops of the Provisional Government ended in May, 1871, when the city was stormed and taken. Atrocities and excesses had been committed by both sides, the Provisional Government's murder of hostages being matched by the Commune's summary execution of clergymen and aristocrats. With the leaders of the Commune discredited, dead, jailed, or exiled, the French body politic was purged of radical elements. Who was left to urge a regime at variance with the designs of either royalists or conservative-moderate republicans?

If republicans had two faces on the issues of the Commune and of war or peace, monarchists showed their lack of unity on how to proceed from provisional to permanent political institutions. Despite their February, 1871, election victory of two to one over republicans and despite their retention of a sound majority in face of subsequent republican successes at the polls between 1871 and 1875, the monarchists succeeded in establishing not the monarchy of their dreams, but a Third Republic of their nightmares. The failure of the monarchists stemmed in great part from an irreconcilable rift in their ranks. The failure also illustrates the thesis that political developments are comprehensible only when considered in relation to the time and circumstances of particular events. The very same peasant who voted for monarchists in February, 1871, to secure peace voted for republicans in July when the foreign and civil wars were liquidated and the question of the type of regime was paramount.

The monarchist majority in the National Assembly was divided into two roughly equal factions each of which represented a contender for the throne. The Orleanists supported the claims of the Comte de Paris, grandson of Louis Philippe, whereas the Legitimists upheld the cause of the Comte de Chambord. A grandson of Charles x, Chambord, the miracle child of 1820, the posthumous son of the Duc de Berri, had not been especially blessed in asserting his rights to the kingdom. First Louis Philippe from 1830 to 1848 and then Louis Napoleon from 1848 to 1870 had kept the descendant of Louis xvi in perpetual exile.

The existence of two Pretenders for one throne need not have been disastrous for the monarchists. The aging Comte de Chambord was childless and apparently had no prospects of altering the situation. The younger and prolific Comte de Paris could serve as the older man's designated heir. Such a reasonable arrangement was concluded in 1871, but it was soon rendered inffective by Chambord's stubborn assertion of nationally unpalatable principles. The Legitimate Pretender unalterably demanded that his family flag, the white banner with the blue fleur-de-lis, supplant the "revolutionary" tricolor. Without this issue, the republican exploitation of other differences between the two monarchist camps could never have prevented a royal restoration.

Although hard-line Legitimists were reluctant to importune their divine-right leader to change his views, many royalists from the clergy and the aristocracy did not hesitate. Each time a spokesman sought to gloss over the divergence of views or implied a possible compromise, however, Chambord emphatically restated his unbreakable attachment to the white Bourbon flag of Henry IV, Louis XIV, and Louis XVI. (It is doubtful that Henry IV would have abandoned the throne of France for a bit of cloth. Converting to Catholicism to become King, had not Henry IV been reported to state that Paris was well worth a Mass?) The Comte de Chambord refused to become Henry V by his perverse obstinacy — or high principle. The Orleanists, judging the temper of the public and the army in the same light as the republicans, withheld their parliamentary support of such a restoration. It was feared that Chambord would provoke civil war by his denial of the tricolor and discredit the entire monarchist cause before the Orleanist heir could ever reach the throne.

Whether revealed as ridiculous and petty for his stand on the flag or portrayed as an unreconstituted Bourbon opposed to constitutional, parliamentary government, the Legitimist candidate hurt the entire monarchist cause at the polls. Having failed to capitalize on their electoral victory of 1871 and provide a royal candidate suitable to their own parliamentary majority, the monarchists went from disunity to disaster. By-elections returned five times as many republicans as monarchists. By 1874, such elections had seated 126 republicans as against 23 monarchists and 10 Bonapartists. In the National Assembly, the combined monarchists commanded but a fragile majority by 1875. French voters had been willing to vote for monarchists as a peace party in February, 1871, but not as an instrument of a royal restoration or a governmental party thereafter. The monarchists' position on church and state relations, foreign policy, and permanent political institutions provided the republicans with leverage to further divide the Legitimists from the Orleanists and to alienate the monarchists from the public.

With diminishing prospects of an immediate royal restoration and with increasing anxiety over republican successes, the monarchists moved in 1873 to set up institutions that would prevent the entrenchment of the Republic and pave the way for a future monarchy. Thiers was shorn of power partially and then totally. He had committed the sin of abandoning his erstwhile neutrality on the question of a regime and had openly espoused republicanism. In his place was installed Marshal Patrice de MacMahon, darling of the Dukes and supposed transitional custodian for a sometime King. To prevent the new President from being dislodged by a parliamentary maneuver, the Law of the Septennate was passed in November, 1873, assuring MacMahon of a seven-year term.

During the first three years of the Provisional Government, both monarchists and republicans had reason to postpone the establishment of permanent institutions. Legitimists lived in daily expectation that their candidate would soon be King. Constitution-making would be more appropriate after the happy coronation day. Most Orleanists shared this hope and joined in the delaying tactics, not wishing to jeopardize the ultimate succession of their Comte de Paris. By 1873, however, many Orleanists betrayed uneasiness about the lack of a constitution lest either a radical republicanism or a revived Bonapartism fill the vacuum. Furthermore, former supporters of the Orleanists found many of their interests more closely connected with the conservative and moderate republicans in the National Assembly than with the ultra-royalists. Often recruited from banking, commercial, or progressive land-owning families, the Orleanists found the socioeconomic line between themselves and those republicans to be a very fine one. Had not the Provisional Government – a republic or certainly a monarchless state – proved its stability in the face of internal disorder? Republicans, too, had been reluctant to press for organic laws during their years of parliamentary inferiority. Only after 1873, with their numbers growing and with possibilities of coalition with Orleanists, dared they contemplate a showdown.

The showdown came in early 1875. A turncoat monarchist, conservative republican Henri Wallon, introduced an amendment to a bill dealing with the succession of the President. If passed, this seemingly innocuous amendment would definitively commit the Assembly to a republic and give permanency to the institution of a republican office. Orleanists in sufficient numbers joined republicans to pass the amendment by a single vote, 353–352. As converts to republicanism or as would-be creators of a structure adaptable to a future constitutional monarchy, Orleanists voted with republicans throughout the succeeding weeks to enact the organic laws that have been informally called the Constitution of 1875. Radical republicans had the good sense to heed their leader Gambetta and swallow provisions repulsive to them. An imperfect republic was better than no republic.

What was the shape of the republic that the monarchist Assembly defined in 1875? From the organic laws, the President emerged as an important official. Carrying over the 1871–1875 practice, the President was to be elected for seven years by an absolute majority of votes in a joint session of the Senate and the Chamber of Deputies. Eligible for re-election, the President was armed with extensive powers in the initiation, promulgation, and execution of laws. Pardons but not amnesties and diplomatic, civil, and military appointments were also within his prerogative. The President was given the power not only to adjourn, but also to dissolve the Chamber of Deputies before the expiration of its four-year term if he obtained the assent of the Senate. Furthermore, he could appoint and apparently dismiss members of the Cabinet (Council of Ministers) of which he was technically the President, although they were responsible to the Parliament. The last clause of Article 3 in the law of February 25, 1875 stated that "Every act of the President must be countersigned by a Minister." Thus, whoever controlled the minister also controlled the executive power. The method of selection and the powers of the President revealed the conservative and even monarchical nature of the constitution makers. With little more than a change of title, the chief executive could easily be a King instead of a President.

Conservative intentions were manifested, too, in the organization of Parliament. The upper house, or Senate, would consist of 300 members, 225 elected indirectly by electoral colleges of prominent citizens in each department and 75 named by the outgoing National Assembly. Even after constitutional amendment in 1884 gave greater weight to larger cities, rural France was more heavily represented than the urban areas. The Senate enjoyed coequal powers with the lower house on legislative matters, with the exception of initiating laws of finance. Refusal to pass bills proposed by the Chamber of Deputies constituted an insurmountable veto. In the Senate's hands rested the decision to allow or disallow presidential dissolution of the lower house. Constitutional amendments also required the Senate's approval. Political and social stability would be hopefully achieved by fixing the senators' terms at nine years and the age requirement at forty. In membership and in powers, the upper house should easily have been a check on ill-considered action by a potentially more radical lower house.

If the spirit and the letter of the organic laws seemed restrictive of the popularly elected Chamber of Deputies, the powers assigned it were a sufficient base for ultimate extension. The right to initiate money bills, to pass on all legislation, to interpellate ministers, and to cause the overthrow of cabinets gave the Chamber a strong influence on legislation and a firm grip on the executive. Since every act of the President had to be countersigned by a minister and since ministers were responsible to Parliament, a recalcitrant Chamber of Deputies could paralyze any government. Bills of the Senate could be vetoed and acts of the President negated. Such actions could be suicidal, for the Senate and the President had formidable weapons in any political war.

Within five years of the adoption of the organic laws, however, both the Senate and the Presidency were blunted as royalist instruments. The monarchists themselves were responsible for the republicanization of the Senate. In the first election under the new system, the embittered Legitimists sought vengeance on the Orleanists who had drafted the Republic's laws. Seventy-five of the 300 new Senators were to be chosen by the retiring National Assembly. In combination with the republicans of the extreme left, the Legitimists passed over the detested Orleanist candidates, despite their being fellow monarchists, and helped install 50 republicans and only 25 monarchists. When the remaining 225 members were finally chosen by the electoral colleges, the Senate was found to have an over-all royalist majority of 4. This slim advantage disappeared in the 1879 elections when one third of the Senate was to be renewed and the republicans swept the field. A monarchist-shaped institution was being transformed into a vehicle of republican power. French voters and the monarchists' vendetta were making the Senate a conservative but not a monarchist body.

Next to fall under republican domination was the Presidency. The elections of 1876 had resulted in a staunchly republican Chamber of Deputies. President MacMahon's efforts to influence the vote did not prevent the republicans from securing 370 seats as against 80 for the monarchists (Legitimists and Orleanists combined!) and 75 for the Bonapartists. With a solidly republican Chamber and a barely monarchist Senate, even a neutral President would have had difficulty maintaining a stable positive government. Ultra-conservative or monarchist ministers in the cabinet might be pleasing to the Senate, but they were galling to the Chamber. Moderate or radical republicans dear to the latter might be challenged by the Senate. MacMahon was not initially adverse to appointing and retaining nonentities like Armand Dufaure or moderate republicans like Jules Simon as Premier. But, essentially, MacMahon was not a "neutral" President. His ideas on the pre-eminence of the presidential office were pronounced. His sympathies for monarchy, Church, aristocracy, and army were clear. He therefore became incensed against Simon when the Premier began taking measures against the Church, the army, and monarchists in the administration. MacMahon forced Simon to resign on May 16, 1877, the date that gives title to this entire crisis, the *Seize Mai*.

Following Simon's dismissal and at the behest of the President, the Duc de Broglie strove to form a cabinet. Composed of monarchists, Bonapartists, and clericals, this government failed to secure the confidence of the Chamber of Deputies. Rather than reform a cabinet acceptable to the republican majority in the Chamber, Mac-Mahon sought and secured the consent of the Senate to dissolve the lower house and hold new elections. The Republic of republicans was in danger. The Republic of Dukes, monarchists, and clerics was asserting itself.

In this struggle over political forms and political powers, conservative, moderate, and radical republicans presented a unified voting bloc. Former enemies like Thiers and Gambetta, conservatives like banker Casimir-Périer, and socialists like Louis Blanc coalesced to vote down the Orleanist–Bonapartist ministry of de Broglie. Before and during the election campaign, republicans of all shades protested and fought the authoritarian, illiberal, censoring, bribing, purging tactics of the monarchists endeavoring to entrench themselves in the nominal Republic of 1875. The momentary alignment of all factions of republicans was touchingly if incongruously demonstrated at the funeral of Thiers. The man who sacrificed Paris to the Prussians in 1871, the ruthless suppressor of the Commune, the arch-enemy of "Red Republicanism" died suddenly in September, 1877, shortly before the elections. With incredible respect and deference, his body was saluted by Parisian workers as it was carried through the proletarian districts that had suffered so much at his hands six years earlier.

That this unity was relative only to the political issue of the moment and not absolute on all issues was manifest by the stand these political allies took on economic and Church questions. Every effort by Gambetta to introduce legislation for an income tax, for example, was frustrated by conservative and many moderate republicans in concert with the monarchists. A republican label, on the other hand, did not help deputies who sided with the Church; many Catholic republicans were defeated at the polls in 1877.

Despite tremendous overt and covert administrative pressure, the republican loss of fifty seats was not disastrous. The new Chamber still contained a republican majority: 320 to 200 monarchists and Bonapartists. Within a month, de Broglie resigned and Mac-Mahon yielded to the Chamber in appointing Dufaure as head of the cabinet. Little more than a year later, MacMahon himself was faced with the decision of whether to resign or do battle with the Chamber over the military establishment. He resigned. With their 1877 majority in the Chamber and the 1879 victory in the Senate, the republicans had no difficulty in installing a candidate of their liking in the Presidency.

The crisis of *Seize Mai* had great significance for subsequent political life in France. Not until the arrival of the Fifth Republic headed by Charles de Gaulle did the French discard many of the precedents established or crystallized during the 1877–1879 period. Increased republican electoral strength might eventually have produced the same results, but *Seize Mai* surely accelerated the rate of change. The Presidency became a comfortable, decorative post, with its powers severely curtailed. Parliament, especially the Chamber of Deputies, gained a predominant position in the Republic. No subsequent President of the Third or Fourth Republics could contemplate dissolving the Chamber. The Senate thereby also lost leverage against the lower house. Over the cabinet, too, the Parliament secured a firmer control. Since no President would dare dismiss or appoint a minister without certainty of the Parliament's confidence, the ministers would tend more to heed Parliament than the President. Furthermore, the Premier was aware that he, through the President, was henceforth shorn of the power of dissolution of Assemblies that might resist the government's program or policy. By 1880, in great part as an outcome of the crisis of *Seize Mai*, the Third Republic remained not only the balcony-proclaimed form of government in France, but also republican majorities of voters had placed republicans in charge of republican institutions.

The republican capture of the state led almost inevitably to a defensive and offensive struggle with the Church. From the opening rounds of the 1880s laic laws on education and social matters to the final knockout blow of separation in 1905, the fight varied in ferocity but was never dropped by extremists of either camp. Efforts at conciliation by moderates were recurrently frustrated, sometimes by voracious priest-eaters or hysterical priest-lovers, at other times by unfolding crises that forced moderates into one corner or another.

Developments within the Roman Catholic Church, the European-wide intensification of anticlericalism, the political circumstances accompanying the founding of the Third Republic, and the temper of French republicans promised trouble for harmonious church–state relations after 1880. Within the Church, Pope Pius IX (1846–1878) was taking an increasingly conservative stand. Disillusioned by the revolutions of 1848, embittered by heavy temporal losses attributable to the wars for Italian unification, aghast at the intellectual currents of midcentury, the Pontiff issued the Syllabus of Errors in 1864. Condemned as errors were some eighty propositions, including liberalism, socialism, communism, rationalism, and freedom of religion. In principle, the French state would be anathema as a liberal or democratic republic or as an advocate of any of the many cited errors – a difficult status to avoid in the increasingly materialistic, secular nineteenth century. Another pronouncement of the Church relevant to the French scene was the Dogma of Papal Infallibility, published by the Council of the Vatican in 1870. Whatever its intentions or implications in other regards, the new dogma strengthened the ultramontane party in the French Church. Ultramontanism tended more to emphasize ties with Rome and subordination to Roman policy than the Gallicanism that recommended greater autonomy, decentralization, and near-independence for French Catholics. To espouse a Catholicism of ultramontanes, thus, would be to espouse the Pope's cause, the Pope's interests, and the Pope's ideas.

The striking changes that had taken place in the Pope's territorial position in midcentury also had bearing on the church–state feud in France. Forced first from the possible Presidency of an Italian Confederation in 1859, then despoiled of vast portions of the Papal States by the military and revolutionary events of 1859–1860, and finally choosing to immure himself in the Vatican when Italian troops occupied the city of Rome itself in 1870, the Pope sought every possible recourse against the stigmatized Italian kingdom. The insistent requests of the Pope for moral, diplomatic, and sometimes military aid against Italy were diametrically opposed to the secular, national interests of the French state. For, having just emerged from the ruinous war with Prussia, the French could ill afford to antagonize another European power. To emerge from their isolated position and to redress the balance of power against the new Germany, the French needed Italy as an ally, not an enemy. Ventures proposed by the Pope and noisily seconded by French ultra-Catholics thus were labeled as ludicrous and possibly "treasonable." For reasons, too, of currying favor with Bismarck, the new leader of European power politics and the Chancellor deeply involved in a Kulturkampf against the Catholic Church in Germany, it seemed appropriate for the French state to maintain an aloof if not hostile attitude to the Church.

Domestic instead of international politics, however, played the greater role in sharpening the division between church and state in France. Century-old animosity between French Catholicism and French republicanism formed the backdrop to the troubles of the 1880s. The breach widened when the Church so firmly attached itself to the monarchist cause during the 1870s. Whether tied to the Legitimists or the Orleanists, the great majority of influential clergymen and many of the Church orders engaged in preaching and teaching against the establishment and entrenchment of the Third Republic. From pulpit, periodical, and parochial schoolroom, laymen heard of the spiritual and political dangers of a republic. Having gained ascendancy over the monarchists in 1875, 1877, and 1879, the republicans possessed the strength to curb the institution considered still to be a threat to them. Unfortunately for

the Church, it had given all too much evidence of its antirepublicanism to avoid a strong dose of anticlericalism.

In a series of acts framed principally by Jules Ferry as Minister
of Public Instruction, the republicans launched their attack first on
the Church's influence in education. On all levels of schooling, the
Church had taken full advantage of the permissive Falloux Law of
1850 and had outpaced the primary and secondary system of the
state by 1880. The republican Chamber of Deputies moved and
passed Ferry's bill of 1879 on the reform of higher education. Central to the bill was the famous Article VII: "No one is to be allowed
to teach in State or private schools, nor to direct a teaching establishment of any sort if he belongs to an unauthorized religious
order." When the more Catholic Senate refused passage into law of
the Chamber's propositions on higher education, Ferry formulated
two decrees in March, 1880, to force all unauthorized religious
associations to regularize their positions within three months. The
Society of Jesus was singled out for dissolution and dispersion
within three months and other religious teaching orders were
offered the opportunity to secure authorization to avoid disbanding.

Two years later, the government assailed the Church's stronghold in French primary education, which was now made free, public, secular, and compulsory for children aged six to thirteen. The
establishment of license requirements and normal schools for
teachers helped to train thousands of replacements for the clergy
and prevent the clergy from perpetuating themselves in the school
system. In 1886, the government passed a law providing forced
eviction of male clerics from all public schools within five years.
Nuns were allowed to remain until their retirement.

Not satisfied with these "laic laws" undermining Church control in education, the republicans proceeded in other ways against
their clerical enemy and against religious manifestations in social
and public life. Civil marriage became compulsory again; civil
divorce, possible. Hospitals and charitable institutions were gradually secularized. The military forces were deprived of chaplains but

given seminarians to train as soldiers. Public displays of religion —
prayers, processions, decorations, Sabbath observance — were curtailed or eliminated.

So far and no farther, however, did the laws or decrees go, for
only the radical faction of the republicans aimed at separation of
church and state. The moderate elements, including Ferry and a
tamed Gambetta, contented themselves with the actions thus far
taken against the Church. Republican unity vanished as the problem was redefined. Moderate republicans stood with royalists and
Bonapartists against further anticlerical action. Laicization of education unified republicans during the early 1880s, but separation
of church and state divided them. Once the circumstances changed
and the Church proved to be a greater threat to the Republic —
which was the republican version of the Dreyfus affair — republicans would reunite to vote more punitive laws and finally separation.

Relaxation — if only temporary — of church–state tensions was
due in part to conciliatory efforts initiated by the new Pope, Leo
XIII. During the late 1880s and early 1890s, Leo officially allowed
Catholics to embrace republican forms. Through Cardinal Lavigerie, French clergymen and laymen were urged to accept the
Republic. Many Catholics, after their setback in the Boulanger
episode, did rally to the Republic. But, if republicans had been
unable to join in a thoroughgoing anticlerical program, neither
could Catholics fuse into a republic-loving group. The *Ralliement*
recommended by the Pope foundered on the Gallican resistance of
monarchist higher clergy and was finally shattered by the Dreyfus
affair.

The clericals were not the sole culprits in fomenting the Boulanger crisis of 1888–1889. Discontent with the moderate republican
regime was mounting among other than Catholic groups. Republican losses on the first ballot in the elections of 1885 might have
become confirmed if not for a last-minute reconsolidation of the
factional republicans. Even so, 202 seats were captured by the
monarchist-Bonapartist bloc. The 247 moderate republicans (Opportunists) needed the support of the 120 radicals to form a

majority and a government. Opportunist policy on Germany, the Church, colonies, and economic distress had produced attacks from republicans and antirepublicans. In agreement with the Opportunists on the virtues of the republican form, the radicals wanted a more stringent anticlericalism, a more virulent anti-German policy but less imperialism, and more radical tax and social legislation.

Into a political scene marked by right-wing unity and republican division stepped the dashing figure of Georges Boulanger. During his brief career, he had attracted groups and individuals of nearly every political shade. As the radicals' choice for Minister of War in an Opportunist cabinet in 1886, Boulanger fulfilled his sponsors' hopes by purging many royalists from high army posts and by insisting that seminary students serve their entire draft term. Conscripts and their families noted with appreciation the improved conditions of army life. Parisian crowds of all classes were thrilled by the striking looks of the General on horseback who led or organized such exciting parades. Patriots everywhere were impressed by the daring phrases and demands he mouthed against Germany. Too popular not to be a threat to the colorless Opportunists, Boulanger was reassigned in 1887 to a provincial post in Clermont-Ferrand where he could turn the heads of fewer Frenchmen.

But for the airing of the Wilson scandal in 1888 and the tactical error of retiring Boulanger and thus permitting him to run in elections, the General might have passed into history as a reforming ex-Minister of War who had been a season's rage in Paris. That all was not pure in the Republic of the Opportunists became public knowledge when deputy Daniel Wilson, son-in-law of the recently re-elected President Grévy, was exposed for having illicitly sold honors and decorations from the Elysée. He had also used his father-in-law's presidential residence as a free mailing center for his own business affairs. Underworld connections gave the whole scandal a most unsavory flavor. Only under the utmost pressure did Grévy resign, making possible the election of an honest but equally insipid Sadi Carnot.

Boulanger's name, meanwhile, increasingly appeared in the

press and on by-election ballots despite his professed noncandidacy. As punishment, the government dismissed him from active duty. This foolish step actually gave him the legal right to enter politics. This he did with a vengeance. Although highly suspect in the eyes of the Opportunists and repudiated by most of his former radical sponsors, Boulanger nevertheless still commanded the loyalites of the ordinary Frenchman in these camps. Secure in this base, he built a following among the right. A monarchist-Bonapartist-Boulanger axis was formed. His ambiguous promise of dissolution of the Chamber and constitutional revision raised hopes for a King, a Bonaparte, or certainly a strong executive. From the disrguntled left, too, there now loomed possibilities of social legislation if the reforming General were placed in office — although which office seemed as vague as his platform. Money and support from the right, especially from the Duchesse d'Uzès, and acclaim from the right, center, and left proved irresistible campaign assets and spelled electoral victories in provincial France in 1888. Paris was next.

The climax of Boulangism took place in the capital in January, 1889. Following the excited speech-making and very sophisticated publicity for a test case rather than a really important public office, Boulanger swept the field by three to two against the republican and socialist candidates. Boulangism had captured Paris; Boulangism had won France. But Boulanger refused to capitalize on his victory to take the spoils on the night of January 27. Despite the urging of his backers and the disarray of his enemies, the General did not march on the Elysée that night nor even appear the next day to be seated in the Chamber of Deputies. Whether because of lack of ambition or of courage or because of preference for his mistress with whom he probably spent the crucial hours, Boulanger killed Boulangism. The crowds had voted for a hero, not another pusillanimous politician; the monarchists and Bonapartists had supported a strong man, not a tender conscience.

The government moved immediately to thwart repetition of such near-catastrophe in the general elections of September, 1889, by changing the electoral laws and disallowing candidacy in multiple districts. *Scrutin de liste* gave way to *scrutin d'arrondissement.* Before September, the government also moved to frighten the fallen idol into flight to Belgium, where he took his own life two years later on the grave of his mistress.

To judge by the elections of September, 1889, the Republic had weathered the storm. Only 40 Boulangists were elected, whereas republicans won 360 seats. The right soon found ammunition, however, first for sniping attacks and then for full-fledged assault on the Republic. The Panama scandal in 1892 and the unfolding Dreyfus affair after 1894 served to revitalize monarchist–clerical groups and to sow discord among otherwise republican Frenchmen.

The Panama Canal Company had been formed in 1881. Shopkeepers, artisans, peasants, and bankers had been enticed into investing their capital in the company, thanks to the prestige and promotional efforts of de Lesseps. However, the perils of digging the Panama Canal far exceeded the vicissitudes of his Suez Canal enterprise. Climate, topography, and disease hampered company operations and necessitated recurrent capital-fund drives at home. In 1892, Edouard Drumont's anti-Semitic newspaper, *La Libre Parole,* broke the story behind the company's bankruptcy. The French public was treated to the sordid details of gambling, lust, and corruption in Panama. More politically significant were the disclosures of the involvement of republican officials. It appeared that the government had been bribed into silence during the 1880s, and, in 1888, a minister had received 375,000 francs for authorizing a national lottery to raise funds. The failure of the lottery and the company's insolvency, followed by the suicide of financier Jacques de Reinach, finally obliged the government to make an inquiry. Of all the directors and politicians brought to trial, only the ex-Minister of Public Works was punished. Although the electoral impact of the scandal and its airing was negligible, the tempo of antirepublicanism in press and pamphlet was quickened. Furthermore, anti-Semitism was intensified.

Never completely absent in France, anti-Semitism had not been so flagrant as in other European states. During the 1880s, however, suspicious signs began to appear. The collapse in the early 1880s of the essentially rural, Catholic-backed bank, the *Union Générale,* was attributed to the Jewish financial monopoly of the Baron de Rothschild and others. The right, too, noted the "disproportionate" numbers of Protestant and Jewish ministers in the anticlerical republican cabinets of the decade and in the laicized educational system. And now, with the Panama scandal, some of the most obvious "corrupters" were the Jewish bankers Jacques de Reinach and Cornelius Herz. To nationalism and clericalism, the right now added anti-Semitism as an arrow in its sling for republic-hunting. The Dreyfus Case gave the right an opportunity to test and sharpen its weapons.

What began as a miscarriage of justice attributable to viciousness and stupidity became an affair embroiling the Presidents, Parliaments, parties, public, and principal institutions of France. The apprehension, arrest, court martial, and conviction of Captain Alfred Dreyfus in the autumn of 1894 formed the initial act in the decade-long drama. From different — and often dubious — sources, French Military Intelligence learned that spying was taking place in its midst. A *bordereau,* or list, of military information available for sale to the enemy was retrieved from the wastepaper basket at the German Military Attaché's Office in Paris. Presuming from its contents that the purveyor of the data must have been an officer working with the French General Staff, Major Hubert Henry and M. du Paty de Clam fixed on Dreyfus as the culprit. To these amateur handwriting analysts, and to some professionals, Dreyfus and the writer of the *bordereau* were indisputably one. To these and other officers in the War Office, Dreyfus was a natural choice, too, since he was Jewish, wealthy, reserved, and talented — all attributes being highly suspect to his Catholic colleagues, who were often titled but poor and convivial but often mediocre. Petty personal animosities and anti-Semitic feelings played a large part in interpreting the purely circumstantial evidence against Dreyfus. Overriding the pusillanimous but probably prudent advice of some cabinet ministers to hush up the matter, the politically ambitious War Minister, General Auguste Mercier, preferred to pursue the investigation and finally authorized the arrest of Dreyfus on October 15.

That the arrest and investigation would not be "dropped" or remain secret was ensured by Major Henry's leaking the story to Drumont. The editor of the anti-Semitic *La Libre Parole* relished the journalistic function of releasing the news – especially since it involved treason in the Republic and treason by a Jew. Drumont feared only that the wealth of the Jew Dreyfus would enable him to escape justice in the same easy fashion as had the culprits of Panama. General Mercier and other members of the government, whatever their share of anti-Semitism, were alerted to the dangers to republican reputations if the case were dropped or allowed to terminate with an acquittal.

At the trial in December, 1894, the inconclusive yet properly submitted evidence of *bordereau* and handwriting experts was followed improperly by a secret packet of documents and false statements to the judges but not to the defense. To strengthen its case and to convince the judges, the prosecution dishonestly claimed to possess reliable proof that it could not disclose without jeopardizing the security of France or provoking a state of war with "foreign powers." Heeding the impassioned lies of Henry, du Paty, and Mercier more than the doubtful evidence or the protestations of the defendant, the court martial unanimously found Dreyfus guilty and sentenced him to life imprisonment as well as to military degradation and dishonorable discharge. The public, with the information at its disposition, could only conclude contentedly that the French army and the politicians of the Republic had acted vigorously and rightfully to safeguard the state against espionage. In fact, at the public degradation ceremony in January, the officials and the crowd enthusiastically expressed themselves against the traitorous Captain Dreyfus. Young Jean Jaurès, soon to be famous on the other side of the affair, deplored the leniency of the punishment in view of the fact that privates were shot for mere disobedience.

There was no Dreyfus affair, only a closed Dreyfus Case, when the convicted officer was sent off to the hell of Devil's Island early in 1895.

Several Frenchmen, each for entirely different reasons, refused to remain inactive or silent about the verdict against Dreyfus. Obvious reasons explained the family's efforts to reopen the case from 1894 to 1898. The prisoner's wife and brothers continued tirelessly to seek political and journalistic aid. Petitions to their fellow-Alsatian, Auguste Scheurer-Kestner, President of the Senate, received a sympathetic personal hearing but did not obtain a retrial. As successor to Colonel Jean Sandherr, head of the Second Bureau and as chief of Major Henry, Colonel Georges Picquart was independently instrumental in re-evaluating the evidence and pointing the finger at the real spy, Count Ferdinand Esterhazy. No particular friend of Dreyfus, no partisan republican officer, no frothing anticlerical, no pro-Semite, Picquart is a refreshing example of a man interested in righting a wrong he had discovered during the performance of his duty. For his pains, however, Picquart was reassigned to North Africa where his honest, inquiring activities could presumably do no damage to the reputations or careers of the frightened War Ministers or officers involved. If any person or group helped keep the case alive for the public though, it was not so much the increasingly interested radical or socialist parliamentarians or press, but rather right-wing, anti-Semitic, and clerical journals such as *La Libre Parole* and *La Croix,* a newspaper of the Assumptionist Order. The intent of these groups was not to reopen the case, but to use it to underscore the villainy of Jews and the ineptitude of the Republic.

In 1898, several striking events occurred that led to the retrial of Dreyfus and the bitter division of Frenchmen into Dreyfusard and anti-Dreyfusard factions. In January, Esterhazy was tried for espionage and acquitted; in February, Emile Zola was tried for libel and convicted; in August, the forger Major Henry was arrested and committed suicide. Esterhazy, protected still by the War Minister and officers of the General Staff and worshipped by the

Parisian crowd, was easily acquitted of espionage charges despite Picquart's testimony. In fact, Picquart's arrest on the morrow of the trial's end caused as much public rejoicing as Esterhazy's release. Zola's inflammatory letter, *J'Accuse,* printed in Clemenceau's newspaper, *L'Aurore,* on January 14 occasioned the novelist's being brought to trial for libel. He had indeed ranged widely in his accusations against War Ministers and General Staff members for their guilt or complicity in the handling of the Dreyfus Case. To prevent a full airing of the Dreyfus Case itself, the government, already having arranged the court martial that found Esterhazy innocent, decided to charge Zola only for libel against the War Ministers. The public found the pronouncement of "guilty" to its taste and menaced the very persons of Zola and Clemenceau. In fear, Zola slipped out of France to a temporary English exile.

The new War Minister, General Godefroy Cavaignac, acted to quiet once and for all the small Dreyfusard agitation by producing evidence in the Chamber of Deputies that purportedly clinched the case against Dreyfus. This ill-chosen action led Picquart to inform Premier Brisson that two of the documents were forgeries. Fearing exposure for his role, Major Henry committed suicide in his cell while awaiting trial. Rightfully suspicious that his erstwhile protectors would make him a scapegoat as well as a revealed spy, Esterhazy fled the country. The Dreyfus Case was soon to be reopened and was fast becoming an affair. Only in 1898 had the anti-Dreyfusards begun to meet their match in numbers and influence.

Social disorder had accompanied the legal and political differences of opinion in the Dreyfus affair by 1898. In cities and villages of metropolitan France and Algeria, Dreyfusards and Jews suffered violence to their persons and property. Street brawls developed between bands of Dreyfusard and anti-Dreyfusard leaguers and students. The trials of Esterhazy, Zola, and Picquart induced scenes of almost uncontrolled mob passion in which the very lives of Zola and Clemenceau were in jeopardy. Early in 1898, the death in bed of President Félix Faure, which stemmed from the lurid circumstances of a personal rather than a Dreyfus affair, sparked an attempted coup d'état by Paul Déroulède. At the end of the funeral procession for the President, the leader of the *Ligue des Patriotes* thrust himself and a small band of followers in the path of the General in charge and implored him to lead the troops to the Elysée. Without sufficient prior planning or reliable confederates, Déroulède's scheme failed. On the heels of this hysterical incident, the newly elected President Emile Loubet, reportedly more sympathetic to revision than his predecessor or his competitors for the office, was treated by Baron Christiani to a public caning at the Auteuil races. In response to this offense to the head of the Republic, the socialist rank and file formed a massive bodyguard for the bourgeois President at the Longchamps in June.

At this juncture, a new government was formed — a broad one of republican defense that included socialist Alexandre Millerand as well as moderate and radical republicans. The new Prime Minister, René Waldeck-Rousseau, was determined to put an end to public disorder and to liquidate the affair that was fomenting strife. Meanwhile, the *Cour de Cassation* (High Court of Appeals) concluded its months of deliberation and set aside the original verdict against Dreyfus. A fresh court martial was ordered to be held. A government of republican and socialist ministers, the civilian law courts, and increasing numbers of Frenchmen were becoming openly Dreyfusard. The issue of Dreyfus and its derivative threat to republican ideals and practices had welded an alliance of groups that, on other issues, were hostile to one another.

To the consternation of the Dreyfusards, the internationally publicized court martial at Rennes returned a bizarre verdict and sentence. Dreyfus was again found guilty but with extenuating circumstances, and was to be punished by ten years imprisonment but not loss of rank. Two weeks later, on September 19, the government succeeded in securing from President Loubet a pardon for the condemned man. Seven years afterwards, with little attention accorded by any except hard-core Dreyfusards, the *Cour de Cassa-*

tion reheard the case and finally declared Dreyfus (and Picquart) innocent of all charges. Promoted and awarded the Legion of Honor, the man who symbolized a frenzied affair was personally rehabilitated, served his country in World War I, and lived on until a quiet death took him in 1935.

An examination of Frenchmen's motives for partisanship in the affair will help to explain why division in France was so deep and why it is hazardous to make absolute categories for party, class, or religious alignment. Anticlerical, antimilitarist republicans and socialists from the bourgeoisie and proletariat did tend to make common cause against right-wing, clerical, aristocratic, authoritarian, nationalist Frenchmen, but notable exceptions existed. For the anti-Dreyfusards, belief in the guilt of Dreyfus provided a starting point. When this supposition was subject to serious doubt in 1898, they based their stand more on the need to assure the nation's security and to preserve the authority and honor of the army. Reasons of state and ability to pursue a revanchist policy transcended one man's rights. The appeal of these arguments was enhanced by the current wave of nationalism and anti-Semitism propagated by such newspapers as *La Libre Parole* and by lay and religious organizations like Déroulède's *Ligue des Patriotes*, the *Action Française*, and the Assumptionist Order. To these anti-Dreyfusard groups rallied Frenchmen who wished the Republic ill and who yearned for either a restoration of monarchy or the establishment of an authoritarian state. The army must be maintained. Was it not the last preserve of aristocratic Frenchmen whose opportunities for careers in the Church had been limited by the anticlerical laws of the 1880s? Public office, too, had become more and more closed to them by the infiltrating bourgeois republicans since 1880.

Without concurring in all respects, many moderate republicans were numbered among the anti-Dreyfusards before and after 1898. Fear of losing office or of diminishing the Republic's prestige made cowards of many republicans who might otherwise have stood for the ideal of justice. Nationalism and anti-Semitism infected both bourgeois republicans and the working class, which was turning to socialism. Among the predominantly right-wing elements in the anti-Dreyfusard camp was also discerned a substantial number of intellectuals. Members of the Institute, the Academy, and the University headed or provided copy for the anti-Dreyfusard pamphlets, newspapers, or associations. Out of principle or traditional adolescent explosiveness, students lent much muscle and voice to these groups.

Growing disbelief in the innocence of Dreyfus led many Frenchmen to press for revision. Picquart was one example of a man whose Catholicism, anti-Semitism, loyalty to the army and lack of vehement republicanism in no way barred his total dedication to upsetting the original verdict. To him and others, the issue transcended Dreyfus, as it had for the opposition. Dreyfusards proclaimed and upheld the principles of liberty and justice for all individuals regardless of the army's fate or the nation's security. To those imbued with the Revolution's ideals and the Republic's forms, the authoritarian nature of the army — especially as manifested in its handling of the Dreyfus Case and in its ties with monarchist, clerical factions — posed a threat to the Republic. Revision of the verdict would thus help weaken the army and its antirepublican supporters. Like their anti-Dreyfusard counterparts, therefore, many Dreyfusards evinced essentially political motives in taking their position. Matching and sometimes exceeding the number of intellectuals and students who had enlisted with the anti-Dreyfusards, the Dreyfusards counted such luminaries as Zola, Anatole France, and Marcel Proust. The League of the Rights of Man, formed during the affair, brought together journalists, politicians, and scholars in an organization dedicated to the principles of 1789. Satisfied finally that more was at stake than a deceptive squabble among expropriating capitalists, many socialists followed Jean Jaurès to defend Dreyfus and the Republic. If anti-Semitism and nationalism helped draw adherents to the anti-Dreyfusards across class and party lines, anticlericalism served the Dreyfusards. For, the Church's intervention on behalf of the army drove the bourgeoisie and proletariat almost automatically into an un-Marxist amity.

As an outcome of the affair, the punishment of the wicked accompanied the reward of the righteous after 1899. The dominant Dreyfusard coalition of moderate republicans, radical republicans (or Radical-Socialists), and socialists moved vigorously against those elements in the army and the Church which had been so vociferously anti-Dreyfusard and antirepublican. Before his retirement in 1902 for poor health, Waldeck-Rousseau had initiated a limited campaign to "republicanize" the army. Notorious anti-Dreyfusard officers were retired. The Prime Minister appointed the unquestionably anticlerical General Louis André as War Minister and transferred to him the ultimate decision over promotions. Not Waldeck-Rousseau but his successor, Emile Combes, gave André free rein to purge the officer corps of anti-Dreyfusards. Formerly, officers with aristocratic, monarchist, and clerical backgrounds or leanings found a smooth path to desirable posts and higher ranks. After the affair, officers with republican and anticlerical sentiments received the plums.

Reversion to unorthodox means of ascertaining officers' political and religious biographies seemed mandatory. Through André's assistant, Captain Mollin, contact was made with a section of the Freemasons who were only too happy to render such services. What a gratifying function to report which officer had attended Mass in his particular garrison town! What a useful task to inform on which officer sent his children to the Church schools! Too many such items in one's dossier spelt probable elimination from the lists of promotions to the next rank or of assignment to a crack unit or choice post. Highly favorable annotations went to those officers who had the good sense (or taste) to be Freemasons, just plain Protestants, or loud anticlericals. That the principles and methods of the Dreyfusards were highly relative and not absolute was clearly exposed when the file system was publicized in Chamber debate. Jaurès, whose probity was otherwise unquestionable, defended the government's double standard and saved the government by rallying enough votes to maintain Combes as Prime Minister. Other equally staunch Dreyfusards in the League of the Rights of Man disagreed, upholding the principles for which the League had been formed even if their application might protect political opponents. While André's system, in the long run, did not prevent many Catholic or right-wing officers from rising to the top — examples being Foch, Joffre, Pétain, and Weygand — the republicanization of the officer corps had been effected. The remaining years of the Third Republic for better or for worse, would be marked by an apolitical or civilian-dominated army.

Punishment of the Church orders for their role in the Dreyfus affair was accorded a more popular reception than the attempt to republicanize the army. Prime Minister Waldeck-Rousseau mildly began the campaign that his successor Combes carried to an extreme. To bring under governmental control those anti-Dreyfusard Church organizations not state-regulated by the Concordat of 1801, Waldeck-Rousseau secured passage of the Law of Associations in 1901. In order not to endanger lay organizations like socialists, trade unions, and Freemasons, care was taken in phrasing the articles demanding that foreign-linked associations be authorized by the Parliament for their formation and operation. Thereby orders like the Assumptionists would be dissolved and only the most simon-pure, nonpolitical congregations would be suffered to exist. More radical adherents to the bill added clauses denying the right of unauthorized orders to teach, reviving the anticlerical tendencies of the 1880s in education. The elections following the enactment of this law gave an overwhelming majority to the Radical-Socialists and socialists, implying public endorsement of this policy.

The passage of the Law of Associations might have ended the church–state controversy that had been resharpened by the Dreyfus affair if the government had applied the provisions moderately and the Church had accepted the reforms gracefully. That the reverse was true was due in part to the obdurate anticlericalism of Combes and to the provocative actions of the new Pope. A former seminary student prepared by the Jesuits for the priesthood, Combes revealed a fanatical detestation of all things clerical in his ruthless execution of the letter of the Law of 1901. Only the most ascetic orders, such as the Trappists, were granted authorization. Between ten and twenty thousand schools were closed with the resulting dismissal and dispersal of thousands of nuns and brothers. Combes pressed the church–state issue, too, by refusing to negotiate with Rome before submitting lists of nominees from which the Pope would, by the 1801 Concordat, choose bishops and arch-bishops. Combes denied permission for two bishops of republican reputation to be cited before a tribunal in the Vatican. Combes used every means at his disposal to poison the atmosphere and finally submitted a bill for the separation of church and state in 1905.

Unfortunately for the Church's century-old convention with the French state, the new Pope Pius x was neither so cosmopolitan nor so conciliatory as his predecessor, Leo xiii. Pius's intransigent attitude and anti-French utterances made Combes' bigotry seem almost like righteous indignation. Papal encyclicals against the Law of Associations placed the French clergy in an impossible position for compromise. The Pontiff's success in forcing the removal of the two bishops would have antagonized even a moderate Premier. The Pope's encouragement and public favors to such organizations as the *Action Française* added fuel to the fire. A final touch was his secret circular letter to all Catholic states protesting the official visit of President Loubet to the Italian Kingdom in 1904. The release of this letter by the socialist newspaper, *L'Humanité*, seemed to range the Pope among the wreckers of France's international status.

Submitted initially by Combes but passed under the succeeding ministry of Maurice Rouvier, the bill separating church and state in France was easier to enact than to enforce. Although long a proclaimed goal of radical republicans, as exemplified in Gambetta's Belleville Manifesto in 1869, separation exceeded the anticipations of many anticlericals. Certain provisions of the act provoked bitter denunciation, as expected, by the Pope and Catholic groups in France and even evoked lukewarm criticism by stalwart anticlericals like Clemenceau. For, the law provided not only for the cessation of salaries, subsidies, and allocations to all religious bodies, but also for the inventory and transfer to laymen's associations of all the property of the Church. Whether viewed as an unnecessary interference with the internal organization of a Church where lay control was nonexistent or as an imprudent provocation of enraged parishioners who refused entry to government inventory takers, the public reaction was violent. Radical-Socialist Prime Minister Clemenceau declined from 1906 to 1909 to carry out completely the provisions on Church property. Not until after the First World War, in fact, did the French government and the Church accommodate each other on this question of property custodianship.

Economic changes and their consequences

WHILE Frenchmen busied themselves with the political events attending the formation and entrenchment of republican institutions from 1870 to 1914, important economic and social developments were taking place. Industry, commerce, agriculture, and finance were undergoing changes that produced challenging problems for that generation. In the world of 1870 to 1914, prosperity and power became increasingly measured in terms of population growth, industrial and commercial expansion, improved agricultural techniques, and concentration of people and production in cities and factories. In all these respects, France made substantial progress but at a far slower rate than her European rivals, Great Britain and Germany. The changes in the French economy, therefore, had not only a great impact on the domestic scene, but also on the international status of France as a great power.

While the French barely advanced in numbers from the 1870 census, the population in England, Germany, and other states "exploded" in the generation preceding World War I. Table 4–1 reveals the degree to which the British and Germans outstripped the French; Table 4–2 shows comparative birth rates of the three powers.

Table 4–1. Population by Country (in millions) *

Year	England and Wales	Germany	France
1870	22.7	41.0	36.1
1900	32.5	56.3	38.9
1910	36.0	64.9	39.6

* Except where otherwise indicated, this and subsequent statistical tables in this chapter have been obtained or adapted from Shepard B. Clough and Charles W. Cole, *Economic History of Europe* (Boston: D. C. Heath and Co., 1941).

Table 4–2. Birth Rates (per thousand)

Years	England and Wales	Germany	France
1891–1900	29.9	36.1	22.2

Whatever the social, economic, or psychological reasons for the leveling off of the French population curve, the effects would be felt in many ways. Far less than in England or Germany, there would appear an excess of population for possible use as factory hands. Far less than in England and Germany would there be a lively market for cheap, mass-produced goods. The stability of the population would help re-enforce the existing French predilection for small-scale enterprise – on the farm, at the workbench, and in the shop. Social values and even social classes would tend to remain more fixed than in a situation of a rapidly expanding population. The political implications would be similar, with more likelihood of perpetuating than discarding existing points of harmony or division. The obvious effect on foreign policy would be to impel the French state to compensate for its demographic inferiority vis-à-vis Germany by colonial manpower and alliances.

As in human reproduction, the production of key items like steel, coal, and iron was also characterized by an absolute increase but a relative decline. Although, as Table 4–3 indicates, French production of steel rose from 83,000 tons in 1870 to 3,506,000 tons in 1910, British and German steel output far surpassed the French.

Table 4–3. Production of Steel (in thousands of metric tons)

Year	United Kingdom	Germany	France	United States
1870	286	169	83	68
1880	1,320	660	388	1,267
1890	3,637	2,161	566	4,346
1900	5,130	6,645	1,565	10,382
1910	6,374	13,698	3,506	26,512

That foreign steel mills benefited more than French was attested to by the fact that more than half the iron ore mined in France was exported for processing elsewhere. As was the practice, less bulky iron moved to the site of more voluminous coal. French iron was thus shipped principally to the German Ruhr for refining and steel-making. The febrile development of the French steel industry is often attributed to the loss of Alsace-Lorraine in 1870. Lorraine did contain extensive iron ore, but, until the introduction of the Thomas Gilchrist refining method in 1878, the high phosphate content of the iron rendered it useless. Furthermore, Bismarck, either unmindful or not caring about the potential wealth of natural resources, had split Lorraine, leaving to the French a substantial share of the iron ore deposits.

The relative lag in French industrialization is also evidenced in the figures relating to domestic consumption of pig iron cited in Table 4–4. Although the French rate of growth exceeded the British, the French base in 1866 was very small, and the final 1913 figures were correspondingly lower.

Table 4–4. Consumption of Pig Iron (in pounds per capita)

Year	United Kingdom	Germany	France	United States
1866	110	41	58	110
1900	292	289	152	351
1913 (iron and steel)	520	575	333	

The production of coal, crucial for steel and a source of power for industry and transportation, showed a similar pattern. The quintupling of French yields (see Table 4–5) in no way compared to the astronomic rates in the United Kingdom or Germany, to say nothing of the United States.

Table 4–5. Production of Coal (in millions of metric tons)

Year	United Kingdom	Germany	France	United States
1860	80	12	8	15
1900	225	109	32	244
1913	292	190	40	617
		(lignite 87	1)	

The loss of the textile establishments of Alsace in 1870 in great part account for the slow rate of expansion of the French cotton industry. Behind England but far ahead of the Germanies in 1850, the French were again outpaced by 1914, according to the statistics in Table 4–6.

Table 4–6. Cotton Industry

Country	Annual Average Consumption of Raw Cotton, 1846–1850 (in tons)	Number of Spindles in 1913	Production of Synthetic Dyestuffs in 1913 (in tons)
United Kingdom	235,000	55,653,000	5,600
Germany	15,500	11,186,000	150,000
France	55,000	7,400,000	2,200

Still an important manufacturer of cottons in 1913, the French had nevertheless failed to capitalize on the advances in chemistry that were making synthetics feasible.

In other sectors of industry, too, French headway was slow. Although Frenchmen were frequently inventors or designers of prototypes of new products or processes, the French evidenced either an inability or an unwillingness to allocate necessary capital and labor to mass-produce automobiles, chemicals, electrical equipment, metals, and other items.

Long a great commercial power, France steadily improved its

foreign trade between 1870 and 1914. Although the French percentage share of world trade declined (see Table 4–7), prosperous extension of commerce was the rule.

Table 4–7. Percentage Share of World Trade

Year	United Kingdom	Germany	France	United States
1880	23	9	11	10
1900	21	12	8	11
1913	17	12	7	10

Nearly doubling exports and more than doubling imports during this period, the French could nevertheless observe that the Germans, starting from an equal base in 1875, had tripled or quadrupled their trade by 1913 (see Table 4–8).

Table 4–8. Foreign Trade Balances

YEAR	UNITED KINGDOM (IN MILLIONS OF POUNDS STERLING)		GERMANY (IN MILLIONS OF MARKS)		FRANCE (IN MILLIONS OF FRANCS)	
	Imports	Exports	Imports	Exports	Imports	Exports
1875	373.0	281.6	3,537.6	2,491.8	3,536.7	3,872.0
1885	371.0	271.5	2,922.5	2,855.7	4,088.4	3,088.1
1895	416.7	285.8	4,120.7	3,317.9	3,719.9	3,373.8
1905	565.0	407.6	7,128.8	5,731.6	4,778.9	4,866.9
1913	768.7	634.8	10,769.7	10,094.9	8,421.3	6,880.2

France's unfavorable balance of trade, as recorded in Table 4–8, was more apparent than real. Offsetting the heavier volume of imports over exports, the tourist trade and swelling French foreign investments brought sizeable returns. Between the 1880s and the outbreak of World War I, for example, the total French foreign investment tripled as did the British (see Table 4–9).

Table 4–9. Total Foreign Investments

Year	United Kingdom (in pounds sterling)	Germany (in marks)	France (in francs)
1880			15,000,000,000
1883		5,000,000,000	
1885	1,302,000,000		
1913	3,763,000,000		
1914		22–25,000,000,000	45,000,000,000

The geographical distribution of these investments was relevant to the formation of French foreign policy as well as to the general economic picture (see Table 4–10).

Table 4–10. Geographical Distribution of French Foreign Investments (1914)

Country or Area	Billions of 1914 Francs
Russia	11.3
Balkan states and Turkey	5.5
All other European states	10.7
French colonies	4.0
Non-French Africa	3.3
United States, Canada, Australia	2.0
Latin America	6.0
Asia	2.2

Russia stands out as the area in which the greatest concentration of investment took place, far exceeding even that in the French colonies.

In transportation, French efforts were noteworthy. Continuing the already well-articulated road and canal network, the French pushed the building of railroads in the late nineteenth century for economic and military purposes. By 1910, total trackage exceeded England's (see Table 4–11).

Table 4–11. Total Railway Trackage (in kilometers)

Year	United Kingdom	Germany	France
1850	4,125	28,000 (1875)	3,000
1910	38,000	61,000	49,500

However, if the French railways hauled vast quantities of freight by 1910, the Germans that year shipped double the tonnage with but 20 percent more trackage. On the seas, the French merchant marine by 1914 found itself outnumbered by the German and, of course, the British. Table 4–12 tells the tale in tonnage and percentage.

Although French industry and commerce were enjoying slow but steady advances, agriculture in France and in much of Europe

Table 4–12. Shipping Steam Vessels (June, 1914)

Country	Net Tons	Percent
United Kingdom	11,538,000	44.4
Germany	3,096,000	11.9
France	1,098,000	4.2
United States	1,195,000	4.6

suffered catastrophic setbacks between 1870 and 1900. By the turn of the century, some recovery was noted, presaging a more prosperous decade before the First World War. The railroads and steamships that had allowed the American West, the Russian Ukraine, and Australia to transport cheaply their abundant grain and meat to European markets adversely affected the French farmer. Prices dropped sharply. A bushel of wheat selling for $1.50 in 1871 brought only $.23 by 1894; meat by 1894 declined 25 percent from its 1873 value. Where France in most previous years had been an exporter of wheat, imports increasingly topped exports during the 1880s. Excess of imports over exports reached nearly 20,000,000 hectoliters in 1891. With wool prices off 50 percent between 1873 and 1896 as a result of the Australian sheep raisers' advantages, sheep herding in France fell markedly. The nearly 30,000,000 sheep in the France of 1862 had dwindled to fewer than 18,000,000 in 1909. German flocks had suffered even more.

Nature, too, took a hand in dealing blows at French agriculture. A disease of the silkworm forced a one-third cut in French silk production. More seriously, Phylloxera struck the French vines during the 1870s. In the wine industry, which occupied one out of five Frenchmen, this disease forced a one-third curtailment of the acreage under cultivation and a drastic reduction in production, from 84,000,000 hectoliters in 1875 down to 23,000,000 in 1889.

By approximately 1896, the "long depression" finally came to an end, and French agriculture gradually recovered some but not all its losses of two decades. Increased costs of production and distribution began to limit the initial advantages of American, Australian, and Russian farmers. Gold discoveries pumped more money into circulation, helping to inflate prices. In France, protective tariffs, and especially the Méline Tariff of 1892, formed a barrier against the flood of overseas goods. The French peasant also undertook to improve his methods of farming and raising livestock. Although the number of sheep remained low, more and heavier pigs and cattle replaced them. Pigs numbered 6,037,543 in the France of 1862 and 7,305,850 by 1909; cattle numbered 12,811,589 in 1862 and 14,313,573 in 1909. German livestock figures, however, showed a 300 percent and 150 percent increase during a similar period.

Mechanization was becoming more common in rural France. Threshers, mowers, and reapers, but not plows, appeared in vastly superior numbers by the end of the century (see Table 4–13).

Table 4–13. Mechanization in Agriculture

Equipment	1862	1892
Plows	3,206,421	3,669,212
Threshing machines	100,733	234,380
Mowing machines	9,442	38,753
Reapers	8,907	23,432

In growing numbers, horses replaced peasants to pull these mechanical devices; there were 2,914,412 horses in 1862 and 3,236,130 in 1909.

New crops were encouraged and showed gains. Sugar beets, for example, were cultivated in three times as much acreage in 1901 as in 1862. The potato crop increased 60 percent from 1882 to 1911. Even the wheat yield mounted 19 percent in 1906–1909 from the 1876–1885 levels. The production of wine had increased to 48,000,000 hectoliters in 1900–1915 as compared with the 23,000,000 hectoliter low of 1889, but it did not reach its former highs.

As a result of the economic changes sketched in above, the French social and political order, as well as the economy, was subjected to modifications and new pressures. Social class structure and mores in France were disturbed but not radically altered. The industrial bourgeoisie counted many new members, and the ranks of the proletariat were augmented. Essentially, however, the emerging industrial and commercial establishments remained small and family-sized. The bourgeois owner-entrepreneur adopted the traditional French pattern of operation and outlook. The new propertyless proletariat still had not replaced the artisan-craftsman whose inclinations continued to be petty bourgeois. Concentration of population in urban centers, like concentration of production in large factory units, proceeded but slowly in France. In 1914, approximately one half of the population still engaged in agriculture and one quarter lived in towns of 2,000 to 20,000 inhabitants.

The impact of economic change on political life was perhaps more observable. Severe competition with foreign farm and factory goods led Frenchmen to seek state intervention and aid. The government responded. For mine owners and shipbuilders as well as for farmers and factory owners, bounties, subsidies, and tariffs became the order of the day. The Méline Tariff of 1892 offered high protection on a wide range of agricultural and industrial products. Also, in support of the stricken peasant, the government sponsored or encouraged cooperative societies, experimental stations, and information agencies. Legislation was tailored to the interests of the peasant and bourgeois majority; it did not, however, suit the expressed demands of the growing minority of working-class Frenchmen. Although real wages, as revealed in Table 4–14, showed more favorable gains than those of the British and German proletariat, French social insurance for old age, accident, and unemployment was negligible.

Table 4–14. Real-Wages Index (1900 = 100 for United Kingdom and Germany; 1895 = 100 for France)

Years	United Kingdom	Years	Germany	Years	France
1869–1879	74	1868–1878	78	1868–1878	83
1880–1886	80	1879–1886	84	1879–1886	90
1887–1895	91	1887–1894	92	1887–1895	98
1895–1903	99	1894–1902	97	1895–1903	107
1904–1908	95	1903–1908	98	1903–1908	114
1909–1914	93	1909–1914	96	1909–1914	114

The French government enacted few and mostly voluntary social security bills.

The French labor movement nevertheless was becoming organized and articulate if not united and effective in the political world of pre-1914. The crushing of the Commune in 1871 had set back the labor movement for more than a decade. The leaders had been executed or exiled; the organizations and associations had been disbanded; the programs of socialist tendencies were discredited. With the amnesty of 1879, the restoration of freedom of association in 1884, and the quickened pace of industrialization, there appeared a revival of trade unionism and political party activity. Craft unions were formed during the 1880s, and in 1896 the *Bourses du Travail* were federated. These *Bourses* were actually labor exchanges acting chiefly as unemployment agencies and as publicity and wage-fixing bodies. A more traditional form of union was the *Conféderation Générale du Travail* (CGT) of 1895, which merged with the *Bourses* in 1902. The emergence of these generally non-political groups was accompanied by the formation in 1905 of a French socialist party, or, officially, the *Section Française de l'Internationale Ouvrière* (SFIO). In 1912, membership in French trade unions, including the half-million in the CGT, amounted to about a million, whereas the British unions numbered 4,500,000 and the Germans 3,000,000. The SFIO in 1914 capped its previous electoral successes by securing 1,400,000 votes and installing 110 deputies in the Chamber.

This strong showing of the socialists, however, was no accurate barometer of labor's strength, for the propertyless Frenchmen had as much difficulty as their propertied compatriots in reaching agreement on a common program or the means of achieving it. Not only did the political philosophy, goals, and methods of the trade unions differ widely from those of the SFIO, but divisions within the unions and the party were deep. The CGT and the *Bourses* tended toward syndicalism, which has been termed the economic expression of anarchism. Deploring the inefficacy and inhumanity of the state and its agencies, syndicalists pressed for a society organized exclusively around the unit of economic activity. To arrive at this ideal, proletarians were urged to band together and engage in constant and preferably generalized violent action against capitalists and the state.

The SFIO under Jean Jaurès, on the other hand, shared the European-wide trend of revisionary Marxism, which allowed for parliamentary means of attaining otherwise orthodox Marxist aims. Jaurès particularly wished to impress on his followers the virtues of some of the past, even if bourgeois in origin, in order to forge the blissful classless society of the future. As much at home in the Chamber of Deputies as at labor rallies, Jaurès practiced and preached parliamentary cooperation with bourgeois parties to secure his ends. Had he not helped save the Republic from reactionary forces during the Dreyfus affair? Might he not lead the workers and intellectuals to a socialist heaven in not many years ahead? Many in his party thought not. The SFIO had its firebrands who preferred the barricades to the ballot box. The more radical unions conversely included many moderate members and leaders.

With the industrial proletariat small in numbers, identified with organizations whose aims and policies conflicted, endowed with interests different from those of still numerous artisans and craftsmen, it is no wonder that the French propertied classes of town and country were able to dominate the political scene. The demands and threats of the labor movement produced fear in bourgeois and peasant circles but no outstanding social legislation. If bourgeois republicans did align with socialists to achieve certain political and social ends, as evidenced in the anticlerical and anti-army policies following the Dreyfus affair, the association ended when the agenda read income tax, social security, or nationalization of industry. On colonial and foreign affairs and on the issue of war and peace, the organizations of the workers set themselves apart, too, from the rest of France. August, 1914, however, would demonstrate how easily the chasm could be bridged between the pacifist left and the militarist right.

The direct effect of French demographic and economic change

on colonial and foreign policy is difficult to assess, even though the importance of colonial resources and international alliances became manifest. Colonial manpower to swell the ranks of the army; colonial raw materials to supply the metropolitan processing plants or to supplement the meager metropolitan resources of iron, coal, or cotton; colonial products to provide exports for foreign trade surpluses; colonial markets to serve as outlets for French goods; colonial areas to absorb French capital – in all these ways the acquisition of colonies might be presumed to have enabled, France to match the economic advance and population growth of Great Britain and Germany. The affirmative avowals of Marx, Engels, and ultimately Lenin notwithstanding, these impelling economic motives for imperialism seemed less operative for the French than possibly for the British or Germans.

France in the imperial race

FRENCH empire-building after 1870 attested to the presence but hardly the overwhelming dominance of the economic factor. In the penetration, acquisition, and consolidation of overseas holdings, the bankers, merchants, planters, railway promoters, and other capitalists often counted far less than the politician, ambitious army or navy officer, adventurer, or missionary. Prominent examples of the last-named group were navy officers Garnier and Rivière for their exploits in Indochina, Cardinal Lavigerie for his founding of the White Fathers in Tunisia, and Captain Marchand for his dramatic trans-African journey to Fashoda. Although financiers and traders were admittedly busy midwives of a newly-born Empire, only 10 percent of French "foreign" investment was placed in French colonial possessions (see Table 4–10). The trade of the colonies, too, was principally with foreign countries and not with France (see Table 4–15). Nor did the French merchant marine benefit from this commerce; most of the trade was carried in foreign ships.

Table 4–15. French Colonial Trade in 1911 (exclusive of Algeria and Tunisia) *

	Millions of Francs
Imports from France	261.3
Imports from French colonies	16.5
Imports from foreign countries	323.4
Total	601.2
Exports to France	273.4
Exports to French colonies	10.4
Exports to foreign countries	357.2
Total	641.0

* From Shepard B. Clough, *France: A History of National Economics, 1789–1939* (New York: Charles Scribner's Sons, 1939), p. 252.

The colonial issue distorted the traditional political alignment found in dealing with metropolitan problems of republic *v.* monarchy, church *v.* state, and so on. Although the French right of the 1880s and 1890s often coalesced on clerical and school issues, it split on imperialism. Much of the nationalist right preferred French strength to be concentrated on *revanche* and the restoration of Alsace-Lorraine. On the other hand, the clerical factions and even many military elements welcomed colonial expansion for the promotion of missionary and army interests. The French left of those years was no more united than the right. Some few stalwart anticlerical, antimilitary republicans – especially of the upper bourgeoisie – gladly joined with segments of the right in the hope of extended business opportunities overseas. Even the skillful parliamentarian Jules Ferry could not, however, bring into the imperialist camp those radical republican Clemenceaus and Gambettas whose egalitarian principles of continental European focus prevented their voting credits for overseas ventures. By the early 1900s, pride in French achievements and acceptance of colonial faits accomplis nevertheless appeared more the rule among Radical-Socialists and even socialists whose party ideologically stood opposed to the exploitation of "backward" peoples.

The Third Republic had inherited a motley assortment of colonies from previous regimes. By 1914, the Republic fleshed out these skeletal holdings, adding a territory fifteen times the area of metropolitan France and peopled by 26,000,000 inhabitants. Table 4–16 shows France ranking second only to Great Britain and far outstripping other contenders in the race for Empire.

Table 4–16. European Colonial Conquests (1871–1900) *

Country	Area in Square Miles	Population
United Kingdom	4,250,000	66,000,000
France	3,500,000	26,000,000
Germany	1,000,000	13,000,000
Belgium	900,000	8,500,000
Russia	500,000	6,500,000
Italy	185,000	750,000

* Table constructed by author.

Southeast Asia, North Africa, and West-Central Africa formed the principal areas of French imperial involvement. In Southeast Asia, the Third Republic added to Napoleon III's acquisition of Cochin-China the remaining pieces of Cambodia, Annam, and Laos to forge the Indochinese Union. Missionary activity antedating the French revolutionary era had already introduced French influence in these feudal appendages of the Chinese Empire. Commercial contacts were quickened in the 1870s, a treaty being signed with Annam in 1874. Often on their own initiative, French naval officers explored and attempted to clear of "pirates" – or were they guerrillas or volunteers? – the northern region (Tonkin-Hanoi) drained by the Red River. The failure and death of Garnier and Rivière at the hand of these Black Flag Pirates only temporarily checked French penetration. From Paris, Ferry spurred on the reluctant Chamber of Deputies to allocate funds for the expeditions. With both China and Annam, he conducted secret and finally successful negotiations. Ferry's fall in 1885 came too late to save the Chinese or Annamites and too soon to allow for extensive exploitation of the French gains. The bourgeois French Parliament apparently would not act as Marx proclaimed an economically determined class should act. Support for the Ferry who had spewed forth the laic laws came from the clerical and right-wing groups interested in missions and militarism. On the imperial issue, the anticlerical radical republicans of the middle class deserted their erstwhile hero. Nevertheless, by 1887, upon the base prepared by Ferry, the Indochinese Union of Cochin-China, Annam, and Cambodia was established; Laos was added in 1893 after a brief war with Siam.

Moving down from Algeria, up from the rivers Senegal and Congo from the Atlantic coast, and down the Niger River from the interior, French explorers, army contingents, and merchants crisscrossed West and Central Africa after 1885. Opposition from the local disease- and slave-ridden tribes melted faster than resistance and countermoves by British competitors. A vast although poorly populated agglomeration of holdings was brought into the French Empire. A dramatic river and jungle journey took Captain Marchand and his party across Africa to the upper reaches of the Nile in 1898. Lord Kitchener had meanwhile been extending the British hold up the Nile into the Sudan and faced Marchand with superior forces at Fashoda in that year. Forced to yield to the British at the risk of an enormous effort, the French were obliged to abandon whatever plans their Empire builders might have conceived for linking French Somaliland in East Africa with the consolidated gains in West and Central Africa.

North Africa was the scene of even more rewards for the French. Already possessed of Algeria by 1870, the Third Republic easily quelled a rebellion in 1871 and began to look beyond the frontiers toward Tunisia. Encouraged by Bismarck at the 1878 Congress of Berlin to release their energies in colonial rather than continental ventures, the French awaited an opportunity to seize Tunisia before the new Italian kingdom moved. In 1881, Ferry used some border incidents as the occasion for punitive and penetrating action. To the delight of French businessmen with enterprises in this feudal remnant of the Ottoman Empire, French forces overcame those of the Bey of Tunisia and brought this state under French control as a Protectorate. Cardinal Lavigerie, Archbishop of Algiers, already active in missionary work in North Africa, established the White Fathers to extend Catholicism (and French "civilization") in the land where Carthage had once stood.

Ferry had less success in Egypt. There, historical memories of Saint Louis had been resuscitated by Napoleon I's brilliant but brief expedition, by continued contacts during the 1830s and 1840s, and finally by the completion in 1869 of Ferdinand de Lesseps' Suez Canal. Unfortunately for the French, British interests, too, were at stake during the 1880s when the Egyptian Khedive plunged deeper and deeper into financial obligations to European bankers. The Khedive's inability to satisfy the claims on him invited intervention and supervision by the states whose interests were most affected. The British government was willing to act; the French was not. The Chamber of Deputies refused Ferry the credits necessary for joint Franco-British action, leaving the field to the British alone. Again, the French bourgeoisie was either too timid or too unaware of how Marx said it should behave.

The French setback in Egypt was offset by French advances elsewhere in North Africa. By recognizing in 1904 the permanent abandonment of French political influence in Egypt, the French secured British support for an ultimate French protectorate in Morocco. Commercial, financial, and strategic interests in the Atlantic- and Mediterranean-washed Sultanate induced the French to negotiate agreements with Spain and Italy as well as with Great Britain. For Machiavellian or other reasons, Germany alone was not accommodated, and, when the French moved into Morocco in 1905, the German government provoked an international crisis. Forced to accept partial domination of Morocco in 1906, the French achieved full control of the Protectorate in 1912, only after the second Moroccan crisis resulted in Germany's receiving a portion of French Equatorial Africa.

Uniformity no more marked the governance of French colonies than it had characterized the motives for their acquisition. The diversity of cultures among and often within particular holdings militated against a single pattern of rule. Where there already existed even a rudimentary state, such as in Tunisia or Morocco, the French administrators remained relatively in the background and dealt with the natives through the Bey or the Sultan. In areas where local tribal conditions prevailed, as in much of West and Equatorial Africa, French civil and military officials assumed direct control over the subjects. Less clearcut arrangements emerged in the case of Indochina where French Governors-General or military chieftains interfered constantly with the Annamite or Cambodian ruling caste, which nevertheless retained nominal authority.

Unlike the British, who in principle aimed at ultimate self-government for many of their colonies, the French wavered between the policies of assimilation and association. Assimilation would hopefully result in the natives' total absorption of French culture and civilization with their ultimately becoming full-fledged French citizens in a unitary French Empire. Association, on the other hand, was the policy of encouraging the subject peoples to evolve in their own culture under the direction of metropolitan French appointees and a local elite that had acquired French attributes. The difference between the two policies was less distinct in practice than in theory. For, in all the French holdings, the French army officer, the schoolmaster, and the missionary worked more diligently to introduce French ideas and practices than to develop Arabic, Indian, or Chinese traditions. In forming and implementing colonial policy, too, Frenchmen in colonial posts often set the pace by individual and on-the-spot action without reference to Paris. Furthermore, French merchant, manufacturing, and mining firms in the colonies were often more concerned with immediate or long-range profits than with the cultural fate of the natives.

France and the world powers

FRENCH imperial achievements were equalled if not surpassed by striking successes in foreign affairs between 1870 and 1914. Emerging from the Franco-Prussian War in 1871 as a defeated and completely isolated state, the Third Republic exultantly declared war on Germany in August, 1914, in close alliance with Russia and Great Britain. In framing foreign policy during this period, French

parties and factions varied and shifted their attitudes. What were
the appropriate interests of state for France: imperial acquisition
or restoration of Alsace-Lorraine? A colonial focus meant alienation of England and lack of common ground with Russia — both of
which powers were essential as allies if Alsace was to be recovered.
Revanche against Germany would require such efforts as would
deprive French overseas forces of the strength to counter British
moves in Africa and Asia. Reconciliation with Germany to block
the British overseas implied abandonment of Alsace.

The choice of allies was not an easy one. Should republicans
link with Russia and thus support an autocratic regime? Should
French Catholic groups associate with an antipapal Italian kingdom? A tie with Italy might strengthen the French against the Germans, but would it not also necessitate accommodation of Italian
colonial demands across the Mediterranean?

War or peace, militarism or pacifism also formed essential
parts of the foreign-policy problems. The peacemongers of 1870–
1871, the French right, became the war party of pre-1914. The bel-
licose French left, like Gambetta's republicans of 1870–1871, became, as socialists in 1914, the antimilitarist, pacifist element of prewar France. As in many previously cited instances, the attitude of
Frenchmen on foreign-policy questions was relative to the time and
circumstances in which the question arose. Socialists talked peace
when there was no war and no direct threat to *la patrie;* monarchists and right-wing groups talked peace when there was war and
danger to the social order. Radical-Socialists were antimilitarist
when the army was an aristocratic–clerical stronghold, as in the
the Dreyfus affair, but they willingly extended military service when
the army had been republicanized.

A detailed view of the evolution of French foreign relations from
the morrow of the Franco-Prussian War to the eve of World War I
will bear out these generalizations. For analysis, three distinct periods may be discerned: 1871–1890, when France was diplomatically
isolated essentially by Bismarck's astuteness; 1890–1904, when
France emerged from isolation by a formal alliance with Russia, an

entente with Great Britain, and a close rapport with Italy; and finally, 1904–1914, when France solidified her connection with England, witnessed with gratification an Anglo-Russian entente, and easily survived several international crises with Germany.

The 1871–1890 period opened with the defeat of France at the hands of Germany and continued with the demonstrable preponderance of German power over the isolated French. The 1871 Treaty of Frankfurt provided for the cession to Germany of Alsace and most but not all of Lorraine, the payment of 5,000,000,000 francs in indemnity, and the accordance of a most-favored-nation commercial status to Germany. Occupation forces would remain in France until the indemnity was completely paid. With understandable unanimity, the French protested the loss of the two provinces; with remarkable speed and facility, the French raised the money for the indemnity and relieved their territory of German troops by 1873. Still at the mercy of a superior Germany, the French were obliged to shape their policy if not their phrases, to the liking of Chancellor Bismarck.

The German leader's diplomacy, even more than French domestic and colonial considerations, prevented the French from obtaining compensating alliances. By adroit maneuvering, Bismarck kept potential French allies tied to Berlin. Until 1887, Austria and Russia were associated in a *Dreikaiserbund* with Germany in the hope of Balkan favors to the respective eastern states. Despite the rupturing effect of the Eastern Question in 1878, when the Congress of Berlin repudiated the advances made by Russia in the Balkans, Bismarck was able to reform the *Dreikaiserbund*. The conclusion, too, of a tight alliance with Austria in 1879 foreshadowed subsequent German policy. Italy was induced to become a partner with Austria and Germany in the Triple Alliance initiated during the 1880s. The "unnatural" connection of Italy to Austria, whereby the former shelved its designs on the Austrian-held Italian Irredenta, was facilitated by Bismarck's diplomacy. His encouragement of France to seize Tunisia deeply estranged Italy from its Latin neighbor. In deference to England's vital interests in imperial and maritime questions, Bismarck held growing German agitation for colonies and navy in check. The French contributed to their own isolation by their moves overseas, which, as we have observed, antagonized Italy and Great Britain. The ultra-Catholic stand for the papal cause after 1870 also hampered any rapprochement with Italy.

Within France during this period, the right and left began to reverse their initial 1870–1871 positions on foreign policy. Whereas the right in 1870 had advocated peace with Germany at all costs, the left under Gambetta pressed for continued resistance. During the 1880s, however, when the republicans had captured the government and were exhibiting much subservience to the enemy, the right became increasingly muscular and vocal in its nationalism and its stress on *revanche*. Rallying behind the outspoken anti-German Boulanger, supporting "patriots" like Déroulède and Drumont, the right attacked the republicans for their docility in face of German provocation. A greater bumptiousness would follow during the 1890s when the Dreyfus affair helped stimulate the forming of such right-wing organizations as the *Action Française* and the *Ligue des Patriotes*.

From 1890 to 1904, Germany was the key to the French emergence from isolation, as she had been the chief contributor to that isolation during 1871–1890. French diplomacy exhibited its virtuosity less by creating circumstances in which alliances could be forged than by profiting from German failures and blunders. German miscalculation or sheer perversity made first Russia and then England available to the French. Even Bismarck might have tried but in vain to check the developments that were embittering relations with Russia and England; the new Kaiser Wilhelm II seemed not even to try. Mounting differences between Germany and Russia appeared during the late 1880s. Pan-Slavism clashed with Pan-Germanism in Polish lands and with Austrian influence in the Balkans. The Prussian Junkers suffered the adverse effects of Russian wheat shipments. Protective tariffs against Ukrainian grain and the closing of the Berlin money market to Russian credit pinched Russia seriously by 1890. The German government refused to renew the Treaty of Reinsurance of 1887, which had only partially substituted for the lapsed *Dreikaiserbund.*

Financially desperate, diplomatically isolated from Austria and Germany, engaged in rivalry with England on the periphery of India, Russia became the inevitable object of French attention. The French government opened the doors of the Bank of France and sought to supplement the capital connection with a politico-military convention. Republican sensibilities about ties with autocracy were assuaged when the Tsar doffed his cap to the *Marseillaise* at a navy ceremony in 1891. Russian reluctance to team up with crisis-ridden France was overcome by the apparent liquidation of the Panama scandal. By the Franco-Russian Alliance of 1894, each power was committed to aid the other if Germany attacked or if any other member of the Triple Alliance, abetted by Germany, was an aggressor. The French and Russians agreed to mobilize, too, in the event of mobilization by any of the Triple Alliance powers. French security against German aggression was henceforth enhanced, but so, too, was the danger of French involvement in wars that might arise because of Austro-German attempts to block Russian expansion in the Balkans.

With England as with Russia, the French were able to come to terms as much through German error as through Gallic brilliance. Centuries-long rivalry between France and England seemed not to abate during the 1890s. The French menace to lands bordering India and the French expedition to Fashoda, which might have destroyed British hopes for a Cape-to-Cairo axis in Africa, intensified the friction. By the turn of the century, however, Germany began to replace France as Britain's greater rival. Kaiser Wilhelm II allowed and encouraged what Bismarck had disallowed and discouraged: imperial thrusts and an extensive navy program. A place in the sun for Germany might mean a place in the shade for Great Britain in light of the solid industrial base on which the Germans could build a dynamic and effective overseas policy. Wilhelm's tasteless words of sympathy to the President of the Transvaal, with whose Boers

thé British were engaged in deadly warfare; Wilhelm's favors to
Admiral von Tirpitz and a navy that could threaten essential British
interests; Wilhelm's constant badgering of the British for a political
commitment as the price of German naval limitation — these and
other twists of the lion's tail caused the British to reflect on the
soundness of their traditional isolation. Could Britain alone face
the continued hostility of the French, the stepped-up Russian drive
into Persia, Afghanistan, and Tibet, and a mighty industrialized
Germany seeking Atlantic and Pacific conquests? By posing a potential threat to Britain, the Germans forced the British to make ac-
commodations with other states. France was one beneficiary; Russia
would be another.

The French withdrawal from Egypt during the 1880s, the
French yielding at Fashoda in 1898, the French delicacy and correctness during Britain's involvement in the South African (Boer)
War were acts that made the French more accessible than the Germans to negotiation and agreement. The purposeful policy of French
Foreign Minister Théophile Delcassé was rewarded in 1904 by the
signing of the Anglo-French Entente Cordiale. Exclusively a colonial "gentlemen's agreement," this Entente contained not a single
phrase implying political or military association of the two powers.
France, as observed, formally acknowledged Britain's status in Egypt
in exchange for British willingness to witness benevolently a French
takeover in Morocco. Siam was neutralized, thereby ending the danger of British expansion toward Indochina or French drives toward
Burma or India. Such long-standing difficulties as the squabble over
fishing rights in the Atlantic were also regulated to the satisfaction
of both states.

Still another diplomatic victory for the French during 1890–
1904 was the improvement of relations with Italy. A two-decade
estrangement because of religious, colonial, and commercial matters
was liquidated by the early 1900s. Tariff warfare was ended by a
commercial treaty in 1898. Agreement was reached in 1900 to con-
done future Italian acquisition of Tripoli in exchange for French
claims to Morocco. In 1905, the separation of church and state in

France relieved the French government of much of the pressure by French Catholics who supported the papal claims to lands seized by Italy. By that date, too, Italy had secretly in 1902 excepted France from being defined as a potential enemy in any implementation of the provisions of the Triple Alliance.

In the ten years preceding the outbreak of World War I, the French noted the effective operation and extension of the Entente Cordiale with satisfaction. Two crises were weathered over Morocco; a Triple Entente emerged through the signing of an Anglo-Russian agreement of 1907. Again, German miscalculation counted more than French astuteness in cementing relations between France and Great Britain. As much to test the newly signed Entente Cordiale as to protect their undeniable interests in Morocco, the Germans moved quickly when the French sought in 1905 to make a protectorate of the North African Sultanate. The Kaiser at Tangiers vehemently upheld the independent status of Morocco and promised full protection for German interests there. In the ensuing crisis and at the Algeciras Conference of 1906, England sided unequivocally with the French, as did Russia and Italy. Austria alone supported Germany. The settlement at Algeciras awarded France not exclusive but joint rights with Spain to intervene in Moroccan affairs. The German government had thwarted the immedate seizure of Morocco by France but only at the cost of frightening England into closer ties with France. For as a result of the threat of war implied in Germany's pronouncements, secret talks were initiated between French and British military staffs. Bitterness against Germany mounted in France after the German-induced dismissal of Delcassé, whose brinkmanship also alarmed many Frenchmen.

Using internal disorders in Morocco in 1911 as a pretext for intervention, the French sent troops into the capital city of Fez while Spanish forces tightened their grip on other portions of that state. Again the Germans refused to stand by while France made gains without paying a price. The gunboat *Panther* was dispatched to the Moroccan port of Agadir to protect German interests and to intimidate the French. In return for German recognition of French suzerainty in Morocco, the French finally ceded to Germany extensive areas of Equatorial Africa, which could ultimately help to create a German bloc from East Africa to the mouth of the Congo.

The Germans, however, had taken another ill-considered although perhaps warranted step and had made ill-conceived although perhaps justified demands. For the appearance of German seapower in the Atlantic port of Agadir posed as great a menace to Great Britain as to France. A possible trans-African collection of German colonies also disturbed the British. Stern warnings to the Germans and firm support of the French characterized the second as well as the first Moroccan crisis. As a tangible sign of closer Franco-British cooperation, a secret Naval Agreement was reached in 1912. Interpreting German diplomacy as indicative of aggressive designs in colonial and naval matters and unable to check by negotiation the multiplying German navy bills, Britain judged it necessary to supplement her own fleet by an arrangement with the French. The 1912 Naval Agreement accomplished this by assigning responsibility for North Sea and Channel zones to the British and Mediterranean duty to the French fleets. Although no formal defensive treaty was concluded, the British had now more than a moral commitment to defend French ports and interests in northern waters while the French concentrated their power in the Mediterranean.

Alliance with Russia proved much less fruitful to the French than anticipated. The Russians offered minimal diplomatic support for French colonial aspirations. At Fashoda and in the Moroccan crises, the Russians made it clear that they would not back up the French in the event of hostilities. The suggestible Tsar Nicholas II had even been persuaded in 1905 to sign a short-lived Björkö Treaty of Alliance with his cousin Wilhelm. Furthermore, Russian rivalry with England placed the French in a peculiar position, allied as they were with one state and in an entente with the other. Several developments rescued the French from their predicament and paved the way for the formation of a Triple Entente of France, England, and Russia. The Russo-Japanese War of 1904–1905 followed by the Revolution of 1905 clearly demonstrated Russia's weakness and sharply curtailed her opportunities for Far Eastern and even Middle Eastern expansion. The British viewed with gratification the stunning victory of their Japanese ally and turned their attention to the greater German threat to English influence in the Near and Middle East.

More amenable to negotiation than to aggressive action after 1905, the Russians willingly heeded British invitations to settle some outstanding differences. The resulting Anglo-Russian Entente of 1907 resolved for the while conflicts over Persia, Afghanistan, and Tibet. By this agreement, too, the Triple Entente was formed. Unlike the Triple Alliance, however, there existed no single treaty binding the three powers nor any stipulation for coordinated military action in the event of aggression on any member. The Triple Entente was no more than an informal connection of France, England, and Russia through the existence of the Franco-Russian Alliance of 1894, the Anglo-French Entente Cordiale of 1904, and the Anglo-Russian Entente of 1907.

That the French could not rely on the solidity of this Entente was amply demonstrated after 1907. France herself acted to deter Russia from taking provocative steps in the Balkans in 1908 when Austria annexed Bosnia-Herzogevina and again in 1912–1913 during the Balkan Wars. England felt free to continue negotiations with Germany in the hope of limiting the naval race. These two powers also came to a "cross-alliance" agreement in 1914 in settling their dispute over the Berlin to Bagdad railway and over contacts with Turkey. This was the nature and extent of French international commitments when news reached Paris of the assassination of the Austrian Archduke Ferdinand in Sarajevo on June 28, 1914.

Unaware of Austria's unformed measures of retaliation for the crime, the initial reaction in Paris was one of quiet sympathy for the loss of the Austrian heir and his pregnant wife. As rumors began to circulate in July of unqualified German support for stern punitive Austrian action, the French government adopted a policy of unswerving attachment to its Russian ally. Despite the mounting international crisis, French President Raymond Poincaré and Premier René Viviani sailed to St. Petersburg on July 20 for a long-planned visit of state. Originally intended as a means of bringing Russia and England into more harmonious relations, the visit served other purposes, as Russia now had to consider her position as protector of Serbia. Poincaré, long convinced of the inevitability of war and the dire need of France to do everything to assure the closest rapport with all possible allies, reiterated the firmness of the alliance with Russia. No sign must be given of French faltering lest the Russians defect from their alliance and make an accommodation with Austria and Germany.

To the Austrian Ambassador at St. Petersburg, Poincaré ominously stated, therefore, that Serbia had very warm friends in the Russian people and Russia had an ally, France. No less than Poincaré, the French Ambassador at St. Petersburg, Maurice Paléologue, encouraged the activist war party in Russia to count unreservedly on French aid and to press the Serbian case forcefully. This faction in Russia needed little prompting. After Austria submitted the famous ultimatum to the Serbian government and then declared war on the Serbs, the vacillating Tsar was importuned to order mobilization. With the French heads of state on their sea journey home at the time of the delivery of the ultimatum, Paléologue continued his prodding advice and the caretakers in Paris did nothing to restrain the Russian moves. Elsewhere the French role in the summer crisis of 1914 was negligible. At Belgrade, the French Ambassador was absent from his post because of a nervous breakdown; in London, Paul Cambon worked unsuccessfully to secure a commitment from Sir Edward Grey; in Berlin, and Vienna, French warnings of caution fell on deaf ears.

The precipitous Austrian declaration of war against Serbia had provoked Russian mobilization; Russian mobilization necessitated German mobilization. French mobilization, with the precaution of withdrawing French forces ten kilometers behind the frontier, was ordered independently and within an hour of the German. Strategically essential but diplomatically disastrous, the German violation of Belgian neutrality brought Great Britain into the war. In a few summer weeks in 1914, Germany had converted into a fighting alliance the loose Triple Entente she had so inadvertently helped to create in the previous decade.

The bald recital of French diplomatic moves on the road to World War I gives little indication of the domestic drama played out in France in the summer of 1914. During the few days immediately preceding and following the August 1 mobilization decree, all France was beset by a wave of emotional demonstrations. In Paris, the main boulevards and the little streets, the railroad stations and the cafés were scenes of parading, chanting enthusiasts. Excitement was rife, too, in the squares of provincial towns. Trains packed with mustered-up soldiers were greeted with shouts of encouragement from peasants in the fields and villagers at the crossings. All Frenchmen seemed united without respect to class or region.

That the day of declaring war on Germany came to General "X" in Proust's last volume of *Remembrance of Things Past* as the day for which he had waited all his life should engender no surprise. The French right had for decades advocated a nationalist, militarist, revanchist policy of war. That the same day should be greeted by socialist and trade union leaders, as well as the rank and file, as the occasion for rejoicing requires explanation. Was not the French left internationalist, antimilitarist, and pacifist in pronouncement and projected action?

The French right had recommended a strenuous nationalism as the basis for political and social change during the early 1900s. A fading but still existent spirit of *revanche* emanated from Léon Daudet, an important member of the *Action Française*. Alone and in concert with others, he agitated for a return match with Germany to secure the restoration of Alsace and Lorraine. His followers were undoubtedly among those responsible for the multiplying demonstrations in front of the statue of Strasbourg on the Place de la Concorde during the 1910s. Maurice Barrès was drumming a similar tune. An old Lorrainer, a President of the *Ligue des Patriotes*, a contributor to the newspaper of the *Action Française*, a member of the French Academy, Barrès devoted his adult life to spreading the gospel of "France for Frenchmen" and of purging "alien" elements. Heartily opposed to any form of internationalism, he was convinced that war was beneficial and advisable in the pursuit of foreign and colonial goals. Building on Barrès, Charles Maurras formulated his own doctrine and launched the *Action Française* and then the newspaper of the same name in 1908. For half a generation before the outbreak of war in 1914, this group and its affiliates pamphleteered and paraded for a quickening of the national spirit and a strengthening of the military forces. It was perfectly logical and understandable that the events of August, 1914, should evoke unbounded enthusiasm from the French right.

For the French left to share this enthusiasm would appear highly illogical and beyond comprehension. Despite their pre-1914 slogains, however, the socialist's stand against war was qualified. Although Jean Jaurès raged against the extension of army service in 1912 and 1913, he did not bar all forms of military service. In 1911, the SFIO chief had proposed a Swiss-type militia, a citizen army. The "new Army" was to be used solely for protecting the nation from unprovoked, irresponsible aggression. This mild, defensive militarism could thus be a causal factor in the left's enthusiasm in 1914 if the workers were or could be convinced that their country was beset by a wicked, unconscionable enemy. The French government and the French press easily accomplished this feat of propaganda, aided often by the mere reporting of provocative German pronouncements and diplomatic (or undiplomatic) moves.

If some of the left needed to be persuaded that the imminent war was defensive to bolster their existent but low-pitched nationalism, others needed to be convinced that a war might produce a radical change in the social system to overcome their resistance to war. How this socialist aspiration might have helped prepare a cordial reception to war was perfectly illustrated by Henri Barbusse's letter of August 9, 1914, to the editor of the socialist newspaper, *L'Humanité:*

Will you count me among the anti-militarist socialists who are enlisting for the present war? Although a member of the auxiliary services, I have sought and obtained [the permission] to be placed in the combat forces and I am leaving in a few days as a private in the infantry. . . . Far from having renounced the ideas which I have always upheld at my own cost, I consider I shall serve them by taking up arms. This war is a social war which will bring about a great step forward—perhaps the final one—for our cause. It [the war] is directed against our infamous and eternal enemies: militarism and imperialism, the Sword, the Boot and, I shall add, the Crown. Our victory will be the elimination of the headquarters of the caesars, crownprinces, lords, and mercenaries who imprison one people and wish to imprison others. The world can become free only by opposition to them. If I sacrifice my life, if I go to war with joy, it is not merely as a Frenchman, it is especially as a member of the human race.[2]

Henri Barbusse, "anti-militarist socialist," postwar antiwar literary light, joined ranks with the militarists of the right and the patriots of the center. The pacifist policy of the French left was thus not absolute but relative to the type of war to be waged and to the possible events war might produce.

The French syndicalist–anarchist left had been even more vehement in its antimilitarism. Long threatening a general strike in the event merely of mobilization, the CGT found its effectiveness blunted by repressive governmental action and by its rank and file's succumbing to the national hysteria. Radical-Socialists had less difficulty in embracing the patriotic cause in 1914. Although vocally antimilitarist, as evidenced in the Dreyfus affair and in their verbal opposition to the three-year service law of 1913, most of the Radicals had followed the lead of the more nationalist deputies in voting the bill's passage. Chance, too, eliminated the leader of the faction of the Radical-Socialists that advocated accommodation with Germany. For, in the spring of 1914, Joseph Caillaux's second wife helped her husband lose his premiership by shooting to death

[2] Quoted in Henri Barbusse, *Paroles d'un combattant* (Paris: Flammarion, 1920), pp. 7–8. Translation by the author.

the editor of the conservative newspaper, *Le Figaro*. Affairs of the boudoir had important bearing on affairs of state.

Perhaps less significant to reputedly aloof historians yet probably more important to the individual Frenchman of August, 1914, were the highly personal, often ulterior motives that impelled him to join his fellow patriots in support of the new-born war. How could young Frenchmen resist the appeal of marching soldiers, resplendent in their red and blue uniformed brilliance, accompanied by gleaming and resonant brass bands? Such scenes had melted even the hard materialistic core of many solidly forged socialists. How could Frenchmen pass up the opportunity of a brief respite from the tedium and monotony of their daily, uneventful lives? Men happy with their wives or mistresses might regret the separation brought about by war, but the aunt of Robert de Saint Loup, in Marcel Proust's novels, was sincerely if erroneously convinced that her nephew enlisted to escape an unpleasant marital situation. Were there those, too, like Robert in André Gide's *Ecole des Femmes* who volunteered before he was drafted in order to be free "to choose the branch of service he preferred – which he did with the utmost precaution and with the help of all the influence he could command"? Or, perhaps, with less soul- and culture-searching, there were Frenchmen like Jean-Paul Sartre's Self-Taught Man in *La Nausée* who went to war in 1914 "without any special reason. . . ."

Often overlooked as playing a role in the French reaction of August, 1914, was the prevailing concept of war – its anticipated duration, nature, and outcome. The many Frenchmen who wrote, read, or shouted *A Berlin!* assumed the time for the excursion would be short, relatively bloodless, and most assuredly victorious. The universally held belief in a lightning war of movement convinced the French that their troops would capture Berlin and be "Home by Christmas!"

5.

THE TRIALS AND TRIBULATIONS OF
THE THIRD REPUBLIC

1914–1918

The great illusion

THE AUGUST, 1914, chant of "Home by Christmas" was no mere popular slogan; it reflected the expectations of the political and military leaders of France. Lest the French generals be charged with a monopoly on obtuseness, it should be noted that all the belligerents' chieftains shared the view that the war would be short and victorious. A narrow reading of history with emphasis on the episodic wars of the nineteenth century deluded almost all the civilian and military heads of the European states.

"Plan XVII" was the name of the strategic and tactical arrangements for French military operations in the opening – and presumably conclusive – months of war; it was the product of decades of reflection and was formalized in the spring of 1914 under the direction of General Joseph Joffre. The basic and clearly stated premise of Plan XVII was that success in battle derived from taking the initiative and conducting unrelenting offensive action against the enemy. The first waves of attacking troops would suffer losses, but the cold steel of the bayonets of successive infantrymen would destroy the defenders and open the way to swift penetration of enemy territory. Artillery would support the infantry after the initial attack and would harass the dislocated, fleeing opponent. To achieve maximum offensive power, the bulk of the French army was to be concentrated along the Franco-German border from Belfort to Thionville, from Switzerland to Luxembourg. The sector along the Franco-Belgian frontier from Luxembourg to the Channel was left relatively uncovered.

At the outbreak of hostilities, the French Command would dispatch the major portion of its armed force across the German border into Alsace and Lorraine, push with unremitting offensives across the Rhine, and move into the heart of Germany on the road to Berlin. Despite familiarity with the broad outlines of the German von Schlieffen Plan, which projected a powerful German thrust through Belgium and a holding action along the Franco-German frontier, the French persisted in leaving their northern flank weak. Why be concerned? While German armies were attempting to penetrate Belgium and before they could enter northern France, French armies would be in possession of valuable German territory if not of the capital city itself. The German Command would be obliged to withdraw its forces from threatened French soil to protect the Fatherland. That the Germans recognized some merit in this French logic was evidenced by the younger von Moltke's modification of the original von Schlieffen Plan. The German Chief of Staff weakened his right (Belgian) flank and strengthened his left where the French were concentrated – one of the many steps to be regretted by the Germans in 1914.

French military preparations before 1914 included measures for overcoming German superiority in manpower and for training, equipping, and mobilizing French effectives. Thanks to the Army Law of 1913, whereby military service was extended from two to three years and an extra class of conscripts was made available, the French Command came close to meeting the Germans with equal numbers of men in 1914. Use of reserve components in rear areas and in fortified zones further enabled the French to close the numbers gap. Armed with rifles and machine guns inferior in firepower to the Germans', the French troops nevertheless had in the 75 mm. gun a piece of artillery unsurpassed for the purposes intended – operation in open country. Unfortunately, this famous artillery

weapon could deliver shells only in a flat trajectory and would be
less effective when high-angle fire would be required against dug-in
troops. Under such circumstances, too, the lack of heavy artillery —
which existed in prototype and on order but not in the hands of the
troops — would constitute a serious drawback. But, then, the anticipated war of movement would presumably not demand such armament. The light, mobile, fast-firing French 75 was considered
adequate. More than adequate were the methods applied to the
problem of the mobilization and initial deployment of the army.
Joffre intended full and proper use of the railroads to bring reservists to their regiments and to dispatch active regiments to the front.

Conceived with hope, executed with zeal, and buried with
venom, Plan XVII became an historical relic long before Christmas,
1914. Within two weeks of the August 4 declaration of war, Joffre
was ready to put Plan XVII to the test. Mobilization had proceeded
smoothly. Without friction or mishap, reservists had been activated
and formed into their military components, and active units had
been shifted to the frontiers. Five French armies had been created,
numbered from south to north (right to left) from Switzerland to
Belgium: the First and Second facing Alsace, the Third opposite
Lorraine, the Fifth deployed near Luxembourg and the southeastern
juncture of the Franco-Belgian border, the Fourth in strategic reserve.

Covering troops had successfully raided Alsace and briefly held
Mulhouse, but the main French attack began on August 14. The
ensuing Battle of the Frontiers involved initially the First and Second Armies. French troops moved with élan crosscountry to sudden
defeat and counterattack. On August 21, Joffre shifted his emphasis
slightly north and ordered an offensive into Lorraine and adjacent
Luxembourg. In this operation, the Third Army, with the Fourth
now added to its left flank, suffered the same fate as the First and
Second. Neither in the rolling countryside of Alsace nor in the
wooded, rocky terrain of the Meuse and Moselle in Lorraine and
the Ardennes could French troops prevail over a sometimes inferior
number of Germans. Offensive action by red-and-blue-uniformed

The great illusion 177

Frenchmen, armed chiefly with rifles and bayonets and ill supported
by artillery, was easily checked by an entrenched enemy dressed in
field gray and equipped with machine guns and heavy artillery. At
fault too was Joffre's miscalculation of enemy numbers. He refused
to believe that the enemy could create so many active combat divisions from the reserves. The cost of the lessons, not yet fully learned
in the Battle of the Frontiers, amounted to three hundred thousand
French casualties.

If Plan XVII was being submitted to severe shocks and setbacks,
the von Schlieffen Plan seemed to bring nothing but success. Moving immediately into Belgium on the expiration of their ultimatum,
the Germans rapidly forced back the defenders. The German victories at Liége and elsewhere in Belgium, however, were persistently
discounted by Joffre. He did not calculate that the Germans had
adequate forces for continued offensives there and into France in
light of the strength of the German center and left wing he was
engaging in the Battle of the Frontiers. He failed to appreciate that
the enemy High Command had used reserve troops to form entire
regiments and divisions. By the end of August, the danger in the
northeast became inescapably evident. The Belgian army had
retreated to cover Antwerp and the coast, the small British Expeditionary Force and the French Fifth Army had fallen back in disarray after a series of delaying engagements, and the remaing French
armies were trying to stabilize the Alsace-Lorraine front after the
Battle of the Frontiers. Still, the German armies pushed on, in the
apparent direction of Paris, past the river lines of the Somme and
the Aisne toward the Marne.

Whether striking back at this juncture was Joffre's or another's
original conception, the French Commander-in-Chief finally re-
directed his thinking and set in motion many of the forces that
helped achieve the "miracle" of the Marne. Already having convinced the British Commander not to retire to the coast and conduct
a Dunkirk a war too soon, Joffre began to reassemble his armies to
outflank or to meet the numerous but ill-coordinated German
armies converging on Paris. Stripping his right wing of all excess

troops and redeploying them rapidly by road and rail to the Paris region and forming new units from garrison reserves in the rear, Joffre re-enforced the weary retreating French troops at the Marne by early September. On the verge of splitting the British and French forces and of breaking through in mass to take Paris, whose Eiffel Tower had already been sighted by advance German cavalry, the Germans were met, stopped, and turned back by the French at the Marne.

Without denying the effectiveness, brilliance, and courage of the French contribution, without discounting or flattening the drama of dispatching several thousand soldiers to the front in taxicabs, the Germans played a large part in producing their own defeat. Von Moltke's lack of daring has already been cited in his unwillingness to leave the German left wing weak. His transfer of forces from the right, or Belgian, wing deprived the Germans of the needed extra mass there. In the same vein, German alarm at Russian drives in the east led von Moltke to divert several corps from the western front to East Prussia. These units might have helped Germany win a victory at the Marne instead of merely helping to celebrate an already concluded Battle of Tannenberg on their arrival on the eastern front. Logistical problems, too, added to the German troubles at the Marne. Outracing their supplies of food and ammunition, German troops at the Marne had less impact than the French, who could draw on the stockpiles and supplies of nearby bases. Furthermore, lack of liaison and excess of personal ambition marked the German effort. Swiftly moving German armies, commanded by generals striving to be first to the Arc de Triomphe, showed little concern for coordinating their offensives or for protecting their fellows' flanks. Too far to the rear and too out of touch with the field commanders the German High Command was unable to correct the situation.

By September 10, the Battle of the Marne was over, but the war was not. The French lack of strength or vision or both permitted the Germans to regroup their dislocated armies north of the Aisne River. Incapable of dislodging the enemy from its entrenched position by frontal assault, Joffre elected the classical alternative of a flanking action. The Germans had read the same manuals and followed the same procedure in a slow, northward course. The mutually fruitless flanking drives led the French and the Germans into the operations subsequently termed the Race to the Sea.

By the end of 1914, a continuous front had been formed from the Swiss border to the North Sea. Monumental efforts and millions of lives would be expended along this front for three long years. Not until 1918 would there be substantial modification of this line, a description of which reads like a listing of famous French cathedrals, châteaux, and textile, mining, and wine centers. Beginning from the northern hinge at the North Sea halfway between French Dunkirk and Belgian Ostend, the line moved in an irregular fashion due south to a point between Compiègne and Noyon. A tiny slice of Belgian territory, including the city of Ypres, which was defended at suicidal cost by the British Expeditionary Force, was held by the Allies. Moving southward, the French cities of Lille, Roubaix, Douai, Cambrai, St. Quentin, and Laon, but not Arras or Compiègne, fell to the Germans. Near Compiègne, the line shifted roughly eastward to Verdun with the French entrenched on the north bank of the Aisne. Soissons, Rheims, and Verdun were barely within the French sector. Just east of Verdun, the line dipped south to German-held St. Mihiel and then east, leaving Toul and Nancy as French bastions. From Nancy southeast, paralleling the Franco-German border, the front followed fairly closely the Vosges mountains to Switzerland, with only a thin edge of Alsace in French possession. On this eight-hundred-mile front, the French would rivet their attention for four long years, despite the assignment of some forces to other theaters of operation and despite anxiety over events on the seas and on the eastern front. The real war for the French was the war on the western front.

Before the end of 1914, battle conditions on the western front began to assume the shape so hideously familiar to the participants and observers of the actions of 1915–1918. The Battle of the Frontiers had early demonstrated the inefficacy of the offensive and the war of movement against troops armed with machine guns and heavy artillery. Forced to retreat and man defensive positions themselves, the French waged a watchful, desultory, outpost war with the Germans along the Vosges frontier for the duration of the war. From Nancy to the sea, however, more massive operations and more typical conditions prevailed, for this sector of the western front displayed characteristics never before witnessed and, unfortunately for the French military strategy of 1940, never again repeated.

As the Race to the Sea resulted in stabilizing the flankless fronts, simple trenches and earthworks at first sufficed to give cover to the opposing forces. Then, more elaborate trenches along the first lines became connected and interlaced with tunnel-like diggings. Safer access was thus afforded to the rear for supplies and re-enforcements. In some areas, heavy timber, concrete, and steel buttressed or covered the trenches for greater protection against such high-angle weapons as the mortar and howitzer. The increased use of the high-explosive shells of heavier artillery demanded a more resistant shield than mere earth or an open trench. Between the opposing forces' continuous and ever more complicated trench lines, there sprouted the barbed wire that was employed to impede movement and to forestall surprise attacks. Unable to move in open country by day without massive preparation, night was the time for patrols to reweave the entanglements that artillery or enemy patrols had torn asunder. With the sky lighted up by flares of Verey pistols and star shells from heavier weapons, nighttime was like a hallucination. Daytime, however, was a nightmare. For, to mount an attack, it became essential — or, at least, the practice — to initiate a massive artillery barrage against the enemy position and then to continue artillery action with a rolling, creeping barrage yards ahead of one's own troops as they crept across the pocked ground and picked their way through the hopefully shattered entanglements. Presumably, the enemy would have been forced under cover, unable to direct deadly machine-gun fire against the attackers. Half-unconscious from concussion if still alive, the defenders would be easy targets for the final rifle bullet or bayonet thrust. The larger tactical and strategic goal of such "normal" operations was to secure a sufficient break in the enemy lines to allow passage of large numbers of infantrymen and cavalry. The aim was to wreak havoc with the enemy flank and rear and perhaps resume a war of movement in the unprepared enemy zone. The next attack, the next offensive might open the road to Berlin – or to Paris.

As the war passed in age from months to years, the stalemate on the western front deepened. Death could not be delivered disproportionately enough for either side to achieve victory. Stalemate, however, was not the equivalent of inactivity. To defend and protect themselves more effectively and yet to deliver fire against the enemy and to launch offensives with greater power and fewer losses, both sides poured increasing masses of men and matériel into combat and introduced tactical variations and new weapons to the battlefield. The use of poison gas, the invention and employment of the tank, and renewed reliance on fortifications were the outstanding examples that gave color to the otherwise monotonous and repetitious but deadly patterns of the unfolding war of attrition.

The year 1915 was marked by French attempts to "nibble" at enemy strength and, more grandiosely, to mount offensives that might achieve strategic breakthroughs and remove the invader from French soil. Sorties in February, March, and April in Champagne and against the St. Mihiel salient cost the French 100,000 men and netted no territorial gains. More renowned for the introduction of poison gas than for any substantial advances, the German April offensive south of Ypres forced postponement of Joffre's campaign in Artois. By May, however, Joffre opened his projected large-scale attack east from Arras, adding 100,000 more casualties but very few acres to the French account. As futile as the spring offensive was the two-pronged autumn maneuver in Artois and Champagne. Aiming east from Arras and north from Champagne, Joffre essayed a giant pincer on the German bulge into French territory. Like previous and succeeding attacks, days of artillery bombardment alerted the Germans to Joffre's intentions. Despite the havoc wreaked by the shell-fire, the enemy recovered its initial losses and prevented any sizeable modification of the front. Nearly 200,000 French (and 50,000 British) casualties were counted as against fewer than 150,000 German.

Verdun and the Somme came next, in 1916, as the highlights of the war on the western front. Whether designed by the German High Command to lure the French into a giant "mincing machine" or to seize a psychologically but not tactically significant fortress city, the Battle of Verdun opened on February 21, 1916. Initial German success in taking some outlying French forts was due to Joffre's discounting intelligence reports on German preparations in the region and to his downgrading and dismantling the forts upon evaluation of the poor record of Liége and other fortresses earlier in the war. By the end of the month, Joffre reversed his policy. Henri-Philippe Pétain was placed in command of the defense of Verdun, and to him was ultimately dispatched more than half a million men and enormous quantities of matériel and ammunition.

The nature of the Battle of Verdun imposed a challenging strain on French logistics. Only one rail line and one narrow road, Bar-le-duc, gave access to the French defenders at Verdun. Over these limited avenues of approach, re-enforcements and supplies had to move in astronomical quantities. Pétain estimated that the Germans and the French had each used approximately 20,000,000 artillery shells in the 140-day period from February 21 to July 15 – an average of 150,000 projectiles per day. Into the "mincing machine" fabricated by the German High Command, more than 250,000 of their own dead and wounded joined about 300,000 Frenchmen. If Verdun confirmed Pétain in his conviction of the ruinous cost of offensive action and the desperate need for masses of men and matériel in modern warfare, it also taught the virtues of fortification and firepower in a defensive complex. French opinion on the value of fortification underwent a sudden reversal when it was observed how well the concrete and steel forts withstood incessant bombardment by the heaviest caliber artillery. In many respects, the Maginot Line of the 1930s was born in the experience of 1916.

A summer offensive by the Russians in the east and the June opening of the Battle of the Somme by the British diverted German forces from Verdun by July, 1916. At the Somme, a new engine of war was introduced: the tank. As a result of the way it was employed, however, the importance of the tank was far less appreciated by the French than was the significance of fortification. For, as used in the Battle of the Somme, the tank was assigned to the fight prematurely in small numbers rather than in mass. The British efforts had already bogged down in the summer of 1916 when the few existing tanks were thrown piecemeal into battle. Despite achieving local surprise and despite combining mobility with protection and firepower, these instruments did little to prevent the recurrence of another stalled offensive. Allied losses totaled more than 400,000 British and nearly 200,000 French as against fewer than 500,000 Germans.

Desperate for victory, the French unhappily heeded the siren calls of General Robert Nivelle for a brief but mournful moment in 1917. Nivelle, who had replaced Joffre at the end of 1916, guaranteed instant success for a final offensive under his command. It did prove to be the final offensive under his command but hardly successful. By the time he launched the attack in Champagne in April, General Ludendorff had withdrawn his frontline forces to well-prepared positions slightly to the rear. Wave after wave of French infantry was murderously cut down by German machine guns or blasted by German artillery. Fifty thousand Frenchmen among 300,000 casualties paid with their lives for a few hundred yards of front.

Victory in the immediate future seemed a grand illusion; death, a reality. To the French troops surviving this battle and to those anticipating the resumption of similar operations, mutiny for self-preservation seemed the only appropriate response. Tens of thousands refused to participate in the mildest offensive action, tens of thousands resisted assignment to the front from replacement depots, tens of thousands evaded return from furloughs or from rest areas. Only drastic corrective measures tempered by liberal concessions could restore the morale of the French army. Pétain, renowned as the Hero of Verdun and as a General sparing of men's lives in his strategic and tactical recommendations, replaced Nivelle to repair the damage. Firm but respected, Pétain proceeded to call a halt to all offensives and to concentrate exclusively on holding the existing and well-entrenched French positions. More rapid rotation of combat assignments, more frequent furloughs, and improvements in feeding and supplying the troops helped to terminate the spontaneous and widespread mutinies of the spring of 1917. The western front became no parade ground for the French armies, but neither was it to be the arena of reckless bloodletting. Henceforth, until the closing months of the war, the French defended their lines with courage and sustained heavy losses but left the initiative first to the British and finally to the Americans.

The United States entry into the war in April, 1917, was followed by a year's training and arming before any substantial American forces appeared on the battle fronts. Meanwhile, for the remainder of 1917 and in early 1918, the British carried the chief burden of attacking the German positions while the French stood on the defensive. Either for the glory of England or for his own personal reputation, British Commander-in-Chief Douglas Haig declined to follow Pétain's cautious policy of armed waiting and pursued a plan of defeating the Germans before the Americans arrived. During the summer and fall of 1917, these plans were buried in the blood of more than 400,000 British casualties in the mud of Passchendaele outside Ypres. Too weak to exploit the stunning local breakthrough achieved by the massed use of tanks near Cambrai in November, the British bitterly watched the Germans reknit the open front and block the chances for strategic Allied success. The British, like the French, would be obliged to await fresh American troops to renew any major offensive.

For the Allies, 1917 had been a year of despair; 1918 promised worse. The Italians had been routed and submitted to a 600,000 casualty defeat at Caporetto in October, 1917. The Russians, despite persistent but deteriorating efforts after the March Revolution, withdrew from the war after the Bolsheviks seized power in November. In early 1918, the German Supreme Command rejected the proffered opportunity of negotiations on the basis of President Wilson's Fourteen Points and chose to essay a knockout blow on the western front. Although fewer than anticipated, substantial numbers of German troops and arms were transferred from the eastern front and served to give the German command a promise of victory in the west before American forces could enter combat.

During March, April, and May, successive attacks nearly separated the British from the French armies and brought the Germans again to the Marne. Closer to total victory than the French dared contemplate, the German armies nevertheless failed to win their desperate gamble. The new Inter-Allied Chief, Ferdinand Foch, threw superior numbers of tanks, artillery, and American as well as French and British troops into powerful counteroffensives against the German armies. Slowly but without any decisive breakthrough, the Allies pushed back the enemy to his prepared Hindenburg line by the end of August, 1918. By Ludendorff's own admission, the Germans were barely capable of maintaining their front and were certainly bereft of further offensive capacity. Still, in October, the Germans held, experiencing some minor breaches but no massive penetration of the Hindenburg line.

Meanwhile, however, on September 29, Bulgaria had deserted the Central Powers; Turkey capitulated on October 31, and, on November 4, Austria was offered the armistice she had earlier sought. Germany stood alone – deep in French and Belgian territory, armed and powerful but faced with the imminent threat of a military debacle and the overrunning of her homeland. Ludendorff signaled his home government to negotiate an end to the hostilities; German soldiers, sailors, and civilians seconded the wish by mutinies and uprisings at home. President Wilson, to whom the German plea was shrewdly directed, instructed Foch to draw up the terms of an armistice. The Germans first had to satisfy the American's demand for establishment of a democratic German government. On the eleventh hour of the eleventh day of the eleventh month of 1918, the war came to an end.

Long before the Armistice of 1918, the French were rudely forced to the realization that modern warfare could not be the exclusive concern of the general staffs and fighting men. *La nation armée,* so often referred to by military and civilian leaders in the prewar era, bore little resemblance to the nation in arms that became necessary in the total war of 1914–1918. To the prewar planners, a nation in arms involved little more than the speedy mobilization of manpower and its dispatch to the front for the lightning war anticipated. Railroads, it is true, would be pressed into military service and would be denied to commercial and business use during the brief period of mobilization and deployment of troops. For the war effort, supplies for about three months of combat would be provided from stockpiles set up in areas where fighting was foreseen. Once war was declared, contracts for artillery pieces or ammunition might even be allowed to lapse, since production could not be expected to be completed before hostilities were concluded. Provision was made for purchase of foodstuffs for the armed forces, but, again, no abnormal measures were deemed necessary. The normal harvest, supplemented by normal importation, would merely be redistributed by army purchasing agents from civilian to mobilized Frenchmen. Were the numbers of mouths not the same? In industry as on the railroads, some deferments of key personnel would be permitted. However, railroad employees were to be ordered to report to their military posts once the rail role in mobilization had been completed. Industrial personnel would follow, too, after a three-month delay.

Like the military concepts of Plan XVII, the economic arrangements for the nation in arms required radical re-adjustment before the end of 1914. As early as September, Joffre had to warn his field commanders to conserve ammunition. The stockpiles were half exhausted, the war was but one month old, and French industry was providing a mere 12,000 shells daily while the army expended nearly 100,000 per day. Industry, idled by the exodus of the worker-turned-soldier, was a poor provider for the hungry artillery piece and machine gun. In fact, as a dislocating result of the mobilization of August, 1914, 47 percent of the factories and shops closed down, and those still open operated with only 34 percent of their former employees.

To complicate further the problem of meeting the escalating demands of the front, valuable French territory had been overrun and occupied by the Germans. With the termination of the Battle of the Marne and the Race to the Sea, the French suddenly awoke to the fact that much of their industrial, mineral, and agricultural resources were in German hands. More than 10 percent of French territory was under German occupation, for the remainder of the war, thereby depriving the French of 50 percent of their coal, with 20 percent of that too close to the front to be mined; they were also deprived of 80 percent of their iron ore, since the Briey basin alone produced fifteen of the twenty-one million tons, and 20 percent of their wheat, 25 percent of their oats, and 50 percent of their sugar beet crop.

To compensate for these heavy losses in the face of swelling wartime demands, the French began in 1915 to take radical steps. By the end of the war, a haphazard but successful set of measures had been applied to the problem and a nation in arms had been organized. The constant goal of providing the necessary supplies for war while satisfying essential civilian needs was achieved by a wide range of methods. Sensitive throughout the war to the persisting interests of large and small capitalists and of labor, however, the government refrained from outright expropriation of property or from any drastic prohibition of higher profits or wages. Subsidies and loans encouraged manufacturers to increase or convert to war production. Allocation of raw materials, regulations and control over standards and prices, establishment of mixed government, business, and labor bureaus — these and other devices were used to maintain private enterprise and yet secure the appropriate product. Agriculture as well as industry came under scrutiny and control for the purpose of waging war. In the former sector, too, price-fixing or decretal of maximum prices, restriction on sale and distribution, and rationing were more typical than sheer requisition of farm goods for military and civilian consumption. Farmers, like manufacturers, were often favored by subsidies and assignment of harvest-time labor to gangs of prisoners of war or furloughed soldiers, as well as other aids.

More than the peasant but less than the manufacturer, the French worker benefited from the government's policies in organizing the nation in arms. The vast majority of French workers had been either mobilized in 1914 or thrown into unemployment by the shutdown of factories and other businesses. When the hope for a brief war failed to materialize and when the need for resuming and even increasing production became urgent, more than half a million skilled workers were demobilized and returned to industry and approximately a third of a million were sent back to the farm. By the war's end, almost a million and a half otherwise draftable men were engaged in civilian employment. Understandable bitterness was the manifest outcome of the fact that peasants, at a soldiers' pittance, found themselves in the mud of the trenches rather than the mud of the farm while skilled workers were more likely to be withdrawn to the factories in well-paid jobs. Such diversion of manpower from military to civilian occupations, however, did not adequately meet the labor shortage. Additional sources were sought and tapped without draining the armed forces: hundreds of thousands of women, foreign workers, and colonial hands joined the ranks of French labor. Lest disputes over wages, hours, or working conditions cause unrest or strikes, the government instituted several reforms hitherto resisted in France. Minimum wages, at least in industries with which the government had contracts, were established. Permanent governmental commissions provided arbitration and conciliation of disputes to avert strikes and lockouts in these and other industries that were deemed essential to the war effort.

The government also extended the scope of its activity in regulating the financial world. Initially, during the summer of 1914, the government closed the Bourse and declared a moratorium on payment of debts and rents, and the semiprivate Bank of France suspended specie payments. Banking and credit facilities were paralyzed, awaiting a return to normalcy once the brief war would be over. Existing capital and credit were no more sufficient in the unfolding total war, however, than were the existing stockpiles of ammunition and weapons. The ghastly truth of the mounting war expenditures is told in Table 5–1 and the government's failure to meet the enormous costs through current taxation in Table 5–2.

Table 5–1. French War Expenditures *

Year	Billions of Francs
1914	10.4
1915	22.1
1916	36.8
1917	44.6
1918	56.6

* Tables 5–1 and 5–2 are from Shepard B. Clough, *France: A History of National Economics, 1789–1939* (New York: Charles Scribner's Sons, 1939), pp. 266–67.

Table 5–2. Tax Yield

Year	Billions of Paper Francs	Billions of Prewar Francs
1913	4.1	4.1
1914	3.4	3.4
1915	3.3	2.4
1916	4.1	2.2
1917	5.7	2.2
1918	7.0	2.1

The gap between the swollen war costs and the shrunken tax revenues was filled by the printing press, flotation of war bonds, sale of foreign investments, and heavy borrowing abroad. The impracticability of burdening a suffering population with heavier charges than the new income tax and many regular or exceptional imposts spelled serious problems for the postwar era. The internal debt rose 71,474,000,000 francs from 1914 to the end of 1919. Where France had been a creditor nation in 1914, she found herself in 1919 saddled with a foreign debt of 67,076,000,000 paper francs.

The organization of the nation in arms was not exclusively a matter of government intervention in economic functions. Industry, agriculture, finance, and commerce were the chief preoccupations of the public authorities, but the area of propaganda was not neglected. In order to maintain civilian morale at home, to present a favorable view of France among the Allies and neutrals, and to demoralize enemy soldiers and civilians, numerous agencies were established during the war. Press censorship and subsidies provided the domestic and foreign audience with highly colored versions of French military and diplomatic efforts. Stimulation of patriotic zeal to offset war weariness became as much a government role as stimulation of production to win the war.

The political unity witnessed in wartime France has been properly ascribed to the danger in which *la patrie* found itself. That national peril did not automatically beget domestic unity in that era, however, should be obvious from the appearance of the March and November Revolutions in Russia, and the Wilson-precipitated but German-consummated overthrow of the monarchy in times of equal if not greater threats to national security.

The formation and endurance of the *Union Sacrée* in France in 1914 and the solid backing of Clemenceau after 1917, therefore, attest to the dynamic pull of patriotism on the otherwise factious French. Within a month of the outbreak of war, Premier René Viviani formed a cabinet whose membership could have been imagined before 1914 only in the most farcial music hall sketches. Joined together in this *Union Sacrée* were the eminent ultra-Catholic Denys Cochin with the notorious priest eater Emile Combes; the Radical Prime Minister Viviani with Louis Malvy, the protégé of the outcast Caillaux. Ex-socialist Alexandre Millerand as Minister of War, Alexandre Ribot as Finance Minister, and Foreign Minister Delcassé were also pressed into service. More surprising in their acceptance than in their being offered posts were Ministers of State Jules Guesde and Marcel Sembat, who had so

explicitly advertised their antimilitarism and their refusal to participate in any bourgeois government before 1914. If the socialists
demonstrated their good faith in France – even in the bourgeois
sector of the country – the exclusively bourgeois members of the
cabinet had already showed their faith in the Frenchness of the
socialists before the *Union Sacrée*'s inception. In a decision of
great wisdom, the government of early August, 1914, refrained from
automatically arresting all those on the *Carnet B*. This carefully
compiled list contained more than two thousand names of left-wing
leaders – politicians, labor officials, professional revolutionaries –
who might attempt to wreck mobilization or other war activities.

   Like French economic activity, French politics came to a relative
standstill in the months following the August call to arms. The
cabinet prorogued the willing Parliament and the ministers joined
the deputies in awaiting news of the battles from the field commanders. The government, including most of the members of the
recessed Chamber of Deputies and Senate, moved from Paris to
Bordeaux to avoid possible repetition of the 1870 plight of governmental isolation. With Joffre in command, the military leaders
were accorded their every wish – or, at least, all the cabinet could
provide. This vacation from politics was extended through the
remainder of the year. The deputies and the party politicians did
not disturb the cabinet; the cabinet and other civil authorities did
not interfere with the military. It was presumed that there would
be time for politics when the three-month war was concluded.
Peacemaking and the resumption of discussion on domestic issues
could then be the proper business of reactivated politicians.

   As the war continued beyond its anticipated duration, Parliament reconvened in late December, 1914, and politics of a sort
revived. Basic unity prevailed, however, and the monarchist, clerical,
aristocratic, authoritarian right scarcely clashed with the republican,
anticlerical, bourgeois center and left over prewar issues. Nor did
the proletarian, socialist left attempt to take advantage of the war
to plague the propertied classes with a serious threat of class warfare
or revolutionary overthrow of the government. Those leaders who

were attracted to an imitation of the Bolshevik Revolution found few followers among the French wartime public. Despite the replacement of Premiers in 1915 and 1916, the SFIOs remained in the government until late 1917. Then, however, the revival of peace talk and the lure of revolution *à la russe* caused their withdrawal from Paul Painlevé's cabinet. The SFIO declined Clemenceau's invitation to join his government in November, 1917, confirming the dissolution of the *Union Sacrée* for the remainder of the war.

Only within the SFIO, and then not until 1917, did there develop a sizeable faction that disclaimed the war and plumped for peace at any cost. The small Radical coterie of Caillaux were peacemongers, but their approach was limited to attempts to seek negotiations with the Austrian, not German, member of the Central Powers. The politics of 1915–1918 involved not primarily war or peace, but rather the dispute between parliaments and governments for control of the war effort and the definition of civilian and military authority and jurisdiction.

After the reconvened Parliament met for its regular session in January, 1915, the members began to reverse the 1914 tendency of allowing free rein to the cabinet and High Command. Instances multiplied of deputies criticizing and interpellating ministers. Demands mounted for parliamentary committees to have authority over executive decisions on the preparation for and conduct of the war. Individual deputies, often soldiers and parliamentarians at the same time, appeared at the front to observe and report back on military operations. War Minister Millerand and Commander-in-Chief Joffre resisted with only varied success the efforts of the parliamentary committees to influence strategy, discipline, and treatment of the troops, war production, censorship, propaganda, and almost any other question dealing with the organization of the nation in arms. And what question did not?

Parliament asserted itself, too, by overthrowing several governments between 1915 and 1917. By the end of October, 1915, Prime Minister Viviani was replaced by Alexandre Ribot. Ribot's tenure of six months was followed by a term of two months for Paul

Painlevé. It is true that the *Union Sacrée* persisted despite the reshuffling of ministers, but with Painlevé and his November, 1917, successor, Clemenceau, the SFIO withdrew. With Clemenceau as Premier, Parliament was obliged to relax its grip on the executive. The deputies continued as legislators and critics, but Clemenceau rode roughshod over attempts to interpellate or challenge his ministers.

The 1915 reversal of the 1914 practice of civil subservience to the military was manifested, as stated above, by increased parliamentary invasion of the presumed prerogatives of the High Command. By 1917, dissatisfaction with Joffre's military performance and his offhand attitude toward the civilian branch resulted in his loss of command. The deplorable failure of General Nivelle, combined with the outbreak of the mutinies of 1917, led the government to name Pétain as chief. With the advent of Clemenceau to the premiership, parliamentary tampering with the High Command diminished. The generals, however, had only exchanged civilian masters. For, Clemenceau, fusing the offices of War Minister and Prime Minister in his own person, scrutinized carefully all the actions of the military. He imposed his will on Pétain even in the matter of the training of the troops. When he named Ferdinand Foch to the position of coordinator of the Inter-Allied Command in France in March, 1918, Clemenceau shielded both Foch and Pétain from parliamentary interference without easing his own control over the two generals. Clemenceau's well-known comment that war was too important a matter to be left to the generals proclaimed his staunch maintenance of civilian authority over political, diplomatic, and even military affairs.

Peacemaking scraped away the thin veneer of inter-allied unity and domestic solidarity in France. The common goal of victory had been achieved. The issue of the moment shifted to the framing of a peace treaty appropriate to the concepts of the respective negotiators. A new problem meant a new orientation – both in the relations among the powers and the relations among the political groups in France. In the effort to draft a lasting peace treaty and to secure the interests of state for France at war's end, Clemenceau found himself at increasing odds with Woodrow Wilson and Lloyd George, as well as with the ultra-nationalist French right and the socialist, internationalist left.

Accentuating and in great part accounting for the emerging peace-table conflict between France and her wartime allies was the sharp difference in the losses sustained by France. Charges against the French of vindictiveness toward Germany and of lack of co-operation with the Allies must be evaluated in light of war casualty statistics offered by the United States War Department (see Table 5–3).

Table 5–3. Casualties of Selected Belligerents in World War I *

	Killed and Died	Wounded	Prisoners and Missing	Total Casualties	% of Total Mobilized Forces
France	1,357,800	4,266,000	537,000	6,160,800	73.3
British Empire	908,371	2,090,212	191,652	3,190,235	35.8
Italy	650,000	947,000	600,000	2,197,000	39.1
United States	126,000	234,300	4,500	364,800	8.0
Germany	1,773,700	4,216,058	1,152,800	7,142,558	64.9

* These figures are available in most encyclopedias and almanacs.

The enemy, Germany, persumed the guilty party by all the victorious powers and by many of the defeated ones, had suffered fewer proportional casualties than the French. The British rate was less than half the French. If the more populous United States had sustained human losses comparable to the French, it would have counted more than 4,000,000 dead instead of 126,000 and more than 12,000,000 wounded instead of 234,300.

Awareness of the stupendous material and human losses also conditioned the attitudes of the peacemakers of 1919. To represent the costs of the 1914–1918 war in terms of goods and services that might have been provided in lieu of military expenditure and damages, it has been estimated that each family in the United Kingdom, the United States, France, Belgium, Germany, Russia, Canada, and Australia could have been provided, in 1934 dollars, with a $2,500 house, a $500 five-acre lot, and $1,000 worth of furniture. Each community of 20,000 people in each of the named countries could also have constructed a $5,000,000 library and a $10,000,000 university. Furthermore, a fund could have been established, the 5 percent interest of which could have provided annual grants of $1,000 each to 125,000 teachers and 125,000 nurses. With the remaining capital, every piece of property and all the real wealth in France and Belgium could have been purchased at a fair market price.

In these losses, as in the human ones, the French claimed to have suffered enormously and disproportionately. Not only had the military effort of the nation-in-arms been onerous, but a substantial portion of French territory had been devastated as a theater of operations and milked as a zone of occupation. The debilitating effect of the war on the French economy may be appreciated by reference to the "balance sheet" drawn up by Shepard B. Clough in his *France: A History of National Economics, 1789–1939.*[1]

French policy at the Paris Peace Conference was based not only on the bitter remembrance of things past but also on fear of the future. Separated from a possibly vengeful enemy by neither a channel nor an ocean, the French were alarmed at the prospect of a Germany with territory, population, and resources far exceeding their own. How to resolve the problem of French security evoked many and contradictory proposals. Secret treaties negotiated and signed by France, Great Britain, Russia, and Italy were apparently a better barometer of official French attitudes than was the lip service paid to Woodrow Wilson's Fourteen Points. While the enemy was in possession of French soil and British and American support was essential, the differences over peace aims among the Allies were muted. With the collapse of the German military machine and the shift from military to diplomatic problems, the differences between the French and Anglo-American position became sharp and public.

For most but not all Frenchmen, long-term security seemed to

[1] See Clough, pp. 292–93.

be attainable through the imposition of terms that would reduce Germany to a size and power the French could dominate. Restore Alsace-Lorraine to France. Detach from Germany the strategically and economically important Rhineland, Saar, and Silesian areas. Prevent any consolidation of Germany with the truncated Austrian state. Encircle Germany with new states such as Poland and Czechoslovakia, which would have the interest and ability to check any resurgence of German strength. Strip Germany of her colonial possessions. Saddle the Germans with heavy reparations, partly to help pay for the reconstruction of devastated northern France and partly to drain Germany of the capital necessary for rebuilding a base for waging modern war.

These French demands at Paris ran counter to much of the spirit and intent of Woodrow Wilson's Fourteen Points. Despite the American President's sympathy for ravaged France, despite his highly moralistic tone toward the "war guilty" Germans, Wilson would or could concede only partially to French interests. Accordingly, Germany should bear the onus of responsibility for the war and make reparations for damages, Germany should return Alsace-Lorraine, Germany should disgorge non-Germans to newly created nationality based states on her frontiers, but here his agreement ended. Germany must not lose territory containing a predominantly German population, Germany should not be saddled with an unpayable debt.

Although to a lesser degree than the United States, Great Britain opposed its erstwhile French ally. Hopeful for a share of German colonies, desirous of some reparations, the British nevertheless carried their traditional view of a continental balance of power into the twentieth century. Not wishing to substitute French hegemony of Europe for the German one just checked, the British preferred a territorially viable Germany in the postwar world. The British, more than the French, hoped for an economically sound Germany that could resume trade to British advantage; a pauperized Germany was no proper customer for British goods and services. A Germany already shorn of its fleet and stripped of its merchant marine posed

no immediate or potential threat to British security or interests.
Too weak a Germany provided no check to French dominance over
a "Balkanized" Europe in which Bolshevik Russia was also a
menace.

Faced with a hostile America and a suspicious Britain and
threatened by Wilson's refusal of further financial aid, Clemenceau
was obliged to soften the French hard policy toward Germany.
Alsace-Lorraine would be returned to France, but no further territory would be denied Germany on her western frontier. Instead,
the Saar Basin would be placed under the League of Nations for
fifteen years and then allowed by plebiscite to choose among return
to Germany, annexation by France, or remaining under the League.
France, meanwhile, would have free access to the resources of the
rich Basin. The Rhineland would remain German, but would be
permanently demilitarized and temporarily occupied by Allied
forces. German losses in the east were more substantial, in deference
rather to the principle of national self-determination than to the
dismemberment aspirations of the French. A corridor to the sea,
separating East Prussia from the main body of Germany, as well
as a sizeable sector of Silesia, was awarded to Poland. Germany was
denied in perpetuity the right to unite with Austria. German disarmament, stipulated as a prelude to general disarmament, was to
be accomplished by reducing her military establishment to one
hundred thousand professionals and by depriving the reduced army
of tanks, airplanes, and heavy matériel. Ruled out, too, was a fleet.
Germany would be obliged to make reparations, but the peacemakers could not arrive at a specific figure and left the amount to
be assessed later by a special commission. The enforcement of these
provisions was added to the other functions of the League of Nations. Such were the compromises reached at the Paris Peace Conference; such were, in essence, the terms of the Treaty of Versailles
that was imposed on the powerless Weimar Republic in June, 1919.

Clemenceau had chosen, if indeed he had a real choice, to
retreat from his original position and accept less than his initial
demands. Allied pressure and his own evaluation of French interests

provided the reasons for his "abdication." Wilson had cajoled and threatened, but Clemenceau independently realized that France alone could not long contain Germany. Instead of alienating the Allies by insisting on the dismemberment of Germany and on tangible material gains for long-term security, Clemenceau preferred to seek compensation by Anglo-American commitments to France for the postwar era. The French Premier thus obtained a draft tripartite agreement from Wilson and Lloyd George by which the United States and Great Britain pledged automatic aid if the integrity or security of France was subsequently menaced by Germany.

Peacemaking further upset French domestic unity, already disturbed by war's end. Clemenceau's revised approach to the French security problem roused the fury of the right and left. The right desired no departure from or concessions on the original hard line toward Germany. Only extensive German territorial losses and the application of harsh military and economic measures would keep the peace and guarantee French security. Clemenceau's concessions were denounced by men like Foch, who saw no safety for France unless, for example, the Rhineland was detached from Germany. Distrustful of the League of Nations as an effective instrument for promoting security, scornful of paper agreements by the Anglo-Saxon powers, the French right ranted against the "sell-out" by Clemenceau.

The socialists, on the other hand, suffered double disillusionment. Pinning their hopes for a lasting peace not on the traditional methods proposed by the right, but rather on the basis of no annexations and the scrupulous allowance of national self-determination of European and even colonial peoples associated in a strong League of Nations, the socialists had been enthusiastic over the apparent idealism of Woodrow Wilson. Clemenceau's refusal to bend sufficiently to this view angered the socialists. The American President's own backsliding participation in secret bargains, exceptions to principle, and framing a weak League left the socialists with no advocate for their approach to ensuring French and, they claimed, European and world interests.

By parliamentary maneuvers and by arguments to the deputies that the Treaty of Versailles represented the best France could obtain under the circumstances, Clemenceau induced the reluctant Parliament to ratify the Treaty by mid-October, 1919. The war was over, the peace was concluded, but the French, in facing the future, would bear the indelible mark of their wartime experience and its effects.

World War I has frequently and properly been portrayed as having had a shattering impact on the historical development of Europe and, indeed, the entire world. The outbreak of the Bolshevik Revolution, the coming of Italian Fascism, the advent of Nazism, the appearance of a world-wide depression, and other phenomena were certainly by-products of the 1914–1918 war. Without denying the cataclysmic and pervasive effects of the war in France, it seems to have produced less drastic political, economic, social and cultural changes there than elsewhere. The war, in fact, seems more to have accelerated than initiated change.

The French parliamentary system had survived the strains and stresses imposed on it by the urgent demands of the nation in arms. The exercise of executive power, the controls, regulations, impositions, and censorship by the wartime governments had probably not exceeded the needs of the moment or undermined loyalty to republican forms. The spirit of nationalist fervor had, on the contrary, smoothed prewar frictions and rallied erstwhile antirepublican elements. French aristocrats, clergy, and military men made their peace with the once-detested "slut" of a Republic. Despite the emergence of the Bolshevik faction in the socialist camp, the majority of the left was still willing to work within the parliamentary system to achieve antibourgeois goals.

Unquestionably heavy financial burdens were placed on France by the costs of war and devastation. The hitherto inconceivable level of the public debt and the anticipated charges for recon-

Changes not drastic

struction would nevertheless be borne without utterly ruinous results. The step-up in industrialization, greater use of women in the labor force, and the increased demands of the working population had not radically altered the balanced, small-scale French economy, whether in the industrial, commercial, or agricultural sector.

In many respects, the war and the peace settlement enhanced the international status and power of France. Germany had been eliminated for the moment as a military force, saddled with a heavy burden of reparations, shorn of territory and resources; Russia was in the throes of civil war, beset by foreign expeditionary contingents, and deprived of Baltic and Eastern European lands; the United States was soon to withdraw into a self-imposed isolation; Great Britain was detaching herself from the close ties to the continent necessitated by the war; and Italy was politically and economically a shambles and ripe for revolution. As a result of the Allied military victory in 1918, the nature of the peace settlement of 1919, and the policies or problems of other major powers, France emerged as the most powerful state on the continent of Europe in the immediate postwar era. Artificial, superficial, or temporary though this supremacy might have been, the fact was incontestable.

Perhaps more difficult to assay is the relationship between the war and the intellectual life of France. At least two questions are involved here. First, what was the reaction of the intellectuals to the war? Secondly, what was the effect of the war experience on intellectual trends and cultural expression? An answer to the first may be offered with more assurance than to the second. The great majority of literary, artistic, and scientific figures deplored but accepted the war as a necessary evil. Such commentators as Georges Duhamel, André Gide, Jean Giraudoux, Marcel Proust, and Jules Romains exhibited varying degrees of dismay and disillusionment with the civilization that produced such a holocaust. A vocal but numerical minority of intellectuals — among whom were Henri Barbusse, Jean Giono, and Romain Rolland — initially or ultimately depicted the war as an unmitigated, unnecessary evil and embraced a militant pacifism.

War's impact on French literature, painting, music, and science seems to have been characterized more by acceleration rather than initiation of change. Nineteenth-century literature, exemplified by the works of Gustave Flaubert and Emile Zola, had already held up to scorn the prevailing bourgeois values, and before 1914 André Gide, Anatole France, and Marcel Proust departed further from traditional mores. Even without the war, the more "formless" ways of Guillaume Apollinaire would probably have emerged. Certainly in painting, the disjointed, distorted, disturbed representations of surrealism during the 1920s was clearly foreshadowed before 1914 by the new cubist-inspired vision of Georges Braque and Pablo Picasso. Igor Stravinsky's musical *succès de scandale* in Paris dated from before the war, and Claude Debussey's atonal scale was no creation of wartime disharmony. The disintegration of the world of scientific matter had also been conceived by Max Planck and Albert Einstein before the world supposedly exploded in August, 1914. Had Sigmund Freud awaited the wartime exhibit of man's aggressive brutality before discerning the thin veneer of civilization and the deeper significance of the unconscious and subconscious in man? To all these and subsequent intellectuals or artists, the war frequently provided a confirmation or substantiation of their already formulated ideas or their already formed visions.

The 1920s' quest for security at home and abroad

THE history of France during the 1920s is characterized by a double quest: a quest for security against defeated but still potentially powerful Germany and a quest for normalcy in domestic politics and socioeconomic affairs. The policies adopted to achieve these goals divide the decade into two nearly equal periods: 1919–1924 and 1925–1929. The elections of 1919 returned a predominant majority of the right to the Parliament for the first time since the

1870s. For the five years of its ascendancy, the *Bloc National* sought to assure French security through punitive and retaliatory measures against Germany. Domestic policy from 1919 to 1924 was marked by a conservative approach to political, economic, and social problems. In 1924, however, the French voters emptied the Chamber of Deputies of the horizon blue, conservative *Bloc National*. The left and center *Cartel des Gauches* (1924–1926) and the more centrist *Union Nationale* (1926–1929) reversed or greatly modified much of their predecessors' foreign and domestic policies. Without abandoning the trumps of military power and tight alliances, the new governments sought to guarantee French security through a rapprochement with Germany, reliance on the League of Nations, and negotiation of collective security pacts. Greater sympathy was also accorded the demands of the labor movement.

The foreign policy formulated and implemented by the *Bloc National* constituted a fairly consistent whole, whether directed by the unrelentingly anti-German, parochially French Raymond Poincaré or by the more supple, more internationalist Aristide Briand. To these statesmen and to the majority of deputies and citizens, France was still in jeopardy. Neither the military victory of 1918 nor the peace settlement of 1919 was considered to have resolved French security problems. Unfortunately for the French, the concessions that Clemenceau had made were drafted into the Versailles Treaty, whereas Wilson's *quid pro quo* of a Treaty of Guarantee had never been ratified by the United States Senate. On impeccably correct grounds of legalism and mathematics, the British had consequently claimed that no Tripartite Pact could be presumed to exist without three parties. Thus, the British, too, reneged on an ironbound commitment to France. Alone, if necessary, or allied, if possible, to smaller European states with similar interests, the French felt compelled to devise a foreign policy to protect themselves against Germany. That the policy of the early 1920s was an intransigent one was due to the nature of the problem, the public temper of the post-Versailles years, and the natural inclinations of the *Bloc National*.

The cardinal and closely interrelated features of French policy included a strict application of the Treaty of Versailles, a strenuous effort to fix and exact enormous reparation payments, and a determined attempt to contain Germany within a ring of states allied to France. In line with the last-named objective, the French capitalized on Belgian fears of German revenge. In 1920, the French procured the willing Belgians' signature to a pact whereby military efforts would be coordinated for mutual defense. Seeking a more substantial bulwark against Germany and deprived of an Anglo-American commitment, the French turned their diplomatic attention to the east. A renewed tie with Russia provided no solution. Russia was torn by civil war and offered little as a military ally. Bolshevism made Russia a social enemy to the *Bloc National* and the new Soviet Union had repudiated the Tsarist debt to France. As a substitute for Russia, the French enlisted the support of the emerging nation–states of Central and Eastern Europe. First Poland, then Czechoslovakia, and the other Little Entente states of Rumania and Yugoslavia became partners in the French venture to encircle Germany with what has been termed a *cordon sanitaire.*

Little Entente interests in French military, financial, and diplomatic connections did not, however, always coincide with the paramount French desire to contain Germany. Poles and Rumanians were often more plagued by fears of Russian aggrandizement or Magyar revival than of German *revanche,* and Yugoslavs felt that they needed support against Italian designs in the Adriatic. The French lent themselves readily to satisfying the anti-Russian motives of Poland not solely, or even primarily, as some observers claimed, to thwart the consolidation of Bolshevism in Russia. An equally impelling motive for French military aid to the Poles in their 1921 campaigns against the Soviets was the effort to guarantee the existence of a strong independent Poland, which could also frustrate potential German resurgence.

More ostensibly repressive of Germany during the 1919–1924 period was the French occupation and reparation policy. According to the Treaty of Versailles, the Allies were entitled to occupy German territory west of the Rhine for a fifteen-year period. Further-more, Germany was obliged to demilitarize permanently the occupied area as well as a zone fifty kilometers east of the Rhine. No fortifications, no garrisons, no military establishments whatso-ever were to be permitted in this sector. The presence of token Brit-ish and American troops among the Allied Occupation Forces did not conceal French predominance in numbers and authority in this operation. The French were able to maintain a substantial portion of their army at German expense. The German burden of occupa-tion costs was made more distasteful to race-conscious Germans by the assignment of French colonial regiments in the Rhineland. Scrupulous enforcement of treaty provisions was demonstrated in 1920 when the German government dispatched troops into the in-terdicted zone to quell civil disorders. The French retorted with a trans-Rhine investiture of the Frankfurt-Darmstadt area, forcing withdrawal of German troops.

Behind the shield of the occupation army, French officials at-tempted to secure a goal not obtained at the peace table: detachment of the Rhineland from Germany. Cultural missions were founded and fed. Pro-French and separatist newspapers, periodicals, and pamphlets were subsidized. Local separatist organizations were en-couraged and supported financially. These French endeavors to foster an autonomous Rhenish state were demonstrably unsuccess-ful. Too often half-hearted in their program, the French failed to elicit widespread popular support for their puppets. In fact, more resentment than sympathy was aroused. British and Americans joined the Germans in decrying the overt and covert activities of the French.

Similarly sharp reaction by the Germans, British, and Americans greeted the unfolding reparations policy of the French. For the French, reparations could be used as a two-edged sword, one side cutting the Germans back from rebuilding an industrial wherewithal to prepare for military resurgence, and the other slashing down the costs to the French taxpayer of reconstructing the devastated north-ern departments. To complicate the latter aim, the government had engaged in fiscal acrobatics. During the immediate post-Versailles era, the French did not await the flow of German reparations in order to begin reconstruction. Rather, special agencies were created to direct and finance the restoration of roads, railroads, mines, factories, and dwellings. These outlays were reported in a separate "extraordinary" budget hopefully to be balanced by reparations payments. The ordinary expenses of government were already swollen to the point of threatening further inflation and trouble for the franc. If the French taxpayer and bondholder had also to liquidate the "extraordinary" public debt, catastrophe might ensue.

In the pursuit of French interests, in spite of German difficulties or recalcitrance, and in the face of mounting Anglo-American hostility, the French government pressed the Germans hard on the reparations issue from 1919 to 1924. The Treaty of Versailles had set a May, 1921, date for the assignment of the precise amount of reparations due from Germany. The Reparations Commission, one month before its deadline, announced 132,000,000,000 marks ($33,000,000,000) as the total due. The enormity of the imposition was somewhat hypothetical, however, since the amount was divided into three categories for payment. One third of the total, or $12,500,000,000 was lumped into Schedules A and B, which the Germans were to begin paying immediately and regularly over an extended period. The other two thirds was put in a third category (Schedule C) of German obligation, to be considered at an unspecified future date. The French share in the reparations had been designated in 1920 as 52 percent; the British, 22 percent; the Belgians, 8 percent; and the Italians, 10 percent.

Even before the reparations figure was fixed, however, the Germans were obliged by the Armistice agreement and the Treaty to begin payments in kind. Timber, coal, locomotives, freight cars, trucks, and other items were delivered to the French and Belgians in addition to the German support of Allied occupation costs. To encourage the hesitant Germans to ship coal to the west, an agreement was made in 1920 to award a five gold mark premium per ton.

On the cessation of the premium, the coal deliveries ceased, implying ability to produce and deliver but political or psychological resistance. When, later the following year, the Germans balked in
negotiations for a final reparations figure and cut off timber shipments, the French had them declared in default and temporarily
occupied some trans-Rhenish towns including Dusseldorf. Again,
in 1921, the Germans refused to transfer immediately a requested
1,000,000,000 gold marks. The French countered with the occupation of an otherwise unoccupied area of the Ruhr and obliged the
Germans to borrow abroad to meet the demand.

By 1922, the French despaired of Prime Minister Briand's policy
of the cudgel and the carrot to secure a smooth flow of reparations.
Nor did Briand's diplomatic activities with the British seem to produce sufficient support for French interests. The stick was not stout
enough for the *Bloc National;* the British tie was not worth the concessions. Briand was replaced by Poincaré in August, 1922. Within
a year, the new Premier's reparations policy led the French into an
"invasion" of the Ruhr and a head-on collision with the British.
If the French between 1919 and 1922 had harassed and nagged the
Germans to secure payments in kind or in gold, Poincaré would
now pursue an unrelenting quest for payments. Easily able to mus-
ter a majority on the Reparations Commission, he had Germany
declared in default in December, 1922, and made subject to seizure
of "productive guarantees." According to Poincaré, the only way
the Germans could be made to assume their obligations seriously
and to meet their debts regularly was for the Allies to show firmness
in their intentions to collect. This firmness could be best manifested
by investing the Ruhr with technicians, supervisors, and economic
management specialists. Some troops would, of course, be necessary
to protect the corps of technicians that was to direct the production
and flow of German goods into reparations channels.

In many respects, Poincaré's occupation of the Ruhr was eminently successful and not the failure so frequently depicted. By late
summer, 1923, the French were in control of German productive
facilities, which were punctually delivering goods according to the

reparations schedule. The cost of French success, however, was pro-
hibitive both to the French themselves and to the Germans, for the
Germans, incapable of military countermoves, had engaged in passive resistance. Spontaneous at first and then organized and subsidized by the government, German workers and trade unions
wielded the strike and slowdown as weapons; the government un-
leashed the printing press. The mark, a much-depreciated currency
even before 1923, became utterly worthless by August, 1923. Passive
resistance had led to financial disaster. The French franc, too, became further weakened by the high costs of the Ruhr invasion. If
the Germans realized that concessions to the French in reparations
were essential, the French observed that their punitive action was
wrecking their own currency, to say nothing of their relations with
Great Britain and the United States. Poincaré and the *Bloc National*
encountered mounting opposition at home, too, culminating in repudiation at the polls in the elections of 1924. Despite their technical success in the Ruhr invasion, the French were thus pressed to a
more accommodating attitude toward Germany.

The Ruhr episode represented the high-water mark of the punitive French policy toward Germany and helped usher in a period of
conciliation, rapprochement, and, to borrow a term more popularly
used for the 1930s, appeasement. From 1924 to 1929, Aristide
Briand led the French on a continued quest for security, but with
an emphasis on negotiated resolution of the reparations issue, withdrawal of French occupation forces from the Rhineland five years
in advance of the Versailles stipulation, fostering collective security arrangements embracing a willing Germany, and efforts to
strengthen the League of Nations as an instrument of international
peace. That the French, even under Briand, refrained from completely dropping their guard against Germany or absolutely reversing the earlier Poincaré policy was demonstrated by significant
diplomatic and military measures. French connections with the
Little Entente were tightened. Although the army reorganization of
1928 did reduce the term of service to one year, great attention was
paid to the needs of an ever alert striking force (*couverture*) at the

frontier. Furthermore, plans were formalized and legislation introduced for the construction of the Maginot Line.

The retreat from a harsh reparations policy after 1923 was due less to French initiative than to British and American moves. At the official behest of Britain and through the unofficial maneuvers of the United States, an international commission under the American General Charles Dawes was established. Its purpose was to investigate and recommend the measures necessary to regularize payments from financially wrecked Germany to suspicious and fear-ridden France. The reluctant French would be obliged to withdraw from the Ruhr but would be better assured of receiving reparations. The total German obligation of $33,000,000,000 was not reduced, but the payments due would be determined by what nonpolitical economic experts judged the German economy could afford. The Commission anticipated a gradual rise in payments between 1924 and 1929 to a regular figure of $625,000,000 per year. As much through American – and British – loans as through German realization of the need to fulfill her obligations, the tentative, temporary Dawes Plan succeeded in its purpose. From 1924 to 1929, the French received uninterrupted payments in gold and in goods; the Germans were treated to greater but still guarded consideration.

By 1929, a new international commission was called into being. Under the chairmanship of the American Owen D. Young, the reparations issue was even more favorably arranged to Germany's benefit. Whereas Poincaré, whose influence and position were somewhat restored after 1926, preferred placing the Dawes Plan on a permanent basis, the other members of the Commission decided to scale down Germany's annual payments and. for the first time since 1921, reduce the total reparations bill to about $9,000,000,000. Enticed by firm guarantees of Germany's willingness and apparent ability to pay, the French submitted to the American and British pleas. As an added concession to the cooperating Germans, the French offered to withdraw French occupation forces from the Rhineland by 1930 instead of awaiting the Versailles date of 1935.

The reparations issue superficially seemed resolved to the mutual satisfaction of the French and Germans, and the French had even sweetened the lump by extra concessions.

The relaxation of the French reparations stand must be viewed also in the light of the new overall policy the French adopted after 1924 during the ascendancy of Aristide Briand. Freed from the hostile grip of the *Bloc National,* backed by a more internationally minded *Cartel des Gauches,* and supported by more sympathetic public opinion, which he carefully and dramatically cultivated, Briand directed French policy toward a peace through conciliation of Germany, collective security, and international cooperation. Neither were all his efforts crowned with success, nor were all his successes pure examples of sweet French charity to Germany or disinterested recommendations for League of Nations' revision.

Along the last-named path – League revision – Briand and other French statesmen stumbled badly. Despairing of containing Germany permanently by their own efforts, the French devised a scheme to strengthen the League as an agency for general security purposes as well as for specific checks on Germany. According to the proposals in the Geneva Protocol of 1924, not only would all nations be obliged to submit disputes to arbitration, as was already provided in the League Covenant, but acceptance of all decisions made by international tribunals in such disputes would become compulsory and binding on the states involved. Any state disregarding the verdict, as well as any state breaking existing international law and engaging in hostile acts, would be automatically considered an aggressor. As such, it would be subject, also automatically, to retaliation by the complete military and economic resources of the League's members. The League, it is true, would have been converted into a powerful organization for keeping the peace, but the Protocol smacked too loudly of French self-pleading, since keeping the peace seemed tantamount to maintaining the status quo of the 1919 peace settlements. Furthermore, the British especially were reluctant to yield to international bodies the decisions traditionally reserved for Parliament on issues of war or peace. Imperial connec-

tions, too, might be jeopardized by such automatic, mandatory operations as envisioned by the Protocol. By the end of 1924, it was evident
that British opposition would block the French proposals for a re-en-
forcement of the League. The French adoption of a more conciliatory German policy stemmed perhaps only in part from positive
principles espoused by the Briand coterie. Conciliation was possibly
merely the result of finding every other path to security filled with
insurmountable obstacles.

Whether pursued for the sake of expediency or lofty ideals,
Briand's new course was charted and followed with vigor and delicacy and a publicity Madison Avenue might envy. Locarno represented Briand's most promising achievement. Months of intensive
and principally secret diplomatic preparations by the French with
Britain, Germany, and Italy led to Briand's October, 1925, meeting
with Gustav Stresemann of Germany and England's Austen Chamberlain in the picture-postcard Italian resort of Locarno. Through
the press, the French public was regaled with an unending scene of
idyllic gatherings of the statesmen and the entourage who were de-
signing in tranquility and harmony the subsequent tranquility and
harmony of Europe. Yesterday's enemies dined and wined as friends.
While the newspapers printed astutely released human interest accounts and Jean Giraudoux wrote of the happy dialogue of *Sieg-
fried et le Limousin*, treaties were drafted to bring into international
law this wondrous reconciliation of the French and the Germans.
The two chief signatories guaranteed the integrity of each other's
territory in western Europe of their free and good will. The German
government relinquished any desire it might have had to revise the
Versailles frontier with France and Belgium. France renounced any
rights it might have assumed to tamper with the Germany of 1919.
The Rhineland and the Ruhr would be inviolably German. Having
so accommodated each other, the French and Germans were rewarded by receiving a written guarantee of automatic aid from
Great Britain and Italy should the pact be broken. Briand had
hereby executed a double coup for the French. Germany had willingly promised to respect French integrity and Britain had been

inveigled into a firm commitment to French interests. Less definitive were the arrangements made at Locarno in respect to Eastern
Europe. Briand could not induce Stresemann to forego expansionist
aspirations for the eastern frontiers of Germany. Stresemann would
and did agree to submit to nonaggression pacts with Poland and
Czechoslovakia, promising to submit to arbitration any subsequent
territorial claims against the new states.

Locarno contained more than territorial guarantees. Germany
was granted not only the right to seek admission to the League of
Nations, but also the right to a permanent seat on the Council of
the League. Might not the Germans be mollified by this apparently
generous re-acceptance into the family of nations and perhaps even
be more strictly bound by their entry into the League to maintain
the strictures of the Treaty of Versailles?

More elusive although surely more sensational than the many
treaties that emerged from Locarno was Briand's 1928 drafting of
a general international peace pact. The Kellogg-Briand Pact, ultimately ratified by almost all the world powers by 1929, made excellent newspaper copy with such stipulations as renouncing war as an
instrument of national policy. Briand, however, failed in his efforts
to include more specific definitions of offensive (and banned) wars
as against defensive (and acceptable) military action. The Kellogg-
Briand Pact, like the Locarno agreements, was part of a trend toward collective security arrangements — in which potential enemies,
rather than exclusively allied states with a common enemy, associated in promising nonaggression upon the cosignatories. The
1930s more than the 1920s, however, would be more afflicted with
what one historian has diagnosed as pactomania.

Pacts of good will, reliance on German pledges, and concessions
to Germany were not the sole pillars of French security even during
Briand's days of dominance from 1924 to 1929. Diplomatic and
military measures were devised or extended to insure France and
Europe against possible German resurgence. On the diplomatic
level, the French were still unable to come to terms with the Soviet
Union, whose Bolshevik leaders could not be convinced of the bour-

geois virtues of settling the enormous Tsarist debt to France. Neither had the accord reached by Russia and Germany at Rapallo in 1922 dispelled French suspicions of the two pariahs of Europe. The French, therefore, treaded the path already blazed of ties with the new Polish state. Increased financial, technical, and military aid flowed into the attempt to build a bulwark against Germany. An alliance was also formed with Czechoslovakia in 1924, supplemented a year later with a promise of armed assistance in the event of German attack.

Less directly aimed at Germany were the French treaties concluded with the remaining Little Entente states of Rumania and Yugoslavia, whose interests were primarily jeopardized by a possible restoration of Hapsburg power. The Little Entente had already been formed in 1921 against such a danger, while French policy was still ambivalent on the Danubian question. The French allied with Rumania in 1926 but begged off any promise of support for that state against Russian claims to Bessarabia. A similar treaty with Yugoslavia in 1927 seemed as much designed to check Italian ambitions along the Danube and in the Adriatic as to blunt German thrusts toward Austria and Hungary. By these various negotiations, the French had created a *cordon sanitaire* around Germany. In some respects, this belt of states might also act to insulate Europe from Bolshevik infection or frustrate the ambitions of the blustering Mussolini. The effectiveness of this "French system" would obviously depend on a unity of purpose not clearly evident, a coordinated military power not yet developed, and a constant diplomatic effort to keep Germany and Russia or Germany and Italy from forming a common front.

While French diplomats and statesmen occupied themselves from 1924 to 1929 with these numerous schemes of securing France through collective security pacts, the League of Nations, and alliances, French military officials and politicians studied and obtained parliamentary approval for military plans to secure the nation against Germany. The nature of the military establishment as well as the military strategy adopted by the government would obviously help determine the diplomatic stance the French would or could subsequently assume.

Under the leadership of Marshal Pétain, the Army drew up plans for its reorganization and for the Maginot Line. Ministers of War Paul Painlevé and his 1929 successor, André Maginot, steered the army committee's proposals through the Parliament. In 1927 and 1928, the Chamber of Deputies and Senate passed three laws that provided the basis for the army with which France entered World War II. Political and fiscal considerations played a more influential role in framing the basic laws organizing the French army than did the recommendations of the acquiescent military chiefs. Republican fears of a professional army and memories of Boulanger and Dreyfus days seemed still vivid. According to the first of the three laws (July, 13, 1927), troops would be formed into three types of units:

1. training regiments, composed of the recruits and their "professional" instructors;

2. units of maneuver, comprising the men who had completed the first cycle of instruction;

3. cadre units, including only career or professional elements.

The second law (March 28, 1928) established the "Table of Organization" for the French army, detailing the structure of the divisions, regiments, battalions, companies, and platoons of the different branches of service. The third law (March 31, 1928) dealt with recruitment procedures and length of service in the army. By its terms, all able-bodied Frenchmen were obliged to serve for twenty-eight years: one year on active duty, three years in *disponibilité* (inactive but on ever ready alert); sixteen years in the first reserve; and finally, eight years in the second reserve.

By the first of the organic laws, metropolitan France was divided into twenty military regions, each of which would provide one infantry division stationed therein or assigned as part of a covering force (*couverture*) in more vulnerable areas. The French government thus possessed a substantial force that could meet any sudden

German attack but that could not engage in large-scale operations unless the citizens in the alert or reserve categories were summoned. Professionals were scattered throughout the many types of units and could not constitute a single, cohesive praetorian guard to challenge the Republic. The French had created a military instrument that presumably would secure the French against a Germany with a Versailles army of one hundred thousand and would avoid the political danger of the rise of an army dictator at home. The containment of Germany and the fulfillment of French commitments to their European allies were possible, however, only if Germany remained disarmed and only if vigorous French governments were prepared to order mobilization of alert and reserve elements in the event of crises.

In harmony with the underlying strategic premises of this essentially defensive army, whose twenty divisions of *couverture* could nevertheless operate as a strong punitive force if commanded energetically, plans for the Maginot Line also took form during the 1924–1929 period. More than four years of intensive study by military and political chiefs led to the 3,300,000,000 franc appropriations bill finally passed by Parliament in late 1929 and signed into law on January 14, 1930. The rationale behind the construction of the Maginot Line well illustrates the direction of the French quest for security during the late 1920s. The anticipated role of the Line had significant implications for the military and diplomatic alternatives available to the French during the 1930s. Proponents of the Maginot Line used as arguments the geographic "deficiencies" of the French frontiers, the location of French industry in vulnerable areas, demographic inferiority vis-à-vis Germany, fear of sudden German attack, and the projected evacuation of the Rhineland. The recommended form of the defensive organization of the frontiers was determined by the French reading of the lessons of World War I and the military strategy largely based on the French experience during 1914–1918.

Although during the 1930s the little-known Captain Charles de Gaulle came to different conclusions from his graphic description

of French geography, he was quick to point out the defensive deficiencies of his country's frontiers. Well-shielded by the Pyrenees
and the Alps along its southern and southeastern borders, the nation was unevenly and poorly protected from Switzerland to the
North Sea. The Rhine, the Vosges, the Moselle, and the Ardennes
formed only feeble barriers to potential German thrusts. From
Luxembourg to the English Channel, the relatively open, flat terrain offered an ideal avenue for invasion. Fortifications, according
even to de Gaulle, could be efficacious as a geographic corrective to
enhance the value of those features cited along the Franco-German
border.

Focus on the frontiers was not merely based on sentimental
attachment to the sanctity of French soil. The natural and industrial resources of France were located in close proximity to these
borders. And, had not the First World War taught the urgency of
reserving for the nation in arms every mine and factory for the
monumental effort of twentieth-century war?

A deteriorating demographic position also served to frighten
the French and to increase their insistence on compensatory measures. A double crisis was foreseen for the 1930s requiring action
in the 1920s. On the one hand, the recruitment law of 1928 had
reduced the term of active service to one year, sharply diminishing
the number of men available to the army at any one time. Worse
still, there lay ahead the *années creuses* – those years in which the
falling birthrate of 1914–1918 would be reflected in a great diminution of conscripts for the years 1935–1939. The gravity of the
situation was statistically demonstrated in a table of potential
military manpower (Table 5-4), which was submitted in 1927 to
the French parliament.

To enable 40,000,000 Frenchmen to withstand 70,000,000 Germans, fortifications were pressed on the Parliament. Construction
was declared mandatory before the "hollow years" of 1935–1939
arrived.

The urgency of establishing the Maginot Line during the late
1920s stemmed also from a recurrently expressed fear of an *attaque*

Table 5–4. Potential Military Manpower (1927–1941) *

Year of Birth	Army Class	No. of Births	Average No. of Effectives Available to the Land Army
1907	1927	421,000	258,000
1908	1928	431,000	265,000
1909	1929	418,500	257,000
1910	1930	419,500	258,000
1911	1931	405,500	251,000
1912	1932	407,500	252,000
1913	1933	407,500	252,000
1914	1934	375,000	226,000
1915	1935	245,000	145,000
1916	1936	195,500	112,000
1917	1937	200,500	122,000
1918	1938	240,000	141,000
1919	1939	258,000	162,000
1920	1940	427,000	260,000
1921	1941	416,000	251,000

* "Tableau B indiquant le nombre des naissances et les effectifs à l'armée de terre," *Journal Officiel, Chambre des Députés, Documents,* 1927, p. 1043.

brusquée – a sudden attack of extreme intensity by a German striking force of small but powerful units. Almost paranoiac distrust of the Germans, despite their peaceful protestations to Briand and the League, led the French seriously to envision a lightning attack in retaliation for 1918. No exaggerated alarmist, Painlevé warned his countrymen that French soldiers might have to defend the nation against "an enemy who would have chosen the hour and the place, have trained and selected his men, and secretly accumulated his means." [2] It was claimed that only the maintenance of a vigorous French army and a strong frontier organization could discourage German hopes for a successful attack on France.

Directly allied to the argument for fortification as a shield against an *attaque brusquée* was the realization that the occupation of the Rhineland could not continue indefinitely. French interest in this regard had been most clearly stated by Marshal Foch ten years earlier in a note of his to the peacemakers of Paris. Foch ominously predicted that,

[2] Paul Painlevé, *Paroles et Ecrits,* published by La Société des Amis de Paul Painlevé (Paris: Rieder, 1936), p. 389. Translation by the author.

If we do not hold the Rhine in a definitive manner, there will be no neutrality, disarmament or written clause of any nature whatsoever that can prevent Germany from taking possession of the Rhineland and issuing forth from it with advantage. There will be no adequate aid arriving in time from England or America to avoid disaster on the northern plains, to spare France complete defeat or the obligation to withdraw her armies . . . without delay behind the Somme, the Seine, or the Loire in order to await re-enforcements from her allies.

The Rhine remains today the indispensable barrier for the safety of the people of Western Europe, and hence of civilization.[3]

By evacuating the Rhineland in 1930 in accordance with the Young Plan, the French lost an allegedly indispensable barrier to German aggression. An accelerated program of fortification was insistently urged on the legislators of 1929.

French military and civilian leaders had produced an impressive rationale for the defensive organization of the frontiers — a rationale that had taken into account such diverse elements as geography and demography, chauvinism and economics. Faced with the bleak prospect of having fewer people to man frontiers that were devoid of natural obstacles, the French turned to "artificial" means of barring any invasion launched by a more populous enemy with superior natural and industrial resources. Despite the emphasis on defensive functions implied in the rationale of the Maginot Line, however, the reader must not be mislead about the role the Line was intended to play. Even the most defensive-minded French strategists recognized the ultimate need for offensive action by French armies to win any war. The fortifications were intended on the one hand to grind to a halt the most weighty onslaught conceivable along the Franco-German border or, on the other hand, to divert an invasion to the Belgian area. French forces, more numerous there because of economies achieved by the Maginot Line, could then meet the enemy in the buffer zone removed from French soil.

Thus conceived, the Maginot Line was predominantly a defen-

[3] Quoted by Maxime Weygand in *Foch* (Paris: Flammarion, 1947), p. 369. Translation by the author.

sive instrument, but, within the context of the grand strategy of the French, the fortifications allowed — in fact, dictated — offensive operations either after a long build-up of French strength or immediately upon a German attack on Belgium. The willingness or ability of the French to devise a military tool appropriate for a threat larger than the one posed by the Weimar Republic was a question not only for the 1920s, but also for the 1930s.

Critics of the Maginot Line have often lamented the French failure to extend the fortifications to the crucial Belgian area. Indeed, if the French anticipated that Germany would be forced to choose the northern route for invasion, why were plans not included for construction of the Maginot Line from Luxembourg to the North Sea? Several reasons were offered. The Ardennes — the woody, hilly, rocky region including parts of Luxembourg, Belgium, and France — was judged by Pétain and others as an impassable, impenetrable zone.[4] From the Ardennes to the Channel, the low-lying, open terrain was considered topographically too difficult or too costly to fortify in a worthwhile manner. There, too, French factories and mines were so close to the frontier that their destruction by German artillery would be inevitable if military operations took place along that border. Protection could be ensured only by French moves deeper into Belgium. Diplomatic considerations also denied the feasibility of fortifications of the northern frontier. Acting on the presumption that fortifications spelled French abandonment of treaty commitments, might not the Belgians make an accommodation with Germany to spare a repetition of the experience of 1914?

Whether labeled as ambivalent and contradictory or as flexible and supple, the quest for French security during the 1920s had led to a diplomatic and military policy of infinite variety. The Poincaré policy of 1919–1923 had been modified but not abandoned completely by the Briand effort of 1924–1929. The French after 1923 may have tempered their anti-German attitude and

---

[4] This judgment would, of course, be regretted by the French in 1940 and by the Americans in the 1944 Battle of the Bulge.

actions in the instances of reparations, Locarno, the League of Nations, and the Rhineland occupation, but there remained more than relics of anti-German feeling and measures in the treaties with Belgium, Poland, and the Little Entente, as well as in the laws passed concerning the army and the Maginot Line.

Like the quest for security abroad during the 1920s, the French quest for normalcy at home exhibited great variety. There nevertheless emerged a similar pattern of initial conservative rigidity yielding later in the decade to more moderate attitudes and policies. The elections of November, 1919, seemed to augur striking departures in French political life. For the first time since the 1870s, an overwhelmingly conservative majority of deputies was seated in the Parliament. Formed into the *Bloc National,* such right and center parties of property as the *Alliance Républicaine Democratique* and the *Fédération Républicaine* swept the field and placed more than 400 members in the 626-man Chamber of Deputies.

Without denying the potency of nationalism and the "Red scare," several factors might be cited to explain or give the lie to the impression that a chastened French electorate had finally embraced the principles of the pre-1914 right. In the first place, the victorious French right of 1919 was not the identical twin of the right of the 1870s. The *Bloc National* was a grouping loyal to republican institutions and not at all inclined to monarchism. The royalist *Action Française* had in fact been excluded from the *Bloc* and received ill treatment at the polls. Neither was the *Bloc* a strictly clerical affiliate. Although more sympathetic to the Church than prewar republican parties, the *Bloc* had nevertheless promised in its campaign to uphold the laic laws. The successful *Bloc* was of the right in its chauvinism, its economic-financial-fiscal orientation, and its virulent anti-Bolshevism.

The failure of the Radical-Socialist Party and the SFIO to halt the tide of the right derived not only from the unpopularity of their platforms, but also from their internal divisions and lack of cooperation. Deeply split at the end of the war, discredited by the questionable or impolitic behavior of some of their leaders, the

Radical-Socialists were temporarily but seriously crippled in 1919. Only about 60 candidates reached the Chamber to which more than 200 had been elected in 1914. To its own disadvantage, the SFIO adopted an electoral tactic of noncooperation with bourgeois parties regardless of certain common interests. The socialists, too, were already racked with tortured internal debate over whether or not to adopt the cause of Bolshevism and the Third International. It was virtually impossible to put forth a united front of their own party, to say nothing of making election arrangements with Radical-Socialists or others. The result was their capture of few more than 60 seats in the Chamber where they previously had more than 100.

The electoral law passed in July, 1919, however, probably accounted as much as other factors for the return of the right and the illusion of a new political world in the making. The socialists, for example, had lost one third of their parliamentary places but had polled 300,000 votes more than in 1914. The new electoral law, in a winner-take-all provision, awarded all the seats to the party or group that secured a majority of the departmental ballot. Proportional representation might be applied, but socialists and Radical-Socialists would have benefited only if they had been willing to combine forces to defeat the more easily coalescing parties of the right and center. For these and other reasons, the election of 1919 did result in the ascendancy of the right, but the victory of the *Bloc National* represented a different right from that of the 1870s and reflected distortedly the French voters' inclinations.

During its five-year tenure in Parliament, from 1919 to 1924, the *Bloc National* revealed its political, social, economic bias through its approach to the many domestic issues facing France in the immediate postwar era: political reform, reconstruction of the devastated regions, the financial dilemma, labor's demands, church–state relations, and the reintegration of Alsace-Lorraine.

Little democratic political reform might be expected from the *Bloc National*. Little was forthcoming. Demands for true proportional representation or for women's suffrage were not heeded. Immediately prior to the election of 1919, the Chamber had passed a bill giving women the vote, but the Senate had withheld its endorsement. Women should release their energies in the kitchen, the bedroom, and the confessional; the polling booth would remain closed until after a Second World War.

If democracy was not extended, the political institutions of the Third Republic nevertheless seemed safe in the hands of the French right of 1919. There was no flirtation with monarchism. There were no attempts to deprive the sovereign assembly of its power, to enhance unduly the power of the executive, or to establish an authoritarian regime in any other way. The *Bloc National* was of the right but not in the royalist-aristocratic-military-clerical sense. This was a businessman's Republic and there seemed no need to change the political system when it was firmly in the hands of the propertied classes' representatives.

If there were few political surprises forthcoming from the *Bloc National*, it must be realized, too, that this group of patriotic and well-meaning deputies lacked experienced leaders. More than half the former Chamber had been retired by the elections of 1919. Clemenceau was shunted aside. The *Bloc* frequently had to rely on politicians not closely tied with it in order to form effective cabinets. The Millerands, Briands, Deschanels, and Poincarés were pressed into service and many of these renowned leaders had come from the ranks of the SFIO or the Radical-Socialists. The political philosophy of these ministers was more attuned to the prewar parliamentary system than to whatever ideology existed in the amorphous right of 1919.

One of the *Bloc*'s most notable achievements was the reconstruction of the devastated regions of France. Already committed to the indemnification of all citizens for losses incurred during the war, the French government itself assumed the responsibility of restoring the road network, bridges, and public buildings. Through the creation of a private joint-stock company fed by public funds and private subscriptions guaranteed by the government, the factories, mines, shops, and residences in the northern departments were replaced or repaired by the mid-1920s.

The financial methods used to accomplish the remarkable feat of reconstruction, however, were less than glorious. We have already observed how the *Bloc National*'s assumption that Germany should foot the bill of war costs had led to a harsh reparations policy. Camouflaged behind the "balanced" 1919 budget of 11,000,000,000 francs expenditures against 13,000,000,000 francs receipts was the "exceptional" outlay of 29,000,000,000 francs that the Germans were expected to cover. Meanwhile, to meet the immediate needs until the Germans retired the "exceptional" budget, the *Bloc National* resorted to the temporary expedient of borrowing. A Bank of France willing to lend to such a "safe" government provided credits; a public with confidence in the *Bloc*'s soundness subscribed to bonds. The public debt, already enormously inflated by wartime obligations, mounted. Where it had stood at 1,500,000,000 francs in 1913, it had risen to 86,000,000,000 by 1921. Retrenchment or austerity was deemed unfeasible; recourse to capital levies or heavy taxation on incomes was inconceivable to the conservative *Bloc*. Additional indirect taxes, the burden of which fell more heavily on the lower classes, were legislated, and the government resorted to the printing press as well in order to service the debt. Pressure increased on the long-declining value of the franc as prices soared in postwar France. The *Bloc* had not really come to grips with the fiscal problem but merely postponed the day of budgetary reckoning.

The rapidly rising cost of living in post-Versailles France and the fiscal policy of the *Bloc* were but two of the factors inducing labor unrest. Before the elections of 1919, the French government had shown some sympathy for labor in the passage of bills for collective bargaining rights and an eight-hour day for workers in industrial and commercial establishments but not in agricultural or domestic employment. With the arrival in power of the *Bloc National*, governmental action against strikes and street demonstrations became more typical. The year 1920 witnessed the repression of the near-general strike that began against the French railways and spread to almost all major industries. The government's use of troops on behalf of the business community succeeded not only in breaking the strike, but also in diminishing the unions' hold over the French worker. To the further dismay of labor, and even of some of the more enlightened entrepreneurs, the *Bloc National* resisted all efforts to enact social insurance legislation so long common in most Western European states.

The plight of labor was the product, too, of its own disarray and its own disagreement on how best to reach a workers' wonderland. The one political party that might have maneuvered in Parliament on labor's behalf was, as noted, beset with internal division since the Bolshevik Revolution of 1917. At the Congress of Tours in 1920, the SFIO formally split. The majority voted attachment to the Soviet-inspired Third International and christened itself the Communist Party of France. The minority, evolutionary rather than revolutionary Marxists, headed by Léon Blum, retained the old party name (SFIO) but lost the treasury, the property, and the newspaper *L'Humanité* to the majority faction. A dozen socialist deputies defected to the new Communist Party, further weakening the parliamentary strength of the socialists. The emergence of a Communist Party in France, dedicated to strict obedience to "foreign" inspiration as well as to intensification of the class struggle, confirmed the fears of the nationalist, conservative *Bloc National*.

This schism was quickly followed by a schism in the trade unions. Instigated only in part by Leninists, a division took place in the *Confédération Générale du Travail* (CGT) in 1921. Unlike the SFIO situation, however, the militants found themselves in a minority when they formed the offshoot *Confédération Générale du Travail Unitaire* (CGTU), which, by 1924, was dominated by the Communists. To compound the confusion and disunity, Catholic trade unions attracted growing numbers of the proletariat in the immediate postwar years. Labor's interests were ill served by the proliferating and squabbling trade unions, which seemed as preoccupied with interunion rivalry as with anticapitalist activity. Labor unrest, however, subsided after 1921 with the full employment and general prosperity enjoyed by the working class.

The founding and flourishing of Catholic trade unions was in-

dicative of the limbo to which the issue of anticlericalism was being relegated in postwar France. Under the auspices of the *Bloc National,* church–state relations rapidly improved. Vastly different from their priest-eating predecessors, the majority of the deputies in the 1919–1924 Chamber were said to be practicing Catholics. Helpful to the rapprochement was the wartime record of Catholics and the presence of more dangerous social enemies. The initiative taken by Presidents Deschanel and Millerand was finally seconded by the Parliament in 1921, when diplomatic relations with the Vatican were restored. By 1924, what remained of Church property sequestered by the state in 1905 was turned over to lay associations similar in form to those demanded by the Separation Bill of 1905 but not hitherto authorized by the Pope. Further than that the Parliament would not go. It balked at bills introduced to give state aid to Catholic schools.

The religious question constituted but one of the difficulties hampering a smooth reintegration of Alsace-Lorraine during the 1920s. A brief but giddy honeymoon in 1919 ended with the realization by the Alsatians more than by the French government that times had changed since their 1871 separation. It was true that Alsatians appreciated escaping their share of the 1871 indemnity by being German and the reparation burden after 1919 by being French. But, the Catholic provinces had also avoided the laic laws of the Third Republic since they were then part of the German Empire. The highly centralizing tendencies of the French educational and administrative systems of 1871–1914 also stood in contrast to the more decentralized, federal experience of the provinces during German rule. For the workers of the industrial provinces, no French social insurance program existed to match that enjoyed since the 1880s' legislation of Bismarck.

The *Bloc National* delayed the division of Alsace-Lorraine into three departments, which would have imposed centralization and direction from Paris. The *Bloc* wisely refrained, too, from revoking the Concordat of 1801 or applying the laic laws in the restored territory. Neither was there decreed immediate and complete conformity in language and other cultural respects. These concessions, although often grudgingly given or only partly executed, reduced some of the friction attendant on the reincorporation of the lost provinces.

General elections were scheduled in France for 1924. The *Bloc National,* never a truly monolithic political force, was opposed by a coalition of center and left parties formed into a *Cartel des Gauches.* Disillusionment with the Ruhr invasion, deepening financial difficulties, and diminution of the Bolshevik peril implied electoral trouble for the conservatives. By their willingness and ability to form electoral combinations and by avoiding the mistakes and divisions of 1919, the SFIO under Blum and the Radical-Socialists under Edouard Herriot improved their chances for gaining seats if not their popular vote. Victory went to the *Cartel des Gauches,* which secured 328 out of 582 seats in the new Chamber. Of these, 103 were socialist, 142 were Radical-Socialist, and the remainder needed for a majority were divided among other center and non-Communist left parties. Excluded from the *Cartel,* the Communists polled nearly a million votes but won only 28 seats, and the disoriented right and center right of the *Bloc National* placed 226 members.

Although the *Cartel des Gauches* initiated and sustained a redirection of French foreign policy, it was eminently unsuccessful in its efforts on domestic issues. The new Chamber of 1924 was able to oust President Millerand in favor of a compromise candidate, Gaston Doumergue, but the campaign promises of the *Cartel* were largely unfulfilled. Precipitate action from which retreat was almost as precipitate was characteristic of the *Cartel's* handling of church–state relations and Alsace. Anticlericalism seemed too weak a tie for the parties of the center and the left. The public was too diffident to support a diplomatic break with the Vatican, a threat to apply strictly the old laws against the religious orders, or a laicization of Alsace-Lorraine. The Church manifested too much goodwill toward the Republic to warrant a return to the harassment of the pre-1914 days. Incredible though it may have appeared to the

French, the Pope himself anathematized the *Action Française,* threating excommunication of Catholics who continued as members of this violently antirepublican organization or who dared read its newspaper. The Pope himself recommended support for programs of social betterment and Briand-like foreign relations similar to those espoused by the *Cartel.* Why distrust this new-found friend of French social republicanism?

It was essentially on financial policy that the *Cartel des Gauches* foundered and finally sank. The decline of the franc was not exclusively the fault of the *Cartel.* Its exchange value had already dropped from five to eighteen to the dollar by 1924. Obviously, the war and reconstruction expenditures as well as the inept, delaying tactics of the *Bloc National* had caused serious fiscal trouble. During the last few months of the *Bloc's* existence, public confidence already seemed shaken and the French failed to subscribe fully to the loan sought by the *Crédit National.* Protests met the *Bloc's* call for indirect taxes, which, although heavy, were nevertheless inadequate to cover the expenses of the Ruhr invasion. With the advent of the *Cartel des Gauches,* monied interests panicked at the mere anticipation of the measures that the leftist Chamber might undertake. In fact, many of the *Cartel's* proposals warranted fear. Capital levies, repudiation of the outstanding public debt, heavy income taxes, runaway use of the printing press — these and other possibilities loomed on the horizon.

Holders of government bonds rushed to cash them in lest there be repudiation or refunding at a confiscatory rate. Subscribers withheld investment in bonds that might become worthless. The Bank of France, after extending heavy credit to the *Cartel,* began to have second thoughts on continuing support by 1926. A capital strike, or, as Herriot termed it, a "wall of money," barred the government's efforts to resolve the financial problem. The franc skidded in value from eighteen to four and finally to two cents. Would the French franc go the way of the German mark?

The "wall of money" had perhaps less to fear in reality than it imagined, for the efforts of more than seven successive finance min-

isters to enact truly radical legislation in less than two years were
frustrated by the Parliament or by the internal divisions within the
Cartel. Either property-conscious factions of the Radical-Socialists
or the conservative Senate prevented passage of socialist-inspired
capital levies or income taxation. The socialists and the Radical-
Socialists in the *Cartel* may have been able to maintain unity on
foreign policy and anticlericalism, but, when the issue of the moment was financial, the harmony disappeared. Other bourgeois parties associated with the *Cartel* in 1924 defected even more readily
when this issue was raised.

Political stalemate and impending financial disaster induced
the French President to call on a broad coalition government (a
Union Nationale) to meet the crisis in July, 1926. No *Union
Sacrée* of 1914, no Popular Front of the next decade, the *Union
Nationale* ranged across the center and right elements with such
figures as Herriot, Briand, and Painlevé teamed under Poincaré.
Benefiting from the frequent practice of according to a sound-
money man the powers denied to radical leaders, Poincaré received
from Parliament those emergency powers that had earlier been refused to the ministers of the *Cartel des Gauches*. Having re-inspired
confidence in the franc by his mere elevation to office, he proceeded
to balance the budget and save the franc by cutting back government
expenses, raising revenues mostly through indirect taxes, and establishing a fund to guarantee bond payments. By these measures and
principally by stabilizing the franc at twenty-five to the dollar, the
French fiscal problem was resolved by 1927. In effect, the French
government was able to discharge its public debt through legalized
but checked inflation. Using the four-cent franc of 1926 instead of
the twenty-cent one of 1914, the state had really repudiated four
fifths of its outstanding debt and made bearable the burden of interest charges in servicing the debt.

With fiscal health restored and with a prosperous economy in
evidence, the French finally instituted a well-developed social insurance program. Deputies of the center and right, who had
previously resisted in principle or in order not to aggravate the

budgetary situation, joined deputies of the left who had long been ideologically in favor, cost what it might. Provision for old-age pensions, accident and death benefits, and allocations for large families became part of the public law as an aid to the workers. Passed before the election of 1928 retired the 1924 Chamber, the legislation was made effective in 1930.

Capitalizing on their financial feat, the parties of the center and right formalized their association as a *Union Nationale* for the electoral campaign of 1928. Without undue difficulty the *Union* defeated the disunited left and secured 320 seats in the new Chamber.

By the end of the 1920s, the quest for tranquility and stability at home appeared to have been as successfully reached as the quest for security abroad. By 1929, the disruptive radical forces of the left and the monarchist right existed only as split minorities, labor tensions had been calmed by full employment and social legislation, church–state relations were nearly idyllic, disorders and protests from Alsace-Lorraine were diminishing, reconstruction of the 1914–1918 damage had been completed, and the economic-financial health of private enterprise and the state was manifestly restored. Euphoria seemed warranted, too, in contemplating the international status of France at the end of the 1920s. Whether through the conciliation or containment of Germany, whether through the Locarno Pact and League of Nations or military alliances and the Maginot Line, the French were convinced that their security had been satisfactorily achieved. The Bolsheviks seemed too preoccupied at home to be able to interfere effectively in a Europe where chastened and superficially prosperous Germans were dominated by a less vindictive France and its Little Entente friends. All was well in the world and all was well in France.

Domestic strife and appeasement without peace: the 1930s

THE euphoria of the 1920s could not long survive the shattering effects of the world depression and the advent of Adolph Hitler. The French response to the double challenge of depression and aggression was feeble and contradictory until the end of the 1930s when the French steeled themselves to the positive but radical and divisive program of the Popular Front and to the final recourse to war instead of appeasement. Further complicating French malaise, measures appropriate to easing the domestic crisis often worked at odds with those feasible and forceful ones needed to stop Hitler. Conversely, a positive policy against Nazi Germany seemed harmful to economic improvement or disruptive of domestic tranquility. Each challenge was in itself awesome; combined, they led the French through a decade of ineffectual, bitterly contested policies culminating in 1940 in the military and political collapse of the Third Republic.

During the 1920s, the economy had made remarkable strides. Not only did it recover by 1926 from the devastation and dislocation of World War I, but also, by the end of the decade, it surpassed most of the records set in the immediate prewar year of 1913. Table 5–5, using the prosperous year of 1913 as a base (100), illustrates the impressive economic growth of France in the postwar decade.

Table 5–5. Postwar Economic Growth

	1919	1926 or 1927
Industrial production	60	125
Railway transport	59	122
Exports	25	166
Imports	87	117

Innovation and the emergence of new industries were as characteristic as mere replacement of destroyed factories. Automobile, chemical, and hydroelectric industries appeared alongside traditional metallurgical and textile complexes in which new techniques and equipment were often introduced. Revival of the craft and luxury trades added to the French ability to sell competitively on the world market. The balance of trade, as indicated in Table 5–5, shifted from the highly unfavorable wartime ratio and that of 1919 to a fruitful one after 1924. The wave of nearly 2,000,000 foreign tourists in 1929 literally flooded France with dollars, pounds sterling, and marks. Agriculture had fared less well, standing at 70 in 1919, rising to 100 in 1925, but dropping to 82 in 1926. If the farm held less and less promise, there seemed sufficient openings in factory and mine for the peasant's son. Full employment was the rule not only for all Frenchmen, but for approximately 2,000,000 foreign workers streaming into France from southern and eastern Europe.

The first dramatic signs of impending disaster did not immediately affect the French economy. The October, 1929, stock market debacle on Wall Street followed by banking failures in Austria and Germany, however, ushered in a world depression from which the French could not remain indefinitely insulated. Balanced though the French economy was in its industrial, craft, agricultural, commercial, and financial sectors, it began to share the fate of other major states by 1931–1932. The serious shrinking of foreign markets for French luxury items as well as for metallurgical and textile products forced cutbacks in France. The volume of foreign trade declined 11 percent in 1931 and 28 percent in 1932 from the 1929 level. The drop in the number of tourists from a spectacular 1,911,107 in 1929 to 944,400 in 1932 dried up a major source of foreign credit and led to drastic losses in tourist-associated enterprises in the hotel, service, transportation, and luxury categories. The American woman's attempt to survive with less perfume and champagne and fewer trips to France obviously affected the Frenchwoman's attempt to survive at all. Agricultural production in the early 1930s remained fairly stable, but the peasant's income was severely reduced as a result of a sharp decline in the prices of his goods.

Unemployment in France mounted appreciably if not as catastrophically as in the more heavily industrialized states of Great Britain, Germany, and the United States. From a ludicrously low figure of 1,000 relief recipients in 1930 (while Britain had about

1,000,000 throughout the 1920s), the official unemployment rolls in France rose to 200,000 in 1932, 350,000 in 1934, and 500,000 a year later.

The tardy arrival of the depression in France and the composition of the Chamber of Deputies elected in 1928 and seated until 1932 largely accounted for the lack of strenuous methods to stem the decline in the economy. The exodus of foreign workers relieved pressure on French laborers. Dangers from budgetary deficits were partly offset by the buoyancy of the franc and the presence of large gold reserves in France. Furthermore, the majority of deputies, grouped initially in the 1928 *Union Nationale* of center and moderate right parties, was highly orthodox in economic doctrine. Despite the innovating recommendations of such men as André Tardieu, the ministries of 1928 to 1932 deemed it unwise or inappropriate to engage the government in a crash program of heavy taxation, devaluation, or pump-priming. Would not the natural laws cure the world economic malaise before France became infected? The answer was in doubt as the voters went to the polls in 1932.

A vague disenchantment with the Parliament's ineffectual administration led to a mild shift of votes to the Radical-Socialist and SFIO camps. Highly reminiscent of the earlier *Cartel des Gauches,* the victors of 1932 secured a majority in the new Chamber by close cooperation in the electoral campaign. As in 1924, however, the electoral marriage soon showed signs of strain as the partners tried to mitigate the effects of the deepening depression on the economy in general and the government's fiscal plight in particular.

At this juncture, the French had several courses open to them to check the downward economic spiral. Taxation to increase revenue, retrenchment to cut expenditures, devaluation of the franc to enable the government to meet its fixed obligations, or borrowing to postpone the decision – these were the chief ways proposed to rectify the growing imbalance of the budget.

The Radical-Socialist and SFIO coalition that had captured the

1932 Chamber was divided within and opposed from without on the efficacy of these solutions. Indirect taxation seemed more consonant to many Radical-Socialists and center right factions than the hikes in the income tax proposed by the socialists. Furthermore, as the socialists themselves recognized, shrinking incomes and the stagnant economy offered less reward to such tax efforts. The problem, too, according to the left, was not to reduce purchasing power, but to increase it to stimulate industry and commerce. The ministries issuing from the 1932–1936 Chamber resisted substantial tax legislation until pressed to it by other forces by 1935. Retrenchment as a policy seemed equally abhorrent to many deputies otherwise supporting the government. Radical-Socialists and more right of center parties urged pruning state outlays by paring down pensions and salaries to civil servants. The SFIO, largely recruited from the ranks of civil servants and teachers, waged a losing battle against the cutbacks finally enacted in 1934. But socialists found themselves in the company of security holders in the "wall of money" in opposing devaluation. Socialists had no desire to be responsible for the national calamity presumably inherent in this action. Too many Frenchmen of all but the poorest proletariat had keen memories of the 1920s and wished no repetition of that experience. Borrowing seemed the only way out of the fiscal impasse.

Raising money by loans principally from the Bank of France was not a simple operation during the early 1930s, however. No more than in 1924–1926 was the Bank generous to coalitions of the left in Parliament. Loans were offered only with the stipulation that the government adopt measures satisfactory to the Bank and its social-class adherents. If the Radical-Socialist ministers and the SFIO deputies desired to avoid bankrupting the state, they were obliged to follow a policy of retrenchment or deflation and refrain from devaluation or confiscatory taxation. Not until the election of the Popular Front in 1936 gave them an apparent mandate would or could the socialists take their revenge against the dictation of public policy by private interests.

The measures taken to halt the more general decline in the

economy reflected an orthodoxy similar to that revealed in meeting the government's fiscal problem. Although some picayune public works were instituted between 1932 and 1936, tariffs, quota systems, and price supports were more the rule than large-scale public works, extensive pump-priming, or nationalization.

In face of the government's halting and demonstrably ineffective socioeconomic policy, the public's increasingly desperate need for radical action and the growing fear of radical change led to a pronounced political polarization. Adding to the economic woes of the government was the emergence of a revitalized right and a massive left, each in its way threatening to transform if not to destroy completely the parliamentary system of the Third Republic.

Among the upper bourgeoisie of bankers, manufacturers, mine owners, and merchants, many dissociated themselves from traditional parties of property that had nevertheless been loyal to republican institutions. Sizeable numbers, but by no means all or even a majority, openly joined or surreptitiously supported groups that leaned toward authoritarian political forms vaguely or closely patterned on Fascist models. The *Action Française,* for example, weakened in previous decades, experienced a revival as it renewed its denunciation of the Republic and the parliamentary regime. The *Camelots du Roi,* composed chiefly of university students (necessarily, at the time, sons of the well-to-do) who sold the newspaper and did street battle as an auxiliary of the *Action Française,* returned to prominence in numbers and violence, which they had not enjoyed since the beginning of the century.

With funds from businessmen inclined to a strong government as a bulwark against radicalism, extraparliamentary, paramilitary organizations of the right proliferated and attracted members from all classes. The roster of such organizations included the *Croix de Feu,* led by the aristocratic Colonel de la Rocque, formed initially as an ex-servicemen's association, and by 1934 manifesting strong antirepublicanism and ambiguously Fascist sentiments; the *Solidarité Française,* a band of malcontents whose fancies of being storm troopers were financed almost exclusively by the wealthy perfume manufacturer, François Coty; the *Jeunesses Patriotes,* one of the competitors of the *Camelots du Roi* for the favors of the generally middle-class youth who was either fearful for his professional and propertied future or was fulfilling his adolescent urge to reform the admittedly corrupt adult world; and the *Francistes,* whose symbol, uniforms, and tactics blatantly resembled those across the Rhine or Alps.

Members of the lesser bourgeoisie often enlisted in company with their social betters in the ranks of these "Fascist Leagues." Many artisans, craftsmen, keepers of small shops, and whitecollar workers in private or state employ were faced with disaster. Their savings, eaten away by the 1920s' inflation and the devaluation of the franc, were near depletion as prices for their goods or salaries for their services dropped. In danger of bankruptcy or unemployment, this sector of the bourgeoisie contemplated with horror being ground into the proletariat. To retain their social status, a corollary often of their occupation, an authoritarian regime held great attraction. Other Frenchmen in the same social strata, reflecting the polarizing effect of the depression, moved in the opposite political direction. The socialists and the Communist Party benefited by persuading many of the lesser bourgeoisie that material and ideological advantages lay on the left. If the upper bourgeoisie held firm or veered to the right in its political sympathies and the lesser bourgeoisie split more substantially between far right and far left, the working class exhibited a natural and overwhelming tendency to return to leftist activism. Both by flocking to the SFIO and the Communist party as well as by returning to the trade unions they had deserted during the prosperous 1920s, the proletariat organized and demonstrated for radical reform.

Where committed at all on socioeconomic questions, intellectuals in university, journalist, literary, and artistic circles began more openly to identify themselves with extremist factions. Often antedating the depression, membership in or fellow-traveling with Communist Party affiliates became *de rigueur* for the majority.

Although some, like Gide, would have only a shortlived flirtation with the left, others held firm to "the God that failed."

Rural France, a traditional bastion of respecters of property, was also subject to the polarization prevalent in the cities. Peasants who had no liking for collectivization of their land or for Soviet-type farm policies nevertheless were more and more attracted by the easy promises of the Communists. Although chained to the cash register, the village grocer's wife, too, might recommend to her husband that he vote for the party that would nationalize big business. The village bootmaker might be diametrically opposed and succumb to the pamphleteering of the right.

A potent element often distorting the social-class alignment in this polarization of the 1930s was nationalism. The siren notes of Marxist-based programs sounded discordant to many bourgeois and even proletarian Frenchmen. Repelled by the internationalist calls of socialists and Communists, many a worker deserted his class brother and many a petty bourgeois found double reasons for joining right-wing groups. Regardless of their apparent economic or social-class interests, professional veterans harked to the right's call for a French solution to the world depression and the ills of industrial civilization. Slogans like "Better Hitler than Léon Blum!" should not be interpreted as the right's desire to submit to Hitler's dictation within France. The adoption of Nazi or Fascist programs and the accommodation of Hitler's or Mussolini's regimes as bulwarks against Bolshevism was not the equivalent of the total surrender of France to the dictators of the right. Even the recrudescence of the anti-Semitism espoused by the French right did not have the same connotation as the rabid persecution across the Rhine.

Whatever the motives and whatever the outcome, the French political scene was marked by extremism in reaction to economic distress and the government's apparent ineffectiveness in easing it. In view of the subversive pressures from the right and left, the Third Republic perhaps deserves more credit than usually accorded it for surviving at all during the 1930s. The Weimar Republic in Germany collapsed, and most parliamentary governments in Central and Eastern Europe succumbed to authoritarian rule long before Hitler overran their frontiers.

In 1934, the airing of the Stavisky scandal brought into the open and accelerated the political polarization of France. During the late 1920s and early 1930s, Serge Stavisky had engaged in numerous financial ventures involving speculative and probably dishonest promotion of stocks and bonds. Frequently investigated by the police and often charged with fraud or misappropriation of funds, he had never been brought to trial and convicted. Connections in the police, judiciary, and even Parliament had apparently shielded him well. In one of its last issues of 1933, a Paris newspaper reported the existence of a warrant for Stavisky's impending arrest. His current difficulties involved an incredibly large flotation of bonds stipulated to be for the backing of the municipal pawnshop of provincial Bayonne. The police search, sensationally covered, especially by the *Action Française*, led to his discovery in the resort town of Chamonix — with a bullet in his head. The official verdict of suicide was derided by the right-wing press, which printed its conviction that Stavisky had been shot to death by the police or other agents of the Republic. Dead, the swindler could not implicate the officials who had aided and abetted his malodorous career. An almost perfect foil for the *Action Française*, the Stavisky scandal could be used to the hilt in attacking the shabby politicians of the Republic. Stavisky's Russian-Jewish parentage was not likely either to escape notice as antiforeign, anti-Semitic grist for the antirepublican mills.

Reacting to the situation in the same foolish, ostrich-like way it had in the days of Panama and Dreyfus, the government of Camille Chautemps refused demands for a parliamentary inquiry. Street demonstrations by the easily provoked *Camelots du Roi*, affiliated with the *Action Française*, were tenderly treated by Chief of Police Chiappe. By the end of January, Chautemps resigned. A worse fate was in store for the succeeding cabinet of Edouard Daladier. After attempting to appease right-wing dissidence by unsuccessful efforts to include that faction's leaders in his cabinet, Daladier was obliged to present a colorless Radical-Socialist government not unlike the outgoing one. Disgusted with the new ministry, the right became infuriated by Daladier's dismissal of the sympathetic Chiappe. The left, too, resented this action of the Premier when it was discovered that Chiappe had been offered the Governor-Generalship of Morocco instead of being forthrightly discharged from government service.

Without contemplating and organizing a coup d'état, several extraparliamentary right-wing groups made ill-coordinated arrangements for protest demonstrations to be held in different sections of Paris on February 6, the first day the new government was to appear in Parliament. The *Camelots du Roi* were less numerous and less the protagonists than the *Croix de Feu* and others of that ilk, but the *Camelots* would be second to none in riot action when the day came. If the Communists had been dedicated to truthful reporting, they might later have been embarrassed by the fact that their own ex-servicemen's association met its scheduled rendezvous, too, and joined the right in the antigovernment fracas of February 6.

By late afternoon on February 6, the various groups began to assemble at their appointed places. The *Croix de Feu* concentrated in the area behind the Chamber of Deputies and filled the Esplanade in front of Les Invalides. Into the unfittingly named Place de la Concorde streamed the other associations. Congestion was heavy enough under normal circumstances as shops and offices closed for the night and their occupants sought their way home by foot or surface transportation across the Place. Police detachments, alerted for the protests, had barricaded the bridge that spanned the Seine in front of the Chamber of Deputies. The right-wing demonstrators, swollen by hordes of curious and circus-seeking Parisians, became more and more excited. Stones, chunks of pavement, pieces of ripped up iron fences were soon being hurled along with invectives against the police. Smoke poured over the scene from a bus set on fire by the crowd. Firemen were assaulted as they tried to put out the fire started by the mob in the Navy Department building facing the Place. In an increasingly ugly mood, the crowd began to rush the police at the barricaded bridge. Having already suffered numerous casualties, the harassed and frightened officers began to fire at their attackers. Not sufficiently armed to overwhelm the police, the mob finally abandoned the effort to cross the bridge and "take" the Chamber of Deputies. By midnight, quiet was restored in the area.

Elsewhere in Paris, the scheduled protests remained within noisy limits. The *Croix de Feu* tired itself out by marching to and fro and shouting oaths but not by what could have been an easy capture of the Chamber of Deputies via the poorly defended side and back streets. Violence took a different form on the following day. Vandals and thieves descended on the shopping district during the evening of February 7 to loot stores and hold up passers-by until the exhausted and disorganized police finally restored a semblance of order.

The immediate political repercussion of the February 6 riots was the fall of the Daladier government. Despite the vote of confidence awarded him on the night of February 6, despite the pleas of socialist leader Blum to refuse acquiescence to the extraparliamentary pressure of the right, Daladier resigned on the morning of the 7th. Daladier was probably correct in his belief that his government could not maintain itself. Would the police continue to keep order for a government that had dismissed its chief? Was the army a reliable force, or had the right infiltrated it? The illustrious Marshal Lyautey had threatened to lead a march on Paris at the head of the *Jeunesses Patriotes* if Daladier did not resign. A new government, formed under former President Gaston Doumergue, embraced all parties except the socialists and Communists.

The street, controlled by the right, had forced out a legally constituted government supported by the center-left majority of Radical-Socialists and socialists. The street had forced the installation of a right-wing government. The Republic was in danger. The socialists announced their intention to join with other non-Communist groups in calling a general strike for February 12. Let the Fascist Leagues be warned. If they attempted to capture the state, they would seize an inanimate body.

Among the Communists, the events of February 6 led to a startling reversal of strategy and tactics. Fresh in their minds was the year-old example of their role in the collapse of the Weimar Republic, whose Nazi replacement boded even worse than the bourgeois republic for the interests of the proletariat, to say nothing of the interests of France (and the Soviet Union). Perhaps the Third Republic, bourgeois though it might have been, was preferable to a Fascist government. Perhaps indiscriminate, irresponsible harassment of all bourgeois parliamentary regimes was a dangerous policy. Perhaps the party of the left had erred in adding to the social strife of February 6 by its participation with the right in the bloody, enervating demonstrations. Whether dictated by the Russian overlords' judgment that the French Republic was worth saving from a Fascist coup and possible Fascist alignment or whether French Communists were now persuaded of the virtues of the lesser evil of the bourgeois regime, the Party switched to a new double line. The Republic was to be defended against the right; the Party was to welcome association with socialist and other non-Communist forces in a formerly anathematized Popular front.

In its shining new role as defender of republican liberties, the Communist Party announced and carried through with vigor its day of violent demonstration on behalf of the Republic on February 9. More importantly, however, the Party chiefs declared their readiness to join in the general strike set by the socialists for February 12. With much misgiving, the socialists responded favorably to the Communists' overtures. Together with some elements of the Radical-Socialists, a united left held Paris in its grip with a gigantic parade. The left had coalesced to warn the government against any abandonment of republican forms and to convince the right of the inefficacy of any coup d'état.

A one-day Popular Front had jelled; a more permanent one was imminent. The SFIO and Radical-Socialists, however, delayed its formalization for more than a year. Socialists still entertained doubts about the Communists' sincerity in their new political, social, and patriotic posture. Only a shade less disdain marked socialist opinion on an alliance with the bourgeois Radicals. But several factors forced the SFIO into the arms of its chief rival on the left and the Radicals of the center. Between 1934 and 1936, the government had allegedly undertaken inadequate measures against the right, leaving the Fascist Leagues as vocally and physically powerful a threat as before the February days. The Doumergue government was accused somewhat unjustly of recommending political reforms that might have allowed a transition to authoritarianism. The government, too, had pursued a woefully inappropriate social and economic course, failing to relieve the average Frenchman of the effects of the depression. Only by participation with the Communists in a Popular Front could the SFIO (and Radicals) envision the perpetuation of republican institutions and the alleviation of economic distress. An alarming intensification of the Nazi threat also must be counted among the elements persuading the SFIO to close ranks with the parties on their flanks.

In an exhilarating July 14, 1935, celebration, the SFIO and the Radical-Socialists pledged their troth to the Communists. Six months later, this Popular Front constructed the platform on which they would all stand in the forthcoming general elections. Published on January 11, 1936, the program revealed both the firm basis on which the Front was founded and the limits of its solidarity. On the one hand, all parties pledged themselves to protect republican liberty, "give bread to the workers, work to the young and a great human peace to the world." On the other hand, these ambitious and glorious goals would be accomplished without "abandoning either their own principles, doctrines or ultimate objectives. . . ." Accompanying this laudatory but hedged campaign promise was a set of precise planks. The most prominent among them dealt with the political laws projected against the Fascist Leagues, whose challenge was probably the firmest link in the otherwise unnatural alliance. Trimming was characteristic of the economic proposals. In obvious deference to the Radical-Socialists, no mention was made of collectivization or nationalization except in the armament industry. Instead, state intervention was proposed to restore the economic well-being of the worker and the peasant without intending grave injustice to the bourgeois citizen. The worker was offered unemployment benefits, cheaper bread, and a reduction of the work week without an accompanying wage loss. For the peasant, farm prices would be re-evaluated from their ineffectively fixed levels of the moment and a government Wheat Office would be established to curtail the alleged evils of middleman operations and to bring an end to disadvantageous speculation. Financial reforms, too, were foreseen, affecting both the tax system and the Bank of France. As for foreign policy, stress was placed on collective security and the League of Nations.

Representing the minimum demands of the Communist Party, the maximum concessions of the Radical-Socialists, and the middling objectives of the SFIO, the Popular Front program of January, 1936, captured the imagination of a great majority of Frenchmen. Here, at last, appeared a dynamic departure for saving the Republic, for checking the deleterious effects of the world depression, and for meeting the threat of a Nazi Germany, which had remilitarized the Rhineland while Fascist Italy was flouting the League over the Ethiopian invasion.

The elections of May, 1936, obtained for the Popular Front a highly deceptive victory. Although the partners of the left won 65 percent of the seats in the Chamber, they had harvested only 55 percent of the popular vote. Electoral combinations in the balloting, more than shifts of votes from the 1932 figures, accounted for the sweeping success in Parliament. The parties to the right of the Radical-Socialists had maintained their more than two million supporters but did not win proportional numbers of seats in face of the interparty cooperation of the Popular Front components on the candidates' lists. The real victor, in number of votes, was the Communist Party, which doubled its 1932 record and reached 1,500,000. Instead of the mere dozen seats in the 1932 Chamber, the Communist Party secured 72. The SFIO held its own by

[handwritten marginal note: in cooperation with other parties, the Com. always seem to come out ahead]

retaining the near 2,000,000 level of 1932 but raising its delegation in the Chamber from 129 to 147. The Radical-Socialists dropped nearly 500,000 votes and saw the number of their deputies shrink from 155 to 109. Despite the left's ascendancy, simple mathematics and the nature of French politics might and later would enable even this Chamber of Deputies to provide governments in which Communists were isolated and socialists and Radical-Socialists were affiliated with center and right parties.

Even before Léon Blum could assume office and attempt to translate into law the campaign platform of the Popular Front, the economic and social situation deteriorated drastically. The desperate and infuriated right urged a repetition – and worse – of the beating Blum had received in February at the hands of *Action Française* followers. Anti-Semitism with a virulence not so manifest since Dreyfus days reappeared in the public press. Wealthy and not so wealthy depositors converted funds into gold and joined those already in possession of bullion in sending their holdings to safer lands. Gold reserves in the Bank of France dropped to a record low. Trouble appeared from other quarters, too. Spontaneous at first and then sometimes directed behind the scenes by Communist or professional agitators, a wave of sit-down strikes inundated France. More than two million workers resisted eviction from their factories, service industries, and department stores. Except for basic utilities and transportation, France was paralyzed by this innovating labor technique.

Immediately on being installed as Premier in early June, Blum attacked the problem of the sit-down strikes by convoking representatives of labor unions and employers' associations. Under his auspices, agreements were reached that gave enormous benefits to the worker. The moribund law of 1919 was revitalized and to its provisions granting full recognition of collective bargaining were added other features protecting labor union activities. Wage hikes roughly averaging 10 percent were also accorded to the workers. From the springboard of these agreements, Parliament acted that very month to legislate further improvements in labor's position:

the forty-hour week at the same pay as previously and the annual two-week paid vacation. To counterbalance some of the increased costs that would thus be incurred by the employers, the government offered subsidies, credit, and certain other aids.

True to its pre-election promise, the Popular Front moved to help the peasant as well as the worker. By creation of a government Wheat Office for fixing prices and quantities of wheat for market, by sponsorship of cooperatives to reduce the farmers' subjection to the middleman, and by other legislation, the peasant's position was enhanced.

As expected, the Bank of France was subjected to significant reorganization. Although not completely nationalizing the Bank, the government transformed the Governor into a civil servant and enlarged the Board of Directors into a body representing not only shareholders but trade unions, farm cooperatives, and miscellaneous economic groups. Forty thousand instead of two hundred families were now reputed masters of the Bank.

Nationalization was more the rule in the Popular Front's policy toward the armament industries. The "merchants of death" were deprived of their wares as the government took over almost all the munitions works, arms plants, and matériel producing factories. Difficulties arose but were surmounted in the nationalization of the aircraft factories and in the delicate separation of parts of companies in which peacetime trucks were produced alongside wartime tanks. In other sectors of the economy, a careful respect was shown for private ownership in deference both to the Radical-Socialist members of the coalition and to the probable public sentiment.

Meanwhile, Blum had not overlooked the earlier promise to curb the Fascist Leagues. Where previous governments had relied on a gentleman's agreement and enacted badly executed legislation to disarm the rightist groups, the new Popular Front passed and enforced laws dissolving them. The results, however, fell short of the intentions. Most of the Leagues merely went underground and operated clandestinely or re-emerged as untouchable political parties. Though weakened, the *Croix de Feu* redesignated itself as the *Parti Social Français* and continued its activities. Many members of the suppressed organizations also were able to find a new home in the *Parti Populaire Français* formed by the ex-Communist leader Jacques Doriot. The new party heaped abuse on the Popular Front and recommended Fascist forms for domestic adoption and pro-Italian, even pro-German, orientation of foreign policy to strike at Bolshevism internationally. For those of the right to whom muscular action held an appeal, there were also the *Cagoulards*, whose hoodlumism and street-fighting became notorious after 1936.

Premier Blum, however, had more to fear from his friends than from his enemies. On his left, the Communists had adopted the old socialist practice of nonparticipation in governments to which they sometimes nevertheless gave parliamentary support. From the Communists there flowed an intensified stream of criticism against Blum and the Radical-Socialist and SFIO ministers of his cabinet. Especially after the Fascist Leagues appeared to be crippled, the Communists condemned the government for its financial policy of devaluing the franc instead of pushing for root and branch reform of the tax system. Blum was further taken to task by the Communists for his February, 1937, "pause" in the extension of public works projects and the social insurance program. On his right, the Radical-Socialists had swallowed the September devaluation measure but began gagging on the possibilities of more socialistic suggestions for meeting the continued economic decline in 1937. As the issue veered from defense of the Republic to the defense of property, the Radicals could no longer be counted on the left. As in so many previous instances, the issue of the moment relatively determined the political stance of the parliamentarian. Begrudgingly, the Chamber of Deputies voted Blum extraordinary decree powers in June, 1937, to execute a more radical program of capital levies and nationalization. The Senate, however, whose composition had not been affected by the 1936 elections, exhibited its more conservative bias and refused assent. Blum resigned.

Based on the Chamber of Deputies elected in 1936, the only feasible government that could command a majority was one sup-

ported by the SFIO, the Radical-Socialists, and scattered right and
center parties. Even if the SFIO had been willing to continue its
alliance with the Communists, they could not together have mustered
sufficient votes. Without the SFIO, the Radical-Socialists would
have been able to carry on only by an unlikely association with the
extreme right. And so it transpired that the same Radical-Socialist
Chautemps of 1934 became Premier again in 1937, with Blum
being named to the ministry without any specific portfolio. Only
the shadow of a Popular Front was discernible.

Aware that the new government would not engage in punitive
taxation or nationalization, the Parliament voted to a safe Chautemps the decree powers it had denied to a suspect Blum. Another
devaluation was palatable only because it was accompanied by
mildness in tax increases and satisfactory reduction of government
expenditures. Too seriously in danger of being compromised by
longer association with a government that showed increasing subservience to vested interests, the socialists brought about the eventual
fall of Chautemps by March, 1938. A brief attempt by Blum to
maintain a cabinet suffered the same fate at the hands of the
Senate as in 1937. The way was open for Daladier to head a
government of Radical-Socialist, center, and all but extreme right
elements. Many of the Popular Front's social and economic reforms
were abrogated, to the delight of the conservatives. Pleading the
urgency of national defense and facing a now disunited left, however, Daladier found that his measures encountered less labor
resistance than he anticipated. Under this government, the French
went to war in September, 1939, when appeasement had failed to
lead to peace.

As the depression of 1929 brought an end to a decade of prosperity and domestic tranquility, so too did it terminate the era
of international good feeling evidenced by Locarno and the
Kellogg-Briand Peace Pact. Still dominated by a concern for security
and under the impression of having made the maximum possible
concessions to Germany, the French pursued a generally unimagina-
tive foreign policy during the early years of the 1930s. Where an

enlightened proposal or two did emanate from France, the British and Americans in turn demonstrated their own short-sightedness.

On the subjects of disarmament and the League of Nations, the French found themselves again ranged against all but some small powers between 1930 and 1933. No more than during the 1920s were the French willing to disarm their land forces until precise commitments were forthcoming from Great Britain and the United States. French agreement to German rearmament was equally inconceivable. The Tardieu proposal at the 1932 Disarmament Conference that the League of Nations be provided with an international police force as a precondition of disarmament received the same aloof consideration it had in the mid-1920s. The League, meanwhile, was suffering a severe blow as a result of the Japanese attack on Manchuria. With negligible interests in that area, the French were less distracted than the more involved but equally ineffectual British and Americans.

Alarmed by the debilitating economic distress of her Little Entente allies and jealous of her right to reparation payments, France kept careful watch on Germany. And Germany at that time bore watching. A tide of nationalist fury accompanied economic collapse in the Weimar Republic. Communist thunder on the left and Nazi lightning on the right imperiled the existence of the Republic. Six million unemployed were clamoring for relief and were seeking a scapegoat for the calamity that had befallen them. Under these circumstances, it seemed the height of foolishness or vindictiveness to insist on continued payments scheduled by the Young Plan. The French, however, did insist until reluctantly forced to accept the 1931 Hoover Moratorium. In 1932, at the Lausanne Conference, the French delegation bowed with bitterness and ill grace to the scaling-down of German obligations to less than $1,000,000,000. The Americans had been quick to postpone German international payments, but the American Congress was loath to excuse the French and others from installments on the war debt. The Chamber of Deputies' rejection of Premier Herriot's demand to honor the due date provoked his resignation.

The Anglo-Saxon powers preferred to see vindictiveness, too, in the French reaction to a German-Austrian customs union in 1931. To prevent such a step, which might lead to an Anschluss and other piecemeal abrogations of the Treaty of Versailles, the French successfully thwarted this effort to strengthen the Weimar Republic's material and public relations status. Briand's reiterated scheme for European federation in 1930 might have obviated bilateral arrangements such as Anschluss, but London and Washington were hardly sympathetic to such advanced ideas. It is doubtful that even the French in any great numbers were either.

For its unaccommodating policy toward Germany in the 1930–1933 period, France has often been labeled the executioner rather than the mere witness of the demise of the Weimar Republic. Whether French concessions could have undercut the nationalist appeal of the Nazis or alleviated the grave economic conditions in Germany is a moot point. Regardless of the French contribution to the collapse of the Weimar Republic and despite the declining popular vote of the Nazi Party in the 1932 elections, Adolph Hitler was invited to the Chancellorship in January, 1933.

Published in *Mein Kampf* and proclaimed in public speeches, Hitler's objectives were as easily known as his blueprint for achieving them. The German Reich would function, as all states should function in Hitler's concept, to promote the interests of the nation. Equating the nation with the race, he assigned priority to the assembling of all German people, all the superior Aryan race, into a single Reich. Anschluss with Austria, detachment of Sudeten German lands from Czechoslovakia, seizure of German-inhabited areas from Poland, reincorporation of Alsace-Lorraine – these were but the initial steps for the one-thousand-year Reich. Contemplating far more than mere revision of the Peace Settlements of 1919, the Führer projected a "drive to the east" in a quest for living space essential to the dynamic flourishing of the German supermen. Inferior Slavs would not be assimilated – this would be mongrelization of the Aryan race. Instead, Eastern European populations would be gradually eliminated as German families mutiplied and the Polish, Czech, and Russian states disappeared or were dismembered. As the home of the despised internationalism called Bolshevism, Russia was even more stigmatized than the rest.

Blocking the access to these goals, according to Hitler, stood France, the same France that had frustrated German aspirations for centuries. England, whether because of her Anglo-Saxon blood or her preoccupation with imperial interest, could be mollified. But, France was implanted on the continent. France was the enemy. France was the perpetrator of the vile Treaty of Versailles. France was the invader of the Ruhr. France was the draftsman of the *cordon sanitaire* around Germany. France had to be isolated diplomatically and overwhelmed militarily before the new order could be realized.

That the French chose to appease Hitler rather than act positively against his aggressive intentions or deeds has appeared foolhardy or inexplicable to subsequent observers. That appeasement poorly served French or world interests is unquestionable. That the policy of appeasement seemed the only appropriate and justifiable one for the French during the 1930s, however, may be demonstrated by reference to the existing climate of opinion and the domestic and international conditions prevailing at the time.

The few Frenchmen (or Englishmen or Americans) who read *Mein Kampf* as well as the greater number who read Hitler's speeches disbelieved or discounted his statements. Were these exaggerated claims not but another example of Teutonic imbalance, reminiscent of Wagnerian music-drama or the ex-Kaiser's ill-chosen outbursts? Many Frenchmen were convinced that Hitler's hyperbolic claims were purely for domestic consumption. Once embarked on his course, he very astutely lulled the awakening dread of Frenchmen by his insistence that the particular demand constituted his last.

What of his initial acts – the renunciation of all reparations claims and the withdrawal from the League in 1933, the official rearmament of Germany in 1935, and the remilitarization of the Rhineland in 1936? Was nonmembership in the League a punishable offense? Were any of these acts a *casus belli?* Did not a nation have the right to exercise sovereign rights in its own territory? The Treaty of Versailles had tied reparations to German moral responsibility for the outbreak of World War I. Had not innumerable eminent American and British historians revealed the inaccuracy of the war guilt charge by the 1930s? The Treaty of Versailles had also stated German disarmament to be but the prelude to general disarmament. Were the victorious signatories of Versailles exempt from the clause? Had they even begun a satisfactory token disarmament of their own defenses?

The much-maligned Treaty of Versailles could be given further sardonic twists for the benefit of Hitler and the neutralization of any French action. National self-determination of peoples, a principle pronounced by Woodrow Wilson in his Fourteen Points as a basis for the peace settlements of 1919, had been improperly applied. Was Hitler not merely fulfilling the spirit of 1919 in his drive for Anschluss with Austria and for the acquisition of the Sudetenland, the Corridor, and parts of Silesia from Czechoslovakia and Poland? Through the clever use of propaganda and the implantation of Nazi-like parties in these countries, Hitler was able to foster the impression that the German people of the lands sought release from foreign masters and union with the Reich. Once Hitler went beyond what might be pictured as "legitimate" expansion, the very government of Daladier that had pursued appeasement *par excellence* at Munich in 1938 stiffened and went to war in 1939.

A fundamental flaw in French policy-making was the premise that stopping Hitler entailed war or, at least, large-scale military operations. The very thought of a recurrence of the 1914–1918 experience – and such was what twentieth-century war implied to the French – was utterly abhorrent. It was the last of last resorts. Too many millions of graves, too many millions of mutilated bodies, too many destroyed homes and factories were too fresh in the French past to repeat the catastrophe. What French government of the 1930s would dare to offer this possibility to the public? The French would not die for Czechoslovakia in 1938, but then neither would the Czechs. The tragedy of France and all of Europe was that no one knew that Hitler's threat of war was an easily called bluff in the early and mid-1930s. To his generals re-occupying the Rhineland in 1936 and to those investing Czechoslovakia in 1938, he had given secret orders to withdraw immediately at the slightest sign of armed resistance. The French would have been able to check Hitler without recourse to war up to the time that the Nazis had incorporated Austria and Czechoslovakia. Public opinion militated against taking the risk. Appeasement was preferable to war.

Appeasement had its source not only in the climate of opinion pervading France (to say nothing of Great Britain and the United States), but also in the soil of domestic and international conditions. Within France, the preoccupation with depression-born problems, the unstable and fragile nature of governments in the politically polarized nation, and the orientation of the political factions — all seemed to spell appeasement. International developments, too, seemed to preclude a dynamic containment of Nazi Germany. Actual or potential allies harbored illusions similar to those of the French. It was no Frenchman who stated the fond hope that concessions to Hitler would lead to "peace in our time." The world depression caused many nations to be most interested in domestic problems, as well as to adopt authoritarian forms of government in which the sibling states of Hitler and Mussolini were viewed sympathetically.

As the economic and social effects of the depression became increasingly apparent within France and as the accompanying political polarization and dissension became more extreme, the French public and parliamentarians fixed less and less attention on the foreign scene. Fewer francs, less time, and diminished energy seemed available for carefully considered, forcefully executed measures against the Nazi threat. Governments lived a day to day existence under fire from easily melted coalitions in the Chamber and from disgruntled demonstrators in the streets. Unable or unwilling to command sufficient authority to investigate a Stavisky scandal or to keep order on Parisian thoroughfares, the governments of 1933 and 1934 could hardly be expected to put down a noisy demagogue across the Rhine. Nor was the caretaker government of March, 1936, pessimistically awaiting the opposition's election victory, likely to mobilize the French — as Commander-in-Chief Maurice Gamelin reported to be necessary — in order to prevent the remilitarization of the Rhineland. Would even the relatively stronger government of Léon Blum dare counter Fascist moves in Spain and expose himself to right-wing retaliation at home?

Preoccupied with domestic issues or paralyzed by fear of overthrow, French cabinets were also led into appeasement by the philosophical premises of the chief political parties and extraparliamentary groups. A strange reversal of the foreign policy orientation of the right and left took place, showing again how the attitudes of a political faction are not fixed but are relative to the time and circumstances of their formation. Throughout the history of the Third Republic, the right had been the sector from which emanated undiluted militarism, extreme nationalism, and boundless detestation of Germany. During the 1930s, the right exhibited almost diametrically opposite tendencies. The days of Boulanger, Dreyfus, and the *Bloc National* had been colored by the most vivid hues of Germanophobia, but, to the right of the 1930s, the enemy was red. The menace of Communism at home and of Bolshevism across depression-bound Europe distorted the traditional views of the right. The Fascist Leagues in France sometimes went so far as to propose alliances with Hitler and Mussolini in an anti-Bolshevik front. Less extreme rightists merely poured out strong sympathy for the authoritarian efforts of Nazism and Fascism. The right contributed to appeasement, too, by its strenuous opposition to government spending during the depression years. A balanced budget seemed more advantageous than a costly military build-up or an expensive repetition of the 1923 Ruhr invasion.

The right's reversal in foreign policy was paralleled by the switch of the left. Most suddenly, the Communists, more gradually, the socialists adopted a nationalist, militarist stance against Germany. The Communist Party, the most highly disciplined party in France, found it easy to move from internationalism, antimilitarism, and near-pacifism to patriotism and belligerency. The Fascist threat to its socioeconomic program, its very political existence, and its policy-determining Soviet homeland induced the Communist Party in France to express in word and vote the ideas formerly typical of the right. The doubling of military service in 1935, the budgetary increases for armaments, the drive for military intervention in Spain – all these were integrally supported by the Communists. The nonappeasing Communists of the left were counterbalanced, however, by the tortured socialists. Appeasement seemed the line of least resistance to the latter as they worked their way tediously out of their ideological predicament. Long suspicious of militarism and nationalism, long dedicated to pacific means of resolving disputes, long supporters of the League of Nations, the socialists refused to recommend the measures necessary to stop Hitler or Mussolini. Preferring to use the scarce government funds for public works and social insurance, the socialists tried to avoid heavy military expenditures. Fearing that policies such as intervention in Spain would either play into the hands of the Communists or would provoke civil disorder from the right, the socialists followed Britain into nonintervention and appeasement.

Whether by design or by drift, appeasement thus prevailed over alternatives weakly proposed and half-heartedly executed from 1933 to 1939. What alternatives were available to the French and to what extent were they pursued? There did exist the possibility of unilateral action, tighter alliances and collective security, reliance on the League of Nations, or the reorganization and refurbishing of the military establishment. Until 1938, unilateral action was militarily feasible but rejected for lack of will and for lack of philosophic sanction for interfering in the "internal" affairs of Germany. The fate of similar punitive action during the 1920s combined with the French focus on domestic issues during the 1930s to negate this choice.

Tightening existing alliances and forming new ones might have been the answer. An attempt was at least made. The Little Entente powers that France had assiduously cultivated during the 1920s were wilting militarily, politically, and economically during the 1930s. Dictatorships had replaced democratic governments and sympathy for authoritarian forms of the right undercut the French chances of close cooperation with the Soviet Union. Louis Barthou, until his assassination in 1934, had fair success with negotiations with the Eastern European states and had even laid the ground-work for a Franco-Soviet Pact. Subsequent statesmen finished his work, although Pierre Laval dragged along slowly and the French right inveighed against the arrangement. Critics pointed out that the Soviet Union was but a weak reed subject to enormous internal stresses, as evidenced by the unpopular collectivization effort and the military purges. Except for Czechoslovakia, the Little Entente powers looked askance at Soviet support. The French could not compel Poland or Rumania to promise permission for the transit of Russian troops across its soil in the event of Nazi aggression in Central Europe. Gaining the Soviets as allies might cause the dis-affection of the Little Entente. The Franco-Soviet Pact also opened France to a debate much like that which the Americans engaged in after Yalta little more than a decade later. As for an Italian connec-tion, the price tentatively paid by Laval was considered too high by French and British public opinion. Mussolini's seizure of Ethiopia frustrated French statesmen's efforts to keep Italy in an anti-Berlin axis. Mussolini's massive aid to Generalissimo Franco during the Spanish Civil War further alienated the French and Italians. And England? Rapprochement with Great Britain proved the lodestar of French governments after 1934 but hardly produced a stiff stand against Hitler. A British government that turned a deaf ear to the loud cries of its own Winston Churchill was equally deaf to the faint murmurs of Frenchmen seeking positive action. Needless to say, the United States offered little promise of material or even moral aid in the event of a militant anti-Nazi French effort.

Collective security pacts, as obstacles to Hitler, were only as effective as the strength and intentions of the signatories. During the 1930s the conditions were not favorable. Collective security pacts to which Hitler was a party were efficacious, too, only if based on good faith or willingness to use force to oblige adherence. The record of the 1930s is replete with Hitler's facility in breaking promises as readily as making them. By the mid-1930s, the League of Nations had little strength to function as an instrument for curbing aggression. The United States had never joined the League, Germany withdrew from it in 1933; Japan flouted it a year earlier in Manchuria; Italy defied it over Ethiopia in 1935. The entrance of the Soviet Union in 1935 and the feeble efforts of the French to bolster the League could not reinvigorate the moribund institution.

French military power was basic to the success of any alternative to appeasement, for it was essential ultimately to secure the integrity of the nation should appeasement fail. Had the French governments of the 1930s provided the nation with a military force consonant with these needs? Lest the reader be blinded by the French military debacle of 1940, let it be noted that the governments of the 1930s did provide France with a gigantic military establishment and a monumental series of fortifications. The strategic use to which the men, matériel, and Maginot Line were put, of course, was not ultimately efficacious. The defensive, inner-directed tone of French military policy was in conformity with the foreign policy of appeasement and clashed with the alternative of dynamic unilateral action, energetic support of allies, or forceful upholding of collective security or League demands. But, despite the climate of opinion of the 1930s, despite the fixation on depression problems, despite the persuasions of right and left, the French did vote the appropriations, did double the military service, did proceed with Maginot Line construction, and did build tanks but fewer airplanes for the defense of French soil.

Urgent appeals were made to reorganize the army to make it an agency for confronting Hitler instead of appeasing him. But the pleas were few in number and poorly supported in public or private places. As parliamentary spokesman for the little known Captain Charles de Gaulle, Paul Reynaud, during the mid-1930s proposed radical reform of the army. A professional army of one hundred thousand men should be created and furnished with armor and airpower. This concentrated striking force of career men could spearhead attacks on aggressors or serve to cover the mobilization of reserves and resources of the nation in arms. Tanks would be massed and airplanes assigned in this *armée de métier* of de Gaulle in a fashion foreshadowing the Panzer Corps of the Third Reich. From right and left came scornful declaimers of the proposals. The right objected to the expense, and the regular army chiefs were satisfied with the defensive strategy to which they were committed. The left was obsessed by the fear of creating a Frankenstein of a praetorian guard, a band of professionals that might turn the Republic of the 1930s into a black-shirted shambles. Wisely rejecting de Gaulle's unfeasible recommendation of a professioinal army, the government unwisely rejected with it the meaningful concepts of massed armor and airpower. Only too slowly during the later 1930s did the army command begin the formation and training of armored divisions within the framework of the existing military institution.

During the 1930s, the French had thus pursued a foreign policy that led to war and a military policy that would lead to defeat. In September, 1939, without a shadow of the enthusiasm and unity of August, 1914, the French went reluctantly to war against Nazi Germany.

6.

THE REGENERATION OF A NATION:
FRANCE SINCE 1939

IN 1939, prophets of doom could not have depicted in dark enough hues the catastrophic fate that hovered over that generation of Frenchmen. Between 1940 and 1944, military defeat, Nazi occupation, and the agonizing division of Frenchmen into Vichyites, collaborators, resisters, and Free French were grim experiences. Colossal problems of postwar reconstruction were complicated after 1944 by the political instability, economic weakness, and exhausting colonial strife that crushed the half-generation-old Fourth Republic in 1958. Without even entering the morass of debate on the virtues or vices of Charles de Gaulle's presidential regime in the Fifth Republic, pessimists can sadly ponder the future of French political life when the President passes from the scene.

Looking to the future of Frenchmen from the 1939 vantage point, congenital optimists, on the other hand, would not have been able to paint in glorious enough tones the renaissance of French hopes, spirit, and unity in the exhilarating days of liberation from Vichy and Nazi rule. Behind the crumbling façade of the Fourth Republic, the Pollyannas could discern the restructuring of the economy and society as the Monnet Plan took life and expanded its operations. On a solid base of soaring productivity and more equable distribution, the French nation could be seen blazing a trail to unprecedented prosperity within the context of Common Market institutions after the popularly supported Fifth Republic liquidated the enervating Algerian war.

Who would have predicted more accurately — the prophets of

doom or the forecasters of good fortune? The French since 1939 in fact plummeted to such depths and scaled such heights as to make both sets of soothsayers sometimes simultaneously correct.

1939–1940

Phony war, military defeat, and political collapse

IN September, 1939, the French government assumed a defensive posture as Nazi legions and Soviet forces carved up Poland in three short weeks. The "all quiet" that reigned on the western front from September, 1939, to May, 1940, earned for these months the title of a *drôle de guerre* (a phony war). With the exception of an initial, small-scale French raid into the Saarland in September and a larger but equally ill-fated Anglo-French expedition against the Nazi sweep into Norway in April, 1940, no major land, sea, or air engagements took place.

Calculation as much as lassitude and internal dissension explain the French failure to take more vital action during the phony war. True to the military doctrine conceived and formulated during the 1920s and 1930s, defensive operations behind the shield of the Maginot Line were dictated by the nature of the anticipated long war of attrition ahead. A careful build-up of modern armaments was essential before any major offensive could be undertaken. One French military expert, whose book had been endorsed by Marshal Pétain, had estimated that an army attacking a continuous front would require three times more infantrymen, six times more artillery, and fifteen times more shells than the defender. The French, no more than the Americans and British in contemplating the opening of a second front later in the war, were not likely to commit prematurely their carefully husbanded resources against a certainly equal and possibly superior enemy. Only after a gradual mobilization of the resources of the far-flung French and British Empires and only after blockade had limited the enemy's efforts could a final offensive be launched.

If there was some wisdom in such cautious concepts, the French government during the phony war demonstrated inability or unwillingness to proceed full speed with the preparation of the nation in arms for the ultimate day of reckoning or for emergencies on the way. Mobilization of the armed forces was smoothly accomplished; reserves were placed on active duty with no serious difficulty. As in World War I, nearly a million soldiers had to be returned to factories and farms to supplement the women and colonial workers pressed into the labor force. The forty-hour week, extended to forty-eight hours in 1938, was lengthened to sixty and sometimes more. Wages, however, were frozen, overtime pay scaled down, but prices were often allowed to find their natural level, to the advantage of manufacturers and merchants. Despite the elaborate bureaucratic organization devised for the procurement, distribution, and production of goods, rationing and price controls awaited the May, 1940, invasion. Purchases abroad were paced to a three-year program as much from fear of financial dislocation as from the dictates of military concepts. By the spring of 1940, serious grievances existed on the part of the ill-paid soldiers whose dreary barracks life seemed petty and unrewarding. Workers enjoyed more benefits than their uniformed compatriots but far fewer than the profiting bourgeois owners of the workplaces.

The political scene was little conducive to stimulating the casual war effort. During the phony war, the poisonous political feuds of the 1930s and the ideological persuasions of rival political factions yielded bitter fruit. The government did little to improve the situation. At the outset of the war, the cabinet was headed by Daladier and supported narrowly by Radical-Socialists and other center and right parties. Within the government and within the Chamber of Deputies were many defeatists who trembled at the thought of a dynamic war effort lest radical social and economic forces be liberated.

A *Union Sacrée* of 1914 was unattainable. The parties of the left, at least, were unavailable. Among the socialists, a large section of persisting pacifists inveighed openly or covertly against the war;

another sizeable wing steered clear of coalition because of opposition to the socioeconomic ideas of the government. The Communist Party, discredited in the eyes of all but a hard core of stalwarts by the startling Nazi-Soviet Pact of August, 1939, became an easy victim of the war government of September. Having reverted to an antiwar position tantamount to a pro-German stand as a result of Stalin's accommodation of Hitler, the Communist Party was declared illegal. With a justice not applied to right-wing antiwar, pro-German elements, the government purged the Chamber of Communist deputies, imprisoned union leaders of that Party, and shut down the newspaper *L'Humanité*.

The only attempt to broaden the base of the cabinet took place in March, 1940. Paul Reynaud's reputation as a dynamic leader, earned as a financial expert and parliamentary spokesman for de Gaulle's army reform schemes, far exceeded his actual accomplishments. He replaced Daladier but succeeded only in enlarging the new cabinet with two lesser lights of the SFIO. Daladier remained as Minister of War alongside numerous defeatist members. Association with Britain in the Norwegian fiasco in April brought no glory to the new government which was faced in May by a more crucial test.

On May 10, Nazi lightning struck Holland, Belgium, and Luxembourg. In accordance with prior and carefully detailed plan, French armies and the ten divisions of the British Expeditionary Force moved quickly and efficiently to prepared positions in Belgium and formed a continuous front against the invader from the North Sea to Switzerland. As the Allies maneuvered their unmolested forces into Belgium, however, the Nazi Luftwaffe obliterated Rotterdam and otherwise reduced Dutch resistance by May 15. Feints and stronger drives against the Maginot Line were blunted, but disaster threatened in the "impassable" Ardennes where inadequate demolition and scanty forces facilitated Panzer Corps penetration. After seizing Sedan on the 13th, the Germans chose not to aim directly at Paris but to move north to the Channel ports. Thereby Allied armies in Belgium would be trapped, leaving easier access to the French capital. In desperation, Reynaud replaced the cultivated, intellectual Maurice Gamelin with the vibrant Maxime Weygand. A reshuffling of the cabinet brought in the venerable Marshal Pétain. All to no avail. The military situation deteriorated.

Once having reached and taken the Channel town of Abbéville on the 20th, the Nazis applied the full strength of their massed armor, Stuka divebombers, and artillery to the mass of surrounded British, French, and Belgian troops. The Belgian King surrendered on the 28th and the Anglo-French armies were submitted to ruthless harassment. Disoriented and deserting soldiers clogged the roads choked with civilians and suffered together the horrors of strafing, machine-gunning, and artillery fire. More than 300,000 men — of whom 200,000 were British — took part in the miracle of Dunkirk in early June. Forced to abandon all their heavy equipment, these men boarded small and large craft and sailed across the Channel to England. A heroic feat or a treacherous withdrawal, the Dunkirk evacuation served to salvage a corps of trained men for future battles, but also marked the end of British participation in the defense of France. Churchill's refusal to commit the R.A.F. to the losing cause completed the separation of the joint military effort.

A contagious sense of helplessness and panic overcame the military and home fronts as Nazi armies concluded their mopping-up operations in northern France. Encountering little effective opposition, the Germans spanned the rivers and crossed the fields on their victorious march toward Paris. On the 10th of June, the "jackal" Mussolini assessed the moment propitious to enter the war with maximum chance of gain and minimum probability of cost. On the same day, the cabinet decided to abandon Paris and began its trek first to Tours and a week later to Bordeaux. During that week, however, the Germans triumphally entered the open city of Paris and fanned out southward toward the Loire River and eastward to the rear of the Maginot Line.

By June 18, the Battle of France was over; the debate on the causes of the debacle was only beginning. From the facts of the Battle and from the evidence produced in 1940 and thereafter, the

French military defeat of 1940 was primarily the result of an inappropriate military strategy poorly executed by the High Command. The Germans unquestionably had advantages over the French in industrial and demographic resources. Political divisions, social strife, and a pacifist-defeatist spirit in France were surely not conducive to a dynamic war effort. Despite the existence in France of a pacifist left, a sometimes Fascist-inclined right, and a population wearied of war and bled by the wound of 1914–1918, the French nation nevertheless put an impressive army into the field in May, 1940. One hundred and one French divisions joined eleven British and twenty-two Belgian to match the numerical strength of the invading Germans. Contrary to the initial impression bred by the overwhelming Nazi victory, the French armies had near equality in equipment and weapons, except in aircraft. Four thousand German armored vehicles were confronted by more than three thousand French tanks. In artillery, machine guns, and small arms, the French were also on a par with the invaders. The Germans were superior to the Allies only in aircraft, probably about two to one. Nor was sabotage or lack of personal courage a determining factor in accounting for the French defeat. Where engaged in the type of battle for which they had been trained and equipped, the French enlisted men and officers performed with as much fear and bravery as exhibited by the citizen-soldiers of other countries. The untold confusion of the French armies dislocated by the Panzer thrusts was not the disorder of treachery or desertion. The discounting or elimination of political, economic, and psychological causes leaves French military strategy as the responsible agent.

However commendable in many of its premises and however consonant with French needs and resources, French military doctrine was tragically in error in the strategic and tactical employment of armor and airpower. The flaw was made more glaringly obvious by the inability of the High Command in 1940 to improvise fast enough to meet the German blitzkrieg. Designed in conformity with doctrine, French tanks had neither the fuel nor radio capacity to operate outside the radius of infantry units. Mass independent action was denied to all but too few armored divisions. Scattered among the regular infantry divisions, distributed in reserve along wide fronts, or parked in the rear areas for use later in the supposed long war of attrition, the three thousand French tanks were strategically and tactically useless against the armored mass of the Panzers. Inadequate attention, too, had been accorded by French strategists to the possibilities of air–ground liaison and the concentrated use of fighter planes and divebombers. French ground forces, ill-prepared for such action, were thus left to the mercy of the more numerous and more versatile Luftwaffe. Whether speedy and vigorous decisions to reorganize the armored units and commit the French fighter planes could have stemmed the German advance is not clear. The effort was not made. Gamelin moved too slowly when he acted at all; Weygand presumed that all was lost soon after he was "recalled to service."

Provided by the government with the manpower and matériel of their asking, but begetters of an ill-conceived strategy, the High Command led the nation to military calamity. Does the assignment of faulty strategy and ineffective command as the causes of the 1940 disaster automatically incriminate the generals as the guilty parties? Or does the pitilessly pushed logic of representative democracy demand that the politicians bear the ultimate responsibility for the strategy? Or was the sovereign French people culpable in accepting the doctrine its elected representatives eagerly accepted from the Generals?

The imminence and then the reality of the French military collapse led Reynaud and his cabinet into an acrimonious debate on whether to continue the war or to seek an armistice. In stirring prose and in impassioned oratory, Reynaud seemed to stand on the side of the sword-wielding angels. In concrete action, however, he did little to prepare for the promised possibility of carrying on the war around Paris, in the provinces, installed in North Africa, or entrenched in the American colonies. On June 16, rather than press the issue to a vote on a cabinet whose majority would still have probably opted against an armistice, he resigned his post and recommended to the President that Marshal Pétain be named as successor.

The new government quickly came to grips with the problem of continued war or immediate armistice. The defeatists, dominating the new cabinet, had already rejected Churchill's dramatic offer of a Franco-British union. A latent anglophobia prevailed, harking back to the British refusal to support the Clemenceau position at the Paris Peace Conference, the British opposition to Poincaré's punitive policy toward Germany during the 1920s, and the British accommodation of the Nazis during the early 1930s. That the British, too, had ulterior designs on the French Empire and the French fleet was an obvious truth in the minds of the anglophobes. Suspicion of "perfidious Albion" was not allayed either by the British contribution – or lack of it – in May and June of 1940. The poorly equipped and miniscule British Expeditionary Force, the Dunkirk evacuation, and the refusal to commit the R.A.F. were vivid and recent reminders of English "treachery." Besides, was not Great Britain doomed to certain defeat? Would not an invincible Hitler soon be able to impose his will on the isolated and powerless British? Would not general peace then ensure Hitler's mastery of the continent? The Soviet Union had come to terms; the United States basked in its splendid isolation without so much as compulsory military training. Was it not wise to salvage what could be salvaged from the wreckage and seek the best possible bargain for France in the new order? Regarding as unfeasible a military redoubt in Brittany, discarding the more reasonable suggestion of a withdrawal to North Africa, declining a move to distant America, the cabinet concluded an armistice with the Germans on June 22.

According to the provisions of the armistice, applied and extended more rigorously over the ensuing four years, the Germans would occupy approximately three fifths of France – the area roughly north of the Loire River and all the coastal region to the Spanish frontier. The remaining and unoccupied zone would retain a French government seated at Vichy that was promised the right to move back to Paris and resume administration over the entire country once Great Britain surrendered. Interzonal travel and trade would be at the discretion of the occupying authorities. The French Empire and fleet remained intact under the control of Vichy. None of the one and a half million French prisoners of war would be released until a final peace treaty was signed. All heavy arms and equipment would be surrendered to the Germans. Only a one-hundred-thousand-man French internal security force would be authorized for the unoccupied zone. The French would assume the obligation of meeting the entire cost of occupation.

From a naked listing of the armistice terms, the French could be seen to hold two trump cards for immediate and subsequent bargaining with the occupying enemy: the colonies and the fleet. Inaccessible to direct seizure by the Nazis in June, 1940, these two assets were allowed to remain in French hands. Fearful that the colonial and naval authorities would put their resources into British hands rather than permit Axis acquisition, Hitler was restrained from more excessive demands in June, 1940, and in the two following years.

Although the armistice had condoned the existence of a nominally sovereign French state and although the French escaped the fate of a Poland or Czechoslovakia, the enemy nevertheless clearly held the whip hand. Under his direct rule lay the greater portion of French population, territory, industry, and natural resources. Nazi control of the interzonal frontier gave the enemy command over the economy and survival of the poorer unoccupied sector as well. Superior Nazi armies stationed in the north could overrun at will the police-army of the south. Further intimidation of the French government was made possible by threatening the million and a half prisoners of war still held in German camps and by the exactions legalized as occupation costs. Although the armistice spared the French from the treatment meted out to the peoples of Central and Eastern Europe, the condition of the French was perhaps worse by its insidiousness.

With the armistice concluded, the French government began a mournful deliberation about the political measures necessary to administer the defeated and divided country. From the temporary coastal capital at Bordeaux, the Pétain cabinet made its way inland to the resort town of Vichy. By early July, there converged on the new seat of government some 650 members of the Chamber of Deputies and Senate of the discredited Third Republic. From the sessions culminating in the crucial sitting of July 10 was born the Vichy regime and the National Revolution it would attempt to perpetrate upon the French people from 1940 to 1944.

By July 9, it was apparent that the overwhelming majority of parliamentarians in attendance agreed on two major points. First, the Third Republic of which they had been illustrious officials had demonstrated fatal deficiencies and stood in dire need of drastic remodeling. Second, the exigencies of the French defeat, the armistice, and the continuing war required for the moment a French government wielding exceptional powers.

To judge from the Taurines proposal of July 9, the deputies would have preferred to separate the two issues. Constitutional changes would be discussed but not adopted until the war's end when a referendum or a newly elected Parliament would pass the final judgment. Meanwhile, Pétain would be vested with emergency, decree power. Although Pétain seemed amenable to this solution, his newly appointed Vice-Premier, Pierre Laval, was not. To this ambitious master maneuverer and to many ultra-conservatives or outright Fascists in Pétain's entourage, the moment seemed opportune to institute an authoritarian regime in France. Whether merely to forestall similar action by the Nazis with whom collaboration was declared essential or to install a long desired government of rightist tendencies, Laval and his côterie countered the Taurines proposal with a recommendation to award constitution-making as well as emergency powers to Pétain. To win his case, Laval alternately enticed, coaxed, and bullied the parliamentarians. Disillusionment with the performance of the Third Republic, exhaustion and shock induced by the military debacle, fear of Nazi recriminations for all but authoritarian gestures, and the veneration for the Marshal in whose hands constitutional changes would be entrusted

– all these elements combined to reward Laval's efforts. By the hands of 569 duly elected representatives meeting in joint session as a National Assembly, the Third French Republic committed suicide on July 10, 1940. A handful of 80 deputies separated from their SFIO and Radical-Socialist colleagues to vote against empowering Pétain as Head of State to promulgate a new constitution. Proclaimed on a balcony of the Hôtel de Ville in Paris by a handful of enthusiasts in 1870, the Third Republic died in a casino at Vichy by the votes of its legal but disheartened representatives in 1940.

1940–1944

Occupation, Vichy, Free France, Resistance, liberation

ALL Gaul, as every school child once learned, was simply divided in three parts. France since the Revolution, as the reader will have observed, was more subtly divided into many more parts, even though its territorial integrity had not been in question. France from 1940 to 1944, as will now be noted, was divided into such countless bits as nearly to defy description. A false impression of tidiness would be conveyed by citing categories of authority such as occupied France, Vichy France, Free France, and the Resistance.

In the occupied zone, where a brutal but monolithic, coordinated system might be presumed to prevail, the courteous, cultivated German officer of one sector ruled differently from the depraved S.S. tyrant in the neighboring town. The Führer would receive no affirmative response to his question, "Is Paris burning?" The French were often equally confused or contradictory in their response to the harrowing occupation experience; to collaborate or not to collaborate was not an easily answered question either.

Vichy France represented even less uniform or stable a system of government, a set of practices, or a command of loyalty. Under the uncertain, aged Pétain there persisted an impermanence of premierships and an incidence of intrigue that made the Third Republic look like a textbook model of solidarity and purity.

The third category of authority under which Frenchmen were grouped from 1940 to 1944 was the Free French movement headed by Charles de Gaulle. But here, too, the self-proclaimed symbol of French unity, who more than any patriot held firm and consistent, found himself the subject and object of dissension and turmoil. A rallying point for many military and civilian Frenchmen, he appeared to others a renegade army officer and an organizer with Britain of raids on French colonies and the navy. Within his fold were followers who venerated him for his mystique of French grandeur and his pronouncements on discipline, whereas others deplored his political, social, and economic ideas – or their absence.

Finally, the organization in metropolitan France of the Resistance exemplified the fourth complex of French association during the war years. Often pitting Frenchman against Frenchman as well as Frenchmen against Germans, liberal Catholic resisters might one day harry clergy who seemed soft to the Nazis or sympathetic to Vichy, yet on the morrow the same resisters worked hand-in-glove with the same cleric to conduct Jews to a safe haven in Switzerland. Within the Resistance were bundled a multiplicity of motives, a diversity of methods, and a host of different goals beyond expelling the Nazi enemy. Suspicion and worse sentiments erupted frequently in the contacts between Communist Party cells and reemerging underground SFIO, Radical-Socialist, and other parties' affiliates.

The cardinal fact of French life from 1940 to 1944 was the German occupation. It gripped not only the great majority of the citizens who inhabited the northern three fifths of France, but also strongly influenced the daily lives of those in the unoccupied zone. It cast its shadow on the activities of the Free French based at first in London and then Algiers; it obviously provoked the rise of the Resistance movement.

The German administrative apparatus for the occupation of France manifested curious overlaps and frequent inner frictions. Vichy and occupied French officials thereby were provided an opportunity to play one branch against another. A German military commander was assigned nominal jurisdiction over all of occupied France except for Alsace-Lorraine and the northern departments. Those northern industrial departments adjacent to Belgium had been detached from France and placed under the German military commander in Brussels. Alsace and Lorraine were being politically and economically integrated and culturally assimilated into the German Reich, notwithstanding the absence of any such agreement in the June armistice. Hierarchically arranged under the German commander in Paris were staffs responsible to him not only for ordinary military matters, but also for general administrative, judicial, financial, and economic questions. At the same time, there existed in Wiesbaden a commission of French and German delegates whose function was to regulate all matters pertaining to the armistice and its implementation. An obvious jurisdictional conflict between Paris and Wiesbaden might arise when occupation costs and French finances were on the agenda. Further complicating the "efficient" German system was the appointment of Otto Abetz as Ambassador to France. His accreditation to Paris and not to Vichy and his ambiguous but near plenipotentiary status often led him to interfere with his fellow Germans' occupation chores. Also established in Paris were such sometimes subordinate, sometimes autonomous, but ever dreaded agencies as the Gestapo and Propaganda Office.

To implement the decrees that emanated from German occupation authorities and that controlled the most minute details of French life, the Germans cleverly reverted largely to indirect methods. At the peril of their lives, French officials — majors, prefects, police, and civil servants — were charged with the responsibility of carrying out Nazi regulations. At the mercy of the Wehrmacht and under the surveillance of the German secret police, local French officials administered the curfew, censorship, rationing, and myriad restrictions imposed on the population.

Whether for reasons of racial delicacy, anticipation of greater gains, or being by chance aside from the main lines of battle, the

German occupation of France was less stringent than that of Slavic Eastern Europe. What the French were spared in the way of indiscriminate shooting or purposeful concentration-camp and slave-labor experience, they often more than lost in the economic drain of their resources. After an initially "comfortable" winter of 1940–1941, the French increasingly suffered the wrath and exactions of the German overlord as his military needs multiplied.

The German occupation siphoned off French resources in three principal ways: direct exaction of the occupation costs, forced trade, and sheer loot. Fixed at 400,000,000 francs per day, the occupation charges of the German armies in France represented payments estimated at four times the reparation payments demanded of a richer Germany under the Dawes Plan during the 1920s. The figures also have been calculated at well over half the amount the Germans received from all the rest of occupied Europe. To no avail, the French protested that 400,000,000 francs was in excess of the cost of maintaining a French army of more than fifteen million men! With these receipts so generously covering the needs of the comparatively scanty German Wehrmacht in France, the Nazis were able to purchase goods and services for other uses. Forced trade yielded a bountiful harvest for the Nazis, too. By an ingenious system of payments and by arbitrary juggling of the exchange rate, French goods were shipped to Germany without balanced returns. In the clearing house account established by the Nazis in Paris, French manufactures, ores, and agricultural products were paid for in francs by the French government. Meanwhile, in Berlin, German exports to France were paid for by the German government in marks. If exports and imports had been equal, a balance would have been struck. However, since French exports to Germany far exceeded imports, the French government was being obliged to support a disguised looting of the French economy. Open plundering, requisition, and confiscation of goods by the Germans provided an incalculable source of tribute. Meats and Matisses, grains and jewelry, vegetables and furniture were seized without compensation from the the helpless Frenchmen.

The Frenchman's person was as violable as his property. In danger of being imprisoned for the slightest infraction of the occupation decrees or being held hostage for ultimate elimination at the ratio of 50:1 if a German soldier was attacked, the Frenchman lived precariously in his occupied country. Although French Jews fared a shade better than non-French resident Jews, more than thirty thousand were rounded up in Paris alone for a final and ghoulish solution. Less success attended German propaganda efforts to enlist Frenchmen of anti-Communist persuasion to join the Nazi legions on the Russian front. Not more than a few thousand exhibited a taste for this enterpise. Ten times the number did succumb to Nazi entreaty and pressure to serve as laborers in Germany. Conditions of work and life varied with the assignment. The rare idyllic situation of a French agricultural worker sharing the plow and sometimes the wife of a German farmer stood in sharp contrast, however, to the deplorable plight of the majority of ill-fed, shabbily lodged, and harshly treated "volunteers."

For the Frenchmen under German occupation and, to a lesser degree, for those under the Vichy regime, three main courses were available: collaboration, sullen submission, or resistance. By choice or by compulsion, some few Frenchmen felt inclined to collaborate. Leaders or members of prewar Fascist Leagues like Jacques Doriot and journalists or other writers had long favored Nazism and now found their opportunity to practice and print what they had long preached. Some manufacturers and merchants actively sought and fulfilled contracts for the production and distribution of goods helpful to the German war machine. Some actors, actresses, and various entertainers willingly performed for Nazi audiences. At the other extreme, and in growing numbers after the initial shock of defeat wore off, many engaged in resistance organizations designed in varying ways to harass the Nazis. When the tide of war began to turn against the enemy and when the enemy raised his demands and intensified his controls, collaboration waned and resistance waxed. By and large, the great mass of Frenchmen submitted to the conqueror with ill grace but no more. In the mines, factories, shops, offices, government bureaus, and brothels of France, men and women worked to earn their dark and rationed daily bread.

The lines between collaboration and submission and between submission and resistance were often imperceptible or greatly blurred. When a worker continued at the assembly line producing cloth for German uniforms was it called collaboration or mere submission? When a French pedestrian returned but an icy stare to a German officer's greeting was he submitting or resisting? Was it profiteering or patriotism that motivated participation in the black market? Fortunes could be made by peasants and middlemen while they diverted from possible German requisition or acquisition the cheeses, meats, and vegetables of Normandy. With apathetic resignation or by agonizing choice, the great majority of Frenchmen mixed submission with petty anti-German acts and gestures. Uneasy consciences probably far outnumbered the cases of deep remorse or joyous righteousness when the Nazi conqueror was swept from the land in 1944.

With somewhat freer rein than possessed by the occupied French, the inhabitants of the unoccupied zone found themselves confronted by somewhat different choices. In the south, the Vichy regime interposed itself between the public and the German victor. Collaboration with the enemy was thus masked by collaboration or noncollaboration with the Pétain government. Submission to that regime and to the enemy were sometimes separable attitudes and acts. Resistance to the Nazis could also at times be distinguished from resistance to Vichy.

Throughout its four-year existence, the Vichy regime was an authoritarian state ruled by Pétain and a shifting set of officials appointed by him. Although remaining titular Head of State to the end, Pétain, in April, 1942, was forced by the Germans to re-enstate Laval as "Premier" for the duration of the regime and delegate to him decree powers. To administer the realm, the Marshal relied on a civil service of *fonctionnaires* carried over from the Third Republic, on the regular police force supplemented by new security detachments, on a judiciary whose procedures and staff became ever more severe, and on a Church that gave its sanction and sympathy to most of the Vichy program.

Criticism against this personal dictatorship and contention among Frenchmen might have been avoided or lessened if the regime had stayed within these bounds. Wartime conditions during 1940–1944, like those of 1914–1918, and the added woes of occupation might have warranted extraordinary and not always democratic measures. The Gambettas and the Clemenceaus had not been overly solicitous of representative government or of civil rights when the *patrie* was in danger. Unfortunately for the unity of the French and the reputations of the leaders of Vichy, the Pétains and Lavals seemed as bent on permanently replacing the institutions of parliamentary democracy as on temporarily suspending them.

Voted emergency and constituent powers on July 10, 1940, Marshal Pétain proceeded both to clear the debris of defeat and to construct a regime to fit the new order of Europe and the old order of France. Yeoman efforts were required and yeoman efforts were applied to rehabilitate the population and repair the damages after hostilities were ended. During the summer and fall of 1940, 90 percent of the four million May and June refugees were evacuated to their original villages and towns in the north; the remainder were lodged in the south. Repairing the transportation and communication system and re-opening many factories and shops absorbed the energies of all but one million workers. To the unemployed, special benefits were offered. On the farms, the peasants brought in good crops to tide the population over its first winter of defeat. Perhaps the least appreciative of Vichy's restoration of order and near-normalcy were the children who had to troop back to classes resumed in the autumn.

Meanwhile, from the capital of unoccupied France sprang a National Revolution – an attempt to redirect the political, social, economic, and moral life of France. If the house that Pétain helped build showed a façade imitative of Fascist models, its foundations were largely of native materials. The basic blueprint and the functioning of the edifice were a curious mélange of expediency and conviction. Politically, the regime began but abandoned in 1942 the framing of a new constitution. Twelve Constitutional Acts, pronounced by Pétain between 1940 and 1942, did away piecemeal with the Presidency and the Parliament. By these acts, Pétain named himself Chief of the French State and armed himself with the power to select a successor. In 1942, however, he suddenly disbanded for the duration of the war the committee earlier appointed to draft a complete constitution. The precise form of government anticipated for peacetime was thus never revealed but could only be expected to follow antiparliamentarian, antidemocratic patterns.

According to the Twelve Constitutional Acts as well as the decrees and pronouncements of the Vichy officials, the role of the state was differently conceived from that under the Third Republic. The trilogy of *liberté, égalité, fraternité* significantly gave way to *famille, travail, patrie*. Deploring the allegedly pernicious individualism and materialism of the Republic, Vichy encouraged instead closer ties for larger families, greater association of youth in patriotic organizations, and a return to religious and moral values of days gone by. To heal the class sores of labor and management, the state prescribed corporate institutions in which the workers and capitalists would be theoretically obliged to cooperate with one another and to heed the directives of government and technical experts in the particular sector of the economy. There was obviously no place for labor unions with autonomous rights or even for employers' associations with monopolistic intent. The greatest blessings of the Vichy regime was poured on agriculture – whether because it embraced the most numerous segment of the population in the unoccupied zone, because it represented the activity most respected by the Vichy ideology, or because its contribution was most sorely needed to feed the people. Individually or ranged in cooperative societies, the peasant landowner received some autonomy of operation and much advancement of credit and tax benefits.

On social questions, related or not to those of family and labor, Vichy worked to remove the strains of two generations of republicanism. It seemed only natural for the Church to be raised from the lowly status accorded it since the 1870s. Church and state regarded each other with greater mutual admiration than at any time since the early nineteenth century. The Church was not, nevertheless, re-established officially nor restored to its one-time ascendancy in political or educational affairs. A brief spell of compulsory religious instruction in the public schools was halted, although the clergy was left with sizeable advantages in state aid and subsidies for its own schools. Church influence was enhanced in youth, family, and patriotic organizations founded by the state.

For its virulent anti-Semitism, Vichy officials later pleaded the urgency of Nazi insistence. Anti-Semitism in France, however, was no German invention. The lie to Vichy's claim may be shown by recalling the France of Dreyfus at the turn of the century and of Blum during the 1930s. That the Jews suffered more than grievous discrimination and flagrant social ostracism in France was another matter. By their military and economic controls, the Nazis not only enabled the most scurrilous French elements to come to the surface, but also applied irresistible pressures to the cowed Vichy regime. Although French Jews residing in the unoccupied zone were some-what safer from extermination than those in the north, foreign Jews enjoyed no such "protection" from Vichy. Laval's bargaining with the Germans led him to the shabby delivery of most of the Spanish and Eastern European Jews who had fled to France. Unsat-isfactorily vigorous in German eyes, Vichy's initially severe meas-ures of social and occupational exclusion of the Jews became more punitive and terroristic as the war wore on. Only by the laxity of some officials, the efforts of sympathetic individuals or resistance groups, and the intervention of certain clergymen (anti-Semitic persecution was one of the few points of discord between the Church and Vichy) did many French Jews survive the rigors of this perse-cution or escape to friendly countries.

Neither in foreign any more than in domestic affairs did the "sovereign" state of Vichy possess or exercise the independence legally recognized by the armistice of June, 1940. Until it was robbed of its trump cards of colonies and fleet, Vichy could play a modified game with Germany as well as with Great Britain and the United States. The invasion of North Africa, the scuttling of the French fleet, and the simultaneous German move into the unoccupied zone deprived Vichy of all but a shadowy freedom.

Relations with Germany naturally constituted the major activity of Vichy in foreign affairs. Whereas Pétain seemed to prefer an aloof and passive attitude toward the conqueror, Laval appeared more bent on active collaboration or certainly constant contacts. Laval and his associates later asserted their "collaboration" was conditioned by circumstances and guided by the hope of shielding Frenchmen from a worse fate. Many of their acts, however, seemed to exceed the need and frustrate the hope. It is true that Laval proved a tireless haggler over questions of occupation costs, release of French prisoners of war, forced-labor drafts, anti-Semitic laws, and general association with Germany in the war effort. At times Laval nevertheless anticipated Nazi threats too readily. He sometimes volunteered the assets entrusted to the French by overrun countries too quickly. Belgian gold and Yugoslav securities were turned over to the Germans without the semblance of a *quid pro quo*. Without completely fulfilling German requests, he yielded able-bodied Frenchmen for labor in Germany without effectively easing the lot of French prisoners of war. He outdid himself in the recruitment and maintenance of a French *milice* whose Gestapo-like police and terroristic activities did much of the Nazi dirty work all too well. And, of course, the very existence and operation of a French government having truck with the enemy presented a degrading spectacle to French and foreign witnesses.

Vichy thus failed to rally Frenchmen to a single cause. With no crystal-clear dichotomy between patriotism and treachery, arguments often flared up as to the degree of treason advisable or the extent of patriotism recommended. Sympathy for Vichy as a conservative regime of desirable social and economic goals turned to loathing for Vichy as a lackey of the Germans, thus splitting Frenchmen further into contending factions. Divided within, the Vichy regime was beset by two chief opposing movements: the Free

French Forces under Charles de Gaulle and the emerging Resistance in metropolitan France. Frenchmen were thus offered these two alternatives in addition to those of direct collaboration with the Germans in the occupied zone or affiliation with Vichy.

On June 18, 1940, a mere handful of Frenchmen heard from London the solitary voice of General de Gaulle pleading that they consider a battle to be lost but a war to be won. Thousands, then millions, would soon listen more attentively as the war progressed. Finally, all would acclaim and salute him as their unquestioned leader in the liberation of France in 1944.

Educated and trained as a professional military man, de Gaulle served brilliantly in that capacity in World War I and during the interbellum years. As head of the Free French, he revealed himself a master statesman. To his everlasting credit and against monumental obstacles, de Gaulle managed to attract Frenchmen of all classes and of plural persuasions to his symbol of the Cross of Lorraine. He imposed unity on his motley following of idealists and adventurers. He dominated the multifaced Resistance. He overcame rival leaders without totally alienating their French or foreign sponsors. He procured substantial Allied economic and military backing yet avoided ever giving justification to charges of being a British tool or an American agent.

From 1940 to 1942, de Gaulle worked in London to elicit the allegiance of all possible Frenchmen who had escaped the occupied or unoccupied zone. Under his command, he enlisted most of those who had been evacuated at Dunkirk and those who later fled France. In Frenchmen at home, he attempted to fan the flame of resistance against the enemy, foster obstructionism against Vichy, and efface the image Vichy tried to convey of his being merely a deserter with a death penalty on his head. To the colonies, de Gaulle also extended the invitation to adhere to Free France and defy the Germans and Vichyites. At the same time, he sought and received official recognition and subsidies from a Churchill who lamented that the Cross of Lorraine was the heaviest he had to bear during the war. But, since Churchill also implicitly confessed his willingness to make a pact with the devil if British interests could be advanced, smooth relations with the British Prime Minister were more possible than with the American President. Roosevelt suspected the French General of colonialism, militarism, and authoritarianism. The ill feeling was unfortunately reciprocal. De Gaulle was firmly convinced of American designs for the liquidation or acquisition of the French Empire.

By 1943, de Gaulle had enlarged his staff and formed a French National Committee that included French political party representatives as "ministers." Without diverting his energies from military and diplomatic concerns, de Gaulle permitted the initiation of discussion on constitution-making and political, social, and economic programs for the future. After the invasion of North Africa and the move from London to Algiers, de Gaulle was able to eliminate General Henri Giraud as competitor for headship of the French National Liberation Committee. In the Consultative Assembly that appeared in 1943 as part of a "Provisional Government," delegates from the principal Resistance groups took their place alongside those of political parties including the Communists. Free France and the Resistance had been adroitly fused, with de Gaulle as chief of the combined whole. French armies under him were poised by June, 1944, to coordinate their operations with the metropolitan Resistance fighters also under his command to liberate their homeland from the Nazis.

The Resistance movement constituted the last but not least category in which some Frenchmen might associate or against which others might inveigh. The tens of thousands of Frenchmen who sacrificed their lives and the hundreds of thousands who survived the ordeal of dedicated heroism perhaps redeemed the greater millions who collaborated with or resigned themselves to the vicious enemy. Certainly the Resistance restored French morale and gave striking evidence to Frenchman and foreigner of a vitality and democratic activism long absent from the final years of the Third Republic.

The origins and motives of the Resistance were highly mixed. To the unifying thread of patriotism was stranded a detestation of

Vichy's collaborating or fence-straddling German policy and Vichy's undemocratic political, social, and economic manifestations. Along with patriots and idealists from all classes in France, opportunists were undoubtedly arrayed who saw a chance for fame or fortune as well as those who temperamentally sought the excitement and violence provided by a hunted, dangerous underground existence. As varied as the origins, motives, and forms of collaboration, the operations of the Resistance ranged from daring armed attacks on German troops to snide remarks about Nazi barbarism.

Organized resistance, in contrast to isolated acts of individuals, began in the unoccupied zone soon after the armistice. Emanating from Lyons and other industrial or mining centers, there radiated a more and more connected network of resistance groups. Demobilized army officers as well as political party leaders, journalists, professors, and students established and gravitated toward three main organizations. Each had a clandestine newspaper or some type of publication. *Combat, Libération,* and *Franc-Tireur* emerged by the end of 1942 as the leading underground units.

In the north, where the German authorities watched vigilantly, more difficulty was experienced and less contact was possible among the nascent movements. Recruited mainly from military and intellectual circles, the *Organisation Civile et Militaire* (OCM) exhibited conservative political tendencies but nevertheless slashed at collaborators and Germans. *Libération-Nord,* on the other hand, was principally socialist in membership and outlook. Students in Paris, who could be found in numerous other splinter groups, were the leading architects and activists in the third outstanding organization in occupied France — *Défense de la France.*

To the Communist Party must be reserved a special place of honor — and dishonor — in the chronicles of the Resistance. Although individual and often defecting members partook in resistance before Hitler's invasion of the Soviet Union in June, 1941, the Party record was a dismal one of watchful association with the Nazis, as per Moscow directive. When Soviet needs finally coincided with French patriotism, the Communist Party plunged into resistance with a vigor and effectiveness that earned the admiration and gratitude of even non-Communists for years to come. The *Front National* was the cross-zone resistance vehicle of the Communist Party, although individual party members had joined (or infiltrated) many other units. Communist and non-Communist elements comprised the bands of young people who were fleeing the Nazi labor draft in ever greater numbers. Seeking refuge in the wooded hills (*maquis*) of the unoccupied zone and later linked with armed bands elsewhere in France, these men constituted a paramilitary resistance organization called the French Forces of the Interior (FFI).

The separate, uncoordinated resistance groups in both zones achieved nominal unity in 1943 under the direction of Jean Moulin, a Free French representative parachuted into France the year before. On his death by betrayal and Nazi torture, the National Resistance Council that he had established chose a new president, Georges Bidault. Friction within the movement and rivalry between the underground and the Free French were minimized so that, by the end of 1943, de Gaulle could be recognized as head of the French National Committee. In it the Free French and the Resistance were joined. Beneath the superficial unity, however, there were three discernible blocs: Communist and Communist-affiliated; socialist, Christian democrat and liberal; and Gaullist. In the Gaullist camp were not only adherents who would follow the General to any destiny, but also men who numbered themselves in the second-named bloc depending on the issue at stake. The implications for postwar French politics would soon become obvious, but rapture preceded despair.

By early 1944, collaboration was confined to a hard core of true believers and a large number of utterly compelled Frenchmen; the Vichy regime was upheld only by diehard reactionaries, congenital trimmers, and the German army. The ranks of the Resistance were swollen by new adherents who acted as generally ready partners under de Gaulle with the formerly separate Free French forces in North Africa. The mass of citizens in metropolitan France continued publicly in their daily routine but reveled privately in the joy of an imminent liberation. Hope had risen in 1943 and 1944 with the Allied victories in North Africa, the invasion of Italy, Russian counterattacks after the Nazi calamity at Stalingrad, massive aerial bombardment of *Festung Europa,* and multiplying rumors of an impending second front.

Rumor became reality on June 6, 1944. Allied parachutists were followed by waves of troops landing on the Normandy beaches south of Cherbourg. By the end of July, the Allies had poured in sufficient manpower and matériel to achieve a breakthrough near the devastated city of Saint-Lô. Striking east, the Allies swept across France to sight Paris by the latter part of August. Meanwhile, on August 15, amphibious Allied forces established strongpoints on the southern French coast, seized Toulon and Marseilles, and began the march north to Lyons. The liberation of Paris was accomplished by August 25 and the fleeing Germans were pursued out of northern France. With the exception of scattered pockets and more sizeable portions of Alsace-Lorraine, France was free of Germans by the end of September.

A bare outline of the events of liberation is easy to sketch; an assessment of the French role is somewhat more difficult. In the D-Day landings in Normandy, French army participation was negligible. Only a token force of fewer than two hundred Frenchmen were permitted to associate with the hundreds of thousands of Americans, British, and Canadians. Barred by a disapproving Roosevelt from the planning and execution of the assault, de Gaulle was understandably stung to the quick. Nevertheless swallowing his pride, and possibly storing the memory for future vengeance, he was shortly given access to his homeland and the right to transfer from England the French divisions under General Philippe Leclerc. Although French army units per se had contributed little to the invasion and breakthrough of June and July, 1944, the French Resistance had assumed a larger role. Allied superiority in manpower and weapons along with German miscalculation as to the location and size of the main Allied penetration was enhanced by the exploits of the Resistance. By daring sabotage of the German communication and transportation system, by outright engagement against German troops, by liquidation of bypassed German enclaves, and by ready reports to the Allies on German military installations and movements, Frenchmen individually, in groups, and in the French Forces of the Interior speeded the Allied victory in Normandy. General Dwight Eisenhower estimated the underground's worth to have been that of several divisions – a valuable but not crucial supplement.

In the invasion and penetration of southern France, the story was different. For there, the operation was essentially a French one – French divisions under General de Lattre de Tassigny coordinated efforts with the Resistance to evict the Nazis from that area. Joining Leclerc's divisions after the liberation of Paris, de Lattre's troops formed a cohesive French army in the field of battle in Alsace-Lorraine. On the other hand, neither Anglo-American nor French armies were the agents of liberation in the southwestern quarter of France. In the quadrilateral bounded by the Pyrenees, the Atlantic, the Loire, and the Rhône, isolated branches of the Resistance and more articulated units of the FFI killed, captured, or expelled the feeble German garrisons.

Perhaps the most dramatic chapter in the history of the liberation unfolded in Paris. Spontaneous uprisings of an excited population, calculated insurrection by late-joiners and early resisters, intervention by neutral diplomats, disobedience of the German military commander, and the proximity of the Allied armies – all combined harmoniously to make a glorious day of August 25, 1944, the day Paris was finally liberated.

Out of the adversity and deep-seated divisions of the war years sprang a France united and bursting with hope. The heinous acts and the declining fortunes of the Nazis reduced the appeal and excuse of collaboration. The fading semi-independence of the Vichy regime after 1942 bred the ineffectiveness of its officials and sympathizers. Teamed together under the dynamic leadership of de Gaulle by 1944, the Free French and the Resistance captured the imagination and support of the French nation. Through the clandestine press and by heroic example, the Resistance helped rekindle the chilled principles of liberty, equality, and fraternity. France aflame exhibited a singleness of purpose in driving out the Nazis and in readying itself for a brave new world. The harmony and exuberance lingered but briefly; the memory would long persist.

In the wake of the advancing Allied armies, there existed a political vacuum in the liberated cities and villages of France. German occupation authorities had been ousted, collaborating French officials discreetly disappeared or less discreetly found oblivion from the firing squads, and Vichy appointees suffered a similar end as a willing Laval and a protesting, 88-year-old Pétain were bundled off on August 20 to a temporary haven (or confinement) in Germany. In anticipation of the absence of authority, the Americans and British had briefly toyed with the idea of establishing an Allied Military Government in liberated France. Wisdom and tact prevailed, however, when it was decided to entrust sovereign responsibility to de Gaulle. On the eve of the D-Day invasion, the Consultative Assembly in Algiers had proclaimed a Provisional Government with de Gaulle at its head. With the blessings of the Allies and with the more respected sanction of the Algiers representatives, de Gaulle was thus not merely the Commander-in-Chief of French military forces but political head of state in France itself.

Armed with these powers, the General proceeded to render another great service to his country — restoring order and asserting his authority. In those areas overrun by Allied and French troops, he immediately appointed prefects, mayors, and other officials. Elsewhere, the red flag was hoisted as often as the tricolor over public buildings, indicating the arbitrary installation of a Communist Resistance leader as local official. To these centers de Gaulle dispatched his delegates and ordered their investiture. By dint of his leadership and military superiority, the exigencies of the continuing war against the Nazis, and the undoubted hopes for future political benefits, the Communist Party organizations bowed sometimes reluctantly, but bowed nevertheless, to de Gaulle's will. By the fall and winter of 1944, more than four years of foreign or Vichy rule was concluded. After a wave of reprisals against tens of thousands of notorious collaborators and prominent Vichyites, order reigned under a free, independent, Provisional French government.

Representative forms were speedily re-established in France in 1945, first on the local and then on the national level. April and May elections in the municipalities and communes resulted in the installation of many Communists as mayors and city councillors, but local government was not of great significance in centralized France. A more complicated and more crucial set of elections was held in October. On the one hand, the French voters – women enjoying the privilege for the first time – were asked to decide between a revived but revised Third Republic and a new republic to be formed by a Constituent Assembly. By an overwhelming majority of 18,584,346 to 699,136, the citizens confirmed the decision of July 10, 1940; the Third Republic was officially discarded. Also, by a two-to-one margin, the preferred Constituent Assembly was urged to favor de Gaulle's plan of according limited powers and tenure to a new legislature instead of creating one of unrestricted sovereignty. The Assembly would have the right to choose the person who would combine temporarily the office of President and Premier.

As deputies in the 586-man Constituent Assembly thus endorsed and instructed by the referendum, the voters seated approximately equal numbers of Communists (152), SFIO's (143), and MRP's (150).[1] The dominant political parties of the Third Republic had suffered as severe a defeat as the Third Republic itself. The SFIO ran third to the Communists and the MRPs; the once mighty Radical-Socialists counted a mere 25 deputies.

One of the first acts of the new Constituent Assembly was to elect the patently sole appropriate candidate for the Presidency-

[1] The last-named party was a new one (*Mouvement Républicaine Populaire*), emerging from the Resistance and composed of liberal Catholics, non-Marxist trade unionists, and democrats of different professions and classes. Its nearest European equivalent would be a Christian Socialist or Christian Democratic Party.

Premiership of the Provisional Government. Despite some scattered opposition, Charles de Gaulle was so selected in November and empowered with a suspensive veto and the right to name a cabinet acceptable to the Assembly. A Provisional Government, elected democratically by liberated Frenchmen and Frenchwomen, was now ready to liquidate the past and chart the future.

1944–1958

The founding and foundering of the Fourth Republic

GODS might have trembled at the problems of the liberated Frenchman as he faced the postwar era; even de Gaulle recognized their enormity. In purely human terms, millions of Frenchmen needed rehabilitation. War had taken a toll of more than a million who could be mourned but never revived; over a million and a half would be released from prisoner-of-war stockades by the Germans. Hundreds of thousands were returned from forced labor or concentration camps as political deportees. Equal numbers clamored for evacuation from their wartime residence in the south to their domiciles – if they existed – in the north. Hundreds of thousands were homeless as a result of the 1940 blitzkrieg, the war-long bombardment, and the liberating invasion of 1944.

Compounding the human misery was the incredible material destruction. The shattered transportation and communications system, demolished factories, wrecked mines, riddled shops, and bomb-strewn farms lay in ruins from the artillery fire and aerial attacks of Germans and Allies, as well as from the patriotic sabotage of the Resistance. Occupation payments, Nazi looting, and black-market operations had helped destroy the financial structure. War costs and loss of overseas investments further depleted the shrunken French capital accounts.

Never an easy task for France, the political problem of establishing permanent forms was urgent. Whatever the form, the role of the state was a consideration, too. Unfulfilled demands and Resistance-bred aspirations seemed to spell out a much more socially conscious and perhaps welfare state at the very moment when the government would be burdened by heightened costs of rehabilitation and reconstruction.

A less tangible but equally real problem existed. A guilt-ridden, remorseful, or dejected population required a moral tonic. The intellectual community had already done much for a moral and spiritual renaissance by its *engagement* in political and social affairs during the war. Much of the defeatism and self-recrimination relating to the 1940 debacle and ensuing wartime experience had been effaced in the heroic days of resistance and liberation, but strong traces remained to be expunged.

Colonial troubles added to French woes. In dire need of the resources and prestige of empire, the French were beset by a rising tide of colonial unrest. Should the French attempt to re-assert their hold over the subject or associated peoples? Should they gracefully relax their grip to avoid the financial drain and moral stigma of repressive action? Or should they withdraw and deprive themselves of access to much-needed raw materials and trade? Should they abandon the long-felt mission of "civilizing" the areas?

Finally, in the realm of international affairs, the French also encountered serious problems. An independent, vigorous foreign policy was impossible. The French military establishment was too weak; the need for foreign aid in reconstruction was too impelling. The French armed forces, reconstituted by mid-1944, were scantily provided with conventional weapons, principally of American origin, and were not at all endowed with nuclear might. The capabilities and resources of France single-handed were no more adequate for the task of reviving the moribund economy. The unfolding rift, soon to become a cold war, between the giants of East and West, further perplexed and limited the scope of French foreign policy. Could the French, alone or in association with other small European states, pursue a neutral course as the United States and the Soviet Union disputed and battled each other's every move

in Europe and beyond? Did the Russian menace, exemplified by
broken promises and aggressive designs in Eastern and Central
Europe and magnified by the presence in France of a large Communist Party, dictate close ties with the United States? Millions of
Communists in France thought otherwise and countless non-Communists deplored French subservience to any foreign power. What,
too, of the German problem? Did the threat of Soviet advances
necessitate the fostering of a German recovery as a counterbalance,
or would a resurgent Germany repeat the dreadful pattern of the
1920s and 1930s?

To the liberated French nation of 1944–1945, the problems
were often painfully clear; the answers were not, although hopes
admittedly ran high. The French did not await the end of the war,
nor even liberation, to delineate their visions of the future. By
March, 1944, the National Council of Resistance was prepared to
proclaim a sweeping program of political, social, and economic
import. The Resistance Charter was more the product of the leaders
of the combined resistance movements than of their chief de Gaulle,
who continued to devote himself to military, diplomatic, and organi-
zational matters. To the disquietude of even staunch followers, he
had long refrained from precisely indicating his political, social,
and economic orientation. After directing understandable attention
to measures designed to punish traitors and undo the work of collaborators and Vichyites, the Charter affirmed the French intent to
restore and expand political democracy and civil liberties. More
innovating were the sections foreshadowing "the setting up of a
true economic and social democracy, entailing the eviction of the
great economic and financial feudalities." Reminiscent of and extending beyond the Popular Front program of prewar years,
nationalization was foretold in certain industries, mining, insurance,
and banking. In other fields, cooperatives were to be developed and
maintained. A planned economy was to be instituted, directed
democratically by management, workers, and government. Social
justice would be enhanced by proclaiming the right to work, restora-

tion of autonomous trade unionism, and the guarantee of subsistence and complete social security for all citizens.

Committed to the implementation of the Charter they had earlier formulated as members of the Resistance, the Communist, SFIO, and MRP victors in the 1945 elections worked also to fulfill the double function of the Provisional Government. First, the job was to provide France with basic legislation consonant with the Resistance Charter while steering the country through the problems facing it at war's end. The second function was to draft a constitution for submission to the electorate before the expiration of the seven-month term of the Assembly. The immediate rise of bitter feuds over an appropriate form of government and the subsequent fall of the compromise Fourth Republic in 1958 often serve to conceal the very substantial achievements of the Provisional Government and, in fact, of the Fourth Republic in its early years. Communist detractors and Gaullist opponents of the Fourth Republic preferred to see only weakness and inefficiency in the Republic they worked so hard to render weak and inefficient and finally buried in 1958.

The Provisional Government and the initial Assembly of the Fourth Republic legislated and put into operation the major portion of the Resistance Charter. Sometimes by vigilante instead of republican justice, notorious collaborators and prominent Vichyites were tried and condemned with loss of life, liberty, and/or property. Popular revulsion against the inequities of the trials and punishment as well as against the re-opening of old sores brought about a slackening of these activities by 1946. Laval had been shot; Pétain had been condemned to death but spared by de Gaulle's commuting the sentence to life imprisonment; thousands of others had suffered similar fates, and others, equally culpable, slipped quietly back to a "normal" existence.

The economic and social reforms of the Charter were more consistently enacted, although criticism of excess or inadequacy was heard. Nationalization took place with relative ease but often with near-catastrophic results for production rates. De Gaulle's limited nationalization of the Renault automobile enterprise, the coal mines of the northeast, and Air France was notably extended. The Bank of France and the four greatest deposit banks as well as the largest insurance companies became public institutions. Gas and electricity and transportation facilities by land, sea, and air soon followed. To the stockholders of the nationalized industries was offered compensation generally in the form of state bonds yielding about 3 percent. The Monnet Plan for the modernization and renovation of the French economy was adopted. Admirably forwarded by the Fourth and Fifth Republics, this Plan anticipated and provided huge appropriations, massive technical improvements, and close cooperation of state and private persons.

Fulfilling the promise of the Resistance Charter, a comprehensive system of social security was put into effect. Re-enforcing or supplementing the Third Republic's and Vichy's contributions, unemployment, sickness, and accident compensation was sizeably augmented, as were old-age pensions, maternity and health benefits, and family allowances. By the last-named item, many a French worker would receive amounts equal to his wage — no small encouragement and support for larger families. For labor, there were still other significant reforms. Trade unions were not only re-instituted, but members were given greater protection in the handling of grievances and more direction in the processes of production and in determining working conditions in the factories. True collective bargaining, however, was postponed, since the government controlled wages in the interest of reconstruction at a minimum expense.

The enactment of this vast program conceived in the Resistance Charter did not take place without the appearance of deep divisions among the dominant parties of 1944–1946: the Communist, SFIO, and MRP. The Communists and many SFIO's expressed disappointment with the feebleness of the nationalization laws, the social security legislation, and the workers' rights to associate in management. In the eyes of the left, too little had been accomplished, either, in expanding the educational system or in democratizing the civil service. Other socialists and most of the MRP feared they had gone too far in tampering with private enterprise and saddling the state with impossible financial burdens.

Not only among the three parties but also between them and President de Gaulle, there developed friction over nationalization and over the share of appropriations due the military forces as against those due welfare. The debate between the Assembly and the General became so heated that, in January 1946, while in the midst of reform and constitution-drafting, de Gaulle resigned. It was not then nor is it yet clear whether the General expected to be recalled by a chastened Assembly or whether he retired with no great political expectations to the quiet of memoir-writing. It was quite evident, however, that he would not play the parliamentary game according to usual French rules which he did not devise. As might be expected, the unity bred by wartime necessity began to evaporate after the Nazi enemy was beaten and the former partners began to examine issues other than the common foreign threat.

Even greater acrimony than that engendered by the reform legislation attended the Provisional Government's endeavor to fulfill its second function — that of drawing up a constitution. Again there arose discord among the three main political parties and complications injected by the initially silent and then intervening voice of de Gaulle. All factions agreed that a democratic constitution was desirable, but each faction had one or several versions of the type of institution that was deemed most suitable.

The two extreme positions were exemplified by the Communists on the one hand and de Gaulle on the other. Essentially reaching for complete control over the state in a drive to collectivize all property, the Communists proposed a unicameral assembly with absolutely sovereign and unchecked powers. Neither an upper house nor an independent executive should be created to thwart the popular will. Behind this superficially laudable democratic suggestion lay the Communist Party's assumption that it would soon secure enough electoral success to dominate the Assembly. The Party wished no further obstacle on its path to power.

Diametrically opposed to this view, but still within the context of a democratic system, stood de Gaulle. For him, a strong executive and an upper house of Parliament should be created to act as a check on a nevertheless powerful Chamber. Mindful of the instability of ministerial regimes in the Third Republic, de Gaulle would arm the executive with the power to dissolve the lower house and with the right to name and control his own cabinet.

Both sides to the quarrel seemed blank or highly selective in their historical memories of France's political past. The Communists apparently preferred to overlook the weakness and inefficiency of French democratic governments in which feuding partners in parliamentary coalitions could wreck or paralyze the government. They seemed neglectful, too, of recalling the fate of liberty when all-powerful committees of Parliament could conduct an unchecked Terror. For his part, de Gaulle discounted or failed to remember the dangers to representative government in France when executives as Kings or Presidents possessed even limited powers. The French experience with Louis Napoleon, Marshal MacMahon, and General Boulanger was alarming. Furthermore, the presence of an upper house had often sufficed not merely to delay but to frustrate completely popular programs of needed reform and urgent action.

Between the two extremes of a sovereign Assembly and a presidential regime were scattered the recommendations of SFIOs and MRPs. Although some socialists sided with the Communists on the constitutional issue and many MRPs rallied to the General, the majority in the two parties worked at a compromise. Especially was this so after the referendum of May, 1946, rejected the draft submitted by the Communists and splintered socialists. The left had obtained a majority in the Constituent Assembly for an "ultrademocratic" draft constitution. At the polls on May 5, 1946, however, 10,583,724 citizens voted against and 9,453,675 in favor of the left's creation. De Gaulle's campaigning, MRP and center-right opposition had won the day in a negative sense. Elections were consequently held in June for a Second Constituent Assembly. The MRP won another victory, increasing its delegation from 150 to 169. The Communists slipped slightly, from 152 to 146; but, to the SFIO factional distress was added the loss of 14 seats of their original 143.

During the summer and early fall of 1946, the MRP and the SFIO prepared a second draft of a constitution. Respectful of the mandate of the people but reluctant to adopt the forms recommended by de Gaulle, the MRP and SFIO reached a compromise. In this second draft, there were introduced a weak upper house and a President empowered to name the Premier. For fear that continued stalemate might play into the hands of de Gaulle and his proposals for a more powerful executive, even the Communists gave their assent. Strenuously attacked by de Gaulle, only half-heartedly supported by the Communists and socialists, condoned with mixed feelings by the MRP, the draft was submitted to the voters in October, 1946. There were 9,257,432 who approved, and 8,125,295 cast negative ballots. The Fourth Republic was born, but it had the blessings of only one third of the registered voters. One third had actively damned it, and another third, by abstention, had revealed hostility or apathy. It was an appropriate beginning for a Republic that would have a sad and practically unmourned ending a dozen years later.

From the provisions of the Constitution of 1946 and clarifications in the ensuing decade, the Fourth Republic emerged as a parliamentary regime of a highly democratic nature. The existence of a President and an upper house (the Council of the Republic) acted as only a mild check on the virtually sovereign lower house (the National Assembly). The President, as under the Third Republic, was elected for a single seven-year term by the combined houses. The ceremonial, titular head of state, he possessed little real power. Although the President, until 1951, enjoyed the right of investing a Prime Minister, that designate could be installed only after receiving a majority in the National Assembly. The Council of the Republic, elected indirectly by a complicated system of local and national bodies, detracted little from the more extensive power of the Assembly. Even though the upper house, in 1954, was accorded coequal rights of initiating legislation except for money bills and treaties, it could delay passage of no legislation for more than one hundred days. The Council, unlike the Senate of the Third Republic, had neither exclusive nor shared powers of dissolving the lower house nor of ousting a cabinet. The National Assembly stood out as the dominant body in legislative primacy and control over the executive and ministers, but it had curtailed powers of constitutional amendment. Under certain circumstances, the President could dissolve the Assembly and call for new elections, but the Presidents of the Fourth Republic declined in practice to exercise this prerogative. The Assembly was king.

The electoral system for choosing deputies in the National Assembly was one of modified proportional representation. By receiving a plurality of votes in a particular district, a single party or group of affiliated parties received all the seats. This method worked to the disadvantage of the two political pariahs of the Fourth Republic — the Communists and the Gaullist *Rassemblement du Peuple Français* (RPF) — but to the advantage of such parties as the SFIO, MRP, and Radical-Socialists, who were willing and able to make pre-election coalitions.

The effectiveness of this type of democratic regime would be determined by the ability of one or more political parties to guide the Assembly in a consistent program. In times of prosperity and domestic tranquility, foreign peace, and colonial order, parliamentary divisions and shifting cabinets might be no more than fare for music hall comedy. Otherwise, lack of consensus in the Assembly and excessive party wrangling could paralyze the sovereign body and thus weaken the state and imperil the nation. Such, unfortunately, would be the fate of the Fourth Republic.

From its birth in October, 1946, until its death in May, 1958, the Fourth Republic was governed by three National Assemblies, elected successively in November, 1946; June, 1951; and January,

1956. The political party composition and popular votes are indicated in Table 6–1.

Table 6–1. National Assembly Election Results (1946–1956) *

PARTY	NOVEMBER, 1946		JUNE, 1951		JANUARY, 1956	
	Popular Vote (in millions)	Number of Seats	Popular Vote (in millions)	Number of Seats	Popular Vote (in millions)	Number of Seats
Communist	5.4	168	4.9	96	4.7	145
SFIO	3.4	105	2.8	94	2.9	88
MRP	5.0	167	2.3	83	2.1	70
Radical-Socialist and allies	1.9	70	2.0	82	2.0	68
Right-wing	3.1	80			2.6	94
RPF			4.1	100	.8	16
Poujadist					2.3	51

* Figures were compiled from newspaper accounts and official releases of the French government.

In the persisting absence of a two-party system, the French resorted to their traditional republican procedure of coalitions of parties for legislative and cabinet-making purposes. Under the Provisional Government during 1945–1946 and under the Fourth Republic until May, 1947, tripartite agreement among the Communists, SFIOs, and MRPs was characteristic of political operations. Despite the serious differences already noted within this bloc, the big three managed to compromise sufficiently to run the country.

Tripartitism broke down in 1947 when the Communist Party detached itself and was henceforth harried out of governmental posts by its former partners. The Party's decision to break with the bloc was based on several considerations. Its association had not resulted in the anticipated political gain of securing a commanding position in the governments. De Gaulle, from 1944 to 1946, and the SFIO-MRP team thereafter had shared only insignificant ministries with the Communists. The important and much-sought portfolios of the Interior, Defense, and Foreign Affairs, which might have enabled the infiltrating Communists to repeat their Eastern and Central European machinations, were guarded jealously by de Gaulle or SFIO and MRP stalwarts. Frustrated in their efforts to control the state through the acquisition of key posts, the Communists in 1947 feared losing control over the labor unions if the Party persisted in reconstruction governments that froze wages and refused to allow strikes. Colonial and foreign issues further soured the Communist Party on tripartitism. Revolt against French rule in Indochina forced the French Communist Party to decide either to vote for appropriations recommended by the "patriotic" government of which the Communists were part or to support anticolonialism as urged by Moscow. Tentative Communist adherence to a repressive colonial policy in early 1947 was repudiated in April and May, and a split in the coalition became inevitable. A month later, the Communist denunciation of the Marshall Plan with its promise of massive economic aid destroyed even the slim chance of reconciling the three major parties.

Despite their withdrawal from the government, the Communists had no intention of relinquishing the offices they had earned since 1945. Socialist Premier Paul Ramadier, however, showed no mercy in eliminating them from police and security forces as well as from much of the civil service. The Communist Party, so successful elsewhere in subverting representative governments by "popular front" associations, suffered a severe setback in France in 1947. The tactics of obstructionism adopted after 1947 were no more fruitful than those of cooperation before 1947 in producing a soviet in France. The Party nevertheless remained a potent instrument, commanding one fourth of the votes, a similar percentage of deputies in the Assembly, and such extraparliamentary weapons as trade unions and *L'Humanité*. Whatever the motives and methods of the Communist Party, a sizeable portion of the French electorate refused to overlook the Party's resistance record, its tripartite contribution to social reform, and its unceasing campaign for the immediate interests of the workers in postwar France.

In 1947, opposition to the government and to the very foundation of the Fourth Republic began to crystallize not only on the left, but also on the Gaullist right. Re-emerging from his seclusion at Colombey-les-Deux-Eglises, the wartime leader and onetime

De Ge l

President appealed for a *Rassemblement du Peuple Français* (RPF).
His avowed intention was not to add another rival political party
to the long list of existing ones, but to rally Frenchmen of all
parties to a movement that would oblige revision of the Fourth
Republic's Constitution. The goal was a presidential regime from
which could flow a more coherent and positive program of reforms, *De*
which de Gaulle only imprecisely defined, and a national revival. *Gaulle*
Into the ranks of the RPF there streamed a widely assorted sampling
of all classes, parties, and professions. The dynamism of the movement attracted intellectuals and politicians wearied of the sterility
of the middle parties, erstwhile Communists despairing of the now
unpatriotic and fruitless obstructionism of their former Party, and
even disgruntled workers. As the 1951 election statistics revealed,
the MRP was the principal source of RPF recruitment; half the
voters had defected to the Rally. Striking successes in municipal
elections in 1947 had foreshadowed similar victory in the national
election of June, 1951. Impelled by the nature of the political
system to transform his Rally into a political party unless he
wished to execute a *coup d'état,* de Gaulle reluctantly became the
titular but extraparliamentary leader of more than one hundred
RPF deputies in the new Assembly.

Having garnished more than half the popular vote and corralled
more than one third of the seats in the Assembly, the Communist
left and the Gaullist right imposed on the center the urgent necessity of unity to save the institutions of the Fourth Republic. The
so-called Third Force of SFIO, truncated MRP, Radical-Socialist,
and center-right independent parties could obtain a parliamentary
majority by coalition. It was a fragile majority, but it was a majority.
When the constitutional question was on the agenda, the Third
Force formed vigorously solid to blunt the attacks from the left
and the right. On socioeconomic matters, Church school aid, foreign
affairs, and colonial policy, however, the motley factions of the
Third Force went their separate ways. To maintain the coalition for
political purposes, therefore, the Third Force frequently was condemned to nonpolicy, nonaction, *immobilisme.* Cabinet followed

cabinet at an alarming rate as the parliamentary coalitions of the Third Force broke down for lack of consensus on almost every problem except that of political forms.

Before plunging into the abyss of nearly total *immobilisme* after the 1954 opening of the Algerian rebellion, the Third Force enjoyed some promise of permanency. After the 1951 elections, the fortunes of the RPF declined. The General studiously refused to organize an insurrection against the detested Republic. The Rally degenerated into a type of maneuvering and splintering parliamentary party so deplored by its original partisans. As a minority party alienated from any major bloc, it was unable to effectuate constitutional reform. By the 1956 elections, the RPF had dwindled to a mere sixteen deputies voted in by fewer than a million Frenchmen. Once more, the General resumed his political aloofness and magnificent literary endeavors.

Unfortunately for the Third Force and its vehicle, the Fourth Republic, the defectors from the RPF did not all rejoin the MRP or the other traditionally republican parties. Instead, many enlisted in such movements as that of Poujade or in right-wing groups of bourgeois and peasant elements. The short-lived Poujadist movement, which rose meteorically to win more than two million votes and fifty-one seats in the 1956 Assembly, was an outpouring of the discontent of craftsmen, shopkeepers, whitecollar workers in private and public employ, and other petty bourgeois citizens. Their precise complaint over taxes masked more nebulous fears of loss of social and economic status in a welfare state and a rapidly industrializing economy. The Third Force weathered this storm, though, as it had the tempest of Communist obstructionism and RPF hostility. From across the Mediterranean, however, came the hurricane that sank the Third Force and, with it, the Fourth Republic.

The political performance of the Fourth Republic was in part determined, in part paralleled, by its economic and social record. Endemic strikes, housing shortages, spiraling inflation, financial distress, and fiscal malaise adversely affected political operations. Behind the tattered veil of economic and social disturbances, however, there materialized an incredible growth and transformation of the economy and an unprecedented program of social security for the masses. Without completely deprecating de Gaulle's later contribution, the much-vaunted prosperity and even the puffed-up nationalist gestures of the Fifth Republic owed much to the maligned Fourth Republic's feat of economic reconstruction and modernization.

Plagued throughout its years by labor unrest, the Fourth Republic seemed incapable of meeting the demands of the mass of workers. The rigid requirements of reconstructing devastated France, the bias of many politicians in the Third Force, and the drain of colonial wars deprived the proletariat of its desired share of the national product. Unemployment was not an issue. In fact, half a million Algerians and hundreds of thousands of Italians and Spaniards were gladly admitted to supplement the metropolitan labor force. The heaven of full employment, however, was clouded by a consistent wage lag as prices steadily and sometimes precipitously rose in postwar France. Pitifully inadequate housing, black-market absorption of food and fuel supplies, and the government's reluctance to permit more extensive worker association in management constituted additional grievances.

As long as the Communist Party remained loyal to its tripartite cooperation during the Provisional Government and the early months of the Fourth Republic, labor agitation presented a serious but not catastrophic political problem. In good faith and often at the expense of incurring losses of adherents, the Communist Party until 1947 curbed the restive labor organizations in its grip. Wildcat strikes of a widespread nature nevertheless broke out, adversely affecting production in 1946 and 1947. Once the Communists detached themselves from the government in May, 1947, partly because they feared losing their hold over the discontented proletariat, strikes became more general and longer lasting. Strikes for economic grievances were accompanied by stoppages to protest against the government's acceptance of the Marshall Plan and against the French repression of colonial uprisings. Strikes against private enterprise were multiplied by strikes of civil servants and of workers in nationalized industries. Guided as much by the desire to ensure social benefits and inexpensive reconstruction as by a calculated favoritism to businessmen, the government replied with insultingly small concessions and aggravating restrictions. By its unacceptable economic and social policy and its strike-breaking activities, the Fourth Republic thus forfeited the undivided loyalty of the masses to its democratic form. A residue of tensions carried over into the 1950s even though the production of consumer goods increased and real wages rose.

Economic and social policy served not only to set the workers at odds with the government, but also contributed to the fragility of the coalitions of the Third Force. Economists in the SFIO would propose different solutions to wage, tax, and inflationary problems from those suggested by the Radical-Socialist financial experts in the governmental team. More traditionalist bourgeois politicians strained to keep wages steady even if prices mounted. Indirect taxes, too, were often preferred to income taxes or more radical revenue measures. The result of these opposing economic interests and philosophies tended not just to make for an ineffective compromise, but to prevent the government from taking any action that might wreck the parliamentary coalition and force out the cabinet. Consensus on political defense of the Fourth Republic thus did not imply automatic agreement on economic issues. The budget's imbalance would thereby be perpetuated, the franc's position in international exchange would deteriorate, and French foreign credit would be dangerously undermined while the government sat by timidly and hopefully awaited some future readjustment by natural or magical laws.

In a land where Jules Romains noted that several contradictory formulas could appear to be simultaneously true, an initially concealed economic miracle was taking place in the midst of economic and social vilification and political *immobilisme*. Labor, capital, resources, and technical skill were applied with zeal and competence to the task of reconstructing and modernizing the economic structure. Transportation facilities were repaired; port installations were modernized; canal and railroad services were improved; roads and highways were extended. All were made available within five years of war's end. Table 6–2 illustrates the noteworthy progess in production in selected but vital sectors of the economy.

Table 6–2. Production in Selected Sectors, 1929–1953 *

	1929	1938	1946	1952–1953
Coal (millions of tons)	55	47.6	49.3	56
Electricity (billions of kilowatt hours)	15.5	20.8	23	41
Oil, refined (millions of tons)	0	7	2.8	22
Steel (millions of tons)	9.7	6.2	4.4	10.5
Cement (millions of tons)	6.2	3.6	3.4	9
Tractors	20,000	30,000	50,000	225,000
Nitrogen (thousands of tons)	73	177,000	127,000	277,000

* Figures were compiled from statistics released by French government agencies.

By 1953, the French had matched and, in many instances, surpassed the high production rate of 1929; total production was 150 percent greater than in 1938. In the last year of the Fourth Republic, 1958, automobiles and other consumer goods were being purchased in quantities four times exceeding those at the beginning of the 1950s. Not only was the output vastly multiplied, but also the plant facilities in steel and electricity were rendered modern and efficient.

Possibly more significant than the raw increases in production was the elevated productivity of the worker. Through mechanization and diligence, he mined one-third more coal daily in 1953 than in 1938 (3,252 pounds compared with 2,165). Productivity in French mines nearly equalled that in the German Ruhr by 1950. Similar advances were characteristic of steel, textiles, and other items. On the farms, the yield per acre of wheat leaped from 23.1 bushels in 1938 to 30.8 in 1952 and 34.1 in 1957. For human and livestock consumption, corn mounted from 20.4 bushels per acre in 1938 to 38.9 in 1957. The use of fertilizers and employment of mechanical devices worked their ways. The postwar spurt in population — another advertised barometer of French vitality — was more than paced by the 5 percent annual growth of the economy. France under the Fourth Republic had become a young country with a modern industrial machine whose quality surpassed British standards and began to equal those of America and Germany.

A host of factors contributed to the startling economic recovery and progress. Most credit should go to French initiative, foreign aid, and cooperation between domestic and international organizations. Brilliantly conceived and adroitly executed, the Monnet Plan began to function under the Fourth Republic immediately after its articulation by the Provisional Government. First established was a General Commissariat for Planning and Productivity, whose original thirty to forty members were engineers, university professors, and public officials in the domain of finance and taxation. The role of the General Commissariat was to advise the government and business on economic policy. At first attached directly to the Prime Minister's office and then to the Ministry of Finance, the Commissariat served as a forum and data-collecting agency for public officials and business executives as well as for trade union leaders.

Under the Monnet Plan there were also formed modernization committees, each corresponding to a particular sector of economic activity (such as steel, coal, cement, and so on) or to principal problems of concern to all sectors (such as financing, labor relations, research, and so on). Permanent but voluntary and unpaid members of these committees came from three sources: business, labor, and government. As in the case of the General Commissariat, specialists from university or other circles were often consulted or pressed into temporary service. Each committee mapped out production and distribution patterns in its own sector, although frequently in consultation with the general Commissariat. Freed from the taint of bureaucratic controls or the imposition of fine schemes from above, this relatively decentralized arrangement engendered much enthusiasm from the members who were both planners and executors of economic change.

The first Five Year Plan began in 1947 with emphasis not on general, across-the-board increases in production, but on six basic sectors: coal, steel, electricity, cement, farm machinery, and transportation. Capital investment in these sectors was derived from three principal sources: public appropriations (30 percent), private funds (40 percent self-financing and 15 percent bank credit), and foreign aid (15 percent Marshall Plan under the European Recovery Program). The proportions reveal the dominance of private over public contribution and of domestic over foreign. Without overlooking the crucial and generous American billions, the French could justifiably point with pride to the bootstrap nature of their operation. Of the total investment, 20 percent was allocated to North Africa and overseas territories. Again, the French could answer American critics by citing the greater relative portion of French than American capital or aid that went to underdeveloped areas.

French economic planning was not restricted to the narrow confines of metropolitan France or even the broader limits of the restive French Union. The Fourth Republic often pioneered ventures involving European-wide economic association and integration. Stimulated by the demands of the American-sponsored European Recovery Program, motivated by a desire to keep a resurgent West Germany within the framework of controlling supranational institutions, spurred on by the needs for markets and resources, encouraged by the Monnet Plan advisors, the French devised or participated in the Schuman Plan and the Common Market.

Two years of debate was capped in 1952 by the inauguration of the Schuman Plan for a European Coal and Steel Community made up of France, Germany, Belgium, Holland, Luxembourg, and Italy. By a complicated set of arrangements, the coal and steel production of these Western European states would be managed by a High Authority of representatives from member states. A free market in coal and steel was inaugurated. Tariffs and national subsidies were eliminated; marginal or inefficient mines and mills were closed down; financial resources were pooled and allocated for modernization; and labor relations were guided by common standards.

With much broader implications for the economic and political future of France and the rest of Europe, treaties were signed in March, 1957, for the formation of the European Common Market. Although Great Britain and all the other Western European states were invited to join, only the six members of the European Coal and Steel Community subscribed. Although some of the authors of the Common Market envisioned ultimate political integration, economic consolidation was the initial concern. Designed to become effective in January, 1958, the Common Market foresaw progressive abolition of tariffs and other restrictions on trade among the members, who also undertook to engage in planning and operations similar to those of the Monnet Plan. The material and prestigious benefits of the Common Market, however, did not redound to the sponsoring Fourth Republic, which expired in May, 1958, but to the succeeding Fifth Republic of Charles de Gaulle.

Despite Communist harassment, nationalist alarm-ringing by Gaullist and right-wing elements, and tedious bickering within the scant majority of the Third Force, the Fourth Republic had rendered a valuable service to French economic development. In foreign policy and in colonial affairs, the record was far less brilliant and finally fatal.

French foreign policy from 1944 to 1958 was determined by several considerations: the German problem, the Russian menace, the need for foreign aid, and colonial disorder. As in domestic matters, in foreign affairs, too, the specific policy adopted by the French at any one moment was guided by the urgency of the particular problem at that moment. Intensification of the Russian menace, for example, led the French to modify their German policy. A threatening U.S.S.R. also pushed the French into close association with other European states in the Brussels Pact of 1948 and with the United States in the North Atlantic Treaty Organization (NATO) a year later. The French were nevertheless more perplexed than the Americans or British in evaluating the relative dangers of a resurgent Germany and an expansive Soviet Union. Relaxation of Soviet pressure in Europe tended to weaken the French attachment to their allies, especially the United States. The harrowing French colonial crises often produced near-rupture with the otherwise protective American ally. The Suez expedition of 1956 was a case in point. As a result of conflicting interests and shifting focal points of the unfolding cold war, French foreign policy thus wavered among several courses: an independent direction, neutralism in concert with other European states, or alignment with the United States in NATO.

As France emerged from the Second World War, attempts to pursue an independent course were foredoomed to failure. The combination of the drastic necessity for foreign aid and the French military inferiority vis-à-vis the two giants of East and West reduced the French to being beggars rather than arbiters in European and world affairs. De Gaulle, as President of the Provisional Governments of 1944 to 1946, nevertheless achieved some slight elevation of France's international status. French prestige was enhanced by de Gaulle's dramatic trip to Moscow in 1944 with the resulting Franco-Soviet Pact of mutual assistance against any recurrence of German aggression. From the Yalta and Potsdam Conferences, to which an infuriated de Gaulle had not been invited, there issued forth more tangible gains for the French. Prime Minister Churchill, fearing that American postwar demobilization and withdrawal from Germany would leave Britain with the burden of military occupation and feeding of the western zones, convinced the reluctant Russians and Americans of the virtues of adding France to the Big Three. The French were thereby assigned a zone, carved out of the British and American sectors, and a place on the Allied Control Commission.

With troops in occupied Germany and with a voice on the Commission, the French could exert greater leverage in shaping the future of Germany to their tastes. Between 1945 and 1948, French interests and policies in German occupation conformed more closely with the Russians' than with the British and Americans'. Bitter memories, economic needs, and military considerations fused to produce a punitive, restrictive French occupation policy. The breakdown of the Potsdam agreement to treat Germany as a single economic unit was signaled by the joining of the British and American sectors into a Bizonia in late 1946. The French refused to amalgamate their zone and continued to reduce it to an agricultural, pastoral level, while in Bizonia the Germans were given Marshall Plan aid and the right to larger quotas of industrial production. The French could not long stand aside, however, when in 1948–1949 the Russian blockade of Berlin imperiled even French interests. With misgivings for their future security as Germany was being economically revived, the French faced up to the urgency of the Soviet threat and in 1949 attached their sector to Bizonia to create Trizonia. The territorial basis of a West German Federal Republic was thus formed, spelling an end to unilateral French activity in treating the German problem.

To meet the Russian threat, the French had yielded their zone of occupation but did not abandon attempts to contain the reinvigorated Germans.[2] Nor did the French immediately align themselves politically and militarily with the United States. Although beneficiaries of American aid, first under Lend Lease and then the Marshall Plan after 1947, the French assumed a pose of independent and associated neutralism in relations with the United States and the Soviet Union. That such a pose was possible was due largely to American willingness to permit the French nearly unrestricted latitude in internal and even international decision-making. Although many Frenchmen would scorn the admission, the United States generally refrained from exerting the pressure that its military power and economic preponderance made possible.

Designed simultaneously to create an obstacle to Russian expansion and to limit the danger of a German revival, the Brussels Pact was signed in 1948. By this agreement, the French sought security in the establishment of a bloc or third force that would be able to arbitrate between the East and West. The French formed, with the British and Benelux peoples, a Union of Western Europe to coordi-

[2] During the 1950s, the admission of the German Republic to NATO, the Schuman Plan, and the Common Market was not purely an example either of boundless largesse to the Germans, but rather a studied French effort to permit German economic revival and even rearmament within a format controlled by France and other European states.

nate political, economic, and military matters. The military organization created for the Western Union consisted of the five Defense Ministers, who were to frame overall defense policies, and the Chiefs of Staff – thirteen senior officers from the five signatory powers – who were to plan overall strategy and decide on the size, disposition, and commanders of the combined forces. Subordinate to the Chiefs of Staff were the Permanent Military Committee and Uniforce, the tactical command located at Fontainebleau. The former included a technical staff whose functions were to draw up military inventories, plan future war production, determine standardization procedures, and establish stockpiles. Military and economic inadequacy, however, impaired the effectiveness of the Western Union to meet the alleged challenge of the Soviet Union in 1948–1949. Without German resources and manpower, without American airpower and the nuclear deterrent, the third force was not feasible for the moment.

At the insistence of the United States, in the face of a hostile Communist Party, and to the despair of many nationalist Frenchmen but with the blessings of de Gaulle, the French government entered the North Atlantic Treaty Organization in April, 1949. To the original members of the United States, Canada, the five Western Union powers, Norway, Iceland, Denmark, and Portugal, strategy rather than geography added such non-North Atlantic states as Italy, Greece, and Turkey. Germany was barred. The supreme body of NATO was the North Atlantic Council, composed of the members' Ministers of Foreign Affairs, Defense, and Finance and of Permanent Representatives. Unanimity in decision-making was the rule. Responsible to the Council was the Military Committee consisting of the Chiefs of Staff of all participants. Subordinate to this Committee was a Supreme Headquarters Allied Powers Europe (SHAPE) whose command jurisdiction embraced four subordinate regional commands in Northern Europe, Central Europe, Southern Europe, and the Mediterranean. According to a communiqué issued by NATO in its first year, problems of four categories were to be treated: (1) elaboration of common strategic conceptions; (2) organization of production of arms and equipment; (3) formulation of general, overall defense plans; and (4) allocation to the regional groups of details of a defense plan.

The protection offered to France by NATO seemed often more paper than real. American absorption in the Korean War and the ever deeper involvement of France in Indochina and Algeria diluted the military strength available to the organization. French mistrust of NATO was twofold: on the one hand, fearing American withdrawal or reduced participation, thus leaving France at the mercy of an angered Soviet Union; on the other hand, regretting Anglo-American domination of the organization whereby France had little effective control over the instruments of power.

As American demands mounted for greater contributions by European states for their own defense and as French manpower and resources were further drained by colonial warfare, the role of Germany became more crucial. The French desired the military miracle that a rearmed West Germany might provide for the defense of the West, but they bridled at the prospect of standing alone on the continent with the reawakened former enemy. Would a remilitarized West Germany, campaigning perhaps for reunification with East Germany, plunge Europe into war by provoking the Soviet Union? Or would Germany repeat its 1939 diplomatic success of buying Russian neutrality in order to revenge itself on France and the West? From 1952 to 1954, the French explored all conceivable ways in which German strength could be used and yet contained. Parliamentary defeat followed two years of debate on proposals to create a European Army or a European Defense Community in which national armies would disappear into an amalgamated cohesive force. By 1954, the French prepared to take the fearful risk of condoning German rearmament and admission to NATO. This departure in French policy was made possible by firm Anglo-American commitments to remain in force on the continent and by French hopes to keep the swelling German economy harnessed within the Coal and Steel Community and more extensive plans of economic integration.

French alignment with the United States in NATO did not preclude the emergence of serious rifts over the colonial question. French efforts to maintain a hold over Indochina were rewarded by begrudging and limited American support; French efforts to crush the Algerian rebellion after 1954 met with unofficial and sometimes official American disapproval.

The Suez crisis of 1956 best exemplified the clash between French and American interests of state. The United States had pursued an ambivalent and sometimes self-contradictory policy of benevolent protection of Israel while at the same time fostering Arab nationalism in a larger game of East-West competition. In Egypt, the new nationalist leader Nasser was recipient of extensive loans from the United States, which the latter hoped would stabilize his regime and orient it to the West. Meanwhile, the French noted with suspicion and some evidence that the Algerian rebels were receiving substantial aid from the Arab leader in Cairo. Action against Egypt seemed essential if Algeria was to be pacified. Nasser posed a similar threat to Great Britain and Israel. His intervention on behalf of the Algerian rebels, his seizure of the Suez Canal, and his provocative statements and measures against the Jewish state elicited Franco-British-Israeli unity of interests, intentions, and preparations. Secret military plans resulted in a coordinated attack on Egypt in late October, 1956. Whether the French and British moves were undertaken in a spirit of avoiding a disastrous appeasement policy or whether the expedition was a reversion to nineteenth-century colonial practices, the outcome was a fiasco for the Allies. The "irreconcilable" United States and Soviet Union joined hands long and firmly enough to thwart the NATO partners and Israel. But, if the Communists within France could take comfort from the government's setback and America's treachery, they were reduced to hypocrisy in trying to explain the ruthless Soviet repression of the Hungarian uprising that occurred the same year.

The international complications of French colonial troubles were nothing compared to the domestic ills that colonial disturbances bred, for it was the colonial issue that so weakened and divided the Fourth Republic that its very survival was jeopardized.

The Fourth Republic somehow maneuvered through political storms, economic difficulties, and foreign crises, but it sank in the colonial morass.

The first and rejected constitutional draft of 1946 charted a more enlightened colonial policy than the second and accepted Constitution. Absent from the latter's provisions were the clauses offering free consent to membership in the French Union and those awarding substantial local autonomy and the right to elect members to the French parliament. Instead, the native populations were allowed no choice but to remain within the French Union and were participants only in an Assembly of the French Union whose body was packed by half with metropolitan French representatives. The implicit promise of continued colonial rule, even if associative and benevolent, was fraught with danger as waves of nationalism swept the Asian and African holdings of France.

Indochina constituted the primary overseas arena of French woes in the immediate postwar years. During the war, Vichy administrators had managed to retain at least the fiction of French rule by mixing collaboration with the Japanese and concessions to the natives. The imminent Japanese defeat had led the Big Three at Potsdam in July, 1945, to assign temporary occupation duty to the Chinese in the northern half and the British in the southern portion of Indochina. With no intention of allowing Indochina to slip out of French control as had Syria and Lebanon, President de Gaulle dispatched a task force under General Leclerc to reassert French authority over territories being abandoned by the retreating Japanese in the summer of 1945. By early 1946, Leclerc announced completion of his mission below the 16th Parallel. He had re-established nominal French control over the provinces of Cochin-China, Cambodia, Laos, and southern Annam. Within these areas there existed enclaves of objectors. In Tonkin and the northern half of Annam, however, hostile forces were dominant. There, the Viet Minh, a Communist-led grouping of nationalists and revolutionaries under the hardy and hardened Ho Chi Minh disputed the French return.

During World War II the Viet Minh, under Chinese Nationalist auspices, had proclaimed the intention of eliminating all Japanese and French authorities and of establishing a Republic of Viet Nam, embracing the provinces of Tonkin and Annam. As Leclerc's troops replaced the temporary British occupation forces below the 16th Parallel, the Viet Minh were forced into underground guerrilla resistance. North of the 16th Parallel, the pending withdrawal of Chinese occupation troops led the French to conclude an agreement with Ho Chi Minh in early 1946. By the terms of this accord, an independent Viet Nam was to be formed as an integral part of the French Union. The new state would possess local political autonomy and the right to raise its own army and to manage its own finances. The French military establishment of fifteen thousand men would be evacuated over a five-year period. Cochin-China would be allowed to join Viet Nam if a popular referendum so decided.

Even the dubious possibility that this agreement could keep peace in Viet Nam was shattered in late 1946. Local French military officials and colonialists in France were not eager to relax the grip on Indochina; elements in the Viet Minh were not given to gradualism. When French units moved to establish control over the north, fighting broke out. In the port of Haiphong, in the northern Viet Nam city of Hanoi, and in many other Tonkinese towns, the French succeeded in removing Viet Minh authority. The Viet Minh fled to the villages and jungle, there to remain organized and ready to engage the French army in a weird and disconcerting type of warfare.

In 1949, the French transformed the rebellion against them into a "civil war" by recognizing and sponsoring Emperor Bao Dai as head of an "autonomous" Viet Nam. Escalation was inevitable in 1950, when Chinese Communists overwhelmed Chiang-Kai-Shek's Nationalist regime and formed a common Communist border with Viet Nam in the north. Although the Korean War precluded more than token military aid from the Chinese Communists to the Viet Minh, the ideological and diplomatic advantages were evident. As the American government would discover a decade later, the French governments of the 1950s found the swelling allotment of troops and almost a billion dollars annually were sinking into a bottomless pit from which no decisive victory seemed to emerge. The 1953 termination of the Korean War worsened the predicament of the French. Communist China was enabled to divert more tangible support to the Viet Minh, more than matching American contributions to the French.

For the French, the military situation deteriorated and a major disaster occurred in 1954. Loath to relinquish its tenuous grip over the north of Viet Nam and noting with alarm Viet Minh advances toward Laos, the French army command committed itself to the defense of the strategic center of Dien Bien Phu. Nearly two months of intense artillery bombardment and murderous infantry assault by the Viet Minh attackers ended on May 7 with their capture of the fortress. This stunning defeat of French troops dictated drastic decisions to the French government. Piecemeal appropriations and regular army units were insufficient to retain French influence in Viet Nam. Choosing diplomacy and withdrawal to the assignment of draftees and the expenditure of more billions, the new Premier Pierre Mendès-France took office in June with the promise (or threat) to end the war in thirty days or resign. The Viet Minh and the Communist powers of China and Russia were brought to the peace table as much by their own domestic economic needs and the possibility of American intervention as by the continued military presence of France in Viet Nam. On July 21 at Geneva, Mendès-France signed the agreement that divided Indochina into four parts. Cambodia and Laos were recognized as separate states, and the 17th Parallel formed an armistice line in Viet Nam. French forces were scheduled to abandon all Viet Nam. As a result two "independent" states emerged similar to those resulting from the Korean settlement.

The Fourth Republic enjoyed but a brief respite from colonial ordeals after its negotiated retirement from Indochina. Mendès-France's dramatic diplomacy at Geneva was immediately followed by a trip to Tunisia where he reiterated earlier French promises to grant autonomy to the Protectorate. Two years of parliamentary wrangling and numerous examples of mutual recrimination were terminated in 1956 by the formal severing of the French and Tunisian tie. A comparable independence was accorded to Morocco in that year after an even worse series of violent acts poisoned relations between France and the Sultanate.

In Algeria, however, the French had a tiger by the tail. The Fourth Republic proved itself unable either to let go of this legal projection of France, in which resided more than a million European *colons* and nine million Muslims, or to pacify the rebellious population. The failure to release or tame the tiger led to the mangling and ultimate devouring of the Republic by 1958.

By the 1954 opening of the Algerian rebellion, one hundred and twenty-four years of French rule had transformed Algeria into a land of striking contrasts and incredible complications. The Third Republic had divided Algeria into three departments over which the citizens had secured a limited degree of self-government. The vast majority of "native" Algerians, however, were classed as French subjects, not citizens, until after World War II, thus confining political power to the *colons* (European settlers). Token legislation in 1919 had enabled Algerians to acquire a qualified French citizenship, but to do so a Muslim was compelled to abandon Koranic law and Muslim customs and to accept French civil status. Even then, the "convert" was not entitled to rights identical with those of Frenchmen in France. Very few Muslims availed themselves of this type of largesse. By a 1944 ordinance, de Gaulle granted citizenship to certain educated Muslims without demanding forfeiture of Muslim status. And finally, in 1946, the French Parliament placed all Algerians on equal legal footing by granting French citizenship to all inhabitants.

Equality before the law did not by any means signify equality to enact the law. A statute of 1947 gave infinitely greater representation than ever before to Muslims in a newly created Algerian Assembly, but the shortcomings were quickly noted by politically hungry citizens. The Assembly's powers were severely limited by the French-appointed Governor-General and the French National Assembly. In the Algerian Assembly, the *colons* held an ascendant position: half the members were selected by 470,000 Europeans and 60,000 Muslims and the other half by 1,300,000 Muslims. The European *colon* minority could dominate the Muslim majority by this two-college system and also by requiring a two-thirds vote on any action on the request of the Governor-General or of one quarter of the Assembly's membership.

Official French publications have frequently presented glowing accounts of the economic and social development of Algeria. In many respects, the French could take justifiable pride in their achievements. The relatively static nineteenth-century population of Algeria mounted from little more than 2,000,000 in 1830 to 4,700,000 in 1901 and 5,700,000 in 1921. The censuses of 1948 and 1954 revealed not growth but explosion (see Table 6–3).

Table 6–3. Algerian Population Growth, 1948–1954 *

	Colons	Muslims	Total
1948	974,000	7,708,000	8,682,000
1954	1,042,000	8,486,000	9,528,000

* Table constructed from official French government figures.

Only one half of the *colons*, it must be noted, were of French origin; the remainder were of Italian, Spanish, or other backgrounds. The country counted eleven cities with more than 50,000 by the 1950s, where only Algiers alone was in that bracket in 1830. Also by the 1950s, Algeria was crisscrossed by thousands of miles of railroads and highways, studded with factories and mines, and endowed with prosperous farms and vineyards. Algeria was no one-crop or one-product colony ruled by leather-belted, pistol-packing European overseers. Neither was it a country peopled predominantly by young Algerians like Albert Camus who studied hard, wrote plays, and swam in the beautiful blue Mediterranean.

A careful analysis and interpretation of the economic and social status of the Muslims do not cover the French with the glory in which they wished to be cloaked. French government surveys conducted in 1955 by Mastiépol and Delavignette revealed the many basic economic and social disadvantages of the Muslims vis-à-vis the European settlers. Although it is incorrect to portray even a sizeable minority of the one million *colons* as lordly plantation holders or as plutocratic merchants, bankers, or industrialists, the *colons* possessed a social and economic status demonstrably superior to that of the Muslims. Of the 15,000,000 arable acres in Algeria, 25,000 *colons* owned nearly half (6,875,000 acres), whereas 15,-000 Muslims held only 1,875,000 acres under modern methods of cultivation. Still entrapped in archaic systems of agriculture were 500,000 Muslims holding 6,250,000 acres. The averages are deceptive: *colons*, 275 acres per farm; "modern" Muslims, 150 acres; traditional Muslims, 12.5 acres. Actually, in 1951, one out of three *colons* held fewer than 25 acres, thus indicating the inequitable distribution even among the European settlers. But at least two out of three Muslims had fewer than 25 acres.

A majority, but not all of the *colons*, thus dominated the modern agricultural sector, leaving proportionately little land for many Muslims. The per capita income of nearly 6,000,000 rural Algerians averaged only $45 per year in 1951. Unable to feed the increasing numbers on the their small farms, many Muslims watched the flight of their families to the Algerian cities, to metropolitan France, or to the armed forces of the rebellion. Still others entered into the category of agricultural laborers on the farms of the *colons*. The population explosion, however, was as responsible for the phenomenon as was French or *colon* policy.

Unlike the Muslims who were 75 percent rural, the *colons* were at least 75 percent urban. In 1954, the size of each group in the nonagricultural sectors of the economy was as follows:

commerce: 64,000 *colons*, 96,000 Muslims
administration and services: 84,000 *colons*, 73,000 Muslims
mining, power, and processing industries: 106,000 *colons*, 172,000 Muslims.

The Mastiépol and Delavignette reports of 1955 shed light on the relative status of these groups. Here, too, as in agriculture, the disparity among the *colons* was not so great as that between *colon* and Muslims.

The per capita income, which is not to be confused with the amount of wages of any individual workman, was $121 per year in 1951 for 1,600,000 out of 2,200,000 urban Muslims. 510,000 reached $240 per year, and 50,000 averaged $502. In contrast, the minimum per capita income for 440,000 *colons* amounted to $240; for 545,000, $502; for 15,000, $3181. Not to be omitted from the income analysis are the funds sent home by the 400,000 to 500,000 Muslims who had migrated to metropolitan France often on a temporary basis. Most observers have calculated that nearly 2,000,000 Muslims in Algeria were entirely or partially supported in this fashion.

One important indication, as well as cause, of these inequities was the lack of education among the Muslims. Until the civil war broke out in 1954, illiteracy was the rule among 90 percent of the Muslims, a fact explained both by the lack of facilities and by the reluctance of Muslim parents to send their children to French schools. Primary and secondary school space and staff were available, nevertheless, for all the children of the *colons*. In higher education, the 6,000 student enrollment at the University of Algiers included only 500–600 Muslims.

From these statistics, it would appear that the *colons* monopolized the executive, managerial, entrepreneurial positions. Yet many urban *colons* were in the same income bracket as the Muslims, both serving as lawyers, doctors, artisans, shopkeepers, taxicab drivers, clerics, civil servants, telephone operators, and as skilled or unskilled workers. However, only one out of twenty Muslims had arrived at the level compared with one out of two *colons;* moreover, it must be remembered that the rest of the *colons* were in upper income brackets, not lower, as were the rest of the Muslims. Although one quarter to one third of the Muslims had or were shifted from a primitive to a modern economy, they had thus not reaped the same benefits as the European settlers. To the credit of the French, this transition did take place in Algeria, whereas other

African and Arab lands were more nakedly exploited without any tangible modernization of the particular "colony" or "subjects." To their discredit, the French and, more especially, the *colons* barred the Muslims from political, social, and economic advantages proportionate to Muslim numbers and contributions.

By 1954, heightened nationalism in Arab and African "colonies," repeated failures by the French to make adequate political concessions to the Muslims in Algeria, mounting misery of the exploding Muslim population — these and derivative factors contributed to the formation of the National Liberation Front (FLN) for organized rebellion against French rule. The FLN challenge and the French response led through the paths of terror and repression to complicate still further the already complicated interrelationships of the French government, the 500,000-man French army, the 1,000,000 European settlers, the 9,000,000 Muslims, and the FLN.

In the early morning hours of November 1, 1954, small bands attacked French army personnel and civilians in scores of villages in the Aurès mountain region of southeastern Algeria. Within a few weeks, spreading raids took place on French army installation while rebel units hampered French relief columns. Over the following months and lengthening years, the rebels engaged in traditional and guerrilla warfare with the swelling French army and the *colons*. Against Muslims, too, the rebels often waged a campaign of sometimes indiscriminate terror to oblige their enlistment in the nationalist cause or to frighten them from association with the French.

From leaflets picked up on the first and succeeding days of the insurrection, the terrorists were apparently part of an organization called the National Liberation Front (FLN) that possessed a military arm, the National Liberation Army. The stated position of the FLN, then and later, showed far greater constancy and firmness than that of the successive French governments of 1954 to 1958. The goal was "the restoration of the Algerian state, sovereign, democratic, and social, within the framework of the principles of Islam." Negotiations were sought between themselves as the representatives of the Algerian people and the French authorities. In return for the

French acceptance of Algerian sovereignty, the FLN offered to respect French cultural and economic interests. Those French citizens who wished to remain in Algeria would be allowed to choose either their original nationality or a new Algerian citizenship. If they selected the latter, they would be considered equals, in rights and duties, to all Algerian nationals.

The initial French reaction to the outbreak of disorder was one of cautious and indecisive action. Not immediately convinced of the extent or organization of the FLN, the French government satisfied itself with assigning some of its 50,000-man army in Algeria to restoring order in the Aurès. When these measures proved ineffectual, Premier Mendès-France dispatched security detachments and parachute regiments to Algeria while police rounded up suspects who often had no part in the rebellion. A new Governor-General, Jacques Soustelle, was appointed. His arrival in Algiers in January, 1955, was greeted by a suspicious reserve on the part of the *colons*. Could any appointee of Mendès-France, who had liquidated the French connection with Indochina and was releasing Tunisia, be sympathetic to an *Algérie Française*? The distrust of the *colons* quickly turned to adulation as Soustelle revealed his dedication not merely to pacification in Algeria, but also to integration, which was later so passionately sought by the *colons*.

In metropolitan France, no such clarity of vision or unity of purpose prevailed. Although the swiftly changing governments of 1955 to 1958 did regularly re-enact emergency-rule legislation, delegating to the Governor-General and the local prefects much arbitrary power, the political parties and the public became increasingly contentious over the Algerian crisis. Although a pattern of center and right alignment for pacification and integration of Algeria seemed to emerge, the pattern was much distorted by inner divisions. MRP, Radical-Socialist, and independent right-wing parties frequently found themselves split between ultra-nationalist, patriotic militarists and those who ideologically or financially abhorred the deeper commitment of France in Algeria. Similar divisions appeared on the left, even in the Communist Party where monolithic anticolonialist unity might be thought unassailable. The small Communist Party in Algeria, in fact, became absorbed into the Muslim nationalist movement of the FLN. Communist trade unions in Algeria, principally composed of *colons*, had never been too benevolently inclined toward the Muslim, and, when the French Communist Party persisted in its anticolonial parliamentary position, the *colons* defected. The SFIO, too, exhibited schizophrenic tendencies on an Algerian solution. One wing was read out of the organization, partly for its expressed desire to abandon Algeria. The majority, though, remained under Guy Mollet, after 1956 a convert to strenuous repression of the rebels.

In the light of these divisions, the governments of 1955–1958 barely succeeded in securing majorities for supplementing the efforts to bring order to Algeria. Proposals for massive expenditures of more men and more money met with immediate and strenuous objections from conscripts, economy-minded deputies, and ideologists. The faintest indication of entering into negotiations with the FLN, on the other hand, roused storms of protest from the French army, the *colons*, and a motley assortment of center and right politicians. After 1956, with the growing public awareness of the brutality and indecencies of the repressive measures of numerous French units, the government was subjected to further criticism from liberals on the MRP and Radical-Socialist benches. Intellectuals entered the fray with pamphlets, articles, and books that often remained undistributed by the censoring state. By 1958, the Fourth Republic had demonstrated its incapacity to crush the FLN or to come to terms with it. Either path was blocked by an array of hostile and powerful opponents. Meanwhile, the French were being drained of men and materials in the unending and large-scale war.

The governments of the Fourth Republic had not only to contend with popular disenchantment and political wrangling over Algeria, but also with an increasingly alienated French army. Many of the officers, although not the conscripts, had adopted procedures and outlooks at wide variance from those of the government. Although most of the army seemed disposed to pursue conventional strategic and tactical methods of warfare against the FLN enemy, a growing number of military leaders crystallized and applied lessons presumably taught by their Indochinese experience and confirmed by Algerian developments. First of all, the army had come to distrust the civilian chiefs who had rewarded its courage and dedication in Indochina with pitifully inadequate support and, finally, weak-kneed surrender. Secondly, the army felt itself to be the custodian of the one and only true doctrine for waging and winning the revolutionary war. According to these theorists, *la guerre révolutionnaire* was the only type of war that could erupt. The Communist fear of nuclear destruction and American reluctance to unleash The Bomb would inhibit large-scale total warfare among the major powers along the lines of World Wars I and II. Underdeveloped peripheral areas, such as Indochina, Korea, and Algeria, therefore, would become the arenas for new conflicts.

Revolutionary warfare was total, however, even when confined to limited areas — total in the army's relations with the population being infiltrated and total in the economic, political, social, and moral support necessarily forthcoming from the home government to its army. To counter the subversions and successes of the Communists — and there was no other enemy — traditional methods of warfare would not suffice. The very tenets of Lenin, Mao Tse Tung, and Ho Chi Minh had to be imitated. The infiltrated, "intoxicated" native populations had to be treated with massive doses of propaganda, economic and social aid, political concessions, and lessons in self-defense. Only then could the Communist fish be kept from swimming, poaching, and feeding in troubled waters. Only then could the French army, using ordinary weapons and irregular techniques of night searches and daytime torture, eliminate the hunted and provisionless revolutionary organizations. For such "total" efforts, the home government and metropolitan population were obliged to demonstrate an unflinching and unstinting support of the army's monumental and costly mission. Negotiations or even rumors of negotiations with the enemy, reduced expenditures or even hints of cutbacks, or moral criticism or even mild doubt on the conduct of the revolutionary war — any of these would encourage the enemy to remain in the field and facilitate terrorization of the native population.

After three years of warfare in Algeria, French army elements were convinced that the government insufficiently grasped the axioms of *la guerre révolutionnaire*. Much progress had been made with the delegation to the army of some of the Governor-General's powers, the establishment of Psychological Warfare Sections, and the resettlement of villagers in compounds safe from FLN influence. Insufficient funds, however, as well as bitter civilian criticism and constant flirtation with ideas of pourparlers with the FLN seriously disaffected the army.

In April, 1958, Premier Félix Gaillard accepted the "good offices" of the insistent United States in order to mediate a heated dispute with neighboring Tunisia. There, a French bombing raid had taken place allegedly to wipe out FLN contingents using Tunisia as a base and an avenue for supplies. For Gaillard's flabby acceptance of the American recommendations, an angry Parliament overthrew his government. The army, the *colons,* and other advocates of an *Algérie Française* could have taken heart. But, who would replace Gaillard? A long list of Prime Ministers from 1954 to 1958 served only to reduce France to paralysis on the Algerian question.

As FLN terrorism spread through rural and urban Algeria, the *colons* remained neither passive nor disorganized. Although not all relished the French army officers' program of uplifting the Muslim, the *colons* nevertheless sided with the army against the wavering policies of the Paris cabinets. A substantial number of *colons* gravitated toward an alignment with metropolitan Frenchmen who felt that Charles de Gaulle alone could lead France and Algeria out of the depths. The silent, uncommitted de Gaulle was less attractive to other *colons* who were centered in Algiers and who organized a conglomerate band of students, shopkeepers, and malcontents. By early 1958, these Algerian activists numbered about ten thousand and gave the appearance of some of the Fascist Leagues of an earlier generation. Desperation and fear dominated the feelings of Gaullist and Algiers activists as the Fourth Republic muddled through its springtime dilemma of Tunisia and overthrown cabinets.

On May 13, Pierre Pflimlin was due to go before the National Assembly to seek investiture after the month-old fall of Gaillard. The army suspected Pflimlin of harboring the unspeakable intention of yielding to Tunisia and of opening talks with the FLN. Was the army to be sacrificed again and ignominiously submitted to a repetition of its Indochinese withdrawal?

On May 13, too, ranking army officers and government officials were scheduled to gather in Algiers in commemoration of three French military hostages whom the FLN had just brutally murdered. Excited crowds would be milling about the Government Building where tribute would be made to the dead.

On May 13, in Algiers, activist *colon* conspirators demonstrated, rioted, and seized the government headquarters, formed with army leaders a Committee of Public Safety, and precipitated the collapse of the Fourth Republic.

1958–

The origins and operations of the Fifth Republic

IF the Fourth Republic had been delivered a lethal blow on May 13, 1958, it nevertheless took two weeks before rigor mortis set in and nearly four months before the Fifth Republic was officially established. During the May 13–28 death throes of the expiring Republic, Premier Pflimlin and a dwindling number of deputies fought a losing battle to save the Republic. In Algiers, the activists easily surmounted the token opposition of army guards at government headquarters. French army Commander-in-Chief Raoul Salan and parachute General Jacques Massu instantly accepted the plotters' request to head a Committee of Public Safety in return for a promise to end the riots. Premier Pflimlin as quickly delegated civil authority to Salan in order to keep at least the fiction of a legal connection between Paris and the revolutionary Committee. Pflimlin failed. For on the 15th, de Gaulle announced himself "ready to assume the powers of the Republic," and Salan fell under Gaullist influence in Algiers to cast his and his fellow "insurrectionists' " lot with de Gaulle.

Again in the self-cast role of savior of France, de Gaulle had his price. Before assuming the powers of the Republic, he insisted that he must be invested as Premier by legal means, that he be voted full emergency powers for six months, and that he be entrusted with the right to draft a new constitution for a later referendum. De Gaulle and his followers worked furiously to convince growing numbers of socialists, MRPs, and Radical-Socialists of the dire necessity of a quick legal investiture. Paratroopers from Algiers had seized control of Corsica; a military dictatorship seemed imminent. Parliamentary and public opposition faded by the end of May. Pflimlin resigned on the 28th; metropolitan police and army units were considered notoriously unreliable; a CGT call for a general strike went largely unheeded; non-Communists of the left marched in a pale procession of ineffectual protest. By threatening resignation, the President of the Republic, René Coty, spurred on the Assembly to pay de Gaulle's price. On June 1, by 329 to 224, it paid. In turn, Charles de Gaulle rededicated his body and soul to framing a new constitution, liquidating the Algerian war, and leading France to an era of unprecedented prosperity and avowed grandeur.

To analyze the Fifth Republic without commenting on Charles de Gaulle would be like writing of the Third Reich without referring to Adolph Hitler, or (lest Gaullists misinterpret the analogy) like treating the New Testament without alluding to Jesus Christ. For de Gaulle was the central and dominating figure in the Fifth Republic – its architect, its engineer, its superintendent, its concierge, and its prophet.

Basic to an understanding of de Gaulle is the appreciation that he is a man of "integrity" – not a petty bourgeois integrity that preaches against stealing five francs from the employer's cash register, but an integrity that makes one and indivisible the person and certain principles or concepts presumed to be rationally, emotionally, and traditionally valid and appropriate. The principles or concepts might be laudable to some or completely abhorrent to others, but the integrity of the General is undeniable. Nor should the fact that he used contradictory methods or inconsistent means to advance to his goal rob him of the label of integrity. His methods or means were varied and relative to the moment of their use, but the objective remained fixed and consistent and he remained true to the objective.

Such generalizations of the General and his integrity could, of course, place him superficially in the company of many totalitarian dictators who, too, were unswerving in their dedication to principles or concepts — be they of state, party, race, or class. In all fairness to de Gaulle, the possible similarities disappear if one considers the nature of the principles with which he identifies himself and the limitations on the methods he employs to advance his cause. His overwhelming concern, or perhaps obsession, is France — its independence, security, power, and grandeur. His fullest efforts are directed to maintaining, recapturing, asserting, or promoting French interests of state in the military and diplomatic field. Not that de Gaulle yearned for a revival of a Napoleonic French imperium in Europe, or for a new order in Europe based on Gallic rather than Aryan hegemony, or for the establishment of French rather than Soviet satellites, or even for an unyielding retention of the far-flung colonial empire ruled over by the Third Republic. Instead, de Gaulle aims at guaranteeing the fullest exercise of independence in charting French foreign policy, the full equality of France in decision-making in such international bodies as NATO and the Common Market in which France was a voluntary or reluctant partner, and the dynamic injection of French influence in crises and struggles from which the French might derive material or prestigious benefits. In short, de Gaulle strives to extract for France every last ounce from the fruit of international bargaining, manipulation, and power play. A strong France would possess more leverage in diplomacy, but even a weak France should insist on and retain its sovereign rights by a proper, often shifting stance in the global duel of giant world powers. Weak or strong, France is de Gaulle's paramount object of affection, attention, and attachment.

Guided by the compelling concept of French sovereignty and grandeur, de Gaulle works to make real his image of domestic France. To de Gaulle, France is democratic, and France is republican. Is de Gaulle? In a special sense and not in terms of the commonplace French definition during the Third and Fourth Republics, de Gaulle is most definitely both a republican and a democrat. Despite his early writings and later emphasis on the virtues of order and authority, despite his frequently galling arbitrariness and imperiousness, despite his caustic criticism of wrangling factions and brawling parliaments, despite the labels stuck on him by detractors of unimpeachable democratic credentials, de Gaulle is no aspiring fascist dictator. Despite his aggravatingly regal, pompous, majestic posing, de Gaulle is no royalist either. His performance as head of the liberation forces in 1944, as head of the Provisional Government and Fourth Republic in 1945–1946, and as the sole acclaimed leader in 1958 reveal a man who scrupulously refrained from capitalizing on his ascendant position to make himself a dictator. Whatever opinions might be held on his constitution for the Fifth Republic, it was not of fascist or monarchist design.

The political system he unsuccessfully campaigned for in 1945 and successfully instituted in 1958 was inextricably related to his image of France as a sovereign, independent, powerful state. At home, there had to be an end to the paralyzing inter- and intraparty warfare, a limit to the enervating interbranch rivalry between executive and legislative, a curtailing of the almost total prerogative of the Assemblies packed with dealing, ineffectual deputies. Governments of stability, order, and authority had to replace the shifting, disorganized, and weak regimes so common during the Third and Fourth Republics.

De Gaulle's integrity, then, consists in his total dedication to a France strong in international position and stable in political functioning. Less clearly delineated in de Gaulle's vision of France are the economic and social attributes. Prosperity and the general welfare, financial and fiscal solidity would all apparently follow inevitably from de Gaulle's remodeling of a revitalized and orderly France. The economic and social features are details — important but secondary — and other Frenchmen might occupy themselves with them. De Gaulle would be active and preoccupied with the essential elements of military, diplomatic, and political affairs.

Whether de Gaulle's image of France is a valid one and whether his activities since 1958 were a service or disservice to France can not yet be fully determined. Tentative judgments may be made while recounting the tale of his forming and guiding his Republic, the Fifth, in and through hazardous times. Ultimate judgments must await the future when the implications of his creation themselves become history. Meanwhile, de Gaulle's policies and practices as President of the Fifth Republic would confirm the thesis of relativism in analyzing historical events. For, despite the absolute and fixed attitudes attributable to the "principled" and "dedicated" de Gaulle, the methods he used to arrive at his destination were determined by the exigencies of the moment. During the 1950s, for example, de Gaulle was a willing advocate of NATO, for French needs desperately dictated it. During the 1960s, however, de Gaulle bitterly and not inconsistently denounced the organization in order to assume different international stances more appropriate to the moment.

Once installed in office in June, 1958, de Gaulle moved swiftly to accomplish one of his most cherished tasks, that of framing a new constitution for France. Working with a freshly picked cabinet of sometimes less than fresh figures and with a newly appointed committee mostly directed by Michel Debré, de Gaulle readied a draft for submission to a referendum on September 28. Acclaimed as much because of its endorsement by de Gaulle as for its intrinsic virtues, the October 4 Constitution of the Fifth Republic was accepted by a rousing 80 percent of the voters.

The Constitution owed its parentage to numerous impulses. The

personal political predilections of Charles de Gaulle, the imposing
need for an Algerian settlement, the alleged imminence of civil war
in France itself — all these elements pointed to modifications of the
Republic's institutions. Long antedating the events of May 13, there
were forces, too, recommending constitutional correction of defects
and weaknesses noted in the political operations of the Third and
Fourth Republics. How was the October 4, 1958, structure to
reach the dual goal of providing a forceful government to resolve
the almost anarchistic situation of the moment and reaching an
ultimate objective of furnishing stable, efficient governments that
would avoid the harrowing fate of the two previous Republics?

Although the presence of de Gaulle as President counted for
more than constitutional provisions in effecting a new political
system for France, the Constitution of the Fifth Republic does
contain several important innovations. The Presidency remained
separated from the Premiership, but the head of state was to be
elected by an electoral college instead of being selected by the
combined houses of the legislature. Election through the electoral
college of local officials gave disproprotionate weight to rural and
provincial France.

The formerly negligible powers of the executive are enhanced;
the previously near-exclusive grip of the Assembly on legislative
and even executive matters is broken. The President is accorded
some few but significant weapons not possessed by his Third and
Fourth Republic predecessors. He can dissolve the Assembly and
he can call for a referendum on bills or items that might become
caught in the slowly grinding or nongrinding parliamentary mincing
machine. His right to dissolve the Assembly is nevertheless limited;
once new elections take place, the President cannot exercise the
power again during the ensuing year. To the customary administrative and honorific functions of French Presidents, the head of state
is enabled further to send messages about policy-making or policy
clarification to the Assembly, to refer matters of disputed jurisdiction and debatable legislation to a new body (the Constitutional

Council), to negotiate treaties instead of merely ratifying them after their being drafted by other officials, and to assume emergency and extraordinary powers on his own initiative.

Through the extension of the presidential office as well as through other means, the executive branch is strengthened vis-à-vis the legislature. Shielded as much by the prestige of President de Gaulle as by constitutional safeguards, the government is also protected from parliamentary wrath and too frequent overthrow by the power of dissolution and by an executive invasion of the legislative sphere. Although the Assembly retains nominal sovereignty, the government responsible to it is given day-to-day privileges of initiating legislation and even framing laws (or "rules") in numerous realms. The Prime Minister, appointed by the President, and the cabinet are thus provided with wider latitude in governing and presumably greater assurance of stability and continuity.

According to the Constitution of October 4, a two-house system of Parliament is perpetuated. The indirectly elected upper house is more reminiscent of the Third Republic's Senate, however, than of the Fourth's shadowy Council of the Republic. The Senate of the Fifth Republic possesses coequal legislative power with the lower house, the National Assembly, in all but fiscal questions. Armed with what is tantamount to a veto over Assembly action, the Senate nevertheless is subordinate. The government is responsible to the National Assembly and not to the Senate.

With these and other provisions, the Constitution of the Fifth Republic created a more balanced and not undemocratic system of government for France. Commendable but possibly dangerous clauses had been inserted — those dealing especially with the attempt to render the tenure and authority of the government more stable. Without the dynamic direction of de Gaulle as President, however, it is difficult to imagine how deadlocks could be avoided in the normal political skirmishing between and within the more distinctly separated branches. Without the self-restraint of a basically democratic de Gaulle as head of state, it is frightening to contemplate how a more narrowly ambitious or less democratic successor might abuse the provision for assuming emergency powers. It remains to be seen whether de Gaulle's attempt to break or modify the long-evolving French variety of parliamentary republicanism will strike roots or be a mere temporary, de Gaulle-long aberration.

Making and adopting a new constitution provoked far fewer debates and created far less difficulty for de Gaulle and the nation than facing and settling the Algerian crisis. The Fourth Republic had discovered, at its peril, that Algeria was not a mere colony to be simply amputated, nor was it a clear cut combat zone to be easily pacified. De Gaulle was to suffer long, too, before he ultimately effected a settlement that would not simultaneously bring down the Fifth Republic.

When de Gaulle came to power in June, 1958, no one – perhaps not even de Gaulle himself – knew to what solution he was partisan. Did he favor an *Algérie Française,* an Algeria integrated completely with France? Many French army officers, *colons,* and right-wing metropolitan citizens were convinced so. Did not the General address the Algiers' multitudes in June with his famous *"Je vous ai compris"* ("I have understood you") speech, leading them to presume his sympathy and support for their cause? Or did de Gaulle prefer an autonomous or independent Algeria, loosely or not at all associated with France? Liberals and moderates in France read de Gaulle in this fashion. Was he not disarming settlers, restoring governmental authority over the army, and appointing a cabinet from which extremists like Jacques Soustelle were conspicuously absent?

If de Gaulle knew his own mind in the summer of 1958, he nonetheless held his tongue. To judge from his subsequent proposals on Algeria and his concurrent treatment of other parts of the French Union, de Gaulle very probably was inclined to give the Algerians the privilege of self-determination with the expectation that their choice would be similar to that of the overwhelming number of other onetime French colonies – autonomy or independence within the framework of association with France. Not a single precise indication of his inclinations slipped from his lips or appeared over his signature, however, until September, 1959. Then and only then did he articulate what had been either long-laid plans or slowly formed ideas. He presented the Algerians with three alternatives from which to select in a future referendum. Pacification was an avowed prerequisite and concurrence by the metropolitan French was declared mandatory. Algeria was offered the right to decide among integration, autonomy, or independence.

In the year and a half between his June, 1958, accession to power and his September, 1959, policy statement on Algeria, de Gaulle had been relatively silent on defining his intentions for Algeria, but he had not been at all idle in preparing the groundwork for a final settlement. His cautious, delicate, almost dilatory approach was dictated by the existence of seemingly insurmountable barriers to any immediate or extreme measures. The strength of the FLN, the nature of *la guerre révolutionnaire,* and the opposition of a liberal and moderate majority in metropolitan France precluded any success for rapid pacification and integration through escalated traditional military action. Sizeable and commanding French army elements linked with well-organized and adamant *colons* were obviously hostile to permitting Algeria to slip into independence or even autonomy. Furthermore, the masses of Muslims were so subject to the vying pressures of FLN and *colons* that they could scarcely indicate freely whatever opinions they might have held. Until the FLN could be mollified, and the army-*colon* combine weakened or brought under control, and the Muslim population relieved of the double harassment of fellow and *colon* organizations, there was no hope for unsnarling the Algerian tangle. In fact, precipitous pronouncements by the General either on integration or independence might have reproduced circumstances conducive of another May 13.

During 1958 and 1959, de Gaulle acted with cunning to demolish the barriers in the path of a lasting Algerian settlement. First, and possibly to undercut the FLN appeal and to woo Muslims into association with France, de Gaulle announced in October,

1958, an ambitious and enlightened "Constantine Plan" for Algeria. A five-year projection, the plan scheduled an investment of $4,000,-000,000 allocated approximately equally among the following sectors: public facilities (education, public health, administration, and communications); housing and urban development; heavy equipment (power, heavy industry, soil conservation and restoration); light equipment (agriculture, light industry, and services). This belated crash program was intended to raise the average per capita income to $400 per year, to introduce more Muslims into modern economic life, and to reduce radically Muslim illiteracy.

Before its premature termination, the Constantine Plan did temporarily accelerate the modernization of Algeria. The discovery, exploitation, and use of Saharan resources promised to achieve even greater results through easy access to natural gas for power needs and the long-range establishment of steel, chemical, and other industries. In housing, much was accomplished by razing many of the *bidonvilles* (shantytowns) around major urban areas. Country "towns" sprang up with better facilities for the inhabitants. Increasing numbers of Muslims received formal education in new schools or in centers established and directed by the French army. Despite the significant material advances, the political and military atmosphere — supercharged with stormy *colon* uprisings, army *putsches*, and unrelenting rebel action — was hardly propitious for strengthening Muslim feeling for France. The Muslims would not or could not be easily wooed.

To remove still another obstacle to an Algerian settlement, de Gaulle gingerly approached the FLN. Immediately after proclaiming the Constantine Plan in the autumn of 1958, the General issued a call to the rebel organization for a "peace of the brave" that was to include negotiations for a ceasefire. The call fell on the deaf ears of the FLN's newly constituted Provisional Government of the Algerian Republic (GPRA). In the December, 1958, elections for the first Assembly of the Fifth Republic, the GPRA's continued resistance and boycott resulted in the candidacy and victory of untypical, "Uncle Tom" Muslims. The FLN refused to lay down its arms; the GPRA persisted in its demand to be recognized as the sovereign representative of an independent Algerian state.

Before wishing or daring to declare himself on his policy of self-determination, de Gaulle also moved inexorably to weaken and divide the army-*colon* combine. He reassigned or removed many officers from key posts, transferred General Salan to Paris, ordered army officers to relinquish their places on the *colons'* Committees of Public Safety, and produced factionalism among the *colons* themselves. Suspicion and even outright detestation of de Gaulle were not absent in army and *colon* circles, but the government's authority had been greatly enhanced by September, 1959.

Although de Gaulle's proposal for Algerian self-determination was greeted with overwhelming approval and relief in metropolitan France, there were adverse reactions of consternation and derision. The GPRA ridiculed the proposal as a trick. Could not election-rigging by the French army in Algeria produce a result favorable to the *colon* minority and the army fanatics? The *colons* and many army officers lambasted the scheme as a complete betrayal of their previous efforts and existing interests. Could the Muslims be counted on to choose an *Algérie Française*?

In Algiers, *colon* vocal indignation turned to armed fury over the January, 1960, Massu incident. The General of the paratroopers had been incredibly indiscreet and vehemently antigovernment in an interview published by a West German newspaper. De Gaulle summoned Massu to Paris and relieved him of his command. In protest, the *colons* responded with a general strike, a massive demonstration against de Gaulle, and a thorough-going insurrection complete with barricades against government forces. The army, for its part, was more divided than it had been in May, 1958. De Gaulle's wiles had worked. Paratroops and even some regular units had fraternized with the rebellious populace, but they stood aside from active support as loyal troops dismantled the barricades, disarmed the insurrectionists, and disbanded most of the extremist *colon* organizations. Within a month, order was restored in Algiers, and de Gaulle sought and secured delegated emergency powers from Parliament for the next fourteen months.

The remainder of 1960 passed without de Gaulle's being able to pacify the FLN or bring it to the conference table on his terms. In January, 1961, a referendum was finally submitted to metropolitan France and Algeria for approval of preliminaries leading to the final choice of Algerians among integration, autonomy, or independence. A solid 75 percent in France and more in Algeria voted affirmatively. De Gaulle's September, 1959, proposals seemed at last possible of implementation, but certain French army generals and the FLN had contrary ideas. During the spring of 1961, de Gaulle imposed his will on the generals but not on the FLN.

In April, 1961, the generals reacted violently to the announced Evian-les-Bains negotiations between de Gaulle and the GPRA. General Salan's replacement, General Maurice Challe, General Salan himself, and other high-ranking French army officers employed several professional army units to execute a coup in Algiers. Their call to fellow officers and regiments for coordinated action in metropolitan France led to a moment of panic in Paris and other cities. Were paratroops and airborne forces going to overturn the Fifth Republic? Swift, well-organized, and nearly unanimous support of the government, as well as the refusal of other professional soldiers and conscript troops to participate in the coup, quickly terminated the crisis.

The collapse of the April, 1961, putsch and the suppression of the January, 1960, insurrection virtually eliminated the army-*colon* obstacle to an Algerian settlement. Over the succeeding months, tens and then hundreds of thousands of *colons* left the land they had helped to transform into a semimodern adjunct of France. They bitterly abandoned hopes for maintaining their special status in Algeria and the special place for Algeria with a French Union. Diehard army officers and fanatic *colon* extremists, however, persisted in terroristic, plastic-bomb tactics in a last-ditch campaign to wreck the chances of the negotiations between the French government and the GPRA. A Secret Army Organization (OAS) worked underground on both sides of the Mediterranean to intimidate Frenchmen and Muslims and to provoke widespread disorders. Attempts on de Gaulle's life were attributed to the OAS as were indiscriminate acts of arson, destruction, torture, and killing. These last acts of desperate men did not prevent de Gaulle and GPRA leaders from meeting and negotiating at Evian-les-Bains from May, 1961, through March of the following year.

When the French government and the GPRA finally met for face-to-face discussions in May, 1961, there was an enormous gulf between the two parties. Although de Gaulle's stand varied tremendously from the earlier French position, it was still far from the FLN's, which had barely budged from the one proclaimed in the opening days of the rebellion in 1954. Like the heads of the Fourth Republic, de Gaulle refused to recognize the FLN's exclusive jurisdiction in Algeria. Until 1961, he had insisted also on a ceasefire before any talks or recognition, whereas the FLN pressed for recognition before a ceasefire. In the midst of the Evian discussions de Gaulle ordered a "ceasefire" or, at least, a halt in French offensive operations against the rebels. Further easing the road to negotiations was de Gaulle's innovation of the ultimate right of self-determination for the inhabitants of Algeria.

During the months of intermittent and often bitter wrangling over terms, the two parties were at public odds over methods of self-determination, guarantees for the *colons* in an "independent" Algeria, and title to the Sahara. On the last item, particular resentment was felt by the FLN since the French had detached the Saharan regions from Algeria proper, thus claiming the oil-rich lands to be outside consideration. At stake, too, was the territorial integrity of Algeria, which de Gaulle implied might be jeopardized by partition for the protection of French and *colon* interests if independence was a chosen option.

In a compromise heavily weighted in favor of the GPRA, final accord was made official on March 19, 1962. By its provisions, de

Gaulle's policy of self-determination would be carried out by a free vote of all Algerians (Muslim and *colon*), Algeria would retain integrally all its existing lands including the Sahara, the remaining *colons* would be respected in their persons and properties on an equal basis with the Muslims, cooperative development of the oil resources of the Sahara would be continued, and French aid would be maintained along the lines of the Constantine Plan. To supervise the forthcoming referendum and to act as an interim government, a mixed commission of French government, GPRA, and non-GPRA Muslim representatives was established.

After 80 percent of the metropolitan French approved the Evian agreements in April, 1962, a referendum was submitted to the Algerians on July 1. Despite an intensified outburst of OAS terror, the foregone conclusion was acknowledged with 5,993,754 to 16,478 favoring independence. For better or for worse, for richer or for poorer, Algeria was free — free of the French army and administrative apparatus and free of metropolitan domination. In the unanticipated mass exodus of the *colons*, the Muslims were now free, too, of their former local political, economic, and social masters but thereby lost the skilled, trained, managerial, entrepreneurial sector of the population that was so essential for a smooth and rapid transition to a modern economy.

If the amputation of Algeria from France brought mixed blessings for the Muslims, it provided nearly undiluted relief for the French. A tremendous drain on the French political, economic, and social body had been ended. France, like Algeria, could now pursue its "destiny" without the cost of a five-hundred-thousand-man army in the field, constant battle losses, and swollen military expenditures. Ended, too, was a major source of domestic political crises and agonizing soul-searching. If de Gaulle had failed to arrive at the solution he desired — an autonomous Algeria associated closely with France — he nevertheless had adroitly supervised an operation that detached Algeria from France without simultaneously imperiling the life of the Fifth Republic.

While de Gaulle was engaged in his four-year struggle against *colon* uprisings, army *putsches*, and FLN adamancy from 1958 to 1962, politics in France was in a moribund state. Essentially, it was reduced to a series of presidential pronouncements punctuated by plebiscites. Immediately after the 1958 referendum approving the Gaullist Constitution for the Fifth Republic, elections for the National Assembly resulted in a smashing victory for a new party dedicated to the Gaullist cause. The *Union pour la Nouvelle République* (UNR) won nearly 5,000,000 votes and captured 188 seats. The Communists, having registered losses in the September referendum, slipped from their 1956 total of 5,500,000 to fewer than 4,000,000. Although they commanded almost 20 percent of the popular vote, the number of their deputies declined disastrously from 145 to a mere 10. The reversion to the single-member district form of election and the refusal of other parties to make pre-election coalitions took their toll more than the loss of popular support. The other political parties did not fare as poorly in vote-getting or as strikingly in loss of seats. The SFIO and MRP continued to poll approximately 3,000,000 and 2,500,000 respectively but saw their deputations decline from 88 to 40 and from 71 to 57. The Radical grouping suffered more substantially, dropping more than 500,000 votes and half their former seats. The first Assembly of the Fifth Republic thus contained a comfortable Gaullist majority of UNR and allied deputies against a disorganized minority of Communists, SFIOs, MRPs, and Radicals.

Backed and not balked by the Assembly, the President was able to secure regular assent when he desired and exceptional powers when he asked. Customary friction between the legislature and executive was minimized, traditional political party maneuvering was halted, and consequent ministerial instability was terminated. But were these political novelties due to the constitutional changes introduced by de Gaulle, to a new spirit infused into the politicians and public in France, to the magnetism or machinations of the President, or to the urgency of the Algerian crisis? Detractors of the General were convinced that historical patterns would repeat themselves. The General would suffer the fate of the Clemenceaus and Churchills of the political world by being repudiated once they had fulfilled their mission of leading their countries out of temporary peril.

In defiance of the soothsayers, however, de Gaulle maintained his ascendancy and the system that he established long past the liquidation of the Algerian crisis. The 'Assembly, although still dominated by his otherwise loyal supporters, did balk in October, 1962. It rejected de Gaulle's debatable demand for constitutional revisions that would make the presidential office a democratically elective one and make constitutional amendments a matter for referendum. De Gaulle overcame the Assembly, however, by placing the issues directly before the voters: 60 percent favored his plan.

Parliamentary elections the following month reconfirmed de Gaulle's sustained appeal. For even without the sword of Algeria poised over their heads, the French voters endorsed Gaullist candidates. The UNR delegation rose from 188 to 234 in the 482-man Assembly. With more than 30 members of associated groups, the UNR had a more generous edge than in the previous Assembly. Although the SFIO and MRP returns showed a drop of approximately 1,000,000 from 1958, campaign coalition tactics accounted for a rise of socialist representation from 40 to 67 and a loss of MRP from 57 to 38. Communist chances were improved by the disorganization of the non-Communist left. With a steady almost 4,000,000 voters, the Communist Party managed to seat 31 more deputies than in 1958.

The Fifth Republic had remained "de Gaulle's Republic" through the elections of 1962. In 1966 and 1967, however, de Gaulle and the Gaullists were shocked to find that they had to try harder to gain less. The first round of the presidential elections of December, 1958, unexpectedly gave de Gaulle only 44 percent of the votes cast – less than the majority required – while François Mitterand polled 32 percent and other contenders garnished the remaining 28 percent. A week of flurried and desperate television, radio, and press activity produced for de Gaulle a bare 55 percent majority on the second ballot. De Gaulle seemed more vulnerable than at any time since 1958.

With revived or newly born hope, the once-shattered but ever present opposition to de Gaulle's principles and practices faced the parliamentary elections of March, 1967. Over the winter of 1966–1967, an anti-UNR, anti-Gaullist coalition, labeled the Federation of the Democratic and Socialist Left, was timidly and tenuously formed from the non-Communist left (SFIO, Radical, and MRP). Real but equally timid and tenuous was the electoral tie between the Federation and the Communist Party. Although not as strongly bound together or as successful as the Popular Front of the 1930s, the new front won an astonishing victory at the polls on March 5 and 12, 1967. The UNR, rebaptized as the *Union Démocratique pour la Cinquième République* (UD), captured only 180 seats and possessed a fragile majority only by alliance with independent groups. The 71 members of the Communist Party and the 116 of the Federation outnumbered the UD but could scarcely act harmoniously on a positive program or attract enough nonaligned deputies to command a workable majority against the Gaullist bloc. Without the still overpowering presence and prestige of de Gaulle, the Fifth Republic seemed on the verge of repeating the factional, multiparty, maneuvering political patterns of the Third and Fourth.

Repeatedly assured of popular and parliamentary support since 1958, released after 1962 from preoccupation with the Algerian rebellion, de Gaulle had wide latitude to pursue the foreign policy of his fancy. The basic aim of de Gaulle as President of the Fifth Republic was not radically different from that of de Gaulle as head of the Free French movement: to promote the fullest respect for French interests in Europe and the world. De Gaulle had not changed; France, Europe, and the world had. He acted, frequently in a highly irritating manner, on the valid premise that French political stability and economic growth coupled with a vastly modified international situation demanded different solutions during the 1950s and 1960s than those required during the 1940s. Ever consistent in his goal of grandeur for France, within and sometimes beyond the limits of the nation's power, de Gaulle set France on a more and more independent, neutralist course.

Although the French President proclaimed his firm allegiance to the "Western Alliance," especially to NATO, and gave corroborating evidence in the instantaneous, solid support for the United States in the 1962 Cuban crisis, he nevertheless acted time and again at ostentatious variance with his American and British partners. Dissatisfaction with the United States was pronounced on several grounds that allegedly kept France in a secondary or subservient position. Particularly rankling was the American refusal to share nuclear information with the French or to elevate France to unequivocally equal status in decision-making and military command functions within NATO. On the first score, de Gaulle insisted that his nation could best shape its own destiny by developing and possessing nuclear armaments. Over some domestic opposition and in the face of adverse opinion abroad, de Gaulle pushed the Fourth Republic's program to build and test atomic weapons. Vis-à-vis NATO, his long-standing feud for equality led him by 1967 to detach French military contingents from that organization while nevertheless remaining a political signatory to the pact.

On three other counts, de Gaulle broke with the United States: recognition of Red China, opposition to American participation in Viet Nam, and neutralism or nearly pro-Arab partisanship in the Middle East crisis of 1967. In almost all instances, de Gaulle gambled on gaining prestige, trade, and diplomatic leverage without foregoing the protection America might provide in another day of French need. Whether the French will benefit from resumed diplomatic and commercial ties with the Chinese, from extended influence in the Arab world, or from anticipated acceptance as arbiters in international disputes remains to be seen. In the long run and under most circumstances, the United States would defend the integrity of France regardless of the bitter and sometimes tiresome anti-American tirades of Charles de Gaulle. He can thus safely assert French independence, proclaim proudly the elevated rank of sovereign France, and pontificate on fulfilling French destiny while denouncing American involvement (and alleged culpability) in the Far and Middle East.

A heightened consciousness of French status, power, and independent action was reflected, too, in de Gaulle's European policy. Two of the cornerstones of this policy include rapprochement with Germany and solidification of the Common Market. That enmity and amity were relative to time and circumstances was manifest when de Gaulle dramatically signed a treaty of friendship with Chancellor Konrad Adenauer in 1963. For the two former first rate powers to wallow in the memories of a century-long duel was deemed inappropriate. De Gaulle most keenly realized that French interests were better served by keeping Germany in a French rather than American orbit and by forestalling possible Bonn-Moscow deals for a reunification of the divided nation. Closer connection with West Germany might also improve French chances of molding the Common Market to the General's tastes.

Toward the Common Market – its nature and its future – de Gaulle has, as usual, decided ideas. By no means opposed to the institution he inherited from the Fourth Republic, the President of the Fifth encouraged and facilitated its phenomenal growth. He proved nonetheless a hard bargainer in the successive rounds of negotiations where special French interests such as agriculture were at stake. On two more substantial issues, de Gaulle used all his influence to block the majority will. No enemy to ever closer economic ties among the six members, de Gaulle was no friend to a rapid transition to political unification. Each state, he claimed, should retain its "personality" in order to make the most valuable contribution; no state – surely not France – should yield basic sovereign political powers or dissolve itself into a common political structure. Perhaps this attitude underlay his opposition to a second move apparently desired by the other members: admission of Great Britain into membership in the club. De Gaulle noted Britain's links beyond Europe, with its Commonwealth and with the United States. Perhaps de Gaulle was concerned, too, that the entrance of the United Kingdom would reduce France's ability to control the economic and political evolution of the Common Market. In any event, de Gaulle continued in 1967 either to deny Britain's bid in principle or to set up impossible conditions for membership.

With a rarely matched consistency in foreign policy goals – if not in specific or permanent alignments – with a striking but declining capacity for maintaining public support and stable political operations in France, and with a commendable resolution of the Algerian crisis, de Gaulle embellished his record with an unprecedented achievement in French economic activity. The strutting and posing on the foreign scene as well as the election victories merely recited above were explicable, in fact, largely in terms of the prosperity widely enjoyed in France under the Fifth Republic. Without the broadened industrial and commercial base and without the freedom from need for extensive foreign capital and technical assistance, de Gaulle's independent, neutralist international position would have been utterly inconceivable instead of mildly ludicrous. Without the vast improvement in the production and distribution of goods and without the sound financial and fiscal situation attributable to the Fifth Republic, de Gaulle would surely have been crippled politically by a bickering Parliament or by a disgruntled citizenry.

Under de Gaulle, the French have built a dynamic and flourishing economy. Frequently overlooked by the Gaullists, however, was the spadework done by the Fourth Republic. The Fifth Republic was fortunate to inherit the foundations laid in the capital goods industries for further expansion and for ultimate extension into consumer fields. De Gaulle was nevertheless no mere passive beneficiary of past accomplishments. Through the confidence he instilled and the measures he fostered, he corrected many of the financial-fiscal faults that the Fourth Republic had been incapable of even approaching. In devaluating and stabilizing the currency, balancing the budget, halting an almost runaway inflation, reversing the unfavorable balance of international payments, and replenishing rather than depleting French gold reserves, de Gaulle provided a financial and fiscal stability never attained by the Fourth Republic. This transformation was even more remarkable in being accomplished before the Algerian settlement further relieved the drain on the French economy.

In industry, agriculture, commerce, and transportation, equally significant advances were made. Where the gross national product had shown an average and enviable increase of just under 5 percent per annum under the Fourth Republic, a 5.5 percent figure was recorded under the Fifth Republic. At a greater rate than in the United States and Western Germany, French industry leaped forward in almost all categories. Automobile, chemical, engineering, and electronic production rose more than 8 percent annually, far ahead of the 6 percent per annum spurt of industry as a whole. Agricultural gains were real but not comparable to industry's. Over the five-year period from 1958 to 1963, the over-all volume of foreign trade grew 50 percent, while trade with countries outside the franc area registered a 75 percent gain. During the same period, 55 percent more road traffic and 50 percent more airline traffic was noted. More than a thousand miles of railroad lines were electrified, the inland waterways system (canals and rivers) were improved, and superhighways were extended or begun. Not only did the production rate surpass the healthy one of the Fourth Republic, but also French industry became more rationalized, modernized, and competitive than ever before.

The social as well as the economic characteristics of this "new" France were often radically different from those of the previous half-generation. A population explosion raised the number of Frenchmen from the once stationary level of approximately 40,000,-000 to 44,500,000 in 1958 and nearly 50,000,000 in 1967. The traditional age pattern was shattered, too, making France one of the "youngest" nations of the West. Despite the burgeoning population and the influx of 850,000 *émigrés-colons* from Algeria in 1961–1962, the French economy was able, until 1967, to absorb all employables.

Full employment was but one of the socioeconomic boons of the 1950s and 1960s. The standard of living, high but often unchanging in France, began to mount spectacularly under the Fifth Republic. Consumer goods became more plentiful as greater productivity and higher incomes boosted purchasing power. A declining portion of the French family's budget went to food, more to lodging, household appliances, automobiles, clothing, amusement, travel, and luxuries. Between 1958 and 1963, the number of television sets, for example, increased from under 1,000,000 to more than 4,000,000. A fourth week of paid vacations was added. Once the Algerian burden was lifted, the Fifth Republic addressed itself to the housing shortage, but a lag persisted between needs and construction. Educational pressures from nursery to university also exceeded the swelling allocations. The already well-developed social security system was extended to cover new groups such as the self-employed, and further benefits were offered to those previously covered for medical, maternity, family, and housing purposes.

In France, the tractor was replacing the horse; the automobile, the bicycle; the ready-made, the hand-made; the supermarket, the corner grocery; the television, the café. Social patterns and economic practices probably underwent as much change since World War II as had taken place in the century and a half following the French Revolution.

From the launching pad of these vast technological and productive achievements, de Gaulle was permitted to project France again into the international limelight. On the basis of the magnificent economic boom, de Gaulle was more easily able to continue the political experiment called the Fifth Republic. It is not to be presumed, however, that Marx's economic determinism has thereby been demonstrated as valid for all time. The change in the mode of production and distribution may, in the instances cited, have been the causal factor for certain historical events, but only in the context of the time and circumstances. The forbearance of the United States in the face of French verbal provocation, the relenting pressure of the Soviet Union on the Western European states, and the détente in U.S.–U.S.S.R. relations provided sometimes as much basis for an independent French foreign policy as exclusively French economic progress. In the domestic realm, too, new political habits were being induced by new material conditions. Less tangible factors were also at work, however. The personal attraction of de Gaulle, the waning divisive force of the religious quarrel, the stilling of class conflict in an era of prosperity, the mysterious rise in reproduction preceding not following the soaring rise in material production – all these have been sometimes results and sometimes agents of economic and political change.

The two-hundred-year history of France since the Revolution has represented an unfolding of continuity and change. Although vastly different in structure and spirit, does not the Fifth Republic reveal, like the earlier republican, monarchical, and imperial regimes, a search for stable political forms? Are not the facile categories of right and left still meaningless unless pinned on specific people in a precise time as they deal with particular issues? Is de Gaulle of the right or the left? His alleged reversion to traditional nationalist outcries and actions seem to place him in the company of an earlier right. His attitude to the United States and to the Common Market, on the other hand, could hardly better conform to the wishes (and applause) of The Party of the Left. His foreign policy may mark him as a Tito of the West, yet his insistence on the private sector makes him no partisan of a collectivizing left. In yet another relativist comparison, de Gaulle's preference for technocratic teams in economic planning would have earned him a leftist label in the days of Saint-Simon. By the 1960s, however, the utopian socialism of Saint-Simon might be regarded as dangerously rightist by Soviet-inclined theorists.

The Fifth Republic, like the previous four Republics and the regimes they intermittently replaced, functions as a result of a multiplicity of "causes" and manifests a variety of tendencies. The test for understanding and explaining the historical experiences remains a close examination of the particular issue or event relative to other issues or events at the precise moment of their appearance and in the context of the special past that is sometimes peculiarly French and sometimes universal.

RECOMMENDED READINGS

The titles below represent a severely pruned and highly selective listing of works in English on France since the Revolution. Many of the books contain extensive bibliographies of aid to the specialized or interested reader.

Some General Works

Albrecht-Carrié, René, *A Diplomatic History of Europe Since the Congress of Vienna.* New York: Harper & Row, 1958.

Cameron, Rondo, *France and the Economic Development of Europe, 1800–1914.* Princeton, N.J.: Princeton University Press, 1961.

Clough, Shepard B., *France: A History of National Economics, 1789–1939.* New York: Charles Scribner's Sons, 1939.

—— and Charles W. Cole, *Economic History of Europe.* Boston: D. C. Heath & Company, 1941.

Kohn, Hans, *The Making of the Modern French Mind.* Princeton, N.J.: D. Van Nostrand Company, Inc., 1955.

Weber, Eugen, *Paths to the Present: Aspects of European Thought from Romanticism to Existentialism.* New York: Dodd, Mead & Company, 1960.

The French Revolutionary and Napoleonic Era (1789–1814)

Brinton, Crane, *The Anatomy of Revolution.* New York: Vintage Books, 1957.

——, *A Decade of Revolution, 1789–1799.* New York: Harper & Row, 1934.

Bruun, Geoffrey, *Europe and the French Imperium, 1799–1814.* New York: Harper & Row, 1938.

Connelly, Owen, *Napoleon's Satellite Kingdoms.* New York: The Free Press, 1965.

Farmer, Paul, *France Reviews Its Revolutionary Origins.* New York: Columbia University Press, 1944.

Gershoy, Leo, *The Era of the French Revolution, 1789–1799*. Princeton, N.J.: D. Van Nostrand Company, Inc., 1957.

———, *The French Revolution and Napoleon*. New York: Appleton-Century-Crofts, Inc., 1933.

———, *From Despotism to Revolution, 1763–1789*. New York: Harper & Row, 1944.

Geyl, Pieter, *Napoleon: For and Against*. New Haven, Conn.: Yale University Press, 1949.

Godechot, Jacques, *France and the Atlantic Revolution of the Eighteenth Century 1770–1799*. New York: The Free Press, 1965.

Hyslop, Beatrice, *A Guide to the General Cahiers of 1789*. New York: Columbia University Press, 1936.

———, *French Nationalism According to the General Cahiers*. New York: Columbia University Press, 1934.

Lefebvre, Georges, *The Coming of the French Revolution*. Princeton, N.J.: Princeton University Press, 1947.

———, *The French Revolution*, 2 vols. New York: Columbia University Press, 1961, 1964.

Markham, Felix M. H., *Napoleon and the Awakening of Europe*. New York: Collier Books, 1965.

Palmer, Robert R., *The Age of the Democratic Revolution, 1760–1800*. Princeton, N.J.: Princeton University Press, 1959.

Philips, Charles S., *The Church in France, 1789–1907*, 2 vols. New York: Russell & Russell, Inc., 1929, 1936.

Stewart, John Hall, ed., *A Documentary Survey of the French Revolution*. New York: The Macmillan Company, 1951.

Thompson, James M., *The French Revolution*. New York: Oxford University Press, 1945.

———, *Napoleon Bonaparte: His Rise and Fall*. Oxford: Basil Blackwell, 1952.

From the Restoration to the End of the Second Empire (1814–1870)

Artz, Frederick, *France under the Bourbon Restoration*. Cambridge, Mass.: Harvard University Press, 1931.

———, *Reaction and Revolution, 1814–1832*. New York: Harper & Row, 1934.

Beik, Paul, *Louis Philippe and the July Monarchy*. Princeton, N.J.: D. Van Nostrand Company, Inc., 1965.

Brogan, Denis W., *The French Nation, 1814–1940.* New York: Harper & Row, 1957.

Case, Lynn, *French Opinion on War and Diplomacy during the Second Empire.* Philadelphia: University of Pennsylvania Press, 1954.

Clapham, John H., *Economic Development of France and Germany, 1815–1914.* Cambridge: Cambridge University Press, 1936.

Fejtö, François, ed., *The Opening of an Era, 1848.* London: Allan Wingate, Ltd., 1948.

Guérard, Albert L., *Napoleon III.* Cambridge, Mass.: Harvard University Press, 1943.

Howard, Michael, *The Franco-Prussian War.* New York: The Macmillan Company, 1961.

Lord, Robert, *The Origins of the War of 1870.* New York: Russell & Russell, Inc., 1965.

McKay, Donald C., *The National Workshops, a Study in the French Revolution of 1848.* Cambridge, Mass.: Harvard University Press, 1933.

Manuel, Frank, *The Prophets of Paris.* Cambridge, Mass.: Harvard University Press, 1962.

Pinkney, David., *Napoleon III and the Rebuilding of Paris.* Princeton, N.J.: Princeton University Press, 1958.

Robertson, Priscilla, *Revolutions of 1848: A Social History.* Princeton, N.J.: Princeton University Press, 1952.

Thompson, James M., *Louis Napoleon and the Second Empire.* Oxford: Basil Blackwell, 1954.

Williams, Roger, *Gaslight and Shadow: The World of Napoleon III, 1851–1870.* New York: The Free Press, 1965.

The Third Republic (1870–1939)

Acomb, Evelyn, *The French Laic Laws, 1879–1889.* New York: Octagon Books, 1966.

Brée, Germaine, *An Age of Fiction: The Novel from Gide to Camus.* New Brunswick, N.J.: Rutgers University Press, 1957.

Brogan, Denis W., *France under the Republic, 1870–1939.* New York: Harper & Row, 1940.

Bruun, Geoffrey, *Clemenceau.* Cambridge, Mass.: Harvard University Press, 1943.

Bury, John P. T., *Gambetta and the National Defence.* London: Longmans, Green & Company, Inc., 1936.

Byrnes, Robert, *Antisemitism in Modern France.* New Brunswick, N.J.: Rutgers University Press, 1950.

Carroll, E. Malcolm, *French Public Opinion and Foreign Affairs, 1870–1941.* New York: The Shoe String Press, Inc., 1931.

Challener, Richard D., *The French Theory of the Nation in Arms, 1866–1939.* New York: Columbia University Press, 1955.

Chapman, Guy, *The Dreyfus Case.* London: Rupert Hart-Davis, Ltd., 1955.

Colton, Joel, *Léon Blum: Humanist in Politics.* New York: Alfred A. Knopf, 1966.

Curtis, Michael, *Three Against the Republic: Sorel, Barrès and Maurras.* Princeton, N.J.: Princeton University Press, 1959.

Earle, Edward M., ed., *Modern France: Problems of the Third and Fourth Republics.* Princeton, N.J.: Princeton University Press, 1951.

Ehrmann, Henry, *French Labor from Popular Front to Liberation.* New York: Oxford University Press, 1947.

Falls, Cyril, *The Great War, 1914–1918.* New York: G. P. Putnam's Sons, 1959.

Foch, Ferdinand, *The Memoirs of Marshal Foch.* Garden City, N.Y.: Doubleday & Company, Inc., 1931.

Gorce, Paul-Marie de la, *The French Army: A Military-Political History.* New York: George Braziller, Inc., 1963.

Halasz, Nicholas, *Captain Dreyfus.* New York: Grove Press, Inc., 1955.

Hayes, Carlton, *A Generation of Materialism, 1871–1900.* New York: Harper & Row, 1941.

Hughes, H. Stuart, *Consciousness and Society: The Reorientation of European Social Thought, 1890–1930.* New York: Alfred A. Knopf, 1959.

Jackson, John H., *Clemenceau and the Third Republic.* New York: The Macmillan Company, 1948.

———, *Jean Jaurès, His Life and Work.* London: Allen & Unwin, 1943.

Jellinek, Frank, *The Paris Commune of 1871.* London: Victor Gollancz, Ltd., 1937.

Joffre, Joseph, *The Memoirs of Marshal Joffre.* London: Geoffrey Bles, Ltd., 1932.

Jordan, W. M., *Great Britain, France and the German Problem, 1918–1939.* London: Oxford University Press, 1943.

Joughin, Jean, *The Paris Commune in French Politics, 1871–1880.* Baltimore, Md.: The Johns Hopkins Press, 1955.

King, Jere C., *Foch versus Clemenceau.* Cambridge, Mass.: Harvard University Press, 1960.

———, *Generals and Politicians.* Berkeley: University of California Press, 1951.

Lorwin, Val, *The French Labor Movement.* Cambridge, Mass.: Harvard University Press, 1954.

Mason, Edward S., *The Paris Commune.* New York: The Macmillan Company, 1930.

Micaud, Charles, *The French Right and Nazi Germany, 1933–1938.* Durham, N.C.: Duke University Press, 1943.

Noland, Aaron, *Founding of the French Socialist Party.* Cambridge, Mass.: Harvard University Press, 1956.

Peyre, Henri, *The Contemporary French Novel.* New York: Oxford University Press, 1955.

Porter, Charles W., *The Career of Théophile Delcassé.* Philadelphia: University of Pennsylvania Press, 1936.

Power, Thomas, F., *Jules Ferry and the Renaissance of French Imperialism.* New York: King's Crown Press, 1944.

Roberts, Stephen H., *History of French Colonial Policy, 1870–1923.* London: P. S. King & Staples, Ltd., 1929.

Tannenbaum, Edward, *The Action Française.* New York: John Wiley & Sons, Inc., 1962.

Thomson, David, *Democracy in France.* London: Oxford University Press, 1958.

Weber, Eugen, *Action Française.* Stanford, Calif.: Stanford University Press, 1962.

———, *Nationalist Revival in France, 1905–1914.* Berkeley: University of California Press, 1959.

Werth, Alexander, *The Twilight of France, 1933–1939.* New York: Harper & Row, 1942.

Wheeler-Bennett, John, *Munich: Prologue to Tragedy.* New York: The Viking Press, 1964.

Wolfers, Arnold, *Britain and France between Two Wars.* New York: Harcourt, Brace & World, Inc., 1940.

France During the Second World War

Aron, Robert, *France Reborn: The History of the Liberation.* New York: Charles Scribner's Sons, 1964.

———, *The Vichy Regime, 1940–1944.* New York: The Macmillan Company, 1958.

Bloch, Marc, *Strange Defeat.* London: Oxford University Press, 1949.

Churchill, Winston, *The Second World War,* 6 vols. Boston: Houghton Mifflin Company, 1948–1953.

Draper, Theodore, *The Six Weeks War*. New York: The Viking Press, 1944.

Farmer, Paul, *Vichy: Political Dilemma*. New York: Columbia University Press, 1955.

Gaulle, Charles de, *War Memoirs of Charles de Gaulle*, 3 vols. New York: Simon and Schuster, Inc., 1960.

Goutard, Adolphe, *The Battle of France, 1940*. London: Frederick Muller, Ltd., 1958.

Huddleston, Sidney, *France: The Tragic Years, 1939–1947*. New York: The Devin-Adair Company, 1955.

Hytier, Adrienne, *Two Years of French Foreign Policy: Vichy 1940–1942*. Geneva: Librarie Droz, 1958.

Pertinax (pseud. for André Géraud), *The Gravediggers of France*. Garden City, N.Y.: Doubleday & Company, Inc., 1944.

Snyder, Louis, *The War: A Concise History, 1939–1945*. New York: Dell Publishing Company, Inc., 1964.

Thomson, David, *Two Frenchmen: Pierre Laval and Charles de Gaulle*. London: Cresset Press, Ltd., 1951.

Werth, Alexander, *France, 1940–1955*. New York: Holt, Rinehart & Winston, Inc., 1956.

The Fourth and Fifth Republics

Ambassade de France, Service de Presse et Information.

Brace, Richard and Joan, *Ordeal in Algeria*. Princeton, N.J.: D. Van Nostrand Company, Inc., 1960.

Earle, Edward M., ed., *Modern France: Problems of the Third and Fourth Republics*. Princeton, N.J.: Princeton University Press, 1951.

Furniss, Edgar, *France, Troubled Ally*. New York: Harper & Row, 1960.

Goguel, François, *France under the Fourth Republic*. Ithaca, N.Y.: Cornell University Press, 1952.

Hoffmann, Stanley, *et al.*, *In Search of France*. Cambridge, Mass.: Harvard University Press, 1963.

Leites, Nathan, *On the Game of Politics in France*. Stanford, Calif.: Stanford University Press, 1959.

Luethy, Herbert, *France against Herself*. New York: Frederick A. Praeger, Inc., 1955.

Macridis, Roger, and Bernard Brown, *The De Gaulle Republic*. Homewood, Ill.: The Dorsey Press, Inc., 1960.

Matthews, Ronald, *The Depth of the Fourth Republic*. London: Eyre & Spottiswoode, Ltd., 1954.

Pickles, Dorothy, *French Politics: The First Years of the Fourth Republic.* London: Royal Institute of International Affairs, 1953.

————, *The Fifth French Republic.* New York: Frederick A. Praeger, Inc., 1960.

Schoenbrun, David, *As France Goes.* New York: Harper & Row, 1957.

Tannenbaum, Edward, *The New France.* Chicago: University of Chicago Press, 1961.

Tillion, Germaine, *Algeria: The Realities.* New York: Alfred A. Knopf, 1958.

Wahl, Nicholas, *The Fifth Republic.* New York: Random House, Inc., 1959.

Werth, Alexander, *France, 1940–1955.* New York: Holt, Rinehart & Winston, Inc., 1956.

————, *The De Gaulle Revolution.* London: Robert Hale, 1960.

Williams, Philip, *Politics in Post-war France.* London: Longmans, Green & Company, Inc., 1956.

————, and Martin Harrison, *De Gaulle's Republic.* London: Longmans, Green & Company, Inc., 1960.

Wright, Gordon, *The Reshaping of French Democracy.* New York: Reynal & Company, Inc., 1948.

INDEX

A

Abetz, Otto, 268
Action Française, 139, 143, 163, 170–171, 242
  excluded from Bloc National, 219
  revival of, 233
  threatened excommunication of, 226
Action Française (newspaper), 171, 236
Adenauer, Konrad, 338
Agriculture, 10, 88, 112, 144, 230, 243, 340
  acreage cultivation, 151
  Algeria, 312, 313, 314
  changes in (1870–1914), 144–155
  crop failures, 28
    of 1788, 12
    1846–1847, 90
  mechanization, 151, 299
  population engaged in (1914), 152
  setbacks (1870–1900), 149–150
  in World War I, 188
  in World War II, 269
Algeciras Conference, 166
Algeria, 306, 311–320, 327–333
  agriculture, 312, 313, 314
  Committee of Public Safety, 320–321
  Communist Party, 317
  Constantine Plan for, 328–329
  Egyptian aid to, 307
  French citizenship in, 311
  independence, 333
  Napoleon III and, 106
  per capita income, 314
  population, 311, 312
  rebellion of 1871, 158
Algerian War, 256, 315–320

  beginning of, 311
  de Gaulle and, 319, 321, 327–333
"Algérie Française" (slogan), 316, 319, 327
Alliance Républicaine Democratique Party, 219
Allied Control Commission (World War II), 303
Allied Occupation Forces (World War I), 204
Alsace-Lorraine, 42, 146, 161, 170, 196, 224, 228
  laic laws, 224
  textile industry, 147
  Treaty of Frankfurt on, 117, 162
  World War I, 176
  World War II, 268
American Revolution, 16
Amiens, Peace of, 58
Anarchism, 153
Anderson, F. M., 49
André, Louis, 141
Anglo-Russian Entente of 1907, 168
Anschluss, 247, 249
Anticlericalism, 67, 140, 157, 227
  of Combes, 142–143
  decline of, 224
  intensification of, 127–130
  Old Regime, 13
  Paris Commune (1871), 118
Anti-Semitism, 133–136, 139–140, 235, 236, 242
  Vichy regime, 274
Apollinaire, Guillaume, 201
Appeasement policies, 207, 248–255, 307
  alternative to, 252–255
  at Munich, 249
  public opinion on, 250, 254
  reasons for, 251–252

Armament industry, 243
Army Law of 1913, 175
Art, World War I impact on, 201
Artois, Comte d', 71
Assignats (legal tender), 37
Assumptionist Order, 136, 139
Aurore, L' (newspaper), 137
Automobile industry, 208, 229, 340, 341
Avignon, annexation of, 42

B

Babeuf, François Emile, 54
Balkan Wars, 168
Bank of France, 59, 90, 164, 189, 222, 232, 241–243
    gold reserves, 242
    reorganized, 243
Bao Dai, Emperor, 309
Barbusse, Henri, 171–173, 200–201
Barentin, 22
Barras, Paul François de, 57
Barrès, Maurice, 170–171
Barthou, Louis, 253
Bastille, the, 16, 27, 30
    fall of, 27, 32
Bazaine, Achille, 114–115
Beauharnais, Hortense, 94
Beauharnais, Joseph, 61
Beauharnais, Josephine, 57, 94
Beaumarchais, Pierre de, 13, 16
Belleville Manifesto, 143
Benedetti, Ambassador, 108–109
Berlin to Bagdad railway, 168
Berlin blockade (1949), 304
Berri, Duc de, 119
"Better Hitler than Léon Blum" (slogan), 235
Bidault, Georges, 279
Birth rate
    1891–1900, 145
    1914–1918, 215–216
Bismarck, Otto von, 107–109, 113, 158, 161, 162–164
    Dreikaiserbund policy, 162, 164
    Kulturkampf policies, 128
    social insurance program, 224
Björkö Treaty of Alliance, 167

Blanc, Louis, 86, 91, 92, 118, 125
Bloc National, 202–203, 206, 209, 220–225
    achievements of, 221–222
    chauvinism, 219
    excludes Action Française, 219
    fiscal policy, 222
    foreign policy, 202–203
    labor movement and, 222–223
    policies (1919 to 1924), 20
    political parties in, 219
    "rightist" affiliation of, 221
    Roman Catholic Church and, 224
Blum, Léon, 223, 225, 238, 245, 251
    criticism of, 244
    ministry without portfolio, 245
    in Popular Front, 243–244
    resignation of, 244
Boer War, 164–165
Bolshevik Revolution of 1917, 185, 192, 199, 223
Bonaparte, Jerome, 104
Bonaparte, Louis, 94
Bonaparte, Louis Napoleon, *see* Napoleon III
Bonaparte, Napoleon, *see* Napoleon I
Boulanger, Georges, 130–133, 163, 213, 290
    background of, 131
Boulanger crisis of 1888–1889, 130, 131–132
Bourbon family, 1, 68–77
Bourgeoisie
    economy impact on (1870–1914), 151–152
    Fascist leagues, 233–234
    labor movement fears, 154
    Old Regime, 7–10
    heterogeneity of, 7–8
Bourses du Travail, 153
Bracque, Georges, 201
Briand, Aristide, 202, 206, 207–211, 216, 218, 227
    League of Nations plans, 209–210
    at Locarno, 210–211
    scheme for European federation, 247
Brisson, Eugène Henri, 137
British Expeditionary Force
    World War I, 177, 179
    World War II, 259

Brogan, Denis W., 116
Broglie, Duc de, 125, 126
Brunswick, Duke of, 44
Brussels Pact, 302
  terms of, 304–305
Buchez, Philippe, 84–85
Bulge, Battle of the, 218

C

Cagoulards (organization), 244
Cahiers, 34
  meaning of, 21
Caillaux, Joseph, 172–173, 190, 192
Cambodia
  acquisition of, 157–158
  becomes protectorate, 106
  independence, 310
Cambon, Paul, 169
Camelots du Roi (organization), 233, 236, 237
Campo Formio, Treaty of, 56, 57
Camus, Albert, 312
Canon laws, 5
Caporetto, battle at, 185
Carnet B (security list), 191
Carnot, Lazare, 52–53
Carnot, Sadi, 131
Cartel des Gauches (1924–1926), 202, 209, 225–227, 231
  excludes Communist Party, 225
  financial policy, 226–227
  political parties in, 225
  Roman Catholic Church and, 225–226
Casimir-Périer, Jean Paul Pierre, 125
Cavaignac, Godefroy, 137
Cavignac, Louis Eugène, 93, 95
Cavour, Camillo, 104–105
Central Committee of the National Guard, 118
Challe, Maurice, 331
Chamberlain, Austen, 210
Chambord, Comte de, 72, 119–120
Chaplains (military), 129–130
Charles X, King, 68, 72–75, 119
  abdication of, 77
Chautemps, Camille, 236
  decree powers of, 245

Chauvinism, 219
Chemical industry, 229, 340
Chiang-Kai-Shek, 309
Chiappe, Jean, 236, 237
Christiani, Baron, 138
Churchill, Sir Winston, 253, 276, 303
  in World War II, 260, 263, 276–277
Civil Constitution of the Clergy, 37–38
Civil marriage laws, 129
Civil War (United States), 107
Clemenceau, Georges, 118, 137, 144, 190, 192–194, 197, 202, 221, 263
  Foch's denunciation of, 198
  peace negotiations, 197–199
  premiership, 192, 193
Clotilde, Princess, 104
Clough, Shepard B., 156, 195
Coal industry, 87, 146, 288
  production
    1860–1913, 147
    1929–1953, 299
  Schuman Plan for, 301
Cochin, Denys, 190
Code of Civil Procedure (1806), 59
Code of Criminal Procedure and the Penal Law (1810), 59
Code Napoleon, 59
Collective bargaining, 243
Colonialism, 106–107, 159–160, 308
  See also Imperialism
Colons (Algerian), 311–320, 327, 328
  agriculture domination, 313
  -army combination, 330–331
  Committee of Public Safety, 320–321
  1960 insurrection, 330, 331
  population, 311
  terroristic tactics, 331–332
Combat (newspaper), 278
Combes, Emile, 141, 142, 190
  anticlericalism of, 142–143
Coming of the French Revolution, The (Lefebvre), 23
Commerce
  changes in (1870–1914), 144–155
  development of, 144, 149, 340
  most-favored-nation policies, 162
Commercial Code (1807), 59
Commercial treaty of 1898, 165–166

Committee of General Security, 46
Committee of Public Safety (Algeria), 320–321
Committees of Public Safety (1793–1794), 46–53
Common Market, 256, 301, 304, 322, 342
  beginning of, 302
  de Gaulle and, 338–339
  members of, 302
Communist Party, 234–235, 237, 239–240, 245, 251–252, 286, 287
  attitude toward Algerian crisis, 316–317
  beginning of, 223
  in Constituent assembly, 283
  election results (1946–1956), 293
  electoral system disadvantages, 292
  excluded from Cartel des Gauches, 225
  Fourth Republic, 289–290
  harrassment tactics, 293–294
    parliamentary, 244
  imprisoned union leaders, 259
  papal condemnation of, 127
  setback (1947), 294
  voting strength (1932), 241–242
  World War II resistance movement, 278–279, 294
Concordat of 1801, 142, 224
  terms of, 143
Concordat of 1802, 60, 142, 224
  terms of, 60–61
Condorcet, Marquis de, 13
Conféderation Générale du Travail (CGT), 153, 321
  schism in, 223
Confédération Générale du Travail Unitaire (CGTU), 223
Congress of Berlin, 158, 162
Congress of Tours, 223
Conseil d'Etat, 98
Constantine Plan, 329–330
Constituent Assembly, 283–284
Constitution of 1791
  nullified, 44
  terms of, 34–35
Constitution of 1814, 69
Constitution of 1830, 77–80
  Roman Catholic Church and, 79
  terms of, 77–78

Constitution of 1875, 122–123
Constitution of 1946, 295
  terms of, 291–292
Constitution of the Fifth Republic, 324–327
  referendum on, 334
Constitution of the Second Republic, 93–94
Constitutions and Other Select Documents Illustrative of the History of France, 1789–1907, The (Anderson), 49
Continental System, 61
Cordon sanitaire (foreign policy), 203, 212, 248
Corsica, paratrooper seizure of, 321
Corvée, the, 23
Cotton industry, 147
Coty, François, 234
Coty, René, 321
Council of the Republic, 326
Council of the Vatican (1870), 127
Crédit Agricole, 100
Crédit Foncier, 100
Crédit Lyonnais, 100
Crédit Mobilier, 100
Crédit National, 226
Crémieux, Adolphe, 91
Crimean War, 101–103
  causes of, 101–102
Croix, La (newspaper), 136
Croix de Feu, 233, 234, 237, 238
  antigovernment demonstration of, 237–238
  renamed, 243–244
Cuban missile crisis, 337

D

D-Day (World War II), 280, 282
Daladier, Edouard, 236–238
  Munich appeasement policy, 249
  resigns, 238
  World War II cabinet, 258–259
Danish War of 1864, 107
Daudet, Léon, 170
Dawes, Charles, 208
Dawes Plan, 208, 269

De Gaulle, Charles, 126, 214–215, 302, 321–342
Algerian War and, 319, 321, 327–333
Common Market and, 338–339
foreign policy, 336–339
Middle East (1967), 337
Fourth Republic, 286–287, 289, 290, 303
Free French movement, 267, 275–279
"Je vous ai compris" speech, 327
liberation policies, 280, 282–285
Moscow trip (1944), 303
nationalism of, 342
NATO and, 324, 337
1930s' army reform proposal, 254–255
nuclear armaments program, 337
peace offer to FLN, 329
World War I, 276
World War II, 276–279
Debré, Michel, 324
Debussy, Claude, 201
Declaration for Assistance and Fraternity to Foreign Peoples, 51
Declaration of the Rights of Man and Citizen, 29, 32, 34, 42
hostility to, 29
Decree for Proclaiming the Liberty and Sovereignty of all Peoples, 51–52
Decree, government by (1792–1795), 48–52
Decrees of Ventôse, 49–50, 51
Défense de la France, 278
Delavignette, 312
Delcassé, Théophile, 165–166, 190
Depression of 1846–1847, 89–90, 92
Depression of 1929, *see* World Depression of 1929
Déroulède, Paul, 138, 139, 163
Deschanel, President, 224
Devil's Island, 136
Dien Bien Phu, battle at, 310
Directory, the, 53–59, 63
Napoleon I and, 55
Disarmament Conference of 1932, 246
Divorce laws, 129
Doriot, Jacques, 244
collaboration of, 270

Doumergue, Gaston, 238, 240
Dreikaiserbund (alliance), 162, 164
Dreyfus, Alfred, 134–139
background of, 134
death of, 139
retrial, 138–139
Dreyfus affair, 130, 133, 134–142, 154, 161, 163, 172, 213, 274
reaction to, 137–140
Roman Catholic Church and, 142
Zola on, 137
Drumont, Edouard, 133, 135, 163
Du Paty de Clam, 134, 135
Dufaure, Armand, 124
Duhamel, Georges, 200

E

École des Femmes (Gide), 173
Economy, 36–37, 66–67, 88–89, 144–155, 285–288, 297–301, 339–342
Algeria, 312–313
effects of World Depression on, 250
effect of World War I on, 195, 199
foreign investments (1880–1914), 148–149
colonial, 155, 156
growth of, 229–230
Old Regime, 11–13
fiscal crisis, 16–20
wage index (1869–1914), 152
World War II, 269
Education, 74, 96, 129, 289
laic laws on, 127, 129
Einstein, Albert, 201
Eisenhower, Dwight D., 281
Electoral laws of 1919, 220
Emigrés, 43, 45, 47, 58, 66–67, 69
Louis XVIII's policies on, 70
Employment (1967), 340
Ems dispatch, 109
Engels, Friedrich, 155
Entente Cordiale, 168
terms of, 165, 166
Era of the French Revolution, 1789–1799, The, 51

Estates-General, 4–5, 19–25
  convened by Louis XIV, 19
  tennis court oath, 23
  votes itself National Assembly, 22
Esterhazy, Ferdinand, 136–137
European Coal and Steel Community,
  306
  members of, 301–302
European Recovery Program, 301
Evian-les-Bains, negotiations at, 331,
  332–333
Exports, 146, 148, 150, 229
  World War II (to Germany), 269

F

Falloux Law, 96, 129
Fascism, 199, 235, 239
  organizations patterned on, 233–234
Fascist Leagues, 239, 240, 251, 319
  bourgeoisie, 233–234
  clandestine operations, 243–244
  collaboration of, 270
Fashoda, Sudan, expedition to, 155,
  164, 165
Faure, Félix, 138
Favre, Jules, 114, 115, 118
Federation of the Democratic and So-
  cialist Left, 336
Fédération Républicaine Party, 219
Ferdinand VII, King, 72, 73
Ferry, Jules, 118, 129, 130, 156, 157–
  158
  imperialist policies, 157–159
Ferry's bill of 1879, 129
Festung Europa, bombardment of,
  280
Feudal system, 5, 9, 28
Fifth Republic, 94, 126, 256, 288,
  302, 320–342
  commerce, 340
  economy, 339–342
  finances, 339–340
  foreign policy, 336–339
  technological achievements, 341
Figaro, Le (newspaper), 173
Financial policies
  Bloc National, 222
  Cartel des Gauches, 226–227

changes in (1870–1914), 144–155
  development of, 144
  Fifth Republic, 339–340
  Napoleon I, 57–60
  Old Regime, 16–19
  World War I, 189–190
Five Year Plans, 300–301
Flaubert, Gustave, 201
Flocon, 91
Foch, Ferdinand, 142, 185–186, 193
  denounces Clemenceau, 198
  on Rhineland occupation, 216–217
Foch (Weygand), 217
Foord, Archibald S., 49
Foreign policies, 245–246, 285–286,
  302–320, 336–339
  appeasement, 248–255
    alternatives to, 252–255
    at Munich, 249
    public opinion on, 250, 254
  Bloc National, 202–203
  cordon sanitaire, 203, 212, 248
  imperialist, 157–159
  of Louis Philippe, 81–82
  Third Republic, 160–173
    1871–1890 period, 161, 162–163
    1890–1904 period, 161, 163–166
    1904–1914 period, 166–173
  Vichy regime, 274–275
Four Ordinances, 75–76
Fourier, Charles, 83–84
Fourteen Points, 185, 196
  self-determination principle, 249
Fourth Republic, 256, 284–320, 325,
  339
  beginning of, 291
  Communist Party, 289–290
  constitution, 290–291
  de Gaulle and, 286–287, 289, 290,
    303
  economy, 285–288, 297–301
  electoral system, 292
  end of, 287, 320
  foreign policies, 285–286, 302–320
  Gaullists in, 295
  industry, 299
  labor movement, 297–298
  National Assemblies in, 292–293
  opposition to, 291, 294–295
  parliamentary coalitions, 295–296
Franc-Tireur (newspaper), 278

France, Anatole, 140, 201
France—A History of National Economics, 1789–1939 (Clough), 156, 195
France under the Republic (Brogan), 116
Francis Ferdinand, Archduke, 168
Francistes (organization), 234
Franco, Francisco, 253
Franco-Prussian War, 68, 99, 101, 109–111, 160
  beginning of, 109
  end of, 116
  indemnities, 162
Franco-Russian Alliance of 1894, 164, 168
Franco-Soviet Pact, 303
Frankfurt, Treaty of, 162
  terms of, 117
Free French movement (1940–1944), 266–267, 275–279
  coordinated to Resistance movement, 279
  de Gaulle and, 267, 275–279
  resistance symbol of, 276
Freemasons, 141
French Forces of the Interior (FFI), 279
French National Liberation Committee, 277, 279
French Revolution, 4–64, 83
  background of, 4–64
  beginning of, 13–32
  causes of, 13–32
    idealist theories, 15–16
    Marxist interpretation, 14–15
    socioeconomic theories, 14–15, 31–32
  Napoleonic synthesis (1799–1814), 56–64
  Old Regime and, 4–32
    Estates-General, 19–25
    fiscal crisis, 16–20
    Necker's dismissal, 25, 26
  the philosophers and, 13
  September massacres, 45
  1789–1799, 32–56
    Committee rule, 46–53
    Directory rule, 53–59, 63
    Roman Catholic Church and, 36–40

rule by decree, 48–52
French Somaliland, 158
French Union, 308, 327
Freud, Sigmund, 32, 201
Freycinet, Charles de, 114
Front National, 279
Frontiers, Battle of the, 177, 179–180

G

Gaillard, Félix, 319, 320
Gambetta, Léon, 111, 113–116, 118, 122, 125, 130, 163
  balloon escape of, 115
  Interior Ministry of, 113–114
Gamelin, Maurice, 251, 260, 262
Garnier, Francis, 155, 157
Garnier-Pagès, Etienne Joseph, 91
General Commissariat for Planning and Productivity, 300
Geneva Protocol of 1924, 209
German-Austrian customs union (1931), 247
German Confederation, 106
Gershoy, Leo, 51
Gide, André, 173, 200, 201, 235
Gilchrist, Thomas, 146
Giono, Jean, 200–201
Giraud, Henri, 277
Giraudoux, Jean, 200, 210
Girondins, 45–46
Gold reserves, 242, 339
Government of National Defense, 113–116
Grévy, Jules, 118, 131
Grey, Sir Edward, 169
Guerrilla warfare, 309, 315
Guesde, Jules, 190–191
Guizot, François, 74, 80, 81, 90

H

Haig, Douglas, 184
Hapsburg family, 43
Haussmann, Georges Eugène, 101
Henning, Basil D., 49

Henry VI, King, 120
Henry, Hubert, 134–136
Herriott, Edouard, 225, 226, 227
    resignation of, 246
Herz, Cornelius, 134
Hindenburg, Paul von, 185
Hindenburg line, 185
Hitler, Adolph, 229, 235, 236, 247–
    255
    appeasement policies and, 248–255
    becomes Chancellor, 247
    Fascist Leagues and, 251
    objectives of, 247–248
    in World War II, 263, 264, 278
Ho Chi Minh, 308, 318
Hohenzollern family, 109
Hoover Moratorium, 246
Hugo, Victor, 118
Humanité, L' (newspaper), 143, 171–
    172, 223, 259, 294
Hungarian uprising of 1956, 307
Hydroelectric industry, 229

I

Imperialism, 155–160, 164–166
    administrative policies, 159–160
    in Africa, 158–160
    in Asia, 157–158
Imports, 150, 229, 269
Indochina, 301, 306, 308–309
    acquisition of, 157–158
    Garnier in, 155
    Governors-General, 160
    split-up of, 310
    Vichy administration, 308
Indochinese Union, 157–158
Industrial Revolution, 66, 83
Industry, 112, 147, 229, 299, 340
    Algeria, 313
    changes in (1870–1914), 144–155
    growth of, 87, 100, 144, 149
    nationalization, 243
    production (1929–1953), 299
    World War I, 186–187
    World War II, 269
    See also names of industries
Iron ore deposits, 146
Italian War (1859), 101, 105–106

J

J'Accuse (Zola), 137
Jaurès, Jean, 135, 140, 141–142, 171
    SFIO under, 154
"Je vous ai compris" (de Gaulle), 327
Jesuits, 129, 143
Jeunesse Patriotes, 234, 238
Joffre, Joseph Jacques, 142, 174, 176,
    183
    World War I, 174–183, 186, 191–
    193
Jung, Carl Gustave, 32
Junkers, 163

K

Kellogg-Briand Pact, 211, 245
Kitchener, Lord, 158
Koranic law, 311
Korean War, 306, 309

L

Labor movement, 153, 297–298
    Bloc National, 222–223
    bourgeois fears of, 154
    Popular Front and, 242–243
    setbacks, 153
Lafayette, Marquis de, 56, 77
Laic laws, 127, 129, 157, 219
    in Alsace-Lorraine, 224
Lamartine, Alphonse Marie Louise de,
    82, 91, 95
Lamennais, Felicité de, 84
Laos
    acquisition of, 157–158
    independence, 310
Lattre de Tassigny, General de, 281
Launay, Bernard René de, 27
Lausanne Conference (1932), 246
Laval, Pierre, 253, 282
    executed, 287
    Vichy regime, 265–266, 271
    Jewish policy, 274
Lavigerie, Cardinal Martial, 130, 155,
    158

Law of Associations, 142–144
 terms of, 144
Law of the Maximum, 48–49, 51
 terms of, 48–49
Le Chapelier Law, 36
League of Nations, 198, 202, 207,
 209–212, 216, 228, 241, 246,
 252
 German withdrawal, 248, 254
 Japanese withdrawal, 254
 proposed revision of, 209–210
 Saar Basin and, 197
League of the Rights of Man, 140
Leclerc, Philippe, 280, 281, 308
Ledru-Rollin, Alexandre Auguste, 95
Lefebvre, Georges, 23
Lend Lease, 304
Lenin, Nikolai, 155, 318
Leo XIII, Pope, 130, 143
Leopold of Hohenzollen-Sigmaringen,
 Prince, 108
Leopold II, Emperor, 43
Lesseps, Ferdinand de, 106, 133, 159
Libération (newspaper), 278
Libération-Nord (organization), 278
Libre Parole, La (newspaper), 133,
 135, 136, 139
Ligue des Patriotes, 138, 139, 163,
 170
Literature, World War I impact on,
 201
Little Entente, 207, 228, 246, 252–253
 reaction of Soviet military support,
 253
 treaties, 212
Livestock industry, 151
Lloyd George, David, 194, 198
Locarno Pact, 210–211, 228, 245
Loubet, Emile, 138, 143
Louis Philippe, King, 67, 77–91, 119
 abdicates, 91
 foreign policy, 81–82
 opposition to, 79–80
Louis XIV, King, 4, 120
Louis XV, King, 4, 5
Louis XVI, King, 4, 5, 13, 14, 40, 43,
 56, 119, 120
 arrested, 44
 convenes Estates-General, 19
 fiscal crisis, 16–19
 rift with National Assembly, 29–30

Louis XVIII, King, 54, 68–73
 death of, 70, 73
 émigrés policy, 70
Ludendorff, Erich Friedrich Wilhelm,
 183, 185
Luftwaffe, 259, 262
Lyautey, Louis Hubert Gonzalve,
 238

M

MacMahon, Marie Edme Patrice de,
 110, 290
 becomes president, 121
 monarchist sympatheies, 124–125
 resigns, 126
Maginot, André, 213
Maginot Line, 183, 217–219, 228, 254,
 259, 260
 construction of, 214
 criticism of, 218
 legislation for, 208
 rationale of, 214–218
Malvy, Louis, 190
Manorial laws, 5
Mao Tse Tung, 318
Marchand, Jean Baptiste, 155, 158
Marie Antoinette, Queen, 43
Marie-Louise, Empress, 61
Marne, Battle of the, 177–178, 187
Marriage of Figaro (Beaumarchais),
 13, 15
Marshall Plan, 301, 304
 denunciation of, 294
 opposition to, 297
Marx, Karl, 85, 118, 154, 155
Massu, Jacques, 320
Massu incident, 330–331
Mastiépol, 312
Maurras, Charles, 171
Maximilian, Emperor, 107
Mein Kampf (Hitler), 247, 248
Méline Tariff, 151, 152
Mendenhall, Thomas C., 49
Mendès-France, Pierre, 310, 316
Mercier, Auguste, 135
Middle East crisis of 1967, 337
Millerand, Alexandre, 138, 190, 192,
 224

Mirabeau, Octave Henri Marie, 56
Mitterand, François, 335
Mobilization
  World War I, 175–176, 186
  World War II, 257, 258
Molé, Louis Mathieu, 90
Mollet, Guy, 317
Mollin, Captain, 141
Moltke, Helmut von, 175
Monnet Plan, 256, 288, 300, 301
Montagnards, 45–46
Montesquieu, Baron de, 13, 15–16
Montmartre (artillery park), 117–118
Moroccan crises, 159, 166–167
Morocco
  becomes protectorate, 159
  French seizure of, 166
  independence, 311
Moulin, Jean, 279
Mouvement Républicaine Populaire
  Party (MRP), 287, 335
  Algerian crisis attitude, 316–317
  in Constituent assembly, 283
  election results (1946–1956), 293
  electoral system advantage, 292
Mussolini, Benito, 212, 235, 250, 251
  World War II, 260

N

Napoleon I, 55–64, 159
  aids Directory, 55
  coup d'état of, 57
  designated First Consul, 58
  divorce of, 61
  fiscal reforms, 57–60
  French Revolution and, 56–64
  One Hundred Days, 64, 70
  overthrown, 62
Napoleon III, 65, 67–68, 82, 94–111,
  290
  free-trade policy, 99–100
  Mexican fiasco, 68
  plebiscite on, 97–98
  popularity, 95
  as president, 95–97
  proclaims himself Emperor, 97
Nasser, Gamel Abdel, 307

National Assembly, 25–26, 28–29, 34
  adopts organic laws, 122–124
  beginning of, 22–23, 24–25
  Bloc National, 202–203
  effect of *Seize Mai* crisis on, 126–
    127
  election results (1946–1956), 293
  Fifth Republic, 325–326, 334–336
  Fourth Republic, 291–293
  parliamentary coalitions, 295–296
  Girondin faction, 43–44
  monarchist faction (1871–1879),
    119–126
  rift with Louis XVI, 29–30
National Guard, 77, 79, 89
  defense of Paris (1870), 115
  disbanded, 76, 99
  formed, 30
National Liberation Army (Algeria),
  315
National Liberation Front (FLN),
  328, 329–331
  de Gaulle's peace offer to, 329
  Evian-les-Bains negotiations, 331,
    332–333
  formation of, 315
  terrorism of, 319, 320
National Resistance Council, 279, 286
National Workshops, 92, 93
Nationalism, 50–51, 81, 82, 139–140
  Arab, 307, 315
  beginning of, 44
  colonial, 308
  of de Gaulle, 342
  1930s' social-class alignment and,
    230
Nationalization, 244, 245, 287–288
  armament industry, 243
Nausée, La (Sartre), 173
Naval Agreement of 1912, 167
Nazi Party, 199, 239, 241, 246, 247,
  267–269
  1932 elections, 247
  occupation policies, 267–268
  Paris clearing house account, 269
Nazi-Soviet Pact, 259
Necker, Jacques, 22, 25, 26
Nicholas II, Czar, 167
Nightingale, Florence, 102
Nivelle, Robert, 183–184, 193

North Atlantic Treaty Organization (NATO), 302, 303, 304, 306–307, 322
de Gaulle and, 324, 337
members, 305
Nouveau Christianisme, Le (Saint-Simon), 85
Nuclear Weapons, 285, 318, 337

O

Oil industry, 299, 332–333
Old Regime, 4–32
anticlericalism, 13
basis of, 4
bourgeoisie, 7–10
heterogeneity of, 7–8
class conflicts in, 10–11
collapse of, 13
economy, 11–13
fiscal crisis, 16–20
end of, 29
Estates-General, 4–5, 19–25
land distribution, 9–10
nobility, 7
classes of, 5
Roman Catholic Church, 6–7
One Hundred Days, 64, 70
Organic laws, 122–124
Organization Civile et Militaire (OCM), 278
Organisation du Travail (Blanc), 86
Orleans family, 76, 77–91
monarchist claims of, 119

P

Painlevé, Paul, 192–193, 213, 216, 227
Paléologue, Maurice, 169
Palmer, R. R., 23
Pan Germanism, 163
Pan Slavism, 163
Panama Canal Company, 133
Panama scandal (1892), 133, 134, 164
Panther (gunboat), 166

Panzer Corps, 255, 259, 261
Papal Infallibility, dogma of, 127
Papal States, 97, 106, 128
Paris
declared open city, 260
liberation of, 280–281
Napoleon III and, 100–101
Nazi clearing house account, 269
round-up of Jews in, 270
Paris, Comte de, 119, 121
Paris Commune (1871), 118–119, 153
Paroles d'un combattant (Barbusse), 172
Paroles et Ecrits (Painlevé), 216
Parti Populaire Français, 244
Parti Social Français, 244
Pétain, Henri Philippe, 142, 193, 213, 218, 257, 282
condemned to death, 287
Vichy regime, 265–267, 271, 272
Constitutional Acts, 273
World War I, 182, 184
World War II, 260, 263
Pflimlin, Pierre, 320–321
Phylloxera (disease), 150
Picard, Ernest, 113
Picasso, Pablo, 201
Picquart, Georges, 136–137, 139, 140
arrested, 137
Pig iron, 146
Pius IX, Pope, 127–128
Vatican seclusion of, 128
Pius X, Pope, 142–143
anti-French utterances, 143
Plan XVII (World War I), 174–175, 176, 186
Planck, Max, 201
Plombières, Pact of, 104–105
Poincaré, Raymond, 168–169, 202, 206–207, 227, 263
reparations policy, 206, 207, 218
Polignac, Jules de, 75
Popular Front, 229, 232, 239–245, 286
Blum in, 243–244
campaign platform, 240–241, 242
criticism of, 244
labor movement and, 242–243
nationalization policy, 243

362 Index

Population, 88–89, 144–145, 152, 157, 299–300
  agriculture (1914), 152
  Algeria, 311, 312
  colon, 311
  explosion (1958–1967), 340
Potsdam Conference, 303, 308
Poujadist Party, 293, 296
Proust, Marcel, 140, 170, 173, 200, 201
Provisional Government of the Algerian Republic (GPRA), 329–330, 331
Psychological Warfare Sections, 319
Public debt, 226, 227
  1913, 222
  1921, 222

Q

Quest for a Principle of Authority in Europe, 1715-Present, The (Mendenhall, Henning, and Foord), 49

R

Radical-Socialist Party, 221, 227, 231, 239–240, 245
  Algerian crisis attitude, 316–317
  in Constituent Assembly, 283
  electoral system advantages, 292
  voting strength (1932), 242
  unpopularity, 219–220
Railroads, 87–88, 340
  growth of, 100
  total trackage, 149
Railway Law of 1842, 88
Rassemblement du Peuple Français (RPF), 292, 295
  election results (1946–1956), 293
Referendum of May, 1946, 290
Reform Bill of 1832 (Great Britain), 77, 78
Reinach, Jacques de, 133, 134

Reinsurance, Treaty of (1887), 164
Relativism, principle of, 2–3
Remembrance of Things Past (Proust), 170
Reparations Commission, 205, 206
Republics
  number of, 1
  See also names of Republics
Resistance Charter, 286–287, 288
Resistance movement (World War II), 267, 276–282
  beginning of, 267
  Communist Party and, 278–279, 294
  diversity of, 267
  Free French coordinated to, 279
  motives of, 277–279
Revolution of 1848, 83, 99, 127
  beginning of, 90–91
Revolution of 1905 (Russia), 167–168
Reynaud, Paul, 254
  resignation of, 262–263
  World War II cabinet, 259–263
Ribot, Alexandre, 190, 192
Richelieu, Duc de, 72
Rivière, Henri Laurent, 155, 157
Robespierre, Maximilian, 41, 50, 56–57
  executed, 47
  pacifism of, 43
Rochefort, Henri, 114
Rocque, Colonel de la, 233
Rolland, Romain, 200–201
Romains, Jules, 200, 298
Roman Catholic Church, 33, 36–40
  Action Française and, 226
  Bloc National, 224
  Bourbon restoration and, 73–74
  Cartel des Gauches, 225–226
  chaplains, 129–130
  Concordat of 1802, 60–61, 142, 224
  Constitution of 1830 and, 79
  in Dreyfus affair, 142
  ecclesiastical courts, 11
  French Revolution and, 36–40
  Old Regime, 6–7
  property losses, 37
  right-wing faction, 39
  Second Empire, 96–97

Third Republic, 127–130
  separation of Church and state,
    142–144, 165–166
  trade unions, 222–223
  Vichy regime sympathies, 269, 273–
    274
Roosevelt, Franklin D., 277, 280
Rousseau, Jean-Jacques, 13, 16
Rouvier, Maurice, 143
Royal Air Force (RAF), 260, 263
Royal laws, 5
Russo-Japanese War of 1904–1905,
    167–168
Russo-Turkish War, 102

S

Saar Basin, 197
St. Mihiel, battle at, 181
Saint-Just, Louis Antoine de, 50
Saint-Simon, Comte de, 85–86, 342
Salan, Raoul, 320–321, 331
Salt taxes, 36
Sandherr, Jean, 136
Sartre, Jean-Paul, 173
Savoy, House of, 104
Scheurer-Kestner, Auguste, 136
Schlieffen Plan, 175
Schuman Plan, 301, 304
  Steel industry, 299
Second Empire, 67, 98–111
  collapse of, 98–111
    reasons for, 110–111
  economy, 100
  Roman Catholic Church and, 96–
    97
Second Republic (1848–1852), 91–98
  Constitution, 93–94
Secret Army Organization (OAS), 332
Section Française de l'Internationale
    Ouvrière (SFIO), 153–154,
    171, 192, 221, 231–232, 234,
    239–240, 245, 287, 335
  Algerian crisis attitude, 317
  in Constituent Assembly, 283
  election results (1946–1956), 293
  electoral system advantages, 292
  split in, 223

unpopularity, 210–220
  voting strength (1932), 241–242
Seize Mai crisis, 125, 126–127
Sembat, Marcel, 190–191
Separation Bill of 1905, 224
Siam War, 158
Sieyès, Emmanuel Joseph, 21–22, 57
Silk industry, 87
  production cutback, 150
Simon, Jules, 118, 124–125
Social insurance, 227–228, 288, 341
  opposition to, 233
Socialism, 153–154, 220, 234
  emergence of, 83–86
  opposition to World War I, 171–
    172
  papal condemnation of (1864),
    127
Solidarité Française, 233–234
Somme, Battle of the, 183
Soustelle, Jacques, 316, 327
Spanish Civil War, 253
Spanish Revolution, 67
Stalin, Joseph, 259
Stavisky, Serge, 236
Stavisky scandal, 236, 250
Steel industry, 146
  Schuman Plan for, 301
Stravinsky, Igor, 201
Stresemann, Gustav, 210–211
Strike of 1920, 222–223
Suez Canal, 106, 133, 159
Suez crisis of 1956, 303, 307
Supreme Headquarters Allied Powers
    Europe (SHAPE), 305–306
Syllabus of Errors (encyclical),
    127

T

Tannenberg, Battle of, 178
Tardieu, André, 231, 246
Television, 341
Tennis court oath, 23
Tennyson, Alfred, 102
Textile industry, 100, 229, 299
  Alsace-Lorraine, 147

Thiers, Adolphe, 80, 91, 114–118
  death of, 125
  ousted from premiership, 81
Third International, 223
Third Republic, 111, 112–255, 265,
      266, 322, 325
  end of, 266, 283
  1870–1914, 112–173
    economy, 144–155
    foreign policy, 160–173
    formation of, 113–144
    imperialism, 155–160
  1914–1939, 174–255
    domestic strife, 228–255
  1919–1924 period, 201–207
  1924–1929 period, 201, 207–228
  Roman Catholic Church, 127–130,
      142–144, 165–166
  World War I, 174–201
Thomas, 91
Tirpitz, Alfred von, 165
Tourist industry, 148, 230
Trade, 148, 230
  balance, 148, 225–226
  colonial, 156
  most-favored-nation policies, 162
  Napoleon III policy, 99–100
Transportation
  development of, 149–150
  Fifth Republic, 340
  growth of, 87–88
  modernization, 299
  railway trackage, 149
  steamship tonnage (1914), 150
Trappist Order, 143
Trench warfare, 180
Triple Alliance, 164
  members, 162
  secret clauses, 166
Triple Entente, 167–168
  terms of, 168
Trochu, Louis Jules, 113
Troppau Protocol, the, 72
Tunisia
  becomes protectorate, 158
  French bombing raid (1958), 319
  independence, 310–311
Turgot, Anne Robert Jacques, 13
Twelve Constitutional Acts (Vichy re-
      gime), 273

U

Unemployment, 28, 92
  World Depression, 230–231
Union Générale Bank, 134
Union Nationale, 202, 227, 231
  political parties in, 227, 228
Union pour la Nouvelle République
      (UNR), 334, 336
Union Sacrée, 190–193
Unions, 153–154, 294
  development of, 153
  permitted to organize, 99
  outlawed, 36
  Roman Catholic, 223–224
  schism in, 223
University of Algiers, 314
Uzès, Duchesse d', 32

V

Verdun, Battle of, 182
Versailles, Treaty of, 197–199, 202–
      203, 211, 248
  terms, 203–205
    moral responsibility, 249
    occupied territory, 203–204
    reparations, 205
Vichy regime, 256, 263–282
  administrative policies, 271–273
  anti-Semitism, 274
  end of, 281–283
  Indochina administration, 308
  Laval and, 265–266, 271
  members of, 265
  opposition to, 275–276
  Pétain and, 265–267, 271, 272
  Roman Catholic Church, 272, 273–
      274
  Twelve Constitutional Acts, 273
Victor Emmanuel, King, 104
Viet Minh, 308–310
  at Dien Bien Phu, 310
  guerrilla warfare, 309
Vietnam, 308–310
  armistice line (1954), 310
Vietnam War, 337

Villèle, Joseph, 72–73
Viviani, René, 168–169, 190
 replaced, 192
Voltaire, 13, 15

W

Wage index (1869–1914), 152
Waldeck-Rousseau, René, 138, 141, 142
Wallon, Henri, 122
Weimar Republic, 197, 239, 246–247
 collapse of, 235, 246
Westphalia, Peace of, 42
Weygand, Maxime, 142, 217, 260, 262
What Is the Third Estate? (Sieyès), 21
Wheat Office, 243
White Fathers (religious order), 155, 158
Wilhelm II, Kaiser, 163
 foreign policies, 164–165
Wilson, Daniel, 131
Wilson, Woodrow, 185–186, 194, 196, 198, 202, 249
 participation in secret bargains, 198
Wilson scandal (1888), 131
Wine industry, 100
 disease curtailment of, 150
 recovery, 151
Women suffrage, 283
World Depression of 1929, 230–233, 235, 241, 245, 250
 beginning of, 230
 economic effects, 230, 250
 unemployment, 230–231
World War I, 139, 144, 148, 160, 174–201, 215, 258
 agriculture, 188
 beginning of, 169–170
 British Expeditionary Force, 177, 179
 casualties, 177, 181, 182, 183, 185, 194
 cost of, 194–195, 189–190, 199
 de Gaulle in, 276
 Eastern Front, 178, 183, 185

 economic effects, 195, 199
 end of, 186
 enthusiasm, 171–173
 finances, 189–190
 French army morale, 183–184
 Hindenburg line, 185
 impact on the arts, 201
 industry, 186–187
 mobilization, 175–176, 186
 moral responsibility for, 249
 Paris Peace Conference, 196–197
 Plan XVII, 174–175, 176, 177, 186
 poison gas in, 181
 reaction of intellectuals to, 200–201
 reparations, 196–197, 200, 203–209
  French policy on, 204–208, 209, 218, 222
  postponement, 246
  reduction, 208
  total, 205, 206, 208
 Schlieffen Plan, 175, 177
 socialist opposition to, 171–172
 trench warfare, 180
 U.S. entry, 184
 Western Front, 179–186
  extent of, 179
  stalemate, 181
World War II, 213–216, 255
 agriculture, 269
 beginning of, 255
 black market, 271, 284
 British Expeditionary Force, 259
 Churchill and, 260, 263, 276–277
 D-Day, 280, 282
 economy, 269
 exports (to Germany), 269
 Free French movement, 266–267, 275–279
 French armistice, 262–265
  terms of, 263–264
 liberation, 280–282
 Maginot Line, 259
 mobilization, 257, 258
 Normandy invasion, 280
 occupied France, 260–271
  hostage ratio of 50:1, 270
  Nazi policy on, 267–268
  round-up of Jews, 270

World War II (*continued*)
    pacifist-defeatist attitudes, 261–263,
      285
    phony war (1939–1940), 257
    resistance movement, 267, 276–
      282
      beginning of, 267
      Communist Party and, 278–279,
        294
      diversity of, 267
      motives of, 277–279
    Viet Minh in, 308–309
    See also Vichy regime

Y

Yalta Conference, 303
Young, Owen D., 208
Young Plan, 208, 217, 246
Ypres, battle at, 179, 181

Z

Zola, Emile, 140, 201
    convicted for libel, 136, 137